FOLKLORE AND FAKELORE

FOLKLORE AND FAKELORE

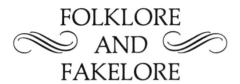

Essays toward a
Discipline
of Folk Studies

RICHARD M. DORSON

HARVARD UNIVERSITY PRESS
Cambridge, Massachusetts
and London, England • 1976

Library of Congress Cataloging in Publication Data

Dorson, Richard Mercer, 1916-
    Folklore and fakelore.

    Bibliography: p.
    Includes index.
    1. Folk-lore—Collected works. I. Title.
GR20.D67   398'.042   75-30734
ISBN 0-674-30715-1

277951

For Jack and Gail Garraty

 Preface

The nine essays reprinted here and the three that appear for the first time show one folklorist in several roles: as polemicist, critic, field collector, library scholar. These roles lead one into another, and seek out anyone who chooses the study and teaching of folklore as a professional career. This book does not attempt to offer a systematic philosophy of folkloristics but rather to support the proposition that folklore is an independent humanistic discipline worthy of academic recognition in every university.

Where folklore courses are offered by professional folklorists, they have pleased students and satisfied faculty concerned with the integrity of their curriculum. Yet the offering of these courses is a haphazard and sporadic affair. Many fine universities have among their thousands of professors no holder of the doctorate in folklore. The consequence is a serious gap in their instruction and research. At fault is the rigid departmental structure of the American university. A holder of a Ph.D. seeks a position in a department whose members have earned the same degree he has just acquired. Where does the folklorist go? Since very few departments of folklore exist, he must attempt to clamber aboard and survive in an alien department. I am not here proposing a direct solution to this difficulty. The intent behind these writings and field forays is to document my own fascination with the subject and share it with others, inside and outside the university. If enough people come to appreciate its lessons, folklore will find a proper place in American higher education as it has in Europe.

Preface

"Folklore in the Modern World" was delivered as the keynote address of the Indiana University Conference on Folklore in the Modern World held in Bloomington, November 28-30, 1973.

"Mythology and Folklore: A Review Essay" is reprinted from *Annual Review of Anthropology*, vol. 2 (Palo Alto: Annual Reviews, 1973), pp. 107-126.

"Is Folklore a Discipline?" is reprinted from *Folklore* 84 (1973): 177-205.

"Sources for the Traditional History of the Scottish Highlands and Western Islands" is reprinted from the *Journal of the Folklore Institute* 8 (1971): 147-184.

"Collecting in County Kerry" is reprinted from the *Journal of American Folklore* 66 (1953): 19-42.

"Tales of Two Lobstermen" is reprinted from *Internationaler Kongress der Volkserzählungsforscher in Kiel und Kopenhagen*, ed. Kurt Ranke (Berlin: Walter de Gruyter, 1961): 74-83, originally titled "The Folktale Repertoires of Two Maine Lobstermen."

"Dialect Stories of the Upper Peninsula: A New Form of American Folklore" is reprinted from the *Journal of American Folklore* 61 (1948): 113-150.

"Comic Indian Anecdotes" is reprinted from *Southern Folklore Quarterly* 10 (1946): 113-128.

"The Career of John Henry" is reprinted from *Western Folklore* 24 (1965): 155-163.

"Paul Bunyan in the News, 1939-1941," is reprinted from *Western Folklore* 25 (1956): 26-39, 179-193, 247-261.

All these essays have undergone some revision. My editor at Harvard University Press, Ann Louise McLaughlin, has given me constant support. As usual my research assistant Inta Carpenter read the manuscript with an improving eye; she has also prepared the index.

Bloomington, Indiana   R.M.D.
August 23, 1975

Contents

ix

Contents

x

FOLKLORE AND FAKELORE

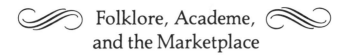 Folklore, Academe,
and the Marketplace

No subject of study in the United States today is more misunderstood than folklore. I can make this statement with some confidence,
for my academic life has been largely spent in attempts to combat
these misunderstandings. A folklorist cannot confine his efforts to
teaching and research but must ceaselessly attempt to explain to his
colleagues and the public the nature of his activities. The historian, the
anthropologist, the literary scholar, and their academic associates face
no such problem. They are the recognized and approved experts in
their disciplines, to whom the layman defers as a matter of course. But
anyone can write on folklore with seeming authority, for its academic
toehold is slippery and its subject matter enjoys wide popular appeal.
Few members of the intellectual community even know that M.A.'s
and Ph.D.'s in folklore are offered at several American universities. A
reviewer of one of my books announced that folklore was a moribund
field of learning in the United States, and in a letter to the editor I had
to recount the phenomenal growth of folklore as an independent discipline in the past half-dozen years.[1] But still there are only about a
hundred holders of the doctorate in folklore, compared with the tens
of thousands in established subjects. Amateurs, dilettantes, popularizers, charlatans—"fakelorists" in my neologism—get into the act.
The Ph.D. is not sacrosanct, and I have my own grievance against
excessive pedantry, but it does serve as one divider between the
trained and the untrained folklorist.

Misunderstandings of folklore studies are intensified by the general
interest in folklore materials. A university professor recognizes that the
world of the academic man seldom intersects with the world of the
marketplace. As a graduate student he soon learns that he must pub-

lish or perish, and that he writes not to be read but to be published, by university presses as opposed to trade publishers, in learned journals not in popular magazines. The scholar addresses himself to his colleagues in the esoteric jargon of their guild and steadily builds up the bibiliographical credits of his vita, the passport to the upper chambers of the university edifice. There are of course exceptions—Samuel Eliot Morison, Margaret Mead, John Kenneth Galbraith—who reach the larger public, but in the act they may forfeit the fellowship of their erstwhile peers, ever suspicious of panderers to popular taste.

From this scene grows the mythology of academe. Supposedly the professor and the businessman inhabit separate provinces. One is learned, contemplative, and indigent, the other practical, active, and affluent. In my years in graduate school pursuing a doctorate at Harvard in a new field, History of American Civilization, I never questioned this script. Nor did I later, until the day I realized that I had become a folklorist. For the folklorist is condemned to hover uneasily between the cultures of academe and of the marketplace.

The reasons are complex and bound up with the history of higher education and the development of the subject in Europe. In a number of European countries—Germany, where the Grimm brothers established the science of Volkskunde in the first half of the nineteenth century, in the Soviet Union and other socialist nations elevating the folk, in the Scandinavian bloc identifying national values with the soul of the countryman—folklore studies have flourished and spawned great research institutes, eminent professorships and chairs, stellar international congresses, and national heroes, like Finland's Elias Lönnrot, or Serbia's Vuk Karadzić, or Norway's Peter Asbjörnsen and Moltke Moe. Then there are surprising soft spots, notably England and France, where bursts of activity by illustrious private scholars from the 1870s to the First World War petered out with little or no effect on the universities.

Folk studies in the United States—whose American Folklore Society was founded in 1888, ten years after the English organized theirs—followed at first the English pattern of private support, then lapsed into a subfield of anthropology, supervised by Franz Boas and Ruth Benedict, and only in the 1950s and 1960s began to assert its independence as a discipline. But few American universities recognize this wayward subject. Indiana University approved a doctoral program in folklore in 1949 and the University of Pennsylvania in 1959. At present these are the only two American institutions of higher learning with departments of folklore. The University of California at Los Angeles has for some twenty years maintained a strong M.A. program, but the request of local folklorists for a doctoral program has run into academic flak. At Harvard, where in 1939 I searched desperately throughout the faculty for some guidance in folklore, and eventually located a young professor of Celtic who introduced me to the mysteries of Stith Thompson's *Motif-Index* in a private reading course, there was introduced three decades later the first undergraduate concentration in folklore and mythology mounted by an American college. The National Endowment for the Humanities awarded Harvard in 1974 a grant of $180,000 to develop a curriculum in oral literature, which is a branch of folklore. Ten courses projected for the fall of 1975 included a practicum in fieldwork, Introduction to Folklore, Colloquium on Mythology, and Oral Wisdom Traditions, a view of traditional word-of-mouth poetry in early societies. This at the university where, combing the catalogue thirty-five years before, I could only find "Legend and Tradition with Especial Reference to Celtic Material," as one small spotlight on the world's store of folk literature!

Yet on balance a mere handful of American colleges and universities include folklorists in their faculties. In spite of their growing commitment to oral traditions, Harvard has appointed no holder of the doctorate in folklore among its professors and lecturers, although as it happens, Yale, Princeton, and Columbia, with much less commitment in this area, have recruited such persons.[2] When an institution does add a folklore Ph.D. to its roster, invariably it faces the problem of where to find him the most congenial departmental home, and the decision varies from campus to campus. In terms of student popularity, folklore does exceptionally well wherever it is offered, and English departments in particular are currently awakening to this fact. Students relish folklore because it informs them of the human values and outlooks of common people so often missing from standard subjects in the humanities and social sciences.

To summarize: the folklorist as academic man speaks with a small voice. For all the pockets of strength there are large tracts of emptiness where the subject matter of folklore is unknown and untaught. The college-educated American knows very well that history and literature, sociology and psychology, philosophy and fine arts, economics and political science are branches of learning with their own pundits and intellectual preserves. But he would probably laugh—and every academic folklorist meets this laughter, or at best polite incredulity—if he were told that folklore belongs with these subjects. "How is the professor of dirty jokes?" my colleagues address me gaily.

Not all academic folklorists fight for the honor of their discipline. The blandishments of the marketplace are tempting and the arguments seductive. Why not appeal to the general reader? Why bother with pedantic annotations? Why not select and adapt tales and songs and rhymes and sayings that please the public (and reinforce existing stereotypes)? It is easy to make the compromises, especially since they promise some measure of fame and fortune for doing less work. Publisher's blurbs, facile reviews, and the beckoning market for frothy folklore give such productions a day in the sun, and further muddle the folklore scene.

Thus the academic side of the coin. On the other side we find the nonacademic man as folklorist, speaking with an authority never conferred on amateurs in the established disciplines. He can do so because there is no powerful guild to whom he must defer.

A Ph.D. does not guarantee wisdom or clarity, and a gifted amateur may far outshine a dusty pedant. The Victorian folklorists, whose history I have written admiringly, were lawyers, publishers, civil servants, and businessmen who did their reading, research, and theorizing on the side. But in the knowledge explosion of the late twentieth century even the academics are hard pressed to keep up with their specialties. Very rarely does a maverick appear like Bernard DeVoto, who taught himself the historian's craft without benefit of higher degrees and regularly sniped at the guild historians who wrote monographs for each other. Yet DeVoto lived in Harvard's shadow and hobnobbed with her historians, who never quite accepted him. Arthur Schlesinger, Sr., stated that DeVoto's prize-winning *The Year of Decision 1846* wasn't history.[3] Because the popularizers are numerous and the professionals few in folklore studies, there is hardly anyone with the temerity to say, "It isn't folklore."

It has fallen to me to make this statement, repeatedly, in a series of encounters with lay experts on folklore over the past quarter of a century. Since the word "folklore" conjures up such a variety of images to the public, from grannies in the hollers spinning old wives' tales to longhaired pop singers to whittling aborigines, any journalist, novelist, travel writer, music buff, local colorist, or even an academic in some other field turned fairy-tale author becomes an instant expert on the folk. A typical treasury contains journalistic rewrites of ghostly legends, concocted tall tales of comic demigods, tearful romances of

4

star-crossed lovers, literary writings about the Devil and his nefarious schemes, regional oddments describing ways of making maple sugar or curing nettle rash, composite ballads splicing together the best phrases of known texts into an artificial version.[4] Let me recapitulate some of my head-on collisions with the folklorists of the marketplace.

The earliest took place in 1950 in the pages of the *American Mercury* in a debate arranged by Charles Angoff, who had succeeded H. L. Mencken as the *Mercury's* editor and sought to keep some of the old fires stoked. My piece was titled "Folklore and Fake Lore" and introduced the word and the concept of fakelore, as a synthetic product claiming to be authentic oral tradition but actually tailored for mass edification. James Stevens, who in 1924 had published a Paul Bunyan story in Mencken's *Mercury*, and in 1925 brought out a bookful of such stories in his highly acclaimed *Paul Bunyan*, replied with "Folklore and the Artist." This exchange presented for the first time the clash of viewpoints between the academic (the Victorians would have said scientific) folklorist and the writer using folklore themes.

"Folklore and Fake Lore" mounted an attack on the growing popularization, commercialization, and resulting distortion of folk materials, as exemplified in the growing shelf of Paul Bunyan books and the treasuries of Ben Botkin. Both these profitable publishing formulas—fanciful whimsies about a giant logger, scrapbooks of folksy Americana—responded to romantic-nationalist tendencies in the American ethos after World War I, tendencies of the sort that have helped produce nostalgic folklore movements in many countries. Botkin's *A Treasury of American Folklore* delighted the American public when it appeared in 1944 and, with the half-dozen regional treasuries he subsequently assembled, has shaped the general conception of American folklore to this day. The success of his first treasury led Botkin to resign from his post as Folksong Archivist of the Library of Congress and devote himself fully to free-lance folklore editing and writing. My article on "Folklore and Fake Lore" drew a distinction between properly documented oral folklore collected directly in the field from the tellers of the tales and singers of folksongs, and the rewritten, saccharine versions of fakelore. On the side of fakelore I placed the treasuries, Paul Bunyan books, and children's story collections, and charged that the authors, editors, and publishers had misled and gulled the public. These parlor folklorists did no fieldwork, adapted printed sources that were in themselves suspect, invented out of whole cloth, emphasized the jolly, cute, and quaint, and contrived a picture of American folksiness wholly false to social reality. The

Paul Bunyan they so adulated had inspired a papier-mâché pantheon of imitations—Pecos Bill the cowboy, Old Stormalong the sailor, John Henry the Negro steel-driver, and more—all equally fabricated, and all trumpeting the American cry of bigness, invincibility, and Manifest Destiny.

Stevens replied patiently and without rancor save toward his competitors whom he felt had defaced the image of Bunyan. He saw himself not as a folklorist but as a literary artist drawing imaginative inspiration from the well of folklore, as Marlowe had done with Faustus, Byron with Don Juan, Homer with Odysseus. For thirty-five years he had been reciting and writing tales of his own invention. In a revealing admission he recorded the one-sentence "text from folklore" on which he based "The Black Duck Dinner," his first Bunyan story, printed in the *Mercury:* "Paul Bunyan's tarp was so big that when he spread 'er out ducks comin' over mistook it for a lake."

This small offhand tall tale rings true to the handful of oral traditions actually collected about Paul Bunyan. Terse allusions, they contain no narrative episodes nor even any development of Bunyan's personality. Stevens wrote up the Bunyan tales on "order" (he uses this term twice) from the publisher, Alfred Knopf, to whom Mencken had shown "The Black Duck Dinner," and expressed "amazement that the subject could interest a publisher." In 1931 Stevens composed a second volume, *The Saginaw Paul Bunyan*, in the same manner. He states his own role honestly, as an American author seeking to emulate Hawthorne, Irving, and especially Joel Chandler Harris in elaborating fiction from nuggets of overheard folklore. But America—publishers, reviewers, readers, schoolteachers, chambers of commerce, other writers, film makers—has insisted on viewing Paul Bunyan as America's foremost legendary hero. (See the documentation in "Paul Bunyan in the News, 1939-41.") When an oldtime lumberjack with varied experience in Canada and in northern states, John Nelligan, submitted his autobiography to the editor of a historical journal, the editor requested the addition of some paragraphs on Paul Bunyan, although Nelligan had never heard any Bunyan stories. The editor deleted unsavory but genuine anecdotes about a local character and requested that Bunyan tales be inserted, because he felt that any work on lumberjack life should pay homage to Old Paul.[5] And this was a scholarly publisher. In point of fact, Stevens readily concedes that the loggers he knew during his woods career spent little time in telling tall tales. After a day's hard work of ten to eleven hours they would read quietly, write letters, or play cribbage. Their most ardent topic of conversation was the Wobblies, the labor radicals of the early twentieth century. "In all the dreams and hopes of my years of hard labor in camps and mills," Stevens recalled, "Paul Bunyan had no part." Today the gusty folklore of the Wobblies remains untapped, and the nebulous figure of Bunyan is exalted to a household word.

Stevens identified strongly with his created Bunyan, "one hero of myth who kept kindness in his heart," and in a curious twist joined my attack on the commercial exploitation of Paul and Babe the Blue Ox. His denunciation of Botkin's *Treasury of American Folklore* outdid my own criticisms, and he sniped at Esther Shephard (whose book on Paul Bunyan had preceded his by a year) for starting the fashion of "hanging any old whopper on Paul Bunyan in the name of 'folklore.' In my view, her book is a prime example of what Dorson calls 'claptrap collections.' " And Stevens ended his piece much as I did mine by castigating "fake folklore."

So the confrontation in this instance turned out to be a triangulation opening a window into the ambiguities of the American folklore scene. Stevens considered himself an epic poet in the Homeric tradition, searching for profound American values in the mythical woodsman. He mentioned his own efforts in script-writing a vast outdoor pageant in Washington's Olympic Peninsula with a Paul Bunyan forestry setting and a theme of reforestation and fire-fighting, and contrasted them with the cheapening effects of tourist promotion and boosterism. Stevens rued the degradation of a noble myth through association with liars' contests, journalistic concoctions, and scatological jokes. Indeed his only counter-criticism of my arguments was to deny my assertion that the real oral tradition contained much obscenity. With the scholar of folk materials he had no quarrel, only with the exploiters who debased the coin of epic literature.[6]

Greater and lesser works of literature have often drawn nourishment from folklore sources. A number of poets, artists, dramatists, and musicians, along with Stevens, have used the Paul Bunyan theme, Frost, Sandburg, and Auden among them. None has produced any work of distinction employing the Bunyan materials. The reason can be provided very simply by the folklorist: there is no body of Paul Bunyan legends for the artist to explore. Stevens said as much in his own essay. Daniel Hoffman in *Paul Bunyan: Last of the Frontier Demigods,* has shown how meager is the oral folk basis for the timber deity. Ironically, the lumberjacks do possess quantities of lore little known to the public but not fitting their preconceptions. Rather than Old Paul, they yarn about the roguish camp bosses who dominate the lumber camps, and who could provide apt subjects for literary treatment.

If Stevens did not object to the term "fakelore," others did, and a vehement controversy over the issue divided the American Folklore Society during the 1950s and the early 1960s. One faction, led by the folklorists at the University of Pennsylvania, which housed the office of the Secretary-Treasurer, wished to keep the society open to all willing to pay membership dues, whatever their image of folklore. The other faction, spearheaded by Indiana University's folklorists, sought to professionalize the society. By 1964, during the presidency of Melville Jacobs, an anthropologist from the University of Washington, the tide had turned sufficiently, with the growing numbers of folklore Ph.D.s from both Pennsylvania and Indiana, to remodel the organization into a learned society. The old nondescript council, filled with whoever was present at a particular meeting, and carrying not only deadwood but deceased members, was replaced by an active executive board of younger professionals and an honorary Society of Fellows elected according to criteria of scholarly accomplishment.

"Fakelore" has now become an accepted word. The *Saturday Review* carried an article in 1970 entitled "Folklore, Fakelore, and Poplore," and the term surfaces in a spectrum of periodicals from the *Journal of American Folklore* to *Time* magazine. Here, for an instance at hand, is a headline in the Los Angeles *Times* for March 3, 1974, "Movies of Old West Called 'Fakelore' by Nevada Historian."[7]

In an encounter some years later in the *Atlantic Monthly* the academic folklorist found himself defending his field methods and understanding of a folk culture against a surprise attack from a seasoned writer. The department "Accent on Living" in the *Atlantic* for November 1958, a sumptuous 101st anniversary issue, contained an item entitled "Research Project" by John Gould. An editorial note thus described him: "A down-East editor widely known for the pungency of the columns he wrote for the Lisbon Falls *Enterprise*, John Gould is also the author of many books and articles about life in Maine." Gould appealed in particular to "Mainiacs," the large clientele of summer visitors to the Maine coast. His writings touched incidentally on traditional folkways of Down-Easters, and, although their forced humor set my teeth on edge, I had noted some local character anecdotes in his *Farmer Takes a Wife* (1946) and *The House that Jacob Built* (1947). Gould customarily titillated his suburban audiences with chatty, tongue-in-cheek vignettes of rural scenes; now he was having fun with a professor who had wandered into the state of Maine with a tape recorder. "Being an old down-East beachcomber from 'way back, I'm astounded to learn that the American Philosophic [sic] Society has been publishing reports from college professors who have recorded the 'folklore' of the old coots in the state of Maine. I've been reading what one of the professors just brought out as his findings."

Then Gould went to work on the savant. First he made the point that the outsider on a short visit to strange community can never learn its ways as effectively as the longtime resident: "you have to play to belong." The nonmember who intrudes into the closed society "creates an automatic artificiality," and will never obtain the genuine article. As a case in point Gould synopsized a story about the dupe who won a raffle on a dead horse, a tale set down by the professor as a prize catch. Actually it was the professor who was duped, held Gould, for Maine "humorists of local reputation" were always trying to fob off the dead horse yarn on him when he was trying to obtain fresh material for a Down-East book. But now the professor has published the yarn, and the "surging-forward motion of American scholarship has been given new momentum." Even at that the professor erred, for his tape-recorded version contained only one damn, and hence was "a fraud on the American Philosophic [sic] Society, in a way, and a deceit on the listening public." Any Maine veteran knew that such a tale would be sprinkled with expletives. Since editors could not well print such dense profanity, he, Gould, jestingly offered *Atlantic* readers a sample text with all the expletives—about half the narrative—deleted. He ended by requesting the American Philosophic [sic] Society to tender him a small grant to spend three weeks in July in Jonesport that he might compile a list of such "folklore words" to be inserted into the publications of folklore scholars.

A sketch of a brawny lobsterman in shirtsleeves talking to a wispy, bespectacled chap in a black suit and felt hat fiddling with a tape recorder accompanied the piece and captured perfectly its tone. In American life the professor is cast as a clown, a bumbling booby with his head in the clouds, and the idea of a professor trying to edge into this masculine society of gnarled Down-Easters and scientifically analyze their commonplace whoppers was a sure laugh-getter.

That unnamed professor was myself, and the article quoted, but not cited, by Gould appeared in 1958 under the title "Mishaps of a Maine Lobsterman" leading off the first issue of a little mimeographed journal called *Northeast Folklore*. "Mishaps" contained half a dozen tales told by Curt Morse of Kennebec as humorous personal incidents dealing with some discomfiture he had supposedly experienced. Some of these anecdotes he had developed from his own realities, some—like the dead horse bit—he had attached to his persona from the floating pool of oral stories. This selection of Curt's repertoire illustrated one facet of his narrative art, his tendency to make himself the mock hero of comic legends. One of Curt's memorates* dealt with a series of misadventures that befell him when he deserted his familiar environment of the coastal fisheries to dig potatoes inland. The whole recital—"performance" as folklorists now call an oral narrative presentation—underscores the culture shock affecting the worker who shifts habitat and occupations. Clearly Curt had often told this well-polished yarn to appreciative audiences, for his daughter interjected to request an episode he had omitted. These points of interest to folklorists did not arouse Mr. Gould, bent on fashioning a salable magazine piece at the expense of the poaching professor, but he had raised a legitimate caveat: how much can the outsider properly learn about an unfamiliar society in a brief period?

I wrote the *Atlantic* requesting opportunity to rebut the charge that my work was a "fraud on the American Philosophic Society." The *Atlantic* allowed me space in the February 1959 issue and printed as well my exchange of letters with the associate editor, Charles Morton. Besides the chance to vindicate myself, I argued that the "questions raised in the exchange between Mr. Gould and myself are of general interest and involve widely held misconceptions about the nature of folklore."

My rebuttal—somewhat overheated, as it seems fifteen years later, so I will recast it here—attempted to explain succinctly some goals of the folklorist. One such goal is to identify the materials of folklore, as a separate part of man's cultural heritage. Not until the nineteenth century did certain scholars, of a philological and antiquarian bent, recognize the existence of folk traditions, among the peasantry or "lower orders," in the parlance of the times. The discovery that unlettered country people possessed their own oral literature and inherited lore, traceable perhaps to the mental outlook of prehistoric man, excited the new genus of folklorists. Intellectuals have always studied primarily the products of other intellectuals, of elite classes, because, even were they interested, the products of the common folk are largely unavailable. But all the culture of the peasantry is not folklore; for example, their religious beliefs may be partly orthodox

---

*Memorate is a term coined by the Swedish folklorist C. W. von Sydow to designate a personal experience narrative that enters oral tradition.

theology, partly folk conceptions. Nor is the culture of the intellectuals devoid of folkloric components. The university campus, seat of
the learned tradition, is also the nucleus for a teeming body of folk
traditions. At any rate, the folklorist sets himself as a primary task
separating out the folktales from the literary writings, the folksongs
from the art songs, the folk art from the fine art, the folk custom and
usage from the formal institutions of society, the folk speech from the
standard language, the folk wisdom from the science. Since the lines
of demarcation are frequently blurred and fuzzy, the folklorist must
continually sharpen his concepts, refine his techniques, appraise his
results. For him the game is very much worth the candle, as he seeks
the greater understanding of the masses of mankind.

To return to the little sheaf of Curt Morse's stories. The first question the folklorist raises is, Are they folktales? That is, do they exist in
tradition, who has told them in the past, and what are their genealogies, so far as they can be recovered? Mr. Gould may not wish to
hear again an oft-repeated story, but the student of folklore considers
repetition a valuable clue in his attempt to capture a folktale. If he can
demonstrate that word-of-mouth repetition has occurred over
stretches of time, in varying forms, he has made his case. To aid him
in his quest, the folklorist has recourse to special classificatory indexes
of types of folktales and of their component parts, known as motifs.
So in the *Type and Motif-Index of the Folktales of England and North
America* compiled by Ernest W. Baughman in 1966, we find a whole
section of references to "Deceptive horse sales or trades," under K134.
The summaries tell of sly owners selling blind, balky, and otherwise
worthless horses through various stratagems, such as literal statements susceptible to double meanings. "Thee would be pleased to see
him pull a load," the Quaker comments to his prospective buyer, who
after the sale ruefully learns this is a correct observation, for the horse
refuses to pull at all. Baughman's index gives as a submotif K134.7(b)
"Raffling off a dead horse," with two examples from Indiana and New
Mexico. They contain a twist not present in Curt Morse's short anecdote, that the winner is given his money back, since he is the only
angry party; the losers are happy not to have won a dead horse, the
owner has profited, and the winner now is mollified, so everybody is
content. This ending would not suit Curt's posture, for he pictures
himself as the perennially unlucky underdog. Back in 1841, under the
title "A Horse Story," the New York *Spirit of the Times,* the
sportsmen's weekly that was a favorite repository for all kinds of
yarns in the ante-bellum decades, printed an anecdote about a dead

horse auctioned off by his owner to save the burial price of $2.50. So horse-trading, horse-selling, and horse-raffling tales belong to a wide network of American folk narratives, reflecting the central importance of the horse in nineteenth-century America and the salesmanship of the Yankee trader, who himself becomes a folk type.

Sometimes, if it does not appear in the indexes or in previous collections, the collector cannot immediately identify a given story as traditional. Yet his putting the item on record may lead subsequent collectors or students to recognize variants. Curt recounted a visit to the insane asylum at Bangor to see a committed friend. Some of the inmates were cutting grass with pruning shears and sickles under the supervision of guards, when a big, black-whiskered, wild-looking fellow carrying a sickle looked at Curt and started after him on the run. Scared, Curt began running too, but stubbed his toe and fell down. The chap with the lethal instrument touched Curt and said "tag." Then the guards led him away. So the tale. This precise incident has been reported as transpiring in Kentucky and Indiana, so the "Tag, you're it" story belongs to the canon of American comic folktales.[8]

Another of Curt's narrations, this time not a memorate (and so not included in the "Mishaps" article), but a serious explanation of how Yoho Cove a couple of miles down the road from Curt's home gained its name, also turned out to be traditional. According to local report, a wild man who had lived there one hundred and fifty years before abducted a village girl and had a baby by her; when a rescue party carried away his mate he tore the baby in half and threw one portion after them. This wild man uttered only the cry "Yoho." The folklorist has encountered this scene set in the Kentucky hills, in French Canada, and in a Persian manuscript of 1830.[9]

A Maine story John Gould published in 1953 in a children's book, *The Fastest Hound Dog in the State of Maine*, told about a dog that outran a train and put out its hot box by peeing on it. In the preface he wrote, "I don't know of my own knowledge, if this story has ever been written down before." He could have found a version from Illinois in Ben Botkin's *Treasury of American Folklore*. Baughman assigns a motif to the tall tale and cites Botkin and two other references.[10] Actually another children's book on the same theme, *The Fast Sooner Hound*, by Arna Bontemps and Jack Conroy, had been published in 1942.

This handful of illustrations shows the often surprising dispersal of oral narratives that the folklorist can trace from what seem like purely local morsels. Having identified the materials of folklore, the student can then pursue a host of questions: the routes of transmission, the nature and appeal of the folk aesthetic, the meaning and function of the item in the community, its structural composition, the role of the performer or carrier, the historical core of legends and ballads, the ethical content of proverbs and sayings, the interpenetration of folk and mass culture. No other discipline is equipped to deal with these questions.

But can the sheltered professor suddenly appear in one or another locality and in a few short weeks master its complex cultural traditions? This query is raised not only by Mr. Gould but by many others skeptical of or sympathetic to the folklorist's operation. The answer is that with proper planning, preparation, and advance research, and a thorough familiarity with field techniques, the folklorist can indeed glean substantial harvests in a limited time. In three weeks in Jonesport on the Maine coast I recorded over four hundred folklore texts; in eight days in Pine Bluff, Arkansas, I obtained one hundred and sixty Negro folktales; in less than a month in Gary and East Chicago, Indiana, I obtained ten tapes and notes on fifty-three interviews divided among nine nationalities, and kept a daily diary running to ninety typed pages; in two days in County Kerry, Ireland, I procured seventeen tales and supporting data later published in the *Journal of American Folklore*. These were all initial visits. Of course every collector maps his own campaign, and noted fieldworkers, such as Vance Randolph in the Ozarks or the Episcopal clergyman Harry M. Hyatt among southern blacks, have devoted many years to their quests. Nonacademics without theoretical axes to grind, they collect primarily to preserve verbal traditions. A few days or weeks may suffice though for the academic folklorist zeroing in on a specific target. Uninterrupted field time stretches out far beyond normal days. Since the collector can follow leads, make contacts, and interview informants around the clock, he immerses himself far more deeply in the alien culture than he ordinarily does in his own culture in the course of his daily narrow routine. With the tape recorder one can accumulate thousands of words in short order, which will require many tedious hours of transcription at a later date. The amount of time actually spent in the field leaves out of account the considerable effort that should be expended in choosing the field site and formulating the field inquiry, before the collector ever leaves home.

The sally to Jonesport was intended to test an hypothesis concerning linguistic relic areas mapped by Hans Kurath and his co-workers on the Linguistic Atlas of America. To gather their lexical samples, the Atlas fieldworkers entered many seaboard communities and recorded oral material from informants in much the same manner as do folklorists. On the basis of the data thus obtained, Kurath plotted geographical zones of speech forms. He noted that certain well-defined regions, which he called relic areas, contained a high incidence of archaic words and locutions. The Atlas collectors occasionally procured tales from their speakers, as convenient vehicles of local speech usage, and Kurath told me of one especially fruitful narrator, Joshua Alley, in the relic area of Jonesport, who had in 1932, at the age of ninety-one, contributed a thick sheaf of tales, songs, and beliefs to the Atlas files. After examining these folders I resolved to make a field trip to Jonesport to determine whether relic areas might prove rich in other kinds of folklore besides folk speech. If the correlation worked out, then American folklorists could plan their fieldwork with far more certain guidelines than presently existed. As matters stood, field collecting in the United States was haphazard, fortuitous, and unsystematic.

This in essence was the proposal I submitted to the American Philosophical Society for a grant-in-aid. The results of the three-week field trip did verify the Jonesport relic area as abundant in a variety of oral traditions and folk beliefs.[11] A nephew of Joshua Alley, seventy-six-year-old James Alley, a lobsterman, alone narrated to me 143 jests, legends, and belief tales. Other relic areas should be similarly tested by folklore collectors.

So too each of the other short-term but intensive expeditions had its rationale and strategy. The sojourn into lower Arkansas was to enable me to compare the southern Negro folktale repertoire with that brought north by southern migrants, which I had collected in depth in Michigan communities. The two days in County Kerry were spent in the company of a full-time collector on the staff of the Irish Folklore Commission, in order to observe their field methods, and to sample the modern Irish repertoire. The foray into Gary and East Chicago represented a pilot run into a racially and ethnically mixed industrial metropolis to test the existence and character of urban folk traditions.

John Gould returned to the dialogue in 1969 with a short book, *The Jonesport Raffle*, which took its title from the dead horse story, opened with a jab at the professor who came to Jonesport on a "nice scholarship grant" to record folklore, and ended with Professor Sigmund Weeps taping "The Tale of the First Cat" from "a humorist with considerable local reputation" (my phrase). Apparently Gould con-

14

ceived the jeu d'esprit as a means of discrediting out-of-state folklorists ("All Maine coastal folklore requires some special knowledge to 'piecen out' the point")[12] and trotting out stories he had heard as an insider. As an example he explained that folklorists had deformed the tale of the becalmed mariner who bought a quarter's worth of wind and raised a storm (the title legend of my *Buying the Wind*) by substituting quarter for shilling, which had originally been farthing, pronounced "fart'in"—too powerful a word for academic folklorists! Gould does include variants of a number of well-traveled yarns in the course of his jottings, but since he places them all in his own waggish prose they offer little substance to the folklorist Gould is trying to set straight.

If the folklorist has difficulties explaining his operations to writers in the marketplace, presumably he should relate more successfully to his academic colleagues. For years I confidently believed that placing folklore books and articles in the hands of historians, literary scholars, and anthropologists, or organizing a session on folklore at one of their meetings, would immediately convert them into appreciative and understanding supporters. Only after a number of painful failures at instant communication did I realize that my own premise would negate such a speedy marriage of minds. If folklore were truly an independent discipline, as I contended, how could it be mastered at one sitting? The reverse situation would never be contemplated, that a historian would pick up anthropology, or a philosopher annex sociology, by reading a book or attending a lecture. The problem was intensified by the fact that folklore is not regularly taught in schools and colleges. "What is folklore?" is asked a thousand times of every practicing folklorist, who is expected to convey the sense of a vast field of learning in a capsule response. The long road to the doctorate in graduate schools leads to the production of highly specialized scholars who can never thereafter speak in each other's language, in spite of occasional valiant efforts by educators at "interdisciplinary" exchange. The folklorist too has his jargon.

Hard evidence of the blocks to communication between folklorists and their fellow academics can be seen in the report of a Newberry Library Conference on American Studies in 1961. At these conferences a sacrificial victim circulated a paper on some controversial aspects of his research to a chosen group of peers for dismemberment. On this occasion I served up "Bogies of American Folklore" to a mixed panel of American historians, including Daniel Boorstin and Philip Jordan, American literary scholars, among them Walter Blair, John Flanagan, and Ernest Samuels, a sociologist, Howard Becker, the publishers Roger Shugg and Carroll Bowen of the University of Chicago Press, and some academic folklorists, notably Francis Lee Utley and Mody Boatright. The presentation paper developed as its main points the shortage of trained folklorists and oversupply of amateurs, coupled with the rejection or misuse of folklore materials by American social, cultural, and literary historians—some of whom were present. The ensuing discussion—a rare moment for the promoter of cross-disciplinary discourse—developed into a question match of the ins (the folklorists) by the outs (the others). How do the methods of the folklorist differ from those of certain capable cultural anthropologists? asked Shugg, who had published Melville Jacobs' *The Content and Style of an Oral Literature*. Is not the definition of folklore too restrictive? Boorstin questoned the insistence on a rigid distinction between oral and written tradition, expecially in a democratic society unmarked by extremes of high and low cultures. Should not the folklorist master history as well as the historian master folklore? How did the social historian use folklore anyway—through the Motif-Index? Why must the English professor learn about Negro folktales before he can appreciate the literary art of Joel Chandler Harris?

So instead of reaching a high plane of theory the conference settled at square one with the primary questions dealt with in a library of monographs. There was no way of responding briefly to these questions. One may only outline rejoinders. The resemblances between Jacobs' study of an American Indian narrator and studies in mainstream American folklore, which seemed so close to the outsider, vanish when scrutinized by the folklorists. Jacobs, the anthropologist, endeavors to make intelligible the tales of a nonliterate tribal culture to readers in an industrialized nation, by filling in parenthetically the givens of the culture, explicating the values and mores, translating and glossing the terms, nuances, inflections, gestures of the reciter. The American folklorist presenting, say, Ozark folktales does not need to deal with the commonplaces of his own culture, but faces a wholly different set of issues, namely how to set Ozark traditions within the regional and national framework of American cultural history. As for the distinction the folklorist insists on between the oral and literary tale or song, it is fundamental to his creed and irrefutable to anyone who has recorded extensively in the field and read bonafide field collections. Oral and written forms do mutually influence each other, but to understand literature based on folklore, as in the Uncle Remus stories, the critic has to develop a competence in folkloristics, for otherwise he has no means of recognizing and assessing the alterations in language, characterization, and story line wrought by the author as he transposes material from one medium into another. No scholar can acquire instant expertise in a discipline; the folk historian must train himself in both folklore and history.

The published report did not convey all the subsurface reverbera-tions.[13] A staff member of the Newberry told me he had never seen such seething emotion at one of their conferences. Several of the panelists fell into one or another of the "bogie" categories denounced in the paper, namely scholars skilled in their own subjects who changed from academics to popularizers when they tried their hand at folklore. Flanagan, keen student of American midwestern and western writers, together with A. P. Hudson had assembled a large anthology titled *Folklore in American Literature* that juxtaposed all kinds of writings and made no attempt to inquire into their widely varied relationships, if relationships existed at all, to folk traditions. Blair, a trailblazer into the neglected realm of American humor, committed a children's book of pure fakelore in *Tall Tale America*. Jordan, one of the very few American historians who also taught folklore, at the University of Minnesota, produced excellent grass-roots historical studies, but on the side wrote adulterated children's fakelore books. These scholars would never dream of tampering with the texts of *Huckleberry Finn* or the Declaration of Independence, but when it came to folklore they abandoned scholarship to recreate arch and fanciful tales as genuine embodiments of the popular genius.

Misrepresentations of knowledge carry serious implications over and above the wounding of a few egos of unhappy folklorists or other crusaders. The doctoring and manipulation of folk traditions plants imposed values and misinformation in the minds of young and old readers. Capitalism distorts the social truths of tradition through chauvinistic fakelore, communism through folklore tailored to the class struggle, and the conscientious folklorist must avoid both ideologies.

How he gets pinned between them can be seen in the controversy involving the National Defense Education Act. In 1961 the Congress of the United States eliminated graduate fellowships in folklore, along with other academic subjects considered marginal, from the revised version of the National Defense Education Act. Under Title IV of the original act of 1958, the Office of Health, Education, and Welfare offered federal grants for new and expanded graduate school pro-grams which would enable the nation effectively to counter its manpower and missiles gap with the Soviet Union, a gap demonstrated by the flight of Sputnik. With the support of Indiana University's administration, I applied for a Title IV grant to develop our folklore program and received an award of five fellowships in 1959 and three in 1960, carrying stipends for three years of $2500 per year, with matching funds to the program for operating expenses. Journalists have long made a practice of combing the printed lists of research projects and proposals receiving foundation or government grants and holding up to ridicule those that seemed excessively trivial or futile, and folklore found itself in this unwelcome spotlight. In 1960 the right-wing weekly newsletter emanating from Washington, *Human Events*, and in 1961 the *Wall Street Journal* carried articles, widely reprinted on editorial pages of leading newspapers such as the Chicago *Tribune*, the Indianapolis *Star* and the Columbus *Evening Dispatch*, mocking federal handouts to folklore. On May 12, 1961, the *Wall Street Journal* ran a front-page headline: U.S. SPONSORS STUDIES OF MUSIC AND FOLKLORE, CLAIMS TIE TO SECURITY. The accompanying article by Jonathan Spivak singled out the NDEA awards in folklore and church music for special criticism. Five days later, on May 17, the paper continued the attack on its editorial page with such wisecracks as "the folklore gap which N.D.E.A. is also out to close" and "Take heart, America, apparently our lead in boondoggling is secure."

Legislators in Washington took due notice of these media slams and the same day that the *Wall Street Journal* ran its editorial, the Appropriations Committee of the House of Representatives cut one million dollars from the bill requested by the Department of Health, Education and Welfare, "after learning that some fellowships were awarded for studies in English and American folklore" (New York *Times*, May 18, 1961). John Fogarty of Rhode Island, chairman of the committee, explained the reduction by saying, "This has been one of the more controversial sections of the Office of Education. It has received some bad publicity with reference to certain of the fellowships that were granted in connection with the teaching of folklore and other things like that." Representative H. R. Gross of Iowa, a perennial budget-slasher, proposed an amendment to eliminate all fellowships in the humanities and social sciences and spoke contemptuously of the fellowship grants given to studies in folklore, the ecology of flowing water (ecology was not charismatic in 1961!), jazz, ballet dancing, and the theater.

In the face of these denouncements the United States Commissioner of Education, Sterling McMurrin, sought to explain and justify the grants to folklore:

I would like to say that I believe that sooner or later we are going to recognize that the real problem of American defense is tied up with the whole strength of our culture. Although it is possible for us to jest a good deal about a thing like American folklore, and this kind of jesting is common in American universities, it is still true that a genuine grasp and appreciation of and capacity for critical analysis of American culture is very considerably strengthened by studies in American folklore. [14]

The Commissioner spoke to no avail. The House sent its recommendations for the revised bill to the Senate, whose Committee on Labor and Public Welfare, chaired by Senator Wayne Morse of Oregon, printed on July 31, 1961, a report of 186 pages titled *National Defense Education Act Amendment of 1961* that excluded folklore (pages 20, 138) from Title IV graduate fellowships. The report contained this statement: "The preparation of college teachers in history, economics, and government, for example, is more directly related to a strong system of undergraduate training to meet the nation's defense manpower needs, than are graduate programs in folklore or church music." On September 5, President Herman B Wells of Indiana University, long a supporter of Stith Thompson and the folklore program he conceived, wired the committee in protest, "Surely there must be some misunderstanding of the nature of scholarly work in this field." Senator Morse wrote back sympathetically on September 9, stating that the difficulty "is one of a breakdown in communication between specialists in this field and legislators" and asking for information from the folklore specialists that he could present to his colleagues. The university administration passed the word on to me, and on October 5, I sent a letter to Senator Morse, subsequently printed in the *Journal of American Folklore*, setting folklore studies in the ideological context of the Cold War. A portion follows:

The recent critics of folklore studies are through ignorance playing directly into the hands of the Communists. Folklore is one of the most powerful propaganda weapons of the Soviet Union, as it was of the Third Reich. The Nazis used folklore to promote their theory of a master-race united by ties of blood and tradition and mythology. The Soviets use folklore to advance their theme of the class struggle. When the Communist Party discovered the possibilities of folklore, in 1936, they promptly ordered their scholars to reverse their established theories, which regarded folklore as a product of the upper classes filtering down to the lower, and instead to proclaim that the working people were the creators of folklore. Soviet scholars have ardently followed the Party line ever since, and condemned the "reactionary" theories of the "bourgeois" folklorists. The Soviet government has encouraged the writing of legends and heroic songs by the collective-farm workers, awarded them prizes, and honored them at the national conventions for Soviet writers.

For the Communist Party ideology, folklore is made to order. The Communists see in folklore the creative literature of the "people." Literature is no longer the exclusive product of the intellectuals. And this literature of the people expresses the passionate protest of the workers against the tsars, the landowners, the bosses, the capitalists.

So runs the Communist line. The Soviets make no bones about their zeal for folklore. . . .

The letter went on to document various techniques and strategies employed by communist countries to bend folklore to their cause. An article in the *Soviet Review* of 1961 on "Folklore Research in the USSR" by V. E. Gusev set forth plans of the USSR Academy of Sciences to solidify the heterogeneous peoples of the Soviet Union through mutual knowledge and appreciation of each other's folklore. A piece in the *New York Times Magazine* (April 23, 1961) explained how Vietminh agents from North Vietnam infiltrated Laos and converted lowlanders and tribesmen to communism by singing communist folksongs and ballads and telling fancy tales of the outside world. An Associated Press dispatch (September 21, 1961) quoted the Bulgarian Communist Writers Association on the need to rewrite children's fairy tales to create new heroes responsive to communist conditions. A 1955 essay by a leading Hungarian folklorist, Gyula Ortutay, spoke of the new branch of Hungarian folklore investigating problems of the working class and of the important tasks ethnography and folklore would perform in building up a culture national in appearance but socialist in essence. A United Press International release (July 27, 1961) from Hong Kong reported how a Chinese communist book of ancient Chinese ghost stories about people who defied ghosts could help the Chinese today to dispel their fears of ghosts and of similar idle fears, such as their apprehension of the West.

In contrast to these manipulative uses, the letter continued, the democracies should utilize folklore for genuine knowledge and insight. No field of study or area of learning reached the heart of a people's values, beliefs, traditions, and ethos so directly as folklore. The older disciplines of history, government, and economics paid no attention to the traditional ideas of the anonymous millions. Unfortunately the study of folklore in the United States had become contaminated by amateurs, entertainers, and charlatans, by "fakelorists." But properly trained folklorists did exist, and to them were coming students from Asia and the Middle East to obtain instruction in folklore methods. Should the United States cold-shoulder these Third World students and scholars, the Soviet Union's folklorists would be delighted to explain to them how folklore expressed the protest of the workers against the capitalists and imperialists. The letter concluded with an objection to congressmen listening to journalists on educational matters without consulting the educators involved.[15]

For a while there seemed hope. Other officers and members of the American Folklore Society wrote their congressmen. I mailed copies of a special issue of the *Journal of American Folklore* titled *Folklore Research Around the World* to the members of the Senate committee to inform them of the scholarly and international character of folklore studies, and received cordial acknowledgments from all except Senators Barry Goldwater and John Tower, the two strongest critics of the bill, who did not reply. Senator Ralph Yarborough of Texas, a good friend of the well-known Texas folklorist J. Frank Dobie, sent a particularly encouraging response. (Years later, in 1971, he read an extract from *Folklore Research Around the World* into the *Congressional Record* in support of his own bill for an American Folklife Foundation, a bill still pending.) I received a polite letter from the secretary of the Senate committee saying that the case I had presented was a strong one and if the committee had received it in advance of their report they might well have made different recommendations. So the bill was passed, with folklore eliminated from consideration under the Act.

If my letter as printed in the *Journal of American Folklore* in 1961 failed to change the votes of congressmen dealing with the Cold War, it angered a later generation of resisters to the Vietnam War, and a decade later I found myself attacked by the New Left.[16] One mid-December day in 1970 a lengthy manuscript, titled "The Establishment and the Tape Recorder: Radicalism and Professionalism in Folklore Studies, 1933-67," arrived in my mail. The writer, John Williams, then an assistant professor of history at the University of Notre Dame, with a doctorate from Yale, had analyzed the recent course of the American folklore movement. He was presenting this paper at the annual meeting later that month of the American Historical Association at a session organized by historians of the New Left and courteously invited me to respond, since he had singled me out for pejorative comment. Interested in the problem of how developing organizations reacted to the contemporary social environment, Williams had selected the American Folklore Society as a case in point. According to his interpretation, in the 1930s and 1940s the American folklore scene was characterized by radical folksingers and activist folklorists outside academe and the Society—Pete Seeger, Alan Lomax, Woody Guthrie, the Almanac Singers. In the 1950s and 1960s the academic folklorists, conspicuously myself, professionalized the Society, identified themselves with the power centers and fund disbursers in American life, namely the foundations and the federal government, and as an organization now associated with elite forces in the larger society, prospered through handsome grants and subventions. After Dorson wrote his letter to Senator Morse committing folklore studies to the ideology of the Cold War, congress renewed the NDEA award to folklore (wrote Williams). Evidence of the elitist nature of the American Folklore Society could be seen in their restricting career opportunities for women members and in their plan, initiated by Dorson when president, to undertake an oral history of their prominent members— actions and attitudes in which this society emulated the elitist American Historical Association.

Taken aback, to put it mildly, I did attend the meeting of the historians and appeared at the panel arranged by the New Left historians, chaired by Staughton Lynd, their most prominent personality, whom the press rushed in to photograph. Soon it became apparent why the New Left, and John Williams, were showing an interest in folklorists. The philosophy of the radical historians called for an overturn of the principle of elitism in the national society and in small societal units. All through the meetings a radical caucus stayed in session debating ways of advancing their cause, and one black-shirted radical interrupted the presidential address and attempted to take over the podium. In their historical writings the New Left sought to rewrite history from the bottom up. At this particular panel Staughton Lynd addressed himself to the topic why the C.I.O. failed to go radical and introduced into his talk tape recordings of interviews with C.I.O. members of the 1930s and their recollections of employer and police brutality in smashing strikes. A number of youths in the audience, engaged in the project, discussed with Lynd problems of using the tape recorder with their labor union informants to obtain accurate historical information.

So the New Left historians had discovered the tape recorder, the technique of the personal history interview, and the presence of the living folk—and incidentally had found out that the folklorists had been doing this kind of thing for years. And where then did the folklorists stand? In Williams' angle of vision, the nonacademic folksingers of the depression decades attempting to radicalize the labor unions through the dispersal of anti-establishment protest songs clearly belonged with the New Left cause. The academic folklorists of more recent years, such as Dorson, meanwhile had allied themselves with the establishment. Titters rose from the audience as Williams quoted various of my remarks on the possible uses of folklore to combat communism.

In my five-minute rebuttal I first stated our common ground. Many folklorists, and myself particularly, sought to give attention to the cultural and historical demensions of the common people, the folk. That was our business. But folklorists, on the whole, did not commence field investigations with a-priori assumptions about the ideology of the folk, whether liberal, conservative, radical, populist, or whatever. Folklorists knew that the folk often contained a considerable conservative streak. As for the American Folklore Society, it was very much an underdog organization, struggling to establish its independence from the giant Modern Language Association and American Anthropological Association under whose shadows it had formerly met. Williams had never attended a meeting of the folklorists, but had constructed his account, heavily buttressed with footnote references, from Library of Congress files and journal reports. Consequently he had made some mistakes. When he said that Congress had renewed the fellowship grants for folklore in the National Defense Education Act following my letter to Senator Morse, he had erred in omitting one key word: "not." They had not renewed the grant. Williams had seen a statement in the *Kentucky Folklore Record* to the effect that the NDEA grants in folklore originally awarded in 1959 had been renewed in 1960. But at issue was the provision for further folklore awards *after* 1961 in the amended NDEA bill. Had Williams ever attended a national meeting of the folklorists, he would have seen women everywhere in evidence, not necessarily satisfied, but highly visible in the corridors, on programs, holding office, unlike the scene at the American Historical Association. Working only from published reports and available files, he had completely missed the turbulent inner history of the American Folklore Society, which at no time presented a united front of academics courting the establishment. When Williams coupled the names of MacEdward Leach, chairman of the folklore program at the University of Pennsylvania and longtime

23

secretary of the Society, with Stith Thompson and Dorson as leading the fight to link folklorists with the power centers, he did not know that Thompson had retired and that Leach and Dorson and their respective institutions were in bitter contention with each other on the policies of the society, a contention that led to a packed business meeting in 1964 and the overthrow of my nomination for the presidency, as too controversial and divisive a figure, the first time in the society's history that the slate was challenged. (I was elected in 1966.) This was the history that never entered the public records, and of which Williams was oblivious.

If Williams had examined my own work he would have found evidence of considerable agreement between us, in terms of interest in folk history, although this convergence of interests would have upset his argument. One study he praised as an illustration of commendable folk history, Lynwood Montell's *The Saga of Coe Ridge*, had actually been undertaken as a doctoral dissertation under my direction.

In a one-minute reply to my rebuttal Williams said graciously that he had not attacked a live man before and was going back to attacking dead men. Still he gave the impression that the New Left historians had looked for allies among the academic folklorists and found them wanting.[17]

So folklore found itself in a murderous crossfire between the right and the left, rejected by the hawks as trivial and irrelevant and pilloried by the doves as establishment toadies. But the exchanges illustrate the ideological implications of folklore which have arisen in the history of one nation after another. An anthropological acquaintance, a seasoned academic entrepreneur, suggested changing the name folklore to a more substantial and prestigious appellation. He recalled how congressmen were once suspicious of the social sciences, whose name smacked of socialism, ergo of communism. When the academics called themselves behavioral rather than social scientists, congressmen looked at them with new respect and ladled out grants.

My most recent folklore debate involves the Ford Foundation and its grantee, Eliot Wigginton, a rural schoolteacher who has edited two best-selling books of folklore, *The Foxfire Book* (1972) and *Foxfire 2* (1973). In a short communication to the *North Carolina Folklore Journal*, titled "The Lesson of 'Foxfire,' " in November 1973, I commented how folklore as a discipline again was being ignored and slighted, in a grant of $196,000 made to Eliot Wigginton and IDEAS (Institutional Development and Economic Affairs Service) "to collect and publish folklore," as the Ford Foundation put it in their Newsletter. The foundation had not consulted any professional folklorists before awarding the grant. Indeed the lack of funding from granting agencies in the United States compelled folklore graduate students and professors to cross the border to Canada, where the National Museum of Man hospitably financed their fieldwork in Canadian provinces. Wigginton admitted readily that in five years at Cornell he had never heard of folklore. Now the Ford grant would extend the Foxfire concept to other disadvantaged communities throughout the United States at the hands of schoolteachers completely ignorant of folklore methods.

The Foxfire idea represented an imaginative concept in education that only accidentally spilled over into folklore. Teaching school at Rabun Gap, Nacoochee, in hill country Georgia, Wigginton found his students hostile and bored with conventional subjects. So he enlisted their energies in a wholly new direction, the consulting of their families, neighbors, and older friends about the traditional ways of life, from butchering hogs to telling ghost stories. The students wrote up their findings in papers that Wigginton helped edit for *The Foxfire Magazine*, which the class put out collectively. Eventually he culled selections from the magazine into *The Foxfire Book*, which became a national sensation.

My paper acknowledged that "Wigginton had recognized a key educational value, in encouraging his charges to explore their own inheritance through fieldwork." But it also contended that he could have developed his concept more fruitfully with the advice of trained folklorists, who could have led students to the library as well as the field to learn of similar cultures, counseled them on traditions they might search for, and advised them on editing the magazine and the book so they would avoid romantic stereotypes of backwoods folk practicing old-timey ways. "Foxfire stands at the crossroads," I wrote. "Properly channeled, the Foxfire concept can lead into valuable fieldwork and interpretation of local cultures; misguided, it drifts into the sands of fakelore."

Wigginton saw the piece and with some indignation issued "A Reply to 'The Lesson of Foxfire'" in the May 1974 *North Carolina Folklore Journal*. He stated that "the people my students found who most excited them, and whom they most wanted to write about, *were* those mountain grandparents they found who *did*, in fact, happen to be separated from the modern world." Aunt Arie Carpenter had never seen television or movies, never been in an elevator or airplane, never eaten in a restaurant, and still lived in a log house with no plumbing and a wood stove. As a teacher he wished to nurture in his students an increased sense of humanity. Turning them into professional folklorists was never in the remotest sense his intention. But "in deference to Dr. Dorson . . . since it appears we are collecting folklore in spite of ourselves, we will attempt in the future to come *closer* to doing a project he would approve of . . . But if, in the end, the project still does not measure up to the academic criteria laid down by the gods of folklore, that's just too damn bad . . . And I would challenge some of those Ph.D. folklorists to get out here in the mud and get their diplomas dirty and pitch in where they can really do some good instead of sniping at little folks from the safety of their certificate-lined walls."

A further brief dialogue followed Wigginton's statement, with my response to his reply and his final rejoinder, in which the communication gap narrowed slightly, as Wigginton invited Dorson to Rabun Gap and Dorson invited Wigginton to Indiana University. Dorson proposed that Wigginton recruit some of the hundred doctoral candidates in folklore at the University of Pennsylvania and Indiana University as resource persons. Wigginton countered by saying they should "commit themselves to *Foxfire*-like projects on their own in some of the thousands of forgotten high schools across this land."[18] (There is though the problem that these graduate students are trained as college teachers and ineligible for teaching in the public schools without acquiring state board of education certificates.)

Here is another crossfire. The foundations ignore folklorists because they do not consider folklore a discipline, while dishing out funds for an educator's package based on folk materials. The educators see folklorists as overdisciplined pedants and criticize them for "going into cultures examining the people there like bugs under a microscope, and then scratching their heads in professional amazement and walking away with their tapes and photographs never to return—never to make one single gesture of affection or personal commitment to the welfare of that group of folks."[19] Wigginton and those who share his stereotype of the folklorist-as-people-dissector simply know nothing of the whole thrust of modern folklore scholarship, which stresses involvement with and recognition of the folk performer. The strongest of personal bonds develop between folklore collectors and their acquaintances in the field. What the Foxfire concept proposes to do is what folklorists have been doing ever since the Grimm brothers founded the discipline: explore the traditions of the people no longer known to the intellectuals.

26

This story stops here because of publishing deadlines; its theme will continue indefinitely. A new episode is unfolding with my most recent book, *America in Legend,* which received more recognition in the marketplace than any of my earlier works. A review in the *Journal of American History,* by Robert Drinnon, savages the book for omitting Afro-American, Native American, and ethnic folk heroes and heroines, and for exalting the bloodthirsty Indian-killer Mike Fink as a legendary hero. Drinnon discovered the Indians in a captivity journal which, as he tells it, produced in him a kind of conversion experience, opening his eyes to ethnology and the Indian perspective in American history. On the wave of current fashion, he demands American folk legends tailored to the existing ideology. Fink and Crockett were indeed violent and even racist personalities. They by no means appealed to all Americans in their time, or in ours. Still, to invent substitutes for them merely produces a new fakelore. Scholars often respond to the psychic pressures of their time as supinely as do the popularizers, and will manipulate folklore, and history, to support their biases.[20]

These are several of the battles on public record that have engaged me in attempts to combat misconceptions about the study of folklore. But many battles are never joined. The handful of professional folklorists cannot control the review media, and, unlike other fields, the book on folklore may be reviewed by almost anybody. To counter all the ill-informed reviews would be a full-time task. For a characteristic example of the anti-intellectual point of view toward folklore scholarship, consider this comment on a children's book of folk stories:

In the foreword, George F. Reinecke, editor of the "Louisiana Folklore Miscellany," points out that in this book the reader is spared the academic folklorists' "excessive attention to nomenclature and methodology." This reviewer agrees with Reinecke that the author's avoidance of codification, structural analysis, and classification of genre is an asset and that the over-academic approach to folklore destroys the color and action of the folktales and decimates the delight of the reader, as well.[21]

The reviewer, an assistant in the Mississippi Department of Archives and History, goes on to say that folklore is an oral art form, that one of the joys of reading folktales is to recognize other versions, and that all the ones in this book "have the stamp of Jagendorf, who wrote them down as he heard them."

Consumers of alleged folklore regularly repeat this mournful plaint against the pedants who spoil their fun by classifying and analyzing tales and ballads. But, in the first place, the contents of the book under review are not folklore, but a literary product passed off as folklore, or what I have called fakelore. If they bear his own stamp the collector cannot possibly have written the tales down as he heard them; each oral narrator possesses his own style, which differs greatly from literary style. Second, writing a book of entertaining stories for children has nothing to do with the serious study of cultural expression and behavior that is the concern of folklorists. If the tales were written down as they were told, they might prove boring, unintelligible, or offensive to children, and to many adults, although once understood the actual folklore can excite readers. The tales themselves are not the prime target of the modern folklore scholar, who seeks to understand the role and techniques of the oral narrator, the social context of each delivery, the construction of the narrative, and the cultural values expressed in the tales. Yet here we have a professor of English writing a foreword to a volume for ten-year-olds and up, composed by a prolific writer of children's books and reviewed by an archivist, all making pronouncements about folklore scholarship with an air of authority. The three have served as officers of state folklore societies, in New York, Louisiana, and Mississippi. Members of such societies for the most part wish to enjoy folk festivals, folk performances, and exhibits of folk arts and crafts, and have little interest in scholarly papers.

What then does the petulant folklorist have to say positively in his own behalf? Let some of my students speak, or at least let me call attention to doctoral dissertations they have published, as evidence of the special contributions that folkloristics can make to man's knowledge of man.

In *The Morphology of North American Indian Tales* (1964), Alan Dundes applied structural principles to the study of folktales, and demonstrated how the structural approach revealed an underlying pattern in the oral narratives of North American Indian tribes, previously regarded as formless and meandering. Following the folksong trail of a Maine woods poet whose songs had passed into oral tradition, Edward D. Ives resurrected a local bard and threw light on the moot question of folksong origins in *Larry Gorman: The Man Who Made the Songs* (1964). Although the Negro community in southern Kentucky whose history he sought to recover no longer existed, William Lynwood Montell reconstructed its story in *The Saga of Coe Ridge* (1970) through skillful use of oral folk history techniques. Analyzing *Folklore in the Writings of Rowland E. Robinson* (1973),

Ronald L. Baker called attention to a regional Vermont author who had captured many forms of local folk traditions in his artistically wrought ethnographic fiction. None of the fourteen critics who praised Robinson's art and craft in the centennial edition of his works recognized that he drew from folklore as his major source. Much of the oral humor and supernatural belief in Western culture involves the erotic, and in his *Analytical Survey of Anglo-American Traditional Erotica* (1973), Frank Hoffmann brought to light hidden bibliographical resources and furnished a greatly needed motif-index of erotic folk literature.

Carla Bianco in *The Two Rosetos* (1974) interviewed residents of the parent town in Italy and its colony in Pennsylvania and contrasted the traditional life and folklore of the same stock in the Old World and the New. The town of Roseto, Pennsylvania, made news in the early 1960s when medical researchers reported that its inhabitants, corpulent eaters of heavy pasta dishes, suffered little or no heart disease. In the course of her field research we agreed that the successful acculturation of the Rosetans, who literally enjoyed the best of both worlds, the folkways of the Old and the well-being of the New, accounted for the contentment, lack of stress, and absence of heart attacks in Roseto. This theory was confirmed when newspaper reports a decade later announced that second-generation Rosetans were now dying of America's number one killer, heart disease, as a direct consequence of the breakdown of the traditional folkways and of the high-pressure living of Americanization.

While tape-recording descendants of slaves, Gladys Fry kept hearing the term "night doctors." Eventually she concentrated on that tradition and uncovered a crucial aspect of slavery life unnoticed in the historical literature. White masters and overseers terrorized slaves into remaining on the plantation with the threat that if they left, the night doctors or night riders would kill them and sell their corpses to medical schools for use as cadavers. Fry presents the tradition in *Night Riders in Black Folk History* (1975).

These are a sampling of the creative research efforts being undertaken by the current generation of folklore scholars interested in the American scene. To such original works the zealous folklorist points with confidence as he expounds his methods, his concepts, his goals, his findings to his colleagues in the university and to the public outside. He believes they will one day share his view that a sympathetic knowledge of humankind must include knowledge of folk utterance and folk wisdom.

I

The Theoretical Side
of Folklore

Ever since the discovery of folklore as a subject matter, students of the new field have puzzled over its meanings. Their interpretations reflect the vogues of Herder, Darwin, Marx, and Freud, the appeals of romantic and ideological nationalism, the currents of mythological, ritual, and structural symbolism. The essays that follow do not espouse a particular system or seek to impose one kind of theoretical grid on folk culture. They are concerned with the directions of folklore theory.

Interpreters of folklore, whatever their differences, have customarily agreed that the materials of folklore hark back to an ancient past. The first essay takes issue with this premise and contends that folklore mirrors the main action of its era. Folklore's philosophers, who began as antiquarians and survivalists, are commencing to relate to the hurly-burly of the world about them.

Some of these up-dated theorists are considered in the second essay, a review article appraising books on mythology and folklore published between 1968 and 1972. The output of this period demonstrates the eclectic nature of the publications on which the folklorist must pass judgment. Unlike scholars in other disciplines, he continually confronts volumes pertinent to his interests that are generated from outside disciplines, and some that reflect no discipline at all.

The last essay in this group faces the question whether folklore itself is a discipline, and develops an answer in terms of academic realpolitik even more than in terms of intellectual rigor. What use is a beautiful system if there is no platform to expound it from and no audience keen for the message?

 Folklore
In the Modern World

The Traditional Concept

From its initial conceptualization folklore has suggested the outlines of a hidden, forgotten, and backward culture. This culture of the folk was hidden in two ways: deep in remote time, in a prehistoric past, when early man perceived the world animistically, or at least in the pre-Christian era, when pagan man indulged in barbarous rites; and far-off in place, away from the busy centers of civilization, in the peasant villages of the countryside and mountain ridges. Among the rural folk, old ways, customs, and beliefs, once vital and central in their epoch, lingered on as outmoded survivals—so ran the formula. In the minds of different folklore scholars the past took varying forms. It might be visualized as the dawn of man in a savage state, or a high ancient culture before its erosion, but in any event folklore was past-minded and past-begotten, the shards and shreds, leftovers and relics of a departed age.

Synonyms of folklore in the nineteenth century plainly indicate this conception: bygones, popular antiquities, survivals. Coupled with this notion of folklore were pejorative terms, such as superstitious, illiterate, backward, primitive, which were applied to the people who possessed this culture. But another set of terms—simple, unspoiled, pastoral, close to nature—viewed them in a nobler light. Whether admired or despised, the folk represented a world different from the centers of power, wealth, progress, industry, and intellectual and political activity in the metropolises. This first formulation of folklore can be presented as a set of almost Lévi-Straussian polarities between traditional and modern cultures:

folk	elite
rural	urban
agricultural	industrial
peasant	factory worker
illiterate	literate
handicrafts	machines
word of mouth	mass communications
backward	modern
superstitious	rational
magical	scientific
marginal	central

These explicitly stated contrasts intrigued the pioneers of folklore studies and aroused them to investigate the newly discovered, unknown, and unsuspected folk culture eclipsed by the high civilization. This theorem of folklore can be readily documented by statements and actions of the great names in the history of folkloristics.

GERMANY

In the late eighteenth century Johann Gottfried Herder, philosopher and poet, expounded a persuasive theory of literary nationalism based on the oral poetry of the common people who transmitted the soul of the Germanic tradition from its medieval springs, before Renaissance influences had imparted an artificial veneer to German literature. He called for volunteers to collect "songs of the people . . . in the unlearned glee-parties of the peasant-folk, songs which often do not scan and which rhyme badly."[1] Jacob and Wilhelm Grimm heard his call and went out to collect tales rather than songs, although they considered all oral literature, prose and verse, of the peasantry as *Naturpoesie*. They described their *Kinder- und Hausmärchen* as a "great treasure of antiquity indispensable for research" and believed they could reconstruct the old Germanic pantheon from village traditions. In the *Deutsche Mythologie* which in 1835 elaborated his sytem, Jacob Grimm called attention to the scholarly values for the cultural historian in such oral sources as a supplement to documentary records: "If these numerous written memorials have only left us sundry bones and joints, as it were, of our old mythology, its living breath still falls upon us from father to son."[2] The example and concepts of the Grimms inspired nascent folklorists in one European country after another to emulate their mode of collecting and interpreting folk traditions as emblems of a people's proud antiquities.

Folklore in the Modern World

The influence of the Grimms's investigations of Märchen, Sagen, and Germanic mythology immediately struck a responsive chord in England, where seventeenth- and eighteenth-century antiquaries had already prepared the way for the recognition of folklore as a word and as a concept. In 1777 John Brand titled his miscellany of notions, customs, and practices culled from printed sources *Observations on Popular Antiquities* and emphasized their pastness. "The *prime* Origin of the superstitious Notions and Ceremonies of the People is absolutely unattainable; we despair of ever being able to reach the Fountain Head of Streams which have been running and increasing from the Beginning of Time." By 1846 another antiquary, William John Thoms, perceived in Brand's accumulated mass of materials the subject matter of a separate branch of learning which he proposed to call "Folk-Lore, — *the Lore of the People*" as a deliberate substitute for "popular antiquities." Fully as much as its replacement, the new term stressed the past: "No one who has made the manners, customs, observances, superstitions, ballads, proverbs, &c., of the olden time his study, but must have arrived at two conclusions: —the first, how much that is curious and interesting in these matters is now entirely lost—the second, how much may yet be rescued by timely exertion."³

Here, in the baptismal rite of folklore, appears the classic cliché of the folkloric enterprise: the old traditions and rites are disappearing; hurry up and collect them as fast as you can. For the next century and more collectors would be motivated by this premise. In a follow-up statement a week later in *The Athenaeum* Thoms correlated folklore with a pastoral, anti-industrial setting by quoting from his contemporary, Thomas Keightley, author of *The Fairy Mythology*, who opined "that the belief in Fairies is by no means extinct in England, — and that in districts, if there be any such, where steam-engines, cotton mills, mail coaches, and similar exorcists have not yet penetrated, numerous legends might be collected."⁴ The sequence is plainly stated: the advent of modern technology and communications drives out the old supernatural beliefs. In an appended note Thoms observes that what Chaucer said of the elves disappearing may now, in 1846, be applied to Keightley's 1838 comment: "But now can no man see non *mails* mo." Even communications have speeded up, as horses gave way to trains. But John Aubrey, the seventeenth-century antiquary, had already mourned the elimination of olden lore by modern contrivances: "Before Printing, Old-wives Tales were ingeniose . . . Now-adayes Bookes are common, and most of the poor people understand letters; and the many good Bookes, and variety of Turnes of Affaires, have putt all the old Fables out of doors: and the divine art of Printing and Gunpowder have frighted away Robin-goodfellow and the Fayries."[5]

Each new generation of folklorists would echo the refrain that modern ways spelled the death of folklore. Max Müller constructed his system of solar mythology around the concept of a "disease of language" in the mythopoeic age of the Aryan race, during which men forgot the original meanings of words and used them metaphorically; "good morning" is a solar myth. Accepting Müller's theory without challenge, Edward B. Tylor directed his attention to an earlier stage of mankind, the savage state of animistic thought, to formulate his doctrine of survivals: the folklore of today represents the survivals of animistic ways of thinking. Under the spell of this persuasive argument, the "great team" of anthropological folklorists explored collections of peasant folklore and stimulated the local vicar to collect such folklore for the purpose of identifying survivals. That was the great quest, the exciting hunt, to pin down the memorial of a prehistoric rite or custom or myth in its fossilized form as a peasant observance or utterance. Each of the Great Team restated the definition and methodology of folklore in terms of its pastness, backwardness, and peasantness:

Andrew Lang: "There is a form of study, Folklore, which collects and compares the similar but immaterial relics of old races, the surviving superstitions and stories, the ideas which are in our time but not of it . . . The student of folklore is thus led to examine the usages, myths and ideas of savages, which are still retained, in rude enough shape, by the European peasantry."

Edwin Sidney Hartland: "Let me try to tell you what folklore is. . . . It is now well established that the most civilized races have all fought their way slowly upwards from a condition of savagery. Now, savages can neither read nor write; yet they manage to collect and store up a considerable amount of knowledge of a certain kind. . . . The knowledge, organization, and rules thus gathered and formulated are preserved in the memory, and communicated by word of mouth and by actions of various kinds. To this mode of preservation and communication, as well as to the things thus preserved and communicated, the name of Tradition is given; and Folklore is the science of Tradition."

Alfred Nutt: "The folk whose lore we collect and study is essentially the portion of mankind which has ever remained in closest contact with Mother Earth, the class upon whose shoulders has been laid the task of making the soil yield food, and of doing the drudgery, the dirty work of humanity. . . . In telling you what folklore is I have emphasized . . . certain features that differentiate it sharply from our modern *civilization*. That is, as the word indicates, a product of town-life, folklore is a product of the countryside."[6]

These were no lip-service definitions. The Great Team devoted their major energies to researches in peasant customs and savage myths based on Tylor's doctrine of survivals. In his encyclopedic three-volume treatise on *The Legend of Perseus*, Hartland traced savage elements coalescing in the familiar narratives of classical Greece. George Laurence Gomme developed his thesis of the mingling of Aryan and non-Aryan layers of ethnic tradition in extant folklore in several books, from *Folk-Lore Relics of Early Village Life* in 1883 to *Folklore as an Historical Science* in 1908. Edward Clodd pursued the primitive idea of magic attached to names in an examination of one well-known English Märchen, *Tom Tit Tot; An Essay on Savage Philosophy in Folk-Tale*, and he alarmed some members of the Folk-Lore Society by his presidential address of 1896 with illustrations of savage folk beliefs and rituals surviving in Christian sacraments.

Collectors of folklore followed the lines marked out by the theorists and sought for survivals among country folk in Britain and backward races throughout the empire. Robert Hunt in Cornwall, Charlotte Burne in Shropshire, and Ella Leather in Herefordshire set the tone for the ample county collection of supernatural local legends pointing back to savage times. Thus, the legend of "The Man with the Hatchet" preserved in an almhouse carving in Leominster, Herefordshire, of a fellow with an axe, above this inscription,

> He that gives away all before he is dead,
> Let 'em take this hatchet and knock him on ye head

seemed a survival from an age when savages killed the elderly with a mallet. The greatest feats of collecting in Britain took place in the Gaelic-speaking outposts of Scotland and Ireland, where a fading language preserved what Celtic folklorists believed to be the remnants of a poetic pagan mythology. As early as 1860 John Francis Campbell was searching the Highlands and Outer Hebrides for the rich veins of narrative tradition he published as *Popular Tales of the West Highlands*. An American of Irish ancestry, Jeremiah Curtin, visited Ireland between 1871 and 1893 to capture oral myths told in the western counties by Gaelic-speaking peasants living in wretched poverty in thatched huts. Other notable field collections to support the survivalist theory came from British colonial administrators and their wives and daughters interrogating peasants in India and tribesmen in Africa.

SCANDINAVIA

In the history of folkloristics the Scandinavian—or Nordic, to include the Finns—scholars have formed an influential bloc, which too has shared the assumptions that folklore belongs to the past and the peasantry. The prime figure in the illustrious record of the Finns, Elias Lönnrot, journeyed to East Karelia in the 1830s to meet singers of ancient Finnish poetry, from whose runes he stitched together the *Kalevala*. As the historian of Finnish folklore research, Jouko Hautala, has written, "the Kalevala opened up dazzling vistas to the few but nevertheless ardent guardians of Finnish culture; it lifted up to the general view a heroic, magnificent past, of which there had been no previous knowledge." So artistic, eloquent, and informative were these oral poems that Lönnrot wondered "how they could have been composed by peasants." Julius and Kaarle Krohn used the national epic as a point of departure for their theoretical formulations. "It is my belief that most of the *Kalevala* material is borrowed from neighboring peoples," asserted Julius.[7] Kaarle Krohn wrote his first major work on the history of the Kalevala runes. His fieldwork, primarily to collect tales, took him to outlying areas in Ostrobotnia, Russian and Northern Karelia, the Forest Finnish districts of Varmland. The historical-geographical method he devised and taught to his students at the University of Helsinki considered the migration routes of tales, runes, and other folklore as they traveled in past centuries from one peasant bard to another. Ultimately the employers of the Finnish method hoped to ascertain the date and place of origin of the tale or ballad type; and if they did not push origins back to the dawn of man, as did the evolutionists, still they looked back in historic time.

In Norway the pioneer collectors Peter Christen Asbjörnsen and Jörgen Moe followed the example of the Grimms in conducting field trips to outlying villages in quest of folktales. As Reidar Christiansen has written, "both were intimately acquainted with the people of the countryside."[8] Jorgen's son Moltke continued the practice, engaging in his first field foray at nineteen and concentrating on the conservative district of Telemark. In the interests of promoting Norwegian nationalism against Danish dominance, Asbjörnsen and the Moes hoped to recover an ancient Norse mythology discernible in peasant traditions.

Magic wishing objects in the *eventyr* appeared to hark back to the Norse god Odin, or "Wish."

The eclectic Swedish folklorist Gunnar Olof Hyltén-Cavallius, who helped lay the foundations for folklore research in Sweden, made capital from his rearing in an old peasant district of Värend in the forests of Småland, although his career took him to Stockholm and Rio de Janeiro. On holidays he collected in Småland; and, as a biographer has written, he "carried his native district with him in his heart and in his suitcase wherever he went."[9] The celebrated theorist of Swedish folklore, Carl Wilhelm von Sydow, also grew up in a rural environment in Småland and enjoyed close contact with servants and cottagers. Though emphasizing the role played by individual bearers of tradition, von Sydow followed Tylor and Lang in ascribing an ancient common inheritance of magic tales to Indo-European speaking peoples.

Similar emphases appear among Danish folklorists. In 1843 Svend Grundtvig made a ringing appeal to his countrymen to send him all known examples of Danish heroic ballads still surviving among the "humblest strata of the population" as a means of recovering the national folk-poetry of the Middle Ages. His writings on Danish mythical ballads stress "their great age, their purely heathen character." Becoming aware well on in his career of the Swedish equivalent of the English "popular antiquities," *folkeminder*, he employed it in the title of his encyclopedic enterprise of 1861, Popular Antiquities in the Mouth of the People: Folktales, Ballads, Legends, and other Relics of the Poetry and Belief of the Past, As They Are Still Alive in the Memory of the Danish People.[10] The tireless Danish collector Evald Tang Kristensen, who published seventy-two books and left a wealth of tale texts unpublished, indulged in little theory about the pastness of folklore but plainly expressed in acts and words his conviction that folklore abounds among the wretched of the earth.

Folklore is mostly in the keeping of poor people; it is as though the comforts of life displace the cultural traditions. It is most reasonable, then, that it is to be found in the poorer moor districts in the middle of Jutland, and it is very seldom . . . that you will meet with rare and well-disseminated folklore in Eastern Jutland, or in the prosperous districts of Western Jutland. . . . As cleanliness and furnishings in the houses of the moor districts ten or twenty years ago [this manuscript is dated 1929, the year of Kristensen's death] left much to be desired . . . I have never come home from a journey without being infested with vermin.[11]

Kristensen adds little vignettes about the impoverished country folk lacking in the world's goods but rich in songs and tales.

Grundtvig's equally famous student, Axel Olrik, is best known internationally for his theory of epic laws which governed the composition of traditional narrative. This theory derived from his own researches in Scandinavian mythology, medieval heroic poetry, medieval ballads, and magical tales descended from ancient myths. In short, the productions of bards and folk narrators along predetermined lines—direct action, the opposition of two active characters, the final resolution of conflict—are shaped by aesthetic principles of oral literature in operation since the myth-creating age.

RUSSIA

The leading theoretical and field-minded folklorists in nineteenth-century Russia shared the assumptions of their European colleagues. Alexander Nikolayevich Afanasyev examined folktales, proverbs, and folksongs from the perspective of the mythological school, which explained the symbolic meanings of folkloric texts through long-forgotten beliefs about the heavens congealed in metaphors—Max Müller's "disease of language": "The greater part of the mythical concepts of the Indo-European peoples goes back to the remote time of the Aryans. . . . Hence it can be understood why the popular traditions, superstitions, and other fragments of antiquity must be studied comparatively. . . . The comparative method provides the means for restoring the original form of the traditions."[12] This method of comparative mythology looking back to an early Aryan age Afanasyev applied throughout the three volumes of his celebrated work, *The Poetic Attitudes of the Slavs on Nature: An Essay in the Comparative Study of Slavonic Traditions and Beliefs in Connection with the Mythical Legends of Other Related Peoples (1865-69)*.

Other interpretations shelved the mythological theory, and Vsevolod Fyodorovich Miller in the 1890s established the "historical school" which, while still pointing backward, aimed its sights at nearer periods of Russian history in the attempt to decipher Russian oral poetry. Disavowing too the diffusionist or migrationist theory as to what routes were traveled by the subject elements that entered the *byliny* (epic ballads) from the outside, Miller concentrated squarely on the byliny as growths on Russian soil. "I occupy myself more with the history of the *byliny* and the reflection of history in them, beginning the first of these studies, not from prehistoric times, not from the bottom, but from the top. These upper strata of the *bylina* . . . can give, not a conjectural, but a more or less exact representation of a period in the life of the *bylina* which is nearer to us."[13] Miller and other members of the historical school then debated each other as to the precise period and area in which a particular bylina was composed. Their speculations ranged widely, from Tartar times down to the sixteenth century. But all agreed that the byliny were at least several centuries old.

The theoretical interest of Tsarist folklorists in byliny was greatly heightened by the uncovering of an active heroic epic singing tradition in the far-off Olonets region of Karelia. P. N. Rybnikov collected and published over two hundred byliny in the 1860s, and A. F. Hilferding recorded over three hundred more in 1871, along with detailed biographies of the bards. In the ensuing decades collectors continued the practice of undertaking field trips to remote areas in search of the prized byliny. Two talented pupils of V. F. Miller, the twins Boris and Jurij Sokolov, journeyed to the Belozersk region in Novgorod province in 1908 and 1909 for the peasant traditions they would publish as *Folktales and Songs of the Belozernsk Region*. Their volume contains vivid impressions of the peasantry whose confidence they painfully sought to win:

> We arrive at a village and ask, "Can we stay somewhere around here?" "Well, whose people are you?" is the first question asked of us, which, in the course of our travels, we have had to answer a thousand times, "From far away, ma, from Moscow." "From Moscow?!" repeats some peasant woman distrustfully and somewhat surprised . . . . "So you say, you're looking for songs. What kind of songs do we have? Are you short of songs of your own in Moscow? Our songs aren't any good. Everyone knows—they're just village songs. We're backcountry people!"[14]

Suspicious, puzzled, distrustful, the villagers conjectured that the Moscow strangers were secret police, politicians, insurgents, even Japanese spies. "Well, they say out there that you were sent for a purpose: to find out where people sing about the tsar and to put those people in jail." The phonograph fascinated the peasants, who considered it an instrument of the devil, and so did the vision of Moscow, which they imagined as a big village.

JAPAN

Japanese folklore studies evolved in relative isolation, but they too emphasize the past and the peasant. The theoretical preoccupation of Kunio Yanagita, founder of folklore science in Japan, and his school has been the historical reconstruction of pre-Buddhist folk religion. In a tape-recorded interview in 1957, seven years before his death, Yanagita expressed his view succinctly: "Although the uncompromising march of Christianity has all but obliterated traces of ancient faiths in the West, Japan offers scholars an opportunity to observe and study still-vigorous traits of old religious ideologies. Beneath the Buddhism of modern Japan, the folklorist will find vestiges of ancient mountain and ancestor worship."[15]

Yanagita acknowledged a debt to George Laurence Gomme's thesis that the folklorist could isolate separate historical ethnic layers in current traditions. From extant rituals, taboos, observances, and legends Japanese folklorists reconstituted the popular deities and the worship accorded them in primeval times. Every essay in *Studies in Japanese Folklore* pursues this goal. Thus, Toshijiro Hirayama perceives in *ta-no-kami* a deity of the rice fields revered by rice farmers in festivals that extend back thousands of years. Nobuhiro Matsumoto analyzes comparative legends of Kogoro the charcoalmaker to conclude that Japanese ironworkers derived their belief system from an ancient immigration of artisans from the Asian mainland. Hiroji Naoe concludes that the family tutelary deity known as *yashiki-gami* is a recent development from an ancient ancestral cult deity of violent disposition, as befits ancestral spirits.

In the fieldwork enterprises he sponsored through the Japanese Folklore Institute, Yanagita set as his targets the small, remote villages of the mountains and seashore. His collecting teams visited hundreds of these villages in compiling the materials presented in *Studies in Mountain Village Life* and *Studies in Fishing Village Life*. These materials cover a spectrum of magico-religious practices and local-historical traditions, and apparently support Yanagita's contention that "outside of the big cities, sixty to seventy per cent of the population still follow the beliefs and way of life traditional to Japan."[16]

UNITED STATES

In the history of American folklore studies the great catalytic library work and the great catalytic fieldwork belong to Francis James Child and Cecil Sharp. From his study at Harvard, Child corresponded in the 1870s and 1880s with a host of British manuscript holders and European ballad scholars in his hunt for the full roster of *The English and Scottish Popular Ballads*. In classifying his famous canon of three hundred and five ballad types Child stressed the qualifier "popular"; these must be ballads that had lived in the mouths of the people, and consequently ones that had endured for a sufficient length of time to demonstrate their popular currency, presumably from the Middle Ages. Their archaic language and chivalric themes bespoke the past; although there were at hand an abundance of recent topical broadside ballads, Child deliberately dismissed these latecomers as not truly popular and of lesser artistic merit. The old ballads were the best. Child hypothesized that ballad poetry preceded art poetry.

In 1916 Cecil Sharp set out on the trail of the three hundred and five as they were still sung in the southern Appalachians. The Englishman hunting British ballads in America adopted the same premises as the American who had, at long distance, sleuthed traditional ballads in Britain. Sharp went to the backlands where he could recapture the pastoral setting of old in which the ballads flourished. The peasant England of yesteryear, eradicated in the twentieth century by the industrial revolution, survived in mountain pockets of the United States. In the noble mountaineer of North Carolina, Tennessee, Virginia, and Kentucky, Sharp found a replica of the preindustrial English peasant—his very descendant. He describes a scene encountered in the Laurel country of North Carolina:

> The region is from its inaccessibility a very secluded one. There are but few roads—most of them little better than mountain tracks—and practically no railroads. Indeed, so remote and shut off from outside influence were, until quite recently, these sequestered mountain valleys that the inhabitants have for a hundred years or more been completely isolated and cut off from all traffic with the rest of the world. Their speech is English, not American, and . . . it is clear that they are talking the language of a past day . . . . The majority live in log-cabins . . . . In their general characteristics they reminded me of the English peasant . . . the majority were illiterate . . . . Although uneducated . . . they possess that elemental wisdom, abundant knowledge, and intuitive understanding which those only who live in constant touch with Nature and face to face with reality seem to be able to acquire.[17]

Here are all the stereotypical qualities associated with the carriers of folklore: remoteness, isolation, illiteracy, poverty, and the nobility of heart engendered by a life close to the earth. Sharp did draw some distinctions between mountaineer and peasant, and found a freer, more independent spirit and greater articulateness in the American type. He admired the bearing, the features, the friendly hospitality of these "primitive peoples," whose lack of suspicion contrasts with the fears of the peasants from Belozersk. Aware of the negative image attached to the mountain folk in the eyes of many city people, Sharp countered with assertions that he heard and saw nothing of bloodfeuding and moonshining. In Thoreauvian vein he lauded these cheerful, leisurely residents of Appalachia who enjoyed the graces of life rather than grinding out their lives "making a living." One of these graces was the singing, naturally and spontaneously in the midst of the daily routine, of traditional songs. The folksong inheritance, like the folk themselves, was pure and unsullied by industrial, commercial culture; if a "modern street-song" invaded the mountains, he perceived a cleansing process through which the singers wedded the tawdry text to a traditional tune and reshaped it into the form of a traditional ballad.

In a revealing aside Sharp contrasted the song repertoire of the cowboys, recorded by John Lomax, with that of the highlanders, as two groups similar in their communal isolation. But in spite of their more colorful existence, the cowboys mustered a sorry song fare, in Sharp's judgment, because they had no fund of traditional song, no imaginative past on which to draw, but must compose their ballads and lyrics about their immediate experiences, in the theme of "the cowboy's life is a dreadful life."

Sharp established for American folklore scholarship the guidelines of pastness and physical remoteness which would be followed for the next half-century. Subsequent collectors combed Appalachia for further treasures of traditional balladry and published volume after volume with such titles as *Folk-Songs from the Southern Highlands, Kentucky Mountain Folk-Songs, East Tennessee and Western Virginia Mountain Ballads,* and *A Song Catcher in Southern Mountains.* As the scope of folklore collecting widened, the uplands proved also to be a reservoir of traditional tales. Isabel Gordon Carter, Richard Chase, and Leonard Roberts unearthed an exciting cycle of magical Jack tales from the hills of North Carolina, Virginia, and Kentucky. In the Ozark hill country of northern Arkansas and southern Missouri, Vance Randolph amassed all kinds of folkstuff in a region characterized in *The Ozarks; An American Survival of Primitive Society.* One of the best field reports in American folklore, Emelyn E. Gardner's *Folklore from the Schoharie Hills, New York* presented a balanced spread of oral traditions from a sequestered German immigrant stock living in mountainous seclusion. She sketched a picture of an ignorant, superstitious people bypassed by time and progress:

As I traveled by stagecoach from prosperous farms and villages of the Schoharie Valley into the hills, where log houses, abandoned grist mills, and long covered bridges still lingered, I realized that I was passing from twentieth-century conditions into those of an earlier period . . . . The customs and beliefs portrayed by Fielding, Smollett, Pepys, and Burns I found to be to a large degree those of the present-day Schoharie hill folk . . . . Of the world outside their immediate environment many of these people know but little. At an election held in Gilboa in 1920, a prospective voter, when asked whether he was born in the United States, earnestly replied: "No, I was born in South Gilboa."[18]

Hillfolk in Schoharie County spoke of Pennsylvania, less than fifty miles distant, as "furrin' parts" and the Atlantic Ocean as "a big river." One old women walked a day's journey to see the "steam cars" but ran for her life when she saw a train coming at her round the foot of a mountain. At first suspicious, the Schoharians took Gardner for a "guvment spy," and hid when she tried to take snapshots of them, fearful lest she injure their likenesses and consequently their persons. When she began taking notes on her conversation with a notorious "law character," who customarily "set the law" on her neighbors, the crusty hillwoman snatched away the notebook and pencil and screamed that Gardner was a witch making magic. Following these vivid vignettes, Gardner set forth a banquet of olden lore.

In other American traditions besides those of white mountain folk, field collectors followed similar assumptions. The black population yielded slave songs in 1867 to a trio of northerners, William F. Allen, Charles P. Ware, and Lucy M. Garrison. In 1880 it gave plantation tales to Joel Chandler Harris, whose collections bolstered the thesis that American Negro folklore, originating in black Africa and nurtured in the rural south, reflected primitive superstitions and ecstatic songs and dances of a childlike race. So too the American Indian, whose verbal traditions were carefully recorded by Franz Boas and his anthropologist disciples, appeared to scholars and public alike as the noble savage harking to wild, fanciful myths about beast and bird culture heroes. Boas always sought the oldest strata of precontact mythology recalled by the Indian nations.

The Revised Concept

All this is familiar ground, covered when we first succumbed to the fascination of folklore studies, but in the light of my present theme it needs a summary review. Outsiders who regard folklore as an antiquarian, self-indulgent, and frivolous subject—attitudes frequently encountered—conceive of folkloristics as dwelling on a faded past and dealing with picturesque but backward and withered subcultures.

Without accepting this value judgment, I concede that folklore studies have been associated from their beginning with antiquities and "primitive" country folk. But another side to the story depicts folklore studies in quite a different light, presents them as contemporary, keyed to the here and now, to urban centers, to the industrial revolution, to the issues and philosophies of the day. In this conception folklore is where the action is, not in some idyllic backwater.

The two views appear so opposed as seemingly to preclude any sutures, and yet they are not irreconcilable. "Folk" need not apply exclusively to country folk, but rather signifies anonymous masses of tradition-oriented people. If country folk move to the city—and in the past decades the metropolises of the world have swelled from the inflow of the rural population—they do not thereby forfeit the interest of the folklorist. Nor do generations born within city limits necessarily fail to qualify as folk groups, for their lives too may be shaped by traditional codes of behavior, dress, cuisine, expression, world view. If we recall the quality in folklore that first attracted the Grimms and the Great Team of Victorians—the sense that its possessors moved in a culture different from that of the intellectuals although living under the same flag—we may redefine folklore to avoid the taint of antiquarianism. If for "popular antiquities" we substitute "oral culture" or "traditional culture" or "unofficial culture" we strike closer to the true concerns of folklorists. "Tradition" too needs reassessment, for traditions are continually being updated. Survivalist Hartland expressed this idea pithily in 1885: "I contend that Tradition is always being created anew, and that traditions of modern origin wherever found are as much within our province as ancient ones."[19] The unofficial culture can be contrasted with the high, the visible, the institutional culture of church, state, the universities, the professions, the corporations, the fine arts, the sciences. This unofficial culture finds its own modes of expression in folk religion, folk medicine, folk literature, the folk arts, and folk philosophy. Yet the unofficial culture reflects the mood of its times fully as much as does the official culture, for both are anchored in the same historical period. And an absorbing interest in antiquities may fuel the spirit of nationalism.

This perspective on what might be called the contemporaneity, as opposed to the antiquity, of folklore, is the thesis of a book I have just published entitled *America in Legend*. This thesis originally evolved in my mind while I was musing over a lecture on "Life Styles in American History" for a course on "History of Ideas in America." Changing life styles being a subject much under discussion, I had conceived an analysis of American history in terms of four major life styles: the Religious, from the beginning of colonization to the American Revolution; the Democratic, from the Revolution to the Civil War; the Economic, from the Civil War to the counterculture; and the Humane, emerging in 1964, the date of the Free Speech Movement at Berkeley. In each life style I perceived a common ideal, characterized by the four captions, and permeating the social philosophy, the educational system, the landmark writings, and the culture heroes. Then one day it dawned on me that the folklore of each of the four periods also mirrored the dominant life style. In the religious era the folklore revolved around the providences of God and the sorceries of the Devil and witches as they set snares for men's souls. In the democratic period a gallery of homespun folk heroes sprung from the people, most notably Davy Crockett, captured the nation's fancy. In the economic life style, a bustling folklore of occupations arose around the cowboy, the lumberjack, the miner, the oil driller, the railroad engineer. Finally, within the past decade, the counterculture has produced a teeming body 'of traditions featuring pill peddlers and draft dodgers as anti-heroes. According to this thesis, the vigorous and vital folklore of each period fades into quiescence or recedes into the hinterland in an ensuing period. Witchcraft beliefs, which permeated society in the seventeenth century, from magistrates and college presidents down to farmers and sailors, still can be heard today, but in the faroff corners of the land. The Davy Crockett who was a living legend in the 1830s and 1840s resurfaced a century later as a Walt Disney boy scout with no folk roots. In our time the cowboy has become a subject for popular films and recordings rather than a dispenser of anecdote and folksong. Meanwhile the youth culture has generated a lively druglore and rock festival scene attuned to the vibrations of the 1960s and 1970s. Many of the themes in this new druglore can be recognized as timehonored in tradition—for instance, the battle of wits between the stupid ogre and the underdog trickster, here represented by the narcs (narcotic agents) and heads (consumers of marijuana and LSD). As Hartland said, tradition is ever being created anew.

This thesis can, I believe, be applied in other places. In his splendid *Religion and the Decline of Magic* Keith Thomas examined the supernatural belief system in sixteenth- and seventeenth-century England within and without the Anglican Church as a consistent and unitary world view responsive to changing historical conditions. Acceptance of magical ideas declined in the eighteenth century, Thomas concludes, not because technological progress eliminated the need for ritual magic but because society had already moved to new ideas of self-reliance and self-confidence. But when the belief in the efficacy of magical solutions or the dread of witchcraft prevailed, it prevailed throughout the society, and not as a cultural lag among an unlettered peasantry.

For the purposes of this essay I will discuss the contemporaneity and modernity of folklore under four rubrics: the city; industry and technology; the mass media; and nationalism, politics, and ideology.

Folklore in the City

The more remote and inaccessible the region, the purer and firmer the traditions, the syllogism went, and so folklorists traipsed from their metropolitan homes to *terra incognita*. The hustle and bustle of the modern city, with its factories, department stores, banks, offices, traffic, and tens of thousands of people heaped upon each other in faceless anonymity, seemed to negate all the conditions most suitable for the perpetuation of folklore. With the explosion of urban populations in the nineteenth century, following on the rise of industrialization, the location of factories in cities, and the demand for cheap labor, the character of the city changed. What once had been a market center for the surrounding area now became a teeming industrial community with a large working class. In a provocative essay on "The City in American Civilization" Arthur M. Schlesinger, Sr., countered Frederick Jackson Turner's thesis of the influence of the frontier on American history with a balancing emphasis on the influence of the city, particularly in the past one hundred years. "The new age of the city," he wrote, "rested upon an application of business enterprise to the exploitation of natural resources such as mankind had never known. The city, as insatiable as an octopus, tended to draw all nutriment to itself."[20] Between 1790 and 1890 the population of the United States grew 16-fold while the number of city dwellers increased 139-fold.

In recent years folklorists have begun to think urban. Although Robert Chambers published *Traditions of Edinburgh*, based on prowls in the old parts of town and interviews with "ancient natives," as early as 1824, he was pursuing antiquities; in any event his book made little impact on folklore science. *South Italian Folkways in Europe and America*, written in 1938 by a social worker, Phyllis H. Williams (reprinted in 1969) presented accounts of feast days honoring patron saints and case histories of beliefs in magical practices from Sicilian families in New York and New Haven. Williams intended her study to serve fellow social workers and hospital attendants dealing with Italian slum immigrants, but her investigation showed the potentialities of urban ethnic folklore. In the 1960s two doctoral candidates in folklore, one in the United States at the University of Pennsylvania, the other in England at Leeds University, undertook fieldwork in cities at or near their university bases. Roger D. Abrahams lived for two years in the Camingerley section of Philadelphia and collected the materials that he published in 1964 in a milestone work, *Deep Down in the Jungle: Negro Narrative Folklore from the Streets of Philadelphia,* an interpretive collection containing such explosive obscenities that the first edition (this was before the impact of the Free Speech Movement) had to be sold under the counter. Abrahams disclosed the existence of a powerful black folk expression in northern cities, quite at variance with southern plantation lore. These northern "toasts" (long, often obscene verse narratives), brutal jokes, and games of "playing the dozens" (ritualized exchanges of insults) reflected the new toughness of ghetto street life. Across the Atlantic, Donald McKelvie was conducting field research in Bradford and its environs, a textile manufacturing area, for his dissertation on the folklore of an English urban industrial region. From this work he has published suggestive essays in *Folk Life Studies* and the *Journal of the Folklore Institute.*

These articles make little effort to introduce texts—although in one McKelvie does append a list of urban proverbs—but concentrate on method and concepts. In directing his attention to industrial cities McKelvie realized that he deals with "living and vigorous tradition," not with "relics and survivals, but with aspects of contemporary custom and social behaviour, usage and beliefs—with folklore, in short, as a living activity of a given community, not as a body of knowledge fixed in time, or as a corpus of survivals which does not become folklore until it has reached a certain degree of antiquity."[21] He maps out his region to discern within the cement jungle of the city its component human parts, which can be reduced to "a street, a square, or a block of houses." The concept of the neighborhood emerges, as an ingrown community with its own fixed sense of physical boundaries. One informant, asked if she knew of another, said, "Yes, but she comes from White Abbey," a reference to the next street and a house not one hundred and fifty yards away. (When I was doing fieldwork in Jonesport on the Maine coast, a local person, in response to my question whether Pompey Grant was a native, gasped and said, "No indeed, he comes from Columbia Falls"—the next little town, ten miles inland.) Within their neighborhoods many residents live in near isolation, fearful of the traffic and the winter cold, limited by their infirmities, and served in or near their homes by corner stores and traveling vendors and agents. McKelvie investigates the degrees and limits of neighborliness: middle-aged women will bring meals to a sick neighbor but never invite her in to tea or to watch television; their husbands meet friends at a pub, club, football match, at the mill, but never at home. Closely inspecting the physical surroundings of three informants in the Westgate district, he finds that, although all dwelt in very poor circumstances, they revealed considerable differences in their domestic arrangements and social behavior. As the city on nearer scrutiny turns out to be a highly differentiated organism, so does the apparently homogeneous working-class district dissolve into individualized persons.

Having looked at city folk analytically, McKelvie scans their lore. He reports little traditional narrative and none of the household tales Sidney O. Addy had collected in Yorkshire and Derbyshire villages in 1895. But he did uncover one cycle of scurrilous anecdotes about the Royal Family—which he does not sample—and another about allegedly true happenings, such as the Death Car sold cheaply because a suicide had left an ineradicable blood stain on the back seat. Other lore included beliefs in good and bad luck, expressed through proverbs, amulets, and rituals, and a corpus of "sub-proverbial sayings" uttered on street corners, in shops, on buses, across the backyard wall by fatalistic working people who "have fought a draw with life" and register their resignation with stock epigrams: "Yo' don't get owt for nowt." McKelvie excluded from his list proverbs of national circulation unless they had been reshaped in the West Riding idiom.

Here we see the folklorist training his sights on the city, rethinking his orientation, adjusting his categories. McKelvie freely acknowledges the layers of urban folklife he could not even touch, deposited by successive ethnic invasions of the Irish, the Slav, the German, the Caribbean, the Indian, and the Pakistani. His discoveries lie not only in the field but also in the library. He shrewdly appraises certain well-known authors as urban folklorists of a kind, particularly Henry Mayhew, the Bohemian journalist who produced between 1851 and 1862 the four volumes of his classic reportage, *London Labour and the London Poor*.

No folklorist can read Mayhew on, for example, "The Habits, Opinions, Morals and Religion of Patterers Generally" without being aware that this is the very stuff of his subject, and that he is in the presence of a collector of the very first rank. Yet Mayhew was not seeking for survivals: he was recording, for quite other purposes, the life of the poor of London in his own time; and the results of his labours is, among many other things, a unique record of some aspects of the folklore of early Victorian London. He was a folklorist by default perhaps, but none the less a folklorist. [22]

Amen. The very phrase that captions Mayhew's first three volumes places its subject matter within the discipline of folklore: "The London Street-Folk." And they do constitute a folk, these street-sellers of many commodities, street-finders or collectors of refuse, chimney-sweepers, street-artists, dock-laborers, watermen, and cab-drivers. In the fourth volume, a collaborative work, Mayhew and his associates wrote of prostitutes, thieves, swindlers, and beggars. Observer and sympathetic interviewer, Mayhew has captured the portraits, accents, philosophies, and personal histories of the London street-folk in a manner delectable to the folklorist concerned with traditional life styles. As an instance of his initiative in field techniques, Mayhew called together a public meeting of "street-sellers, street-performers, and street-labourers" in the National Hall, Holborn, to ascertain "what were the peculiarities and what the privations of a street-life." A thousand persons attended, and a representative from each occupation spoke about his calling. What John Brand called "vulgar Rites and popular Opinions" strew Mayhew's pages. This incident, for instance, involving a "street-Jew" displays a folk prejudice of long standing:

A gentleman of my acquaintance was one evening, about twilight, walking down Brydges-street, Covent-garden, when an elderly Jew was preceding him, apparently on his return from a day's work, as an old clothesman. His bag accidentally touched the bonnet of a dashing woman of the town, who was passing, and she turned round, abused the Jew, and spat on him, saying with an oath: "You old rags humbug! You can't do that!"—an allusion to a vulgar notion that Jews have been unable to do more than *slobber*, since spitting on the Saviour. [23]

In the midst of city life Mayhew has caught on the wing an act, and its pithy verbal accompaniment, embodying an esoteric belief, which he glosses. His volumes continually yield such folkloric nuggets.

Another urban study, by an academic scholar, not a folklorist, R. P. Dore's *City Life in Japan* (1958), provides evidence of the persistence of living traditional culture in the world's largest metropolis.

The magico-religious practices of folk religion, or *minkan shinko,* which the contributors to *Studies in Japanese Folklore* all treated as rural phenomena, adapt surprisingly to urban conditions. *Kami,* the household deities so prominent in village Japan, maintain themselves in Tokyo wards, especially in the kitchen, where 68 out of 255 households in Shitayama-cho reverenced Kohin-sama, the kitchen-god. Water-taps and flush toilets did cause attrition among water and lavatory kami who guarded the spring-water bamboo pipes and outdoor privies in the country. Still, the whole complex of ancestor-worship, shrine rituals, faith in *fuda,* the wooden or paper tablets carrying the name of the shrine's kami, continues in the city. Owners of fuda not only place them in the *kamidana,* the household altar to the deity, but at times display them over men's bath-house locker rooms with their caption "spirit which prevents robbery," or on lightning-rods on rooftops. Sometimes they paste or nail them to hallways at home to prevent disasters from entering. Worn on the person, fuda ward off injury. "Yes, I am sure they have an effect. One day when I had the Narita *fuda* on me, I was at work and fell off a high shelf with a pile of things in my hands. Fortunately the things I was holding fell underneath me and I wasn't hurt. But the *fuda* was broken in two. I was overcome with awed gratitude and burnt the *fuda* and buried the ashes in the earth."[24] Another fuda wearer attributed his survival from a serious train accident entirely to the power of the amulet. Some fuda possessors regarded their potency as spiritual and symbolic rather than magical, in maintaining a link with the kami of the shrine.

In recent years folklorists have consciously undertaken urban investigations. Inquiring into industrial folklore, a research group of Hungarian folklorists, led by Linda Dégh, selected as one of its targets the traditions of factory workers in Budapest. After joining the Folklore Institute of Indiana University in 1963, Dégh turned her attention to urban Hungarian immigrants who had come to Gary and East Chicago, Indiana, to work in the steel mills. In one paper published from this research, she describes in depth two Hungarian narrators in Gary, women of eighty-six and of seventy-five, who employ the telephone to exchange personal experiences, obscene anecdotes, jokes, and witch stories. The television set, continually turned on, stirs their memories and imaginations; the serial "Bewitched" led Katie Kis to recall Old Country witch legends. Deprived of their accustomed village audiences and storytelling occasions, Katie Kis and Marge Kovács have discovered in the telephone a substitute channel for their narrative instincts and art, and in their American urban life new sources of gossip and amusement for their memorates. Dégh's article is a model study of how peasant immigrant tale-tellers adapt to American city life.[25]

The work of Dégh and her husband, Andrew Vaszonyi, in these cities of smoke and steel led me there in February 1968, on a brief pilot field trip. My aim was to attempt a *Bloodstoppers and Bearwalkers* of the city: that is, to pursue in Gary and East Chicago the multigroup targets I had aimed at in the Upper Peninsula of Michigan in a remote, rural, and small-town situation. Could a folklorist ply his trade in the city and make contacts and collect among varied ethnic and racial groups in a short space of time? What could he learn about the accommodation of black and ethnic traditions to each other and to their new urban frame? My preliminary answers in an essay, with extracts from a field diary, "Is There a Folk in the City?" indicated that the folklorist from the outside can operate within the city as readily as in the southern mountains, and that layer upon layer of folk-cultural traditions lie heaped up in the metropolis. In less than a month it was possible for a folklorist without previous acquaintances to record from southern blacks, southern whites, Greeks, Serbs, Croats, Romanians, Italians, Poles, Czechs, Slovaks, Mexicans, and Puerto Ricans and to obtain intensely dramatic and moving personal histories and experiences.

One of the surprises for the urban folklorist has been the relative paucity of his conventional harvest—tales and songs—and the abundance of saga, as we might call the vivid memoirs of migrants to the city from the countries of eastern and southern Europe and Latin America and from the deep south. Several hypotheses about urban folklore resulted from my trip: the processes of retention and loss of imported folk custom operate at different rates for various nationalities, depending on historical factors (Serbs seemed more culturally conservative and homogeneous than Croats because of their national church and national history); individuals often reveal unexpected deviations from their ethnic bloc; the city is breeding a new lore enveloping its diverse residents. In the case of Gary and East Chicago, elements of this lore derived from traditions of steelworkers, stories of violent crime, and *blason populaire* (ethnic slurs) about the many nationalities and races jostling each other on the city pavements.[26]

American folklorists formally took note of the city in a symposium held at Wayne State University in Detroit in 1968 on The Urban Experience and the Folk Tradition. The papers, with prepared comments and taped discussions from the floor, were published two years later in a special issue of the *Journal of American Folklore* and reprinted the following year in book form with a select bibliography. Besides my own paper the symposium included reports on Negro folklore and the city riots of the 1960s, by Roger D. Abrahams; medical beliefs of southern mountain whites as transposed to Detroit, by Ellen Stekert; and the evolving of an urban hillbilly music from country-western music, by D. K. Wilgus. One paper by a nonfolklorist, Morton Leeds, holder of a doctorate in political science, discussed problems of the rural migrant to the city in socioeconomic terms. The prepared comments on each paper and most of the floor comments from the audience were offered by Wayne State University faculty members from several disciplines and from interested Detroit residents, sometimes referred to in the volume as "unidentified black woman." Because of the composition of the discussants, the diversity of the papers, and the concern of some of the speakers and most of the audience with solutions to problems of the urban ghetto, the symposium almost turned into a discussion of applied folklore techniques, and sometimes into defensive postures on behalf of blacks or Mexicans or southern whites, and dealt little with questions of urban folklore theory. As one floor speaker, "second unidentified black woman from Detroit," remarked, "I sit here and listen, and presumably people are trying to solve social problems."[27] True, Abrahams' paper analyzing black riots in terms of folk performances on the grand scale and Stekert's reporting on the gulf between folk medicine practiced by southern Appalachian white women and the city medicine of doctors, nurses, and hospitals inevitably invited the questions how can the folklorist help prevent the riots? how can he help build a bridge between doctors and their poor white patients? The very words "folklore in the city" evoke images of the culture of poverty, racial districts, the cement jungle. One discussant, Reverend Hubert Locke, a black theologian, warned against romanticizing the ghetto, and a speaker from the floor reminded the panel of the need to collect from businessmen as well as from ghetto dwellers.

Fieldwork in the city has barely begun. So modest a start has yet been registered toward the tasks of urban folklore and ethnography that any talk of problem-solving through folklore is premature and presumptuous. We should regard the cities as teeming laboratories for the folklorist offering almost endless possibilities among ethnic, occupational, socioeconomic, professional groups. From Detroit two ample volumes of Polish folksongs and Armenian wonder tales reveal the retention by first generation immigrants of Old Country traditions. These well-preserved texts elicited by the collectors contain slight traces of their American setting and constitute "memory culture." But the relation of memory culture to New World hyphenated folk culture deserves its own study. In his dissertation on Romanian-American folklore, Ken Thigpen distinguishes between immigrant retentions and new ethnic lore but places them in a continuum. He writes, "What a contrast to the Transylvanian village is an American city like Detroit! What a reorientation must occur in the mind of the budding folklorist whose preparation for fieldwork is anchored in the folklore classics based on rural folk cultures!"[28] In New York City Barbara Kirshenblatt-Gimblett is leading a foray among east European Yiddish folksingers, shortly after completing her folklore doctoral dissertation on folk narrators in the Toronto Jewish community.

One of the most remarkable tradition carriers I ever met resided in Oakland, California, a bearer of Portuguese supernatural lore who had never seen Portugal. Mrs. Florinda Pereira Freitas was born in Honolulu in 1903 to parents from San Michael Island in the Azores who went to Hawaii to work in the pineapple and sugar cane plantations. She moved to Oakland at twenty-one, part of a considerable Portuguese-American migration attracted between 1910 and 1930 by the fruit-packing and textile factories and dairy and fishing industries of the California coast. With eloquence and passion, unlettered Florinda Pereira Freitas recited saint's and biblical legends and accounts of the *feiticeiro* (witch) and the *quebrante* (evil eye). These were in no way dormant deposits of memory culture but vital experiences. Right in her own home where I recorded her on 26th Street in Oakland in 1968, a suspected feiticeiro, also from San Michael Island, came into Florinda's house to see her new baby, and surreptitiously cut the baby's hair. The baby, Vivian (in 1968 a grown-up daughter), groaned, and Florinda rushed to the bedside, to discover a big piece of hair on the pillow where the feiticeiro had licked the baby with her tongue. "They have sand or some salt and when they lick it's just like a razor blade. They can cut. Sometimes it [the hair] grows or sometimes it never grows in." Florinda rushed around to her mother-in-law, wise in such matters, who took the present the feiticeiro had brought—a *camisinha*, baby's blouse—and said, "I'm goin' to fix this so that woman no harm nobody no more. She'll never be no more feiticeiro." And shortly after the feiticeiro hastily departed the neighborhood. This happened not in the southern mountains but in the heart of an industrial city.

Folklore and Industrialization and Technology

In the older theory of folklore, Mother Earth and the peasant and pastoral life cradled the seasonal rituals and traditional culture that folklorists studied, not only in oral but also in physical forms. Craftsmen of village and farm, along with oral narrators and bards, transmitted folk skills and products. The industrial revolution silted up the wells of folk energy, so ran the theory, both in terminating the rural rhythms so conducive to storytelling, folksinging, and the persistence of folk belief and in replacing the craftsman by the machine. In common usage "folklore" has meant preindustrial traditions and artifacts. The machine, the factory, the assembly-line method of mass production, and the wholesale distribution and consumption of goods supposedly mark an end to folklore and folklife patterns in the steadily expanding domain of the world they occupy. Have not the old Märchen and Child ballads disappeared in the Westernized, industrialized nations? Urban industrialism has destroyed the old folk community and created in its place a traditionless, faceless labor force, bound to machines.

A body of counter-evidence and counter-theory is beginning to appear. Hermann Bausinger in *Volkskultur in der technischen Welt* challenged the traditional view of tradition. He speaks of a "fundamental new approach in folklore studies":

> For about a century, the field of German Volkskunde studies had seen its principal objective in the attempts to grope back to the era of Germanic antiquities, using clues provided by still living folk traditions. Today, this study of survivals, predominantly mythological in orientation, has by and large been transformed into a historically oriented investigation of contemporary patterns. We no longer believe that industrialization necessarily implies the end of a specific folk culture, but rather we attempt to trace the modifications and mutations undergone by *folk culture in the industrialized and urbanized world.* [29]

Bausinger adds that this changed perspective requires a shift in methodology, which has not yet been satisfactorily accomplished, but recent projects clearly demonstrated that the "folklorist brings to the job a set of tools" quite distinct from the tools of the sociologist. Some inquiries of his institute at Tübingen deal with the relation of the tourist industry to folk culture. Examining tourist centers in the Black Forest and the Tyrol, the investigators concluded that the vast influx of visitors into villages catering to tourists did not destroy the old traditions, although the intrusion of alien ways did alter the existing social and economic institutions. Rather, the Tübingen folklorists perceived a complex phenomenon involving processes both of integration and disintegration. This whole question of the conscious commercialization of folk festivals, dances, costumes, and crafts has led to the neologism "Folklorismus" to which the *Zeitschrift für Volkskunde* devoted an issue in 1969. Not only the tourist villages but the whole countryside has responded to the forces of industrialization represented by increased mobility, resulting from the advent of the automobile, the mechanization of agriculture, policies of land reclamation and resettlement, and the spread of small-scale industry into the countryside. Industrialization is seen as a rural as well as an urban development affecting folk traditions. An example Bausinger offers concerns a broadened concept of folk drama to include Christmas plays, local historical performances celebrating anniversaries of an event or a birth- or death-day, and the open-air theater "treating romantic-patriotic themes—which in recent decades has established itself in market squares, parks, stone quarries, and on romantic sites strewn with ruins."

In the Institute for Central European Folk Research at the University of Marburg, directed by Gerhard Heilfurth, a specialist in European miners' folklore, one section is devoted to "Research on Industry and Mining." Projects include "(a) Mining in its key sociocultural position as a link between primitive patterns of production and advanced technology; (b) The vocabulary of mining on the basis of specialized industrial technical terminology; and (c) Forms of industrial life and 'worker's culture.' "[30]

Similarly a team of folklorists in Hungary in the 1950s formed a Group for the Research of Workmen's Folklore, supported by the Hungarian Academy of Sciences, to undertake the "systematic disclosure and study of Hungary's industrial folklore." Directed by Linda Dégh, the group set up such targets as the mode of life, culture, and folklore of skilled iron workers; unskilled workers from the country in the building trades; and apprentices in the new industrial songs of 1860-1945 and the traditional customs and folklore of the agrarian proletariat. This proletariat included such groups as the navvies or seasonal construction workers and the small craftsmen—also remarked on by Bausinger—who shared both agrarian and industrial traditions. In a comparative study of two coal mining villages, Kishártyan and Karancskeszi, the group found preindustrial folklore well preserved among a male population composed almost wholly of miners or factory laborers and much less retained in the other, where 38 percent of the men were agricultural laborers resented by the local authorities and classroom teachers.[31]

The redirection of folklore studies in the Soviet Union since 1936 toward Party ideology has strongly stimulated interest in the folklore of factory and mill, not merely in the contemporary period but from earlier times as well. Research in printed sources uncovered songs of workers in foundries and mines in the eighteenth and nineteenth centuries. A characteristic feature, distinguishing workers' from peasants' songs right from the start, lay in the attention to industrial tools and processes:

> Oh, you, who bathe us in our own sweat,
> The Zmeyevsky foundry!
> Sharply, loudly she beats on a board,
> And invites people to visit her,
> Beside the cord, the side,
> There is a trough and a rake,
> A poker, a hammer;
> We pour a charge into the furnace
> Of four hundred poods in weight;
> When we have put in the four hundred poods in weight—
> In one shift we will burn it all up. [32]

A pood is approximately seven tons. The song was recovered from an 1865 newspaper.

Another element in this and similar songs stressed the resentment by workmen of their repressive authorities, who are directly named, and the Soviet folklorists also see in these pieces anticipations of the workers' collective, in their spirit of defiance and boldness, as the workers strike back at foremen (often German) and overseers. Yury Sokolov underscores the community of interest between peasant and worker in the early stage of industrialization, when the factory was yet a manufactory with much work done by hand, and the factory workman was usually a transported peasant.

Besides songs and song-poems descriptive of factory life in an earlier day, Soviet folklorists unearthed "secret tales" of Ural workers which related legendary accounts, unknown to the oppressive mill owners and tsarist police, of worker and bandit heroes who conceal treasure in the mountain until the toiling masses inherit the riches of the earth.

After the October revolution the new Soviet folklore, especially the chastushkas (short popular rhymes) celebrated not only industrial workers in the city but also country workers on the now mechanized collective farms. The tractor itself becomes a symbol of felicity:

> I did not love the tractor driver,
> I was not a tractor driver myself.
> But when I got behind the wheel myself,
> I fell in love with the tractor. [33]

Other chastushkas hymn the power and efficiency of the tractor, its appeal to girls after their initial shyness, and their romancing of the tractor driver and dreams of some day becoming a tractor driver's wife, or even a driver themselves: "There behind the tractor's wheel / The girl is sitting like a king." With the introduction of machinery and collective management to the farms the successful young workers declared their resentment against the derogatory label "country bumpkins" and composed a chastushka leveling all distinctions between city and countryside. Industrialization has thus linked the erstwhile peasant and the city factory worker in a common newfound self-confidence.

A sign of new research in England is Alan Smith's forty-eight-page pamphlet, one-third given over to illustrations, on "Discovering Folklore in Industry."[34] Smith provides no references or sources, and his headings—Ships and seafarers, Miners and quarrymen, Apprentices and beginners, Printers and machinery, Unions and factories, The industrial community—promise much more than they deliver. Primarily he deals, as did Sebillot before him in fuller scope, with the curiosa of trades and occupations—the odd belief, saying, or custom, as the rite of "trussing the cooper" or "banging out" the apprentice printer, initiation ceremonies of long standing in which the newly accredited workman is besmeared with soot or ink. Smith's instances of performances by Morris dancers in Cheshire and Lancashire, who wear clogs and who substitute hanks of untwisted cotton rope for the sticks and handkerchiefs they customarily carry, seem small revisions of village observances in an urban, industrial setting. More to the point are the folk beliefs in sterility caused by machinery (such as welding tools), or by service in airplanes at high altitudes; and the legends attached to Ned Ludd, a fictitious apprentice framework knitter of Nottinghamshire, who allegedly smashed his frame with a hammer after being whipped by a magistrate, and so initiated the underground movement of craftsmen against shoddy machinery, or, as others have it, against technological progress. Smith suggests as a preliminary typology survivals of preindustrial traditions in the industrial era, such as Pace Egg plays enacted in factory towns; new growth, for instance, the Londoners' belief in luck brought by chimney sweeps at weddings; and transfers of folk ideas connected with older objects to modern ones, such as the shift from ships to airplanes of the notion that traveling priests or nuns bring bad luck.

In spite of the advanced technology and industrialization of the United States, American folklorists have as yet done little probing into industrial traditions. The chief successes to date are registered by George Korson with anthracite and bituminous coal miners and by Mody Boatright with oil drillers and other oil field types. Korson brought to the surface an extensive repertoire of miners' songs reflective of underground work, cave-ins and disasters, loyalty to the union, and the ethnic strains among the colliers.[35] Boatright performed a still more difficult feat, since the folklore of the oil industry included little in the way of songs and no folktales of the Märchen variety. But his interviews with oilmen yielded a cycle of tall tales, many highly technical, attributed to the yarn-spinning of Gib Morgan, a Münchausen of the oilfields, and a corpus of legendary anecdotes connected with the location of "black gold," the "Coal Oil Johnnies" who dissipated their sudden fortunes, and the "McCleskeys" who handled theirs frugally. In an ingenious analysis, Boatright identified oilfield types such as the prospector, the driller, the shooter, and the promoter, and associated them with earlier known figures in American folklore, such as the wizard, the ringtailed roarer, and the Yankee trader. He broadened his inquiry to include oral history and so moved from the strict categories of folklore to the related realm of personal reminiscence and experience in the oil fields.[36] *Folklore of the Oil Industry* demonstrated the continuity of preindustrial and industrial folk themes. The waterwitch slides into the doodle-bugger, the search for buried treasure glides into the quest for liquid gold, the tall tales of hunting and shooting merge with technological whoppers about drilling.

American industrial folklore lies open as a vast, uncharted field. A recent catch-all anthology entitled *Folklore from the Working Folk of America* concentrates on the older occupations and contains little that can be called industrial.[37] Two folklore doctoral dissertations at Indiana University are exploring the subject: one by Bruce Nickerson, who has worked in industrial plants, on blue-collar folklore, and another by Betty Messenger on traditions of the linen industry in northern Ireland. In a preview article she samples songs and rhymes circulating in spinning mills:

> The yellow belly doffers,
> Dirty wipers down,
> The nasty, stinking spinning room,
> The stink will knock you down. [38]

Doffers are the young apprentice spinners who replaced the filled bobbins of yarn with empty ones, and wiped down or cleaned the wet spinning machines while wearing yellow oilskin aprons, hence the "yellow belly." The doffers sang mill songs, often about themselves.

Meanwhile we await penetration of the steel industry, the entertainment industry—a borderland between mass communications and mass manufacturing—the transportation industry (B. A. Botkin's and Alvin Harlow's *A Treasury of Railroad Folklore* is primarily a literary compendium), the automotive industry, and other industrial giants. Any consideration of industrial folklore should include traditions gravitating to specific machines, such as automobile legends and computer jokes. Two of the great technological symbols of the machine age, the automobile and the computer, have captivated the folk fancy. A series of macabre migratory legends pivots around the auto: the Death Car, the Stolen Grandmother, the Killer in the Back Seat, The Ghostly Hitchhiker. [39] As for the computer, seemingly the most remote and dehumanized of man's modern inventions, it has generated its own stock of terse and elaborate jocular narratives.

Folklore and the Mass Media

In the traditional concept of folklore the spoken word is paramount. Oral tradition and oral transmission are supposedly the sine qua non, blighted in our time by the printed word and the new electronic channels of communication—radio, cinema, television. Only in hidden pockets of our civilization, deep in mountain hollows, out on scrub country flats, or among extreme orthodox sects like the Amish and the Hasidim, impervious to modern ways, do the undefiled word-of-mouth tradition and face-to-face audience still persist. The enemy of folklore is the media that blankets mass culture: the large circulation newspapers and magazines we read, the movie and television screens we watch, and the recording industry whose disks we listen to. So runs the lament. What is distributed to the millions, after an elaborate, expensive packaging process, does seem the antithesis of the slow drip of invisible tradition.

But there may be linkages between the folk and the mass cultures. Marshall McLuhan has talked about the new oral-aural ambiance of the media which in a way reverts to the early tribal community. The millions share the same spectacles, laugh at the same comedies, idolize the same stars. Some folklorists have already recognized that the mass media transmit, in suitably adapted form, folk items that enjoyed currency in limited circles. Several excellent studies—Charles Keil's *Urban Blues*, Bill Malone's *Country Music U.S.A.*, Archie Green's *Only a Miner*—have examined the complex relation among folksongs, folk music, and folk singers in their natural habitat and the end products of popular hits, studio recording artists, and cabaret performers. A song like "Casey Jones" can coexist in tradition, on the vaudeville stage, as a sheet music best seller, and in obscene parodies —all related in greater or lesser degree. Keil inspects the mechanics and techniques of the recording industry that remold southern Negro blues singers like B. B. King and Bobby Bland into successful entertainers for urban audiences.

As yet few folklorists have ventured into large interpretations of folklore in the mass media, but in 1972 in *Myth and Modern Man* Raphael Patai drew bold analogies between classical myths and expressive formulations in western industrial society. He compares Heracles with Mickey Mouse of Walt Disney's film cartoons:

> The basic similarity of the two hero types lies primarily in the power relationship between the hero and his adversary. Whether Mickey or Herakles, the hero in each case faces overwhelming odds. In fact, in the course of the almost ritualized combat sequence, there are invariably one or more junctures at which the hero is quite clearly trapped and defeated . . . . A second and equally important similarity between Mickey and Herakles is that both partake of a double character . . . superhuman hero and ridiculous buffoon . . . . [Mickey's] very appearance provokes laughter. But then, after sufficient provocation by the Cat, he shows his mettle: underneath the mousey exterior he is, in reality, a great little hero. Inasmuch as he defeats the Cat, he is Superman. [40]

So Patai brought a second mass media hero into his equation: Superman of the comic books. In other analogies he likens the magico-mythical qualities of the ambrosia and nectar quaffed by the gods with the Coke sipped by modern mortals, and the smoke and incense rituals of yore with the balm conferred by cigarettes. Madison

Avenue advertising in pictures and text underlines the excitement, gaiety, youthful transport, and ecstasy induced by Cokes and Smokes. The admen also utilize mythical heroes and beasts in advancing the claims of their products through television commercials and magazine ads. The bald, half-naked giant known as Mr. Clean, who magically vanquishes kitchen floor dirt, is a jinni from the *Arabian Nights.* A Green Giant gazes benevolently at dwarfs preparing green peas for market. "Put a Tiger in Your Tank!" advertised the makers of Esso gasoline in the most effective ad ever for an automotive fuel. Posters of the tiger, animated cartoons in TV commercials of the tiger pushing a car, stuffed tigers placed inside cars—all carried further the mythical identification of the automobile with the power of a wild animal.

Magic metamorphosis, according to Patai, characterized much of the advertising for products that can assist the harried housewife in her incessant battle against dirt, odors, and germs. No appliance wins more respect and awe on this score than the washing machine; accordingly, admen stress the "masculine, phallic aspect of this most powerful, active, and aggressive of all major household appliances." In the modern myth of the sexual superman, best characterized by James Bond and known not only through successful films but also from ten million copies of books about his adventures, recurs the "archetypal mythical hero," who descends into Hades and wanders like Theseus through a labyrinth of dangers. The man in the street admires and seeks to emulate the virile life style of "007." Although Patai's analogies seem strained, they suggest lines of inquiry that the folklorist more readily than the mythologist might undertake. Patai does touch base with Stith Thompson's *Motif-Index* on one occasion for instances of the mouse in folktales, but for the most part he proceeds by tenuous analogies on supposed myth resemblances.

For the past several years I have assigned graduate students an exercise on culling folklore from the mass media. They clip items from printed sources and note examples from television, radio, and films. Their directions are, first, to identify folkloristic themes; second, to comment on the relation of these themes to oral folk sources; and, third, to interpret the use or purpose to which this mediated folklore is being put. Most students compile intriguing scrapbooks that reveal the wealth of folkstuff encountered in their daily exposure to the media over a period of a couple of months. Some of these reports have been deposited in the Folklore Archives of Indiana University; two have developed theories and typologies original enough to merit publication in the *Folklore Forum*.

Priscilla Denby first catalogues the kinds of media she has combed: "magazines catering to different interests; newspapers; Sunday magazines; plays; television; radio; cartoons; greeting cards; records (pop, folk, classical, rock); illustrations, such as book and record jackets; posters; films; novels; local festivals and customs; children's books and coloring books; advertisements; trademarks; names of places, such as restaurants, inns, and camps; crossword puzzles and games; and various miscellany such as linguistic folklore (puns, dialects, etc.) and a curious chain letter I received in the mail." She then adds potential sources she could not consider at the time, "comic strips, billboards, speeches, cookbooks and recipes, the backs of cereal boxes and other products, pamphlets describing various American tourist attractions and landmarks, recorded tapes for tourists, placemats and matchbook covers from restaurants and gift shops, bumper stickers."[41] This inventory fairly suggests the bombardment of printed, placarded, spoken, sung, screened, and spectacled messages that engulf us all in the age of the media.

To bring order to the folkloric materials gleaned from these diverse sources Denby proposes three large divisions: Folklore qua Folklore; Folklore as Folklure; and Folklore as an Aside. The first category applies to items that deal directly and specifically with folklore, legends, and myths under those terms. "Folklore qua folklore" subsumes more or less informed discussion about our discipline and its processes, and Denby cites as an instance a five-minute segment of an ABC television show on April 6, 1971, explaining the rise of Lieutenant William Calley, accused of the massacre at My Lai, as an American folk hero, and playing the recording of the "Ballad of Lieutenant Calley" that had sold a million copies the previous week. A recording that denounced Calley as un-American was mentioned but not played. Had the ballad simply been played or sung, the rendition might be classified as folk-emulated, but the commentator's attempt to analyze the making of a legendary hero, using the record for documentation, gives the nod to theory, however attenuated, over entertainment. By the neologism "folklure," a happy addition to our terminology, Denby suggests the use of folkloric associations to help sell a product. The film title "Grimms' Fairy Tales" lured moviegoers, including myself, into a skinflick. "Folklore as an Aside" refers to stylistic devices that enhance a topic by giving it a folkloric touch, such as journalistic references to Paul Bunyan feats or objects; and visual devices for the same end, such as the cartoon of an angelic businessman with a magician's wand in his hand and fairy wings clipped to his suit sitting under a large sign reading LOANS.

The other essay, by Tom Burns, concentrated exclusively on television. Burns plunked himself down before the tube at 6:15 A.M. on May 15, 1969, and did not come up for air until 1:30 A.M. the next day. During that time he recorded programs on tape while entering comments on the visual portions in his notebook. To assess his folklore gleanings Burns devised a fourfold test, of text, performance, situation, context. All four elements must be rated "traditional" for the entire item to be considered "true" folklore. A pop artist singing a Child ballad before a studio audience would rate low on the scale because only one element, the text, is met. Burns concluded:

> The survey of one day's television programming has revealed that there is a good deal of traditional material (101 items) covering a wide range of genres (twelve) in the television media. There is, however, little "true" folklore. "True" folklore and the material approaching it seem to be present in primarily two areas: (1) in the peripheral regions of the programming on locally produced shows which are directed to a more or less specific subculture audience, and (2) in those programs where the performers on stage can be said to compose a kind of folk group which the mass audience is simply overhearing and viewing. [42]

The least "true" folklore he found to be in advertising. Folk beliefs, especially with supernatural motifs, proved the most prevalent genre, penetrating even prime-time shows but quite divorced from traditional contexts, as in the "kitchen magic" of advertising already remarked on by Patai.

A good example of an in-depth treatment of a single genre is "Folklore in the Mass Media: Head Comics," an unpublished paper of John Cicala, deposited in the Folklore Archives. [43] Head comics are a counterculture mockery of the crime-fighting Superman and the establishment values in newsstand comic books. They appeared in the late 1960s in centers of the youth culture, such as Haight-Ashbury, created, it was reported, by potheads and acidheads while they were stoned. Pictures and text replaced Superman with hippie anti-heroes and savagely caricatured straight-world character types. Here Cicala describes two protagonists:

> Two characters one often comes across in Head Comics are Projunior and his teenage companion Honeybunch. Projunior is the prototype of the "freak"

revolutionary whose rhetoric is a form of self-lampoon. Usually he doesn't know what is going on around him until it is nearly too late. Honeybunch speaks the clichés of the "teeny-bopper" and has the innocence which gets her into difficult situations, though in some stories about her, she can be a nagging bitch. Both lovers wander in a bleak capitalistic landscape trying to eke out a few pennies in order to exist. This economic necessity often gets them into situations where only their cleverness (as tricksters) or their powers as superlovers can free themselves from "Mr. Man," the personification of capitalistic greed and lust.

In the attached cartoon sequence, Projunior and Honeybunch are out scrounging the streets for pennies when a well-dressed businessman, Mr. Man, passes by. Honeybunch asks him for spare change; he puts his arm around her, expresses his admiration for anti-establishment kids, leads her back to his studio, and gets her stoned; meanwhile Projunior, clad in an animal skin, wanders off musing how to save the world. Suddenly waking from his reverie, Projunior senses through his vibes that an establishment pig is about to seduce Honeybunch and sends her warnings on an astral plane. Honeybunch comes to just in time and lying on her back, spins Mr. Man dizzily around on the heels of her heavy boots, then bounces him off with an epithet, "Take a flying fuck, ya phony liberal fascist fraud!!" But Mr. Man loves it and comes slobbering back for more. Honeybunch defecates in his face; Projunior rushes back into her arms; and the final frame shows them graphically in the sixty-nine position.

For folklore motifs Cicala suggests T41 "Communications of lovers" and F610.0.1 "Extraordinary strong woman," but he finds fewer motifs and folktale analogues for this particular episode than for other of his analyses. The case for folkloric implications can best be made in terms of folk-hero patterns. Projunior conforms to the formulas of the anti-hero in druglore legends about pill-peddlers and draft-dodgers who triumph over police and army officers. He too, with his girl friend, overcomes the evil spokesman for the system, Mr. Man; "the man" in counterculture parlance signifies the enemy, sometimes specifically a narcotics agent.

These few examples indicate the wealth of possibilities for examining folklore in the mass media. The problems of methodology, typology, morphology, aesthetics, cultural analysis are formidable. It is difficult enough to screen the tons of newsprint that engulf the modern world, although, were funds available, a news clipping service clued in to key words (I had great success once with "Paul

Bunyan") could salvage a great deal of fleeting folklore. But how to capture folklore on the screen or the air waves? If scholars direct their attention to these questions, they will find answers—for example, in Burns's using one electronic system against another by taping the audio portion of television programs. European folklorists are already actively considering the relation of folklore to mass culture. Hermann Bausinger declares that one of the most pressing questions of folklore research is "whether the basic need for narrative in our time is not now being satisfied by completely different media, such as motion pictures, television, and, above all by certain kinds of reading material which today undoubtedly enjoy a far greater currency than ever before."[44] At the University of Hamburg the folklore institute has sponsored studies on "Radio and Folklore," "The Movies—A Subject for Folklore Research," "Folk Literature and Reading Material for the Masses," and "Television and Folk Culture." The Hamburg school of folklorists has revised the older concept of the folk as the "lower orders" in favor of the idea of a community of individuals who form a folk group and share a basic common property (*das Grundständige*). Therefore, *Volkskunst* or folk art must appeal to everybody and be understood by everybody within the larger folk group or people concerned.[45] No longer is the concept of folk art limited to narrow circles and regions. This train of thought readily leads toward acceptance of a mass culture species of folklore.

Folklore and Nationalism, Politics, Ideology

Far from being an antiquarian hobby, folklore has throughout the history of its study been connected with national issues and concerns. The appearance of folkloristics as a discipline coincided, not by chance, with the heightening of nationalism in a number of countries, since folklore traditions could help reinforce the sense of national identity, once the intellectuals and policymakers became aware of their existence. They faced a paradox in seeking national traits and characteristics in tales, songs, proverbs, and customs found in similar forms in many lands, but the nationalists chose to emphasize seemingly local and indigenous elements. Their quests for a national language, literature, history, mythology, and folklore often overlapped, and folklore proved of special use, for it could be embedded in regional dialects, suggest literary themes, and contain remembrances of the mythological and historical past.

Jacob and Wilhelm Grimm clearly associated their work in folklore with the reconstruction of a proud Germanic past. Their researches in philology, legal history, and mythology as well as in folklore proper were directed at reversing the stereotype of wild, savage Teutonic forebears and substituting the vision of an advanced and civilized people, as Jacob forcefully states in the preface to *Germanic Mythology.* Not a Greek and Roman heritage, but the indigenous Germanic tribes furnished the sources of nineteenth-century German culture. "I do not suppose," observed Jacob drily, "that the old German fancies about beasts crossing one's path, or about the virtues of herbs, were in themselves any poorer than the Roman." Later in the century, in 1858, Wilhelm Riehl developed the nationalist implications of *Volkskunde* in terms of a national folk community, and in the 1930s the Nazi politicians exploited Riehl's thesis. An American scholar has written that under Hitler "the study of folklore was raised to a special place of honor. . . . a large part of Nazi literature designed for children was merely a modernized version of the Grimms' tales, with emphasis upon the idealization of fighting, glorification of power, reckless courage, theft, brigandage, and militarism reinforced with mysticism."[46]

The Nazis' use of folklore involved and interwove nationalism, politics, and ideology. As a nationalistic strategy, folklore would restore the old peasant values of community bonds being weakened by urban impersonality; hence political folklorists sought to reverse the trend of migration from country to city. Hitler considered the "preservation of our folkdom" dependent upon the preservation of the peasantry. The Nazi architects followed the Grimms' initiative in exalting the Germanic tribes of old and downgrading the artificial intrusions of Roman civilization which had sapped German folk unity. A new, greater Germany would derive its national purpose and cultural unification from renewal of the pure Nordic-Germanic myths, customs, and rituals. The task of the Nationalist Socialist folklorist was to screen out alien elements. In 1937 Hans Strobel stated, "The aim of folklore is and remains to give an unfalsified representation of that which is true to the *Volk.*"

In terms of politics, folklore provided practical opportunities for the Nationalist Socialist Party. Otto Schmidt devoted a treatise of 1937 to *Volkstumsarbeit als politische Aufgabe* (The Work of Nationhood as a Political Duty). Professor Hans Strobel inferred the need for political action when he wrote, the same year, "If we want to walk safely into the future, then we will have to walk upon the firm soil of our folklore." Party policy produced peasant schools and institutes seeking to revive German folk consciousness through courses on folklore and history and through encouragement of peasant festivals, folk music, and folk dance. The Party's Folk Education Program endeavored to instruct the German people in their role as bearers of Germanic culture.[47] Ideology underscored the special heroic qualities of the fighting German peasant, qualities needed to expand Germany's political boundaries in the drive for "living space." The folk spirit was construed as a martial spirit.

Instances connecting folklore research and the rise of nationalism can be multiplied. That the composition of the Finnish epic *Kalevala* by Elias Lönnrot became a platform and rallying point for the cause of a Finnish language, culture, literature, and mythology is now a commonplace. William A. Wilson is completing a doctoral dissertation in the Folklore Institute at Indiana University exploring the detailed history of the interdependence of folkloristics and nationalistic strivings in Finland. Caught between German and Soviet domination in the twentieth century, and before that submerged by Sweden up to Finland's independence in 1917, Finnish scholars were obliged to shift their philosophical as well as political allegiance between theories of aristocratic and proletarian sources of folk materials. In a paper delivered before the American Folklore Society in November 1972 on "Folklore and National Consciousness in Pre-Nineteenth Century Finland," Wilson traces the story back before Lönnrot to seventeenth- and eighteenth-century figures, such as Daniel Juslenius and Henrik Gabriel Porthan, who exalted the Finnish heritage through the study of antiquities and folk poetry. He states:

In the careful, scholarly work of Porthan we see folklore used as a mirror for Finnish culture, as a means of gaining insight into the mind of the people. In the searing, patriotic writing of Juslenius, we see the tendency in periods of national stress to turn to an imagined heroic past for strength to face the future, and also the tendency to shape the cultural mirror of folklore to reflect the political predispositions of the man holding the mirror. Both these approaches have persisted in Finnish folklore study to the present.[48]

In Norway, as Oscar J. Falnes has shown in *National Romanticism in Norway*, the movement for Norwegian independence from Denmark that achieved political success in 1814, but strove for cultural independence throughout the nineteenth century, depended importantly on folklore. Jörgen Moe, in a prospectus of 1840 for the collection of Norwegian folktales he was undertaking with Peter Asbjörnsen, commented that "No cultivated person now doubts the scientific importance of the folk tales . . . they help to determine a people's unique character and outlook." And, following Moe's thought, George Webbe Dasent characterized the Norse tales as "bold, out-spoken, and humorous, in the true sense of humour. In the midst of every difficulty and danger arises that old Norse feeling of making the best of everything, and keeping a good face to the foe." Moe perceived in the fairy-tale hero Askeladden the spirit of the *landsman* guided by providence, and an Oslo newspaper in 1957 visualized Askeladden as "a crafty, glib Norwegian farmer with the necessary sense and power to win half a kingdom."[49]

In Ireland the drive for cultural nationalism preceded and fed the movement for political independence. The Irish literary renaissance involved such major personalities as William Butler Yeats, Lady Gregory, and John Millington Synge, who actively collected Gaelic folk traditions and incorporated them in poems and plays. Their friend Douglas Hyde published scholarly collections of Irish folk narratives and literary histories of Ireland and became the first president of Ireland. All fought for the revival of the Gaelic tongue and heritage against the stifling cloak of English culture. Hyde mourned that "story, lay, poem, song, aphorism, proverb, and the unique stock-in-trade of an Irish speaker's mind, is gone for ever."[50] Through the Gaelic League, founded in the 1890s, Hyde exhorted the Irish people to recover their inheritance of Gaelic song, dance, music story, and speech.

In Greece too political and cultural nationalists utilized folklore and enjoyed an advantage over other European scholar-patriots who sought to reconstruct a shadowy Celtic or Norse mythology from fragmentary hints in Märchen and Sagen. Olympus beckoned invitingly across the centuries, and modern Greek folklorists strove to connect their peasant tales with the classic myths. One Greek scholar commented in 1964 that the "science of folklore and the new independent nation of modern Greece were born almost simul-taneously; the term folklore was not officially minted until 1846 when Greece already had its new constitution for three years . . . the study of folklore became a nationwide project and a number of studies and collections of folk-literature were published in Greece together with the first modern Greek publication of the ancient authors, for both were deemed equally important."[51] In pursuit of their claims, folklorists such as Stilpon Kyriakides beheld vestiges of the Dionysiac revels in the masquerades of the Twelve Days of Christmas, the nymphs of old in the *nereids* of current belief, and myths of the Olympian gods and goddesses in saints' legends and Virgin Mary miracles.

Not only the sentiment of nationalism but also a particular nationalistic ideology may derive support from the content and interpretation of folklore. The course of folkloristics in the Soviet Union provides a ready case in point, well-documented by Felix Oinas.[52] As he recounts the story, government controls over writers, critics, and scholars—including folklorists—tightened from 1929 on with the introduction of Stalin's five-year plans and the organization in 1932 of one inclusive Union of Soviet Writers. In the keynote speech of the first All-Union Congress of Soviet Writers in 1934, Maxim Gorky stressed the values of folklore as an expression of the realities and aspirations of the working classes. From then on government policy strongly supported widespread collecting activities and socialist interpretation of folklore. In November 1936 the staging in Moscow of the comic opera *Bogatyri* (The Epic Heroes), written by Demian Bedny, Soviet poet laureate, evoked the ire of Party officials for disparaging the *byliny* heroes. The opera was withdrawn from the repertoire, and articles in *Pravda* attacked the distortion of Russian history and epic traditions by folklorists. In time folklore scholars shifted their view of the origins of the *byliny* from aristocratic to peasant sources. In his standard work on Russian folklore Y. M. Sokolov expresses the current ideological attitude of the Communist Party and the Soviet government toward folklore: "what a vastly important artistic force this is in the propagandizing of the resplendent ideas of Communism, what a great place folklore occupies in Soviet socialist culture." And: "Never, in all the history of Russia, has the oral poetic word served the social aims so broadly and powerfully as in the Soviet period. Soviet folkloristics has helped to reveal the agitational and propagandist significance of folklore. And thereby, Soviet folkloristics has firmly allied itself with the practical tasks of our social life."[53]

This shift in general attitudes toward the national body of folklore, and indeed the expressed desire for a new and different content of folklore, seems to substantiate my thesis of the contemporaneity of folk traditions. Not only were the older epic songs reinterpreted, but a whole new corpus of revolutionary and industrial-labor lore was collected by trade-school students and workers on collective farms and machine tractor stations. By the 1930s such collectors had recorded a new folklore of Soviet *byliny*, laments, tales, and new songs called *noviny*, often glorifying Lenin, Stalin, Voroshilov, and other political and military figures. So too did folk heroes of the new democracy like Davy Crockett, Mike Fink, and Mose the Bowery b'hoy appear on the American scene half a century after the American Revolution. The same social forces are operating in different countries to produce a folklore, and a folkloristics, reflective of the ideology and ethos of the times. Governments in Finland and Ireland have supported national folklore archives in order to place on record folklore materials that exalt the heritage of their people.

The pressures of government in the United States on the scholar are considerably less than the pressures of the marketplace, and the publication of folklore responds not to official ideology so much as to popular taste, which contains its own latent ideology. In the depression decade of the 1930s leftist folksingers in the United States sought to arouse the working man to a sense of social injustice and a mood of political radicalism through the singing of protest songs. The history of this movement, embracing well-known personalities such as the Almanac Singers, Woody Guthrie, Pete Seeger, Burl Ives, and others, has been ably told by R. Serge Denisoff in *Great Day Coming: Folk Music and the American Left* and Richard Reuss in "American Folklore and Left-Wing Politics: 1927-1957." In spite of the individual reputations of these singers their strenuous endeavors came to little, since they misunderstood the underlying philosophy of the American workingman. One observer pointed out that he had never heard Arkies or Okies singing the Dust Bowl ballads that Woody Guthrie had written expressly to dramatize their distress.

All sorts of questions about ideological, political, and nationalistic uses of folklore invite exploration. The new African nations are a wide open field. In a suggestive article on folklore as an agent of African nationalism, James Fernandez discusses how folk traditions furnish pan-Africanists and new-state Africans with an oral history and references for statements of negritude and African personality.[54] Folklore can be divisive as well as unifying and contribute to separatist feelings: witness French Canada, Scotland, Wales, Brittany. Political folklore and the relations between politics and folk genres have inspired new courses at the University of Pennsylvania and Western Kentucky State University. Gyula Ortutay, the noted

Hungarian folklorist, has related "the way I turned from folklore research to work in politics and how the two came to be united inseparably."[55] As he studied the folk life of peasants and realized their difficulties he perceived, as a folklorist, the need for a political action program. The political philosophies of the modern world, whether following the trail of democracy or socialism, embrace the peoples of the world, and sooner or later will levy on the traditions of the people.

Mythology and Folklore: A Review Essay

Although the terms mythology and folklore are frequently linked together in both lay and academic discourse, the students of the two subjects have steadily grown apart. In the eighteenth century mythology was its own science; but today it has become an uneasy adjunct to anthropology, classics, literature, and theology. None of the recent writers on mythology cited below are folklorists by primary allegiance, and, although all make gestures toward folklore, they appear surprisingly ill-informed on current folklore scholarship. In their scanty references they refer to the old standbys of a past generation—Franz Boas, Stith Thompson, Archer Taylor—and make no mention of, say, the *Journal of the Folklore Institute* or the Folktales of the World series, both initiated in 1963. Still, the study of mythology continues to attract powerful minds and to produce stimulating works.

Conversely, folklore has within the past two decades achieved the status of an independent discipline in the United States, with close to a hundred doctorates being granted by Indiana University and the University of Pennsylvania. These folklorists chiefly concern themselves with traditions within their own cultures, where myth as a form has disappeared.

Because of the scope and vast, uneven literature on these topics, this review will eschew journal articles and deal only with books, in English, published mainly between 1970 and 1973 but reaching back a year or two more if they fit into a theme under discussion. My aim has been to select titles that illustrate theoretical and research trends in studies of mythology and folklore.

Current interest in myth and mythology has extended to a historical concern with past interest, and in *The Rise of Modern Mythology,*

Mythology and Folklore: A Review Essay

1680-1860, two associate professors of English, Burton Feldman and Robert D. Richardson, constructed a bounteous history-cum-anthology.[1] They chose their dates to encompass immediate predecessors of the well-known modern philosophers of myth, and they selected their authors to illustrate the widely eclectic variety of writings about myth during the period. In the Enlightenment the surge of rationalistic inquiry coupled with the new literature of exploration and travel induced a reexamination of pagan and heathen myths. The editors point out that by the nineteenth century myths had become invested with qualities of creative literary art and spiritualizing religious principles. Meanwhile mythology, formerly an independent study devoted to Greek and Roman myths, had broadened to cover myths of many peoples but had lost its status as a separate branch of learning and become an adjunct to various subdivisions of the humanities and social sciences.

To illustrate this development Feldman and Richardson resort to a compromise between intellectual history and anthology. They preface each selection or group of selections with succinct brief essays placing the myth writer in his philosophical setting. These essays, with their bibliographical notes, maintain a high standard of scholarly excellence and illuminate the excerpts. In their net the editors catch a host of German, French, English, and American antiquaries, churchmen, philologists, poets, critics, historians, social theorists, and professed mythologists, the great and the obscure, all united in a sensitivity to the force of myth. Essays and selections indicate how myth is directed by Jacob Grimm toward folklore, by Marx toward ideology, by Goethe into literature, by Wagner into musical drama, by Bulfinch into bowdlerized fairy tales, by Blake into poetic symbolism, and so on through scores of ingenious commentaries. Only in their last section, "The Nineteenth Century to 1860," do the editors attempt more than chronological sequences, with headings on German, English, and American romanticism and myth, and only in the romantic movement—a loose designation—does a unitary attitude toward myth as a high mode of truth achieve some dominance in a given period.

The myth writing of yesteryear seems very far removed from that of today. In the 1970s the scholarly impulse to interpret and even to create myth finds its foremost exponents in Joseph Campbell, an American professor of literature, and Claude Lévi-Strauss, the French anthropologist. Another mythologist, Raphael Patai, in *Myth and Modern Man* describes both men as mythopoets, makers as well as students of myth, and quotes Lévi-Strauss as calling his book *The Raw and the Cooked* a myth of its own, "the myth of mythology."[2] In terms of style the ornate, rhapsodic prose of Campbell and the relentlessly logical narrative of Lévi-Strauss suggest creative rather than pedagogical writings.

Since completing his tetralogy on world mythology, *The Masks of God*, in 1968, Campbell has brought out two volumes of papers and talks elaborating his mythological system. In 1969 he published *The Flight of the Wild Gander: Explorations in the Mythological Dimension*, assembling pieces written and read between 1944 and 1968. Two years later he presented in *Myths to Live By* transcripts of tape-recorded talks he delivered at the Cooper Union Forum in New York City from 1958 to 1971.[3] Campbell's lurid body of work is highly repetitive, and one essay or book melts into another. He admires Jung and the Jungian view of omnipresent archetypal symbols, and he sees recurrent themes—theft of fire, virgin birth, incarnation, the returning hero—linking the world's folktales, legends, and myths and reflecting basic human biological and psychological demands. His pronouncements verge on the mystical. "Mythology is the womb of mankind's initiation to life and death," he writes; mythology is "dreamlike and, like dream, a spontaneous product of the psyche."[4] Toward the particularism of field anthropologists and their American Anthropological Society (*sic*) he betrays a defensive edginess, and praises Bastian for placing universal elementary ideas ahead of local factors. The psychoanalytic keys of Freud and Jung added to Bastian's thesis give Campbell his springboard.

In *Myths to Live By* Campbell moves from the role of mythographer to the role of prophet. While stressing the psychic unity of mankind, he dwells on the ideal of self-obliteration in the East as contrasted with the assertive individualism of the West. Regarding religious mythologies of the West as outdated and sterile, he advises the churches to dispense with talk and renew their rituals. In this same vein he chides James G. Frazer for assuming that a rationalist exposure of superstitious customs would lead to their disappearance. In his mystical posture, Campbell retells myths in the form of pretty fables and inflates his rhetoric in an incantatory pitch. Lowering his voice, he descends to down-to-earth homilies about the boy at the lunch counter who had boldly defied the fundamentalism of his teacher and mother. Then he is off again, dazzling his audience with quotations from the *Upanishads* and the *Bhagavad Gita*. Yet for a modern Occidental man, as he prides himself, he finds the youth culture regressive and schizophrenic, untuned to the vibrations of the true mystics.

Campbell appeals firstly to a literary constituency, Lévi-Strauss to an anthropological constituency, although they have reached far wider audiences. The myths that Campbell cites from variegated sources are literary and artistic reworkings of the oral originals or fluent renderings of field sources. To illustrate his books he chooses artistic devices representing mythic themes. In *The Raw and the Cooked* Lévi-Strauss exclusively cites field-collected oral myth texts of Brazilian and other South American Indian tribes, among whom he himself has done extensive fieldwork. Working from opposite ends, Campbell from the prehistoric and classical and Lévi-Strauss from the contemporary tribal, they move toward the same central goal: a universal system of mythology. Campbell says: "Essentially the same mythological motifs are to be found throughout the world . . . such images stem from the psyche . . . they cannot be interpreted properly as references . . . to local historical events or personages."[5] Lévi-Strauss writes: "The layered structure of myth . . . allows us to look upon myth as a matrix of meanings, which are arranged in lines or columns, but in which each level always refers to some other level, whichever way the myth is read. Similarly, each matrix of meanings refers to another matrix, each myth to other myths."[6] Their ultimate meaning lies in the mind that generates them and in the image of the world perceived by that mind.

So Lévi-Strauss begins with one Bororo myth and works his way through 186 more, diagramming the binary oppositions of such empirical categories as the "raw and the cooked, the fresh and the decayed, the moistened and the burned." Everything fits beautifully, under the master's touch, into tables of opposites, and if a piece seems to be missing, he gently guides the reader to its restoration. Thus, when one myth apparently lacks an incest episode, he shows that the act of a grandmother squatting over the head of her sleeping grandson and farting in his face is properly to be interpreted as inverted incest.[7] One recalls the mythological schemes of the solar and the sexual mythologists who interpreted all myths with similar neat finality and excited such admiration in their day.

Raphael Patai, the prolific Judaic scholar who collaborated on *Hebrew Myths* with Robert Graves in 1964, seeks not to unlock the world's myths with a new key in *Myth and the Modern Man* but to show their relation to cigarette ads, Mickey Mouse cartoons, and

James Bond movies. After summarily reviewing schools of myth interpretation, he turns to consider mythologizing tendencies in America of the 1960s. His aim is twofold: to demonstrate that contemporary Americans develop myths much as did the ancient Greeks, and that these myths respond to the psychic needs of particular followings. As middle America identified with Mickey Mouse, so did the Greeks of old identify with Herakles, likewise a buffoon-hero, in his series of mighty labors. One sector of black Americans accepted the myth of the Godhead with which Father Divine invested himself. Contrary to customary myth process, he managed to become a legend in his lifetime, and, through the manipulation of his wife, to transcend the fact of death. Radical student activists at the peak of SDS violence chose for their mythic hero a fantasized five-year-old, whom they named Marion Delgado and invested with their own infantile spleen toward, and imagined power over, the authoritarian system. They selected a superchild because in permissive America the errant child never gets punished. *Playboy* magazine and its clubs and bunnies foster a new sex myth of a virile, dominant, but blasé male fending off hypermammalian young women. The *Playboy* rabbit evokes images of sexuality and seeming weakness that, like Mickey Mouse, conceal inner strength. In forced analogies such as these between classical myths and the blandishments of mass culture Patai has strained the concept of myth beyond any recognizable meaning. Mickey Mouse is nobody's demigod.

In *Myth: Its Meaning and Functions in Ancient and Other Cultures* Geoffrey S. Kirk refuses to deal with "modern myths," although he concedes that a proper comprehension of these "bastard modern forms" may be aided by a study of the genuine article.[8] Himself a professor of classics at the University of Bristol, and the deliverer of the Sather classical lectures at the University of California on which his book is based, Kirk takes a refreshingly broad view of his subject by exposing classical myths to light from folklore and anthropology. An introductory chapter considers and rejects prevalent conceptions of myth that associate myths exclusively with gods, or rituals, or religion. Kirk contends, quite correctly, that myth narratives cannot be precisely categorized since they flow into other kinds of folk narratives such as fairy tales and legends. Most folklorists would agree with his assertion that myth implies no more than a traditional story, which may deal wtih deities or explain origins or involve religious matters or sanction customs. Recognizing that myths contain folktale elements and reflect the styles of individual storytellers is a large step forward in comparative mythological study.

A second chapter offers an astute analysis of Lévi-Strauss's structural theory as applied to South American myths. Kirk proposes certain plausible modifications: that Lévi-Strauss not attempt to fit all myths into his model of polarities resolved by a mediator; that he seek meaning in content as well as structure; that he allow for the non-structural elements contributed by narrators, and indeed begin his analysis by empirical observation of myth tellers rather than with a priori dogma about the structure of the human mind. In the main Kirk gives high marks to Lévi-Strauss for advancing the state of mythological study beyond all previous systems, and for his convincing analysis of how Brazilian myths functioned to mediate between the contradictions of nature and culture.

In subsequent chapters Kirk brings to bear folklore perspective and Lévi-Straussian structural theory on Sumerian, Akkadian, and Greek myths. His approach yields fresh rewards, as when he perceives the nature-culture contrast in the Gilgamesh epic, but not among the Greeks, for whom the natural environment posed no formidable problems. He sees a special quality of Greek myth in its emphasis on heroes—elsewhere usually found in legend—and a flaw in its poverty of fantasy. Subsequently, Kirk extends his comparative treatment to Germanic, Egyptian, and Hindu myths and finds their relation with the mythic expression of ancient Greece less meaningful than with that of Mesopotamia. A final chapter weighs certain theories of mythic formulation, particularly those of Cassirer and Jung, and proposes a myth typology based on narrative, operative, and speculative functions. Kirk himself supports the thesis that many myths can be classed as speculative in their concerns with man's life, death, culture, and environment. His own work represents a high level of speculative scholarship resting on a sound comparative and folkloric base.

History of Folkloristics

One sign of the coming of age of folklore studies is the appearance of historical and biographical explorations of the great nineteenth-century folklorists who developed the subject. The past decade has seen histories of Finnish and British folkloristics, two biographies of the brothers Grimm, a biography of the Serbian folklorist and linguist Vuk Karadzić, and a volume of biographical essays on the Scandinavian folklorists. Hitherto the most elementary information about the pioneer collectors and scholars of folklore has been lacking in English-language sources.

Finland occupies a special position in the history of folklore scholarship. In the late nineteenth and early twentieth centuries Finns took the lead in collecting and explicating oral peasant traditions and developing an analytic system which attracted international attention, the so-called Finnish historical-geographical method. The monograph of Jouko Hautala, *Finnish Folklore Research, 1828-1918*, sets the illustrious figures now so well known—Elias Lönnrot, collector of the Kalevala poems, Julius Krohn and his son Kaarle, who formulated the Finnish method, and Antti Aarne, pioneer tale cataloguer—in a full perspective.[9] It was the collections of oral epic poems, mainly from Karelia in eastern Finland, published by the country doctor Elias Lönnrot in 1835 as the *Kalevala*, that inspired cultural drives toward a Finnish national civilization and formed the foundation for the Finnish achievement in folklore studies. To ensure that ample variants were available for comparative folklore studies, Kaarle Krohn stimulated the Finnish Literature Society to increase their archival holdings, which rose from forty-three thousand items in 1877 to over half a million by 1930. (Today they approach three million.) In his Finnish folklore seminar at the University of Helsinki, Kaarle trained dozens of young scholars, including Antti Aarne, who propagated his methods.

Less familiar names also come into view: A. E. Ahlquist, the first outspoken critic of Lönnrot's *Kalevala* scholarship; M. A. Castrén, theorist of Finnish mythology; E. Salmelainen, the first major Finnish collector and scholar of folktales; V. Salminen, who collected and compared Ingrian wedding songs; and E. N. Setälä, critic of the historic-geographic method and exponent of the mythical interpretation of ancient Finnish poetry. For the American scholar the information on these and other relatively unknown figures is especially useful. Hautala's history turns into a catalogue of Finnish folklorists and a summary, often with extensive quotations, of their publications. This is a digest of academic scholarship by a member of the guild. One dissertation after another on a folklore subject produced at the University of Helsinki is mentioned and synopsized. Hautala recognizes the major trends of folklore theory, from early-nineteenth-century romantic nationalism through nature mythology and positivistic evolutionism to the historical-geographical methodology, and he comments temperately on their weaknesses. But lacking is any human side of scholarship or of the Finnish folk who are being so assiduously studied.

The story that unfolds in Dorson's *The British Folklorists: A History* is almost wholly a nonacademic chronicle.[10] Some parallel points are notable. Although the central magnet of the *Kalevala* is absent, the successive waves of interest in folkloric matters by antiquaries, nature mythologists, evolutionists, and diffusionists wash over Britain as well as Finland. But literary and antiquarian societies, culminating in 1878 in the Folk-Lore Society, rather than universities, supported folklore research in England, a situation that accounts for its decline after the First World War and for the anomaly of an American writing the history of British folklore. The Great Team of the Folk-Lore Society that carried its prestige to a peak in the International Folklore Congress held in London in 1891 were all private scholars: Andrew Lang, a free-lance writer; George Laurence Gomme, a London civil servant; Edwin Sidney Hartland, a solicitor; Edward Clodd, a banker; and Alfred Nutt, a publisher. Unlike the Finns, none engaged in field collecting, although their large body of theoretical writings, suggesting analogies between the beliefs of peasants and contemporary aboriginals, did generate collecting activities in the English counties and throughout the Empire. In Scotland, Ireland, and Wales impulses of cultural nationalism have in the twentieth century led to institutional folklore centers that sponsor considerable fieldwork. *The British Folklorists* traces the vigorous but largely forgotten efforts of folklore enthusiasts who built upon each other's labors from the first national history of William Camden in 1586 to Edward B. Tylor and the Great Team of anthropological folklorists whom he so powerfully influenced. Tylor established anthropology firmly at Oxford, but folklore never gained entry into Oxford or Cambridge.

Selections from the major figures in *The British Folklorists* were edited and published by Dorson in a two-volume anthology, *Peasant Customs and Savage Myths*, aimed at presenting the continuous development and spirited controversies of British folklore theory in the nineteenth century.[11] Writing for a general rather than a scholarly audience, although maintaining high standards of research methods as they sought to construct a "science" of folklore, the Victorians expressed themselves with grace, fluency, and zeal, and, in the cases of Lang and Clodd, with wit and charm. Yet their work has vanished from the scene. At international folklore congresses the names of the Great Team and their associates are rarely mentioned; the Finns, on their much narrower academic and cultural base, have maintained their eminence. In England social anthropology has rejected folklore and new developments in folklore have come in the name of social history and oral literature. The moral is obvious: in the twentieth century the fate of folklore studies has for better or worse rested with the academic professional and his university sponsor.

Complementing and to some extent overlapping Hautala's history is a volume of collective biographical sketches dedicated to him on his sixtieth birthday, *Biographica: Nordic Folklorists of the Past*, edited by Dag Strömbäck and others. Twenty-four folklore scholars of Finland, Sweden, Denmark, Norway, the Faroe Islands, and Iceland (the last two with single representatives) reviewed the accomplishments of twenty-six of their predecessors, some internationally known, like Carl von Sydow, Svend Grundtvig, the Krohns, and Axel Olrik, and others of local reputation. This volume testifies to the vigorous and continuous activities, past and present, of Scandinavian and Finnish folklorists who held chairs at the universities of Copenhagen, Oslo, Lund, and Helsinki, museum curatorships, pastorates, and teaching positions from which they embarked on lifelong collecting and publishing careers. Unlike the inner circle of the English Folk-Lore Society, the Nordic folklore enthusiasts almost without exception possessed roots in the country soil and engaged in frequent field trips. A number, like the indefatigable Evald Tang Kristensen of Denmark and Jón Árnason of Iceland, expended their energies in amassing rather than theorizing about oral traditions.

Although more personal and revealing than Hautala's wooden history, *Biographica* displays the unevenness one might expect from two dozen humanists turning their hands to the critical biographical sketch. Some essays, like Tillhagen's on the folk-medicine expert Ingjald Reichborn-Kjennerud, Nesheim's on the Lappish collector Just Knud Qvigstad, and Strömbäck's on the talented but unproductive Moltke Moe, do little more than abstract or quote from the writings of their subjects. Matti Kuusi dealt with an unknown, A. A. Koskerjaako, who was overshadowed by his great Finnish colleagues; Kuusi writes persuasively that "in the history of scholarship, fame seems to be a cumulative affair: he who has, gets more" and makes a case as a neglected pioneer for the headmaster who abjured popularization or sweeping sensational theories and who wrote only in Finnish, and little at that, on a neglected subject, legal proverbs.[12] For the most part the essays avoid filiopietism and often indulge in hard-hitting criticism. In her sketch of Henning Feilberg, the Danish teacher, minister, and compiler of the dictionary of the vernacular language of Jutland,

Mythology and Folklore: A Review Essay

Bente Alver challenges the assumptions of his 1904 study *Jul*, interpreting Christmas customs as a festival of death. Alver finds Feilberg's methods deficient in source criticism and genre analysis and in failure to distinguish between individual and collective elements of tradition. In a solid essay appraising Axel Olrik's scholarship, Bengt Holbek, who contributes a judicious preface to the volume, declares that for all Olrik's esteemed writings on Danish heroic poetry, Scandinavian mythology, and theories of folk-epic composition, he customarily overlooked the individual informant. The Nordic folklorists have chiefly plowed their own vineyards and influenced each other. Yet they have advanced folklore studies to a greater degree than any other body of regional scholars. This tentative volume affords some clues to their thought and motivations.

In the history of folkloristics the role of the brothers Jacob and Wilhelm Grimm is crucial, and two biographies have recently appeared in English. Since the brothers were born a year apart and died within four years of each other (Jacob's dates are 1785-1863, Wilhelm's 1786-1859) and since they collaborated on much of their scholarly work and shared their professional lives, one biography inevitably serves both. *The Brothers Grimm*, an impressionistic portrait by Ruth Michaelis-Jena, who had previously edited lesser known folktales collected by the brothers, paints in homely details of their lives, drawn in large part from published correspondence and materials, iconographic as well as printed, from the Brüder Grimm Museum in Kassel.[13] *Paths Through the Forest: A Biography of the Brothers Grimm* by Murray Peppard, chairman of the German department at Amherst College, is far more the academic biography with a surer command of the historical and intellectual setting. Both biographies retell the basic narrative of the brothers' youth in Steinau, their college days at Marburg, their posts as librarians in Cassel, their move to the university at Göttingen when denied promotion by the Elector of Hesse, their defiance of King Ernest Augustus of Hannover on his repeal of the liberal constitution of 1833 and Jacob's subsequent exiling, and the final phase as revered lecturers at Berlin University. Bachelor Jacob emerges as a research mole, vexed at every interruption to his labors (such as the Congress of Vienna in 1815, which he was obliged to attend as a minor functionary). More outgoing, and finally marrying at thirty-nine, Wilhelm achieved somewhat less as an original scholar. What strikes the modern academic is the similarity of his problems with those of the Grimms: the struggles for a position, advancement, recognition, academic freedom, scholarly principles versus commercial rewards. The opus that won them their greatest fame, the *Kinder- und Hausmärchen*, was the one on which through successive editions they steadily compromised with the demands of the marketplace.

Both biographers are deplorably ignorant of folkloric scholarship. Michaelis-Jena barely rises above the level of reciting titles and repeating clichés about the brothers' works. Because he pretends to more authority, Peppard fails even more dismally to comment intelligently on their folklore publications. His translation of *Sagen* as "Folk Tales" and his constant comparisons between the "Fairy Tales" (Märchen) and the "Folk Tales" (Sagen), which every folklorist refers to as legends, make a mockery of basic folklore terminology. His statement that the "true fairy tale . . . will be characterized by prudery" is another shocking piece of ignorance.[14] It is the old story of the competent literary scholar who lacks any basic training in folklore. Campbell, for all his rhapsodizing, gives a much sounder brief treatment of the work of the Grimm brothers on the folktale, with a crisp definition of Sagen, in a 1944 essay, "The Fairy Tale," reprinted in *The Flight of the Wild Gander.*

Like Jacob Grimm, whom he met and with whose ideas he sympathized, Vuk Karadzić devoted his lifelong energies to propagating a national language and folklore. His biographer, Duncan Wilson, has written in *Vuk Stefanović Karadzić, 1787-1864*, "The various branches of Vuk's work were all undertaken with the one aim in view of reviving the Serb popular language for the greater use and glory of the Serb nation."[15] Toward this end Vuk collected and published oral poetry and folktales sung and recited in the folk dialects that he knew from his own village childhood, while in his *Dictionary* of the Serb popular tongue (1818), as well as in his posthumous *Life and Customs of the Serb People* (1867), he recorded many folk beliefs and rituals. Accordingly, he ranks as one of the founding fathers of national folklore studies in early nineteenth-century Europe, and Wilson gives full recognition to Vuk's folkloric and ethnographic activities. Disclaiming any pretense to new knowledge and excusing himself as a working diplomat, Wilson provides a highly informative, scholarly biography based on Vuk's extensive writings and on secondary studies in Serbian, French, German, and English. His narrative combines the political-chronological account of Vuk's career in Serbia under the Turks and in Vienna under the Austrian Empire with his ethnographic activities in Croatia, Dalmatia, and Montenegro. For the folklorist there are vignettes of heroic singers, such as Tešan Podrugović, a destitute reed-cutter in the Srem who recited a hundred heroic songs about outlaw leaders; discussion of the favoring conditions in Vuk's early life for the folk creation of heroic poetry about the wars of liberation against the Turks; examples of Vuk's stylistic revision of folktales; as well as appendixes of translated texts of traditional poems, tales, and beliefs collected by Vuk, and Jacob Grimm's sympathetic review of Vuk's 1823 collection of Serb popular songs. Biographical studies of this caliber are sorely needed for the Grimms and for other major European folklorists of the nineteenth century.

General and Theoretical Works

No single theory or school has emerged from the younger generation of American folklorists, but a definite point of view and community of interest are recognizable and have found expression in a special issue of the *Journal of American Folklore* separately issued as a book titled *Toward New Perspectives in Folklore.*[16] Co-editors are the editor of the *Journal*, Américo Paredes, and his colleague at the University of Texas, Richard Bauman, who conceives of the symposium as emphasizing the "event" rather than the "item" aspect of folklore. Of the thirteen contributors, eight hold doctorates in folklore, one in American studies, one in psychology, and three are anthropologists. They evince strong interest in linguistics communication theory, the sociology of small-group interaction, developmental psychology, and structural and symbolic forms of analysis. To a large extent they conceive of folklore as communication. Dan Ben-Amos states that "folklore is a communicative process," and he eliminates from his definition the long-established criteria of tradition and oral transmission. If a popular song or anecdote enters into the communication of a small group, it should be treated as folklore, and if a traditional tale or ballad appears on television, it ceases to be folklore. Bauman emphasized the use of folklore in "communicative reaction." Dell Hymes sees the new perspective as a "focus on the communicative event." Elli Maranda begins her analysis of Lau riddle texts with the "hypothesis that verbal art is a form of communication."

Another favorite term is performance. To Roger Abrahams, "Folklore is folklore only when performed." Kenneth Goldstein contends that a given individual actively performs only certain items in his repertoire, and that performance, not passive knowledge, is the test of whether a tradition can be labeled active or inactive. Bauman argues that attention to "folklore as doing . . . folklore performance" holds the key to the future of empirical folklore studies.

Still another approved term is continuum, with its suggested transcendence of the conventional categories of the genres and space-time divisions. Working on a corpus of Israeli legends, Heda Jason redefines the Grimms' definition of historical and local legends into a "linear continuum" with separate tales distributed along the continuum. In seeking to develop a methodology for analyzing festival behavior, Robert J. Smith prepared a "simple hedonic continuum" to determine normative and actual affective responses to two folktales. Defining folklore in context, Ben-Amos asserts that "the narrator, his story, and his audience are all related to each other as components of a single continuum." Attempting to point out related interests of folklore and linguistics, Hymes describes speech in terms of genres and of esthetic quality, and allows that "folklorists will be most concerned with the more highly organized, more expressive end of the two continua." Gary Gossen views Chamula oral tradition in holistic terms rather than under the rubrics of European genres. So too Brian Sutton-Smith examines various expressive forms "such as dreams, stories, folktales, rhymes, cartoons, and games as if they could all be part of the same conceptual domain," and arrives at what he considers an "expressive profile" of a youthful age group. In these studies the tendency is to soften not only the genre distinctions within folklore but also the boundaries between folkloric and nonfolkloric expressive behavior. The article by Alan Dundes on "Folk Ideas as Units of World View"—refreshingly jargon-free, in contrast to the balance of the papers—steps outside the genres to suggest that folklorists record traditional attitudes, often referred to as myth in the derogatory sense, which represent inherited values and fallacies in the folk community. Such values may be expressed in proverbial form—"money talks"—or in ordinary discourse.

In the end there is little that is novel in *New Perspectives*. The contributors have for the most part written previously on the points they make here. Attention to "artistic verbal performance" is already becoming something of a cliché, and rather than enlarging the scope of folkloric investigation the concept excludes material culture and all nonverbal folk forms. The anthropologists included continue to interpret the one culture in which they have done their fieldwork. Perhaps the most valuable contribution, involving no new perspective but a refinement of method, is Dennis Tedlock's proposal for more faithful translation of Zuñi oral narratives by attention to all linguistic and paralinguistic features. One curious byproduct of the "new perspective" is the disappearance from view of the folk, who are shunted aside in favor of models, graphs, and social-science terminology.

Two volumes of essays devoted to structural theory were published by folklorist Elli Köngäs Maranda and anthropologist Pierre Maranda. They co-edited *Structural Analysis of Oral Tradition*, heavily weighted toward the analytic method of Lévi-Strauss, who supplies one chapter explicating three Guianese myths. Although all the essays deal with folklore materials—tribal folktales and ritual, Finnish riddles, Javanese folk drama, crosscultural folksongs—they belong to the discipline of structural linguistics rather than folkloristics. Only three of the thirteen contributors—Elli Köngäs Maranda, Alan Dundes, and Alan Lomax—are folklorists, and the folk whom they study make few appearances in these papers full of diagrams and computer statistics. Commenting on the necessity to identify before interpreting folk narrative, Dundes points out that "to someone trained in folklore, it is clear that the narrative [a Sherente myth] is not simply a retelling of Genesis. It is in fact a standard European narrative, a tale found in the Grimm collection," and he furnishes the type and motif numbers. Responding, the ethnographer Maybury-Lewis concedes his ignorance of the folktale type he had collected and accepts the label of a "folkloristically naive anthropologist." Lévi-Strauss frankly states that the need for ethnographic knowledge recedes as the semantic universe of the myth becomes clearer.[17] The Marandas also published *Structural Models in Folklore and Transformational Essays*, reprinting a 1962 essay they had jointly written and adding a transformational myth analysis by Pierre and a transformational riddle analysis by Elli Köngäs. The few vivid pages describing their recent field experience recording Lau folklore in Melanesia, "where myth and ritual are fully alive and form the core of the culture," contrast with the main content of the diagrammatic papers.[18]

At the opposite end of the folklore spectrum fall two volumes of collected articles by Richard M. Dorson, *American Folklore and the Historian* and *Folklore, Selected Essays*.[19] In the humanistic tradition these essays discuss questions of oral narrative style, concepts of myth and legend, the historicity of tradition, and the future of folklore as an academic discipline. A folklorist of the "new perspectives" school reviewing these volumes would point out the absence of computerized conclusions and models of communicative behavior.

Two contrasting attempts surveyed the subject matter of folklore comprehensively. In *Folklore and Folklife: An Introduction*, edited by Dorson, sixteen contributors deal with specific folklore genres and research techniques, and the editor discusses twelve schools of folklore theory in an introduction.[20] The faculty and former students of the Folklore Institute of Indiana University constitute the core of the authors, reinforced by three specialists from Britain and one from Switzerland. Recognizing the extension of the folklore concept to cover material culture as currently acknowledged by European and American folklorists, the volume gives attention to folk costume, folk cuisine, folk architecture, and folk crafts. In between the clear-cut areas of oral folklore and physical artifacts are placed the performing arts of folk drama, folk dance, and folk music, and such matters of social belief and custom as folk medicine and folk religion.

Nonliterate and non-Western cultures, which are not discussed in *Folklore and Folklife*, receive considerable attention in *Lore: An Introduction to the Science of Folklore and Literature* by Munro S. Edmonson, who calls his book "an introduction to the science of lore . . . commonly described by such terms as *folklore* or *comparative literature*, here defined as the study of connotative meaning." No professional folklorists use these terms in these ways, or deal with materials in his manner. He tabulates all the world's cultures and all the world's literatures, oral and written, from prehistoric times to the present, under the rubrics of Speech, Song, Story, Plays, and Style, and in a lengthy Chronological Outline of the World's Written Traditions. His examples come indiscriminately from everywhere. Under "Plays" he includes excerpts from a Filipino riddling game, the dozens from United States blacks, Vietnamese courtship verses, the Middle American ritual ball game Tlachtli, a hypothetical Reindeer Dance ritual drama of Cro-Magnon hunters, a ceremonial preparation of Alacaluf whalers of southern South America, a Mayala Negrito ritual drama for propitiating mountain spirits, a New Year's ritual in Kuntunso in Ghana dedicated to the god Tano the Hyena, a Pueblo Indian raingod ceremonial (in which the text has the Chief Raingod striking the first clown with his yucca whip to elicit the response, "Ouch, goddam, that hurts!"), and so on. In providing his miscellaneous texts of speech, song, story, and play, Edmonson intends to illustrate the power and range of metaphor. He sees "connotative relationships" as metaphors, and he believes that "some part of the building of a world political structure rests on the development of comprehensible and acceptable metaphors on which to base it—in short, it awaits the further elaboration of a world literature."[21] This work seems to be the stuff rather than the study of folklore.

British Folklore

The most exciting folkloric studies of recent years came from an unexpected direction. They were written by two English social historians familiar with British social anthropology and working closely together. Keith Thomas, author of *Religion and the Decline of Magic*, directed the dissertation at Oxford University of Alan Macfarlane, published as *Witchcraft in Tudor and Stuart England*, and both express deep debt to the other's work. Thomas's history is the more comprehensive and philosophic, a densely annotated, panoramic examination of the supernatural belief systems within and without the church in sixteenth- and seventeenth-century England. Macfarlane concentrates on beliefs in witchcraft in three Essex villages, Hatfield Peverel, Boreham, and Little Baddow, in the same period. Their work goes far beyond anything in print in delineating the social functions of magical beliefs in preindustrial England. They seek to establish— one on a national, the other on a local scale—the precise manner in which ideas now regarded as superstitions operated in English society after the Reformation. Where folklorists customarily list and describe beliefs in general terms, Macfarlane and Thomas are determined to pin down as far as possible the nature, extent, genesis, and social utility of supernatural concepts. On witchcraft, for example, they ask who in the community held such beliefs, over what periods of time, exactly what the villagers believed, what counter-measures they pursued, from magical to legal, and to what kinds of individuals they imputed their charges. (Thomas reports that an accusation against a witch for riding a broomstick occurs only once in an English trial.) The wealth and orderliness of the information they have presented, and the convincing nature of their evidence, make these volumes landmarks in a field plagued by popularizers and dilettantes.

Ironically Thomas and Macfarlane have approached the study of folklore materials not from the great humanistic tradition of the Victorian folklorists, whose day ran out with the First World War, but through what they consider hard-nosed social sciences of today, quantitative history and social anthropology. It is only plausible that, folklore never having gained a foothold at Oxford and Cambridge, these historians of witchcraft should exchange notes with anthropologists of witchcraft at the High Table, and so add a comparative dimension to their insular concerns. Thomas incorporated into his work a paper he presented to the Association of Social Anthropologists on "The Relevance of Social Anthropology to the Historical Study of English Witchcraft," and Macfarlane includes three chapters of anthropological field data. Avant-garde too in historical method, they pursue statistical conclusions, and Thomas defers to the computer that has made the "historian's traditional method of presentation by example and counter-example . . . the intellectual equivalent of the bow and arrow in a nuclear age."[22]

Yet the success of these studies rests on time-honored methods rather than new magic formulas. Thomas has done what a good historian must do: he has mastered an enormous, complex literature of primary and secondary writings, and he had analyzed them to show lines of force and change. His canvas covers the magical system within the medieval and Protestant Church, exemplified by acts of divine providence and the efficacy of prayer; the folk magic of healers and "cunning men"; the intellectually fashionable dependence on astrology; the role of witchcraft and related beliefs in ghosts and fairies, auguries and apparitions. Always he seeks to explain the social reasons for the emergence, persistence, and decline of supernatural ideas. Thus, he accounts for the abandonment of the once-popular belief in lucky and unlucky days by the changing conception of time contingent on the shift from a seasonal agricultural calendar to a more technological routine, the acceptance of Newtonian time regularity, and the invention in 1657 of the pendulum clock. Widespread sentiments of rebellion at the time of the Reformation and the Civil War induced the belief in prophecies, Thomas contends, rather than prophecies stimulating rebellion. To answer the question why witchcraft reached a peak in the one hundred and twenty years after the accession of Elizabeth I in 1559, he suggests that in this period it assumed a particularly menacing aspect because the continental theological concept of witchcraft as heretical Devil-worship fused with the English popular notion of witchcraft as malevolent magic. Such conclusions represent processes of historical reasoning, buttressed by substantial evidence. But the new tools contribute little. Thomas concedes the unavailability of firm statistics for the large questions he is covering. As for insights from social anthropology, he considers Malinowski's thesis that magical ideas decline when technological advances render the old magical rites for controlling phenomena unnecessary, and finds it wanting. The eighteenth century had moved away from the sixteenth century's reliance on magic, and magical techniques had lost their appeal well before new technical solutions had come to hand. The key, Thomas finds, lay not in the new achievement but in new aspirations, in an altered mental set that stressed self-help.

If he deplored his own pursuance of conventional historical method, Thomas still could praise the statistical and anthropological mold of *Witchcraft in Tudor and Stuart England*. Macfarlane's reworked dissertation bristles with maps, tables, figures, diagrams. Every item of information that can be tabulated about witchcraft is given its statistical identity. We learn that 473 indictments of 299 persons accused of witchcraft in Essex in the Home Circuit resulted in 112 executions between 1560 and 1700; that 23 of 49 husbands of accused witches reported in the Essex Assizes between 1560 and 1680 were alleged victims; that in the three Essex villages under survey between 1560 and 1599 witchcraft lagged behind sexual offences and nonattendance at church but considerably exceeded murder and drunkenness; that assize indictments from 1560 to 1680 recorded the bewitchment of 124 pigs, 123 sheep, 110 cows, 63 horses, and 11 chickens valued from fourpence to four pounds. Besides this scrupulous amassing of documentary data, Macfarlane adds to his pot summary statements of beliefs about witches in African tribal societies and among the Navaho. And where does it all end? "A close examination of the records for one English county has shown that witchcraft beliefs were an important part of village life." When Macfarlane turns from specifics to generalities, he admits that his hypotheses about the rise and decline of English witchcraft require knowledge of "the total intellectual and social background of sixteenth- and seventeenth-century England." He defers to Thomas as Thomas deferred to him. As for the new light to be shed from anthropological field studies, well, Macfarlane muses, some suggest a correlation between social change and witchcraft fears—and some do not. He regrets the lack of studies of witchcraft in African towns which could offer possible analogies with Tudor and Stuart England. In the end the evidence that remains most firmly in the reader's mind is the individual oral testimony sought by the folklorist, as in this outburst over a garden fence by a parson railing at a suspected witch, recorded in a pamphlet of 1582: "I am glad you are here you vield strumpet (saying) I do think you have bewitched my wife, and as truly as God doth live, if I can perceive yt she be troubled any more as she hath been, I will not leave a whole bone about thee, and besides I will seeke to have thee hanged."[23] This is the authentic voice of the folk, not the whir of the computer.

An invaluable resource for the folklorist is the four-volume *Diction-*

ary of British Folktales (omitting Celtic examples), assembled by Katharine Briggs.[24] Hitherto England has appeared woefully lean in oral traditional narratives, compared to the treasures in Ireland, Scotland, and on the continent. By diligent sleuthing of myriad printed sources that have captured traditional narratives in texts close to the spoken word, and by giving due recognition to the legend and jest, Briggs has confounded disparagers of the English storytelling tradition.

Ewart Evans continues his informative interviewing of traditional craftsmen and farmworkers in East Anglia in *Where Beards Wag All: The Relevance of the Oral Tradition.* In associating himself with David Thompson in an old-fashioned work stringing together comparative myths and folklore about the hare, and suggesting their debt to man's observations on the hare's enigmatic behavior, Evans is less successful.[25]

American Folklore

American folklore as a subject-matter field has been characterized by lack of a theoretical base, random field collecting often following vogues of the moment, and the dominance of commercial over academic goals. The past few years have seen some reversals of these trends. An attempt at formulating "A Theory for American Folklore" grounded in the social realities of American history was first presented by Richard M. Dorson in 1957 in a paper, reprinted with other of his pieces supporting the argument, in *American Folklore and the Historian.* A conference devoted to the genre most closely linking American history and folklore produced an unusually coherent and stimulating set of papers, published as *American Folk Legend: A Symposium,* edited by Wayland D. Hand.[26] The fourteen participants, all professional folklorists, in exploring general and specific legendary themes arrived at a surprising consensus on the need to recast the concept of legend in North America. Rather than the static notion of a simple narrative summarized on a three-by-five card, the participants one after another spoke for a fluid, complex form coalescing with other genres, dipping into the popular culture, susceptible to psychological and functional analyses. In terms of suggestive theory and vivid empirical data covering Pennsylvania-German, Mormon, Navaho, Kentucky mountain, Mexican, and urban legendry, this work merits high praise.

Two disappointing studies dealt with the relation of folklore to

American history and American literature. Tristram Coffin turned to a near virgin subject in *Uncertain Glory: Folklore and the American Revolution.*[27] A book successfully exploring the folklore associated with the American Revolution would indeed be a contribution, but this work merely confuses the issue. A twenty-page introduction explains what folklore is. Five chapters follow under "Part I: Folklore Goes to War," and five more under "Part II: Fakelore Goes to War." There are chapters on the song repertory of a Revolutionary soldier as reflected in the 1823 Sandgate, Vermont, ballad book *The Green Mountain Songster;* on the folksong "Yankee Doodle"; on five Revolutionary War ballads; and on William Billings, composer of hymns during the Revolutionary period. Part II deals with "Three Spies" of fiction and balladry—Harvey Birch of Cooper's *The Spy*, Nathan Hale, and Major André—and chapters are devoted to Timothy Murphy the Indian fighter and Ethan Allen the Green Mountain Boy as forgotten heroes and to Paul Revere and Benjamin Franklin as remembered ones. The author's intentions, he informs us, are to show the kinds of oral traditions extant during the Revolution, those materials developed during the War by "highly literate propagandists" that drifted into tradition, and the Revolutionary lore that "we educated Americans have created or borrowed or nurtured for our own purposes." He proposes as a "seminal idea" the proposition that fakelore is winnowed in a highly literate society to serve needs much like those served by folklore in a folk society. So, of the three spy figures, one is "fake" (Birch), one "partly fake" (Hale), and one "folk" (André), but the processes that shape them are not, he feels, all that different.

Much of Coffin's argument rests on the distinction between folklore and fakelore. That the production of fakelore should be considered and not summarily dismissed by the professional folklorist I readily concede. But his handling of the term is baffling. Under true folklore he places an imaginary reconstruction through nineteenth- and twentieth-century texts of a tale-telling session at Valley Forge, with weather-beaten soldiers staring into the glowing coals, but this is a prime example of fakelore and indefensible as a scholarly procedure. He himself says that a text of the present tells us more about today than about the period it describes. That Paul Revere is remembered because of Longfellow's poem has nothing to do with either folklore or fakelore. What Coffin seems to mean by *fakelore* could probably be described as popular culture or national taste; it is the pseudo-scholar creating folklore for the mass culture who is guilty of fakelore. Nor does he use *legend* precisely when he equates ballad stories that have no independent prose existence, such as the ballads of Hale and André, with legends. Benjamin Franklin should be viewed as a culture hero rather than a folk or fake hero. Generalizations, concepts, terms are fuzzy. Coffin never cites the richest repository for the popular literature of the Revolution, Moses Coit Tyler's classic *Literary History of the American Revolution*, which gives verses of the André and Nathan Hale ballads and samples of poems attacking "pernicious tea" at the time of the Boston Tea Party. Nor does he allude to the genre of personal narratives by Revolutionary veterans, clearly based on oral memorates, which represent the strongest link between the Revolution and the formation of indigenous traditions.

There are ideas here worthy of pursuit, such as the distinction between the occupational folklore shared by soldiers and the impact of the war on folk tradition. Revolutionary folklore—and Civil War folklore—deserve close attention from American folklorists, but that attention should be based on a firmer methodology and a more intimate acquaintance with the historical matrix than is evident in *Uncertain Glory*.

In *The Voice of the Folk: Folklore and American Literary Theory*, Gene Bluestein wove together Johann Gottfried von Herder, Emerson, Whitman, Constance Rourke, John and Alan Lomax, and Ralph Ellison, with an epilogue on rock performers such as Bob Dylan, to contrive a thesis that the central achievement of American letters rests on sustenance from folk traditions.[28] Herder supplied a "folk ideology," by reversing the Enlightenment's scorn for the peasant and asserting that higher cultural values in society blossomed from the folk arts of the lower strata. Folk tradition was actually the instrument for cultural change and development; it produced a healthy nationalism and, ultimately, a sympathetic internationalism. Emerson and Whitman applied Herder's principles, according to Bluestein, in their symbolic esthetic, which perceived in American speech a freshness and vitality available to writers and poets. Whitman in particular reveled in the slang of New York waiters in low-class restaurants. Bluestein then pays his respects to Rourke, whose thesis he has adopted, particularly its statement of the Traveler and Squatter confrontation as endemic in American folklore, humor, and fiction.

Up to this point Bluestein has accomplished the remarkable tour de force of devoting four chapters to a discussion of American folklore and literature without ever citing an example of the folklore, save for a text of "The Arkansas Traveler" quoted from Botkin's *The Pocket*

Treasury of American Folklore. His discussion of Emerson and Whitman is couched entirely in the literary criticism of the F. O. Matthiessen – Perry Miller – Henry Nash Smith – Leo Marx school that seeks, praiseworthily enough, to relate American writing to American thought and experience. These scholars admire Constance Rourke, but in following them Bluestein merely compounds her error of confusing folklore with subliterature.

To include folklore, Bluestein then extolls John and Alan Lomax for fulfilling the precepts of Herder, the Americanism of Emerson and Whitman, and the analysis of Rourke in their series of folksong collections. Some of Bluestein's remarks on the hierarchy of the ballad genre over lyric folksongs and the constricting influence of Child and Kittredge, who considered balladmaking a lost art, make good points, but overall he romanticizes the Lomaxes as much as they romanticize the cowboy, hobo, and sharecropper. Except for one uneasy footnote, he makes no distinction between rightwing, unspeculative John Lomax and his leftwing, idea-happy son Alan; he neglects Alan's intellectual shifts from Marxist to Freudian to hard social science commitments; and he fails to note the Lomaxes' scholarly inadequacies in publishing composite texts, musical arrangements, and commercially attractive all-American omnibuses. (I once heard John Lomax say that the chief reason for the success of *American Ballads and Folk Songs* was the American in its title.) Bluestein excuses the Lomaxes' inattention to ethnic folksong through the concept of "hybridization" of imported traditions, a concept as inaccurate as that of the melting pot.

Throughout his treatise Bluestein makes gestures to black folklore, and he assigns one chapter, "The Blues as a Literary Theme," to the affirmation that black traditions of blues and jazz and other expression form part of the folk subsoil in American literature. His chief example is Ralph Ellison's *The Invisible Man,* a work almost wholly devoid of black folk belief and narrative folklore elements. The one small passage of Peter Wheatstraw rapping with the narrator, which he duly quotes, is an unrepresentative instance of black folk speech. Bluestein seems to have little knowledge of folklore (other than folksong and folk music) or folklorists. He states that "Most academic folklorists . . . tended to place black tradition outside the main lines of American development" when, four years earlier, I had written as the opening sentence to my own collection *American Negro Folktales,* "One of the memorable bequests by the Negro to American civilization is his rich and diverse store of folktales." Three years before that, Roger Abrahams had produced his classic portrayal of black street folklore from Philadelphia, *Deep Down in the Jungle*. Blue-stein's efforts to associate Ellison and Cleaver, Eliot and Joyce, James and Fitzgerald, Emerson and Whitman with "folk ideology" carry little weight because he never relates them—if it were possible—to the body of field-collected American folklore.

Imaginative regional fieldwork beyond single-genre collecting still lags in the United States, but the recent period has registered one notable credit in George Carey's *A Faraway Time and Place: Lore of the Eastern Shore*.[29] Carey concentrated on the white watermen of the lower Eastern Shore of Maryland's Chesapeake Bay between the Nanticoke and Pocomoke rivers. These "proggers" living off the crabs, oysters, terrapin, eels, ducks, and other creatures of the bay and marshes possessed a distinctive subculture filled with a traditional lore of anecdote, legend, tall tale, jest, belief tale, folk speech, and folk naming that Carey has captured in a fluently written ethnography. As in any such collection, many familiar narratives and folk beliefs can be recognized, and it is deeply regrettable that the publisher excised the author's appendix of tale types and motifs.

Another work of regional collecting, but with an emphasis on the traditions of material culture rather than of oral expression, is *The Foxfire Book*, which became something of a national phenomenon on its publication in 1972. Its astonishing appeal lies in satisfying certain vogues: interest in ecology and primal nature, the revival of manual skills, nostalgia for the good old simple ways and days. Much of the book proves to be a do-it-yourself guide to building a log cabin, making chairs and baskets out of split oak, cooking mountain recipes on wood stoves and in Dutch ovens, even constructing a moonshine still. Oral lore is represented in realistic tales of hunting turkeys and bears, accounts of the properties of snakes, faith-healing experiences of bloodstopping, burn healing, and curing thrash, and statements on planting by the signs. Photographs of the mountain people and their artifacts supply a valid visual documentation of these topics.

A product of high-school pupils and a teacher untrained in folklore, *The Foxfire Book* does surprisingly well in presenting accurate tape-recorded texts, graphic informant sketches, and genuine examples of Appalachian cultural traditions. But overall it seriously misrepresents folklore. The *Foxfire* premise rests on the discredited cliché that the old lore must be gathered speedily from the aged before it vanishes, and ignores the fact that folklore belongs as well to the young and to the present even more than to the past. Eliot Wigginton romanticizes mountain folkways: "There is something about a quilt that says people, friendship, community, family, home, and love."[30] He renders mountain speech in unnecessarily folksy dialect (what is the purpose of spelling "the" as "th"?). He provides no conspectus of the community with which he is dealing, and no comparative information to indicate that much of the Foxfire material has been collected elsewhere. Some of the main genres of Appalachian folklore—local historical legend, for example—are almost wholly unrepresented. The stress on chimney-building and straw-mattress-making is better suited to a homeowner's manual than a serious cultural study.

Three first-rate treatments of what might be called cultural histories of American popular folk music all deal with the period since the 1920s, before electronic media and political ideology reshaped traditional folksongs. In *Country Music, U.S.A.*, Bill C. Malone considered the history of American rural southern music sung and performed for gain.[29] His narrative covers such favorite styles as hillbilly, country, mountain, western, honky-tonk, and bluegrass, and performers such as Jimmie Rodgers, Vernon Dalhart, the Carter Family, Roy Acuff, Hank Williams, Bill Monroe, and Earl Scruggs, who profoundly influenced them. Malone demonstrates the importance to the folklorist of these and other popular singers and instrumentalists who disseminated many traditional songs through recordings, radio and television shows such as the Grand Ole Opry, and cabaret, tent-show, vaudeville, and honky-tonk appearances. He is alert to the distinctions between folk and nonfolk music, and points out that in the 1930s left-leaning urban intellectuals appropriated the term "folk music" for composed urban protest songs far removed from folk tradition, while "hillbilly music," disparaged by the same intellectuals, remained firmly within a folk milieu. Malone recognizes that southern country music reflects industrial and social changes in northern cities, that the South itself changes, and pastoral images yield to moralizing songs about railroad wrecks and truck-driving.

In a more specialized vein, Archie Green in *Only a Miner* has investigated the tangled histories of coal-mining songs recorded on ten-inch discs at 78 rpm by a variety of recording artists ranging from local traditional singers to the celebrities of country music.[32] He unravels the genealogies of such pieces as "Only a Miner," which he calls "the American miner's national anthem," and "Nine Pound Hammer," popularized by Merle Travis, in intricate but lucid accounts of field and commercial recordings, white and black sources, and emotional and technological ingredients. A new kind of research is opened here, based on recording company files, interviews with company technicians, artists, and executives, and the fugitive song literature of the recordings themselves. Green addresses himself to larger questions of folklore theory, such as the impact of electronic culture on the folk society, and differences between traditional and popular songs. Bibliographical and discographical check lists appended to each chapter and well-chosen illustrations of miners and musicians enhance the work.

Complementing Malone's history of country music, R. Serge Denisoff in *Great Day Coming: Folk Music and the American Left* concentrates on those urban intellectuals from the 1930s to the present who have actively associated protest and dissent with the singing of purported folksongs.[33] Here is a different cast of characters, featuring Woody Guthrie, Pete Seeger and the Almanac Singers, Alan Lomax, Paul Robeson, Bob Dylan, Burl Ives, and Irwin Silber, editor of *Sing Out!*, the organ of the movement. This is an ironic story of frustration, internal splits, and ideological doubts as these talented and in many ways successful singer-socialists failed almost completely to win an audience committed to their objectives. They idealized a working class but evoked little response from the labor unions; they vainly sought to attach European communist values to American traditions; they anguished over the problem of commercialism and forfeited opportunities they desperately needed, as when the Almanac Singers refused to wear Lil' Abner costumes and so lost a coveted Rainbow Room contract in New York. Denisoff maintains an impartial stance in handling these sensitive issues but he does not hesitate to make value judgments. He sees Guthrie as a unique hybrid of rural and urban cultures, none of whose protest dustbowl songs were sung by the Okies and Arkies he represented. Burl Ives emerges as a turncoat playing the "innocent dupe" role before the McCarran Committee in the Senate, when investigation of communist folksingers threatened his career. Using the term "folk enterpreneur" to denote a conscious spokesman for proletarian values and a composer of "agit-prop" songs, Denisoff avoids confusing traditional singers with reform-minded performers.

Afro-American folklore continues to flourish as a subfield of American folklore. For the volume and sensitivity of its raw data on Negro hoodoo beliefs, the publications of Harry M. Hyatt, a retired Episcopalian clergyman, have no match in American folklore. Noteworthy collections of blues from Louisiana prisons and worksongs from Texas prisons have been issued by Harry Oster and Bruce Jackson. An oversize volume by John Lovell, bringing together a miscellany of information on the spiritual and its worldwide impact, badly needs the pruning of an editor and consultations with a folklorist on basic concepts. Valuable for theoretical statements by both black and white scholars is the anthology of previously published but widely scattered writings on many aspects of Afro-American folklore assembled by Alan Dundes.[34]

What might be called the great bamboozle in American folklore, namely the effort of author and commercial publisher to reach the mass market with sentimentalized folklore claiming scholarly value, is exemplified in Duncan Emrich's *Folklore on the American Land.*[35] This kind of production, superficial and chauvinistic in its selections and comments and ludicrous in its concepts (the author singles out Santa Claus and The Cowboy as the two chief American legends), damages folklore studies in the eyes of other disciplines. At the other extreme lies the laborious research monograph undertaken in a limited regional area, represented by Vance Randolph's magisterial bibliography of Ozark folklore.[36] The great field collector has here produced a model regional inventory, culling every kind of printed source from novels to newspapers, organizing his entries by coherent genres, and enriching them with flavorsome and judicious annotations. This is a pioneer work in revealing the wealth of printed sources available to the American folklorist.

African Folklore

In recent years Africa has moved from a position of marginal folklore activity conducted by practitioners in other disciplines—anthropologists, linguists, political scientists, historians—to one ever closer to the professional center. In the 1960s the Oxford Library of African Literature, under the general editorship of E. E. Evans-Pritchard, Godfrey Lienhardt, and W. H. Whiteley, published a dozen volumes of traditional oral poetry and prose. The volume editors deal with the materials of folklore but employ the methods of the literary scholar or the ethnologist. A climax and synthesis to this approach appeared in Ruth Finnegan's *Oral Literature in Africa.*[37] Finnegan addressed herself to the full range of oral expressive forms throughout sub-Saharan Africa, and adeptly utilized the accumulated monographs of tribal ethnographers to present a depth survey with copious examples. At every point she stressed the performance situation of the particular oral genre: praise poems, dirges, hymns, divining songs, hunters' songs, war songs, political songs, children's game songs, and folktales. This emphasis on social context wins the folklorist's approval, but he regrets the downgrading of oral narrative forms, the absence of comparative annotation—characteristic of the whole Library of African Literature series—and the unfamiliarity with current folklore theories and methods. Finnegan seeks to apply the techniques of literary criticism to her materials when her own evidence fully demonstrates the gulf between written and oral literature and the need to formulate distinctive criteria for appraising verbal performances.

A conscious contrast to Finnegan's point of view is proposed in *African Folklore,* edited by Richard M. Dorson, which espouses a folkloristic approach to African cultural traditions.[38] This volume developed from a Conference on African Folklore held at Indiana University in 1970, at which Africans and Americans presented research papers on a variety of oral genres. Sixteen of these papers, dealing with aspects of the folktale, the proverb, tongue twisters, the heroic epic and heroic songs, folk drama, visions, oral history, and literary uses of folklore, formed Part II of the volume. An extended essay on Africa and the Folklorist by the editor formed Part I, and field-collected texts furnished by the contributors and annotated by the editor formed Part III.

Indexes

Useful indexes of traditional narratives were issued by Bacil F. Kirtley for Polynesian folktale motifs and by Hiroko Ikeda for types and motifs of Japanese folktales.[39] Ikeda's index represents an attempt to fuse the systems for classification developed by Kunio Yanagita in Japan and Stith Thompson in the United States. Since Japanese oral narratives run strongly to the local legend, they do not fit harmoniously into the magical fictional tale types that occupy a large part of the Aarne-Thompson index. It is regrettable that Kirtley has published only the Polynesian section of the type and motif index of Oceanic tales he originally prepared as a doctoral dissertation. Those wishing to consult his Micronesian and Melanesian classifications will need to refer to the dissertation in the Indiana University library.

 Is Folklore
a Discipline?

At a meeting of the American Folklore Society back in 1957, a panel of two well-known scholars and a dentist who wrote children's books on folklore addressed themselves to the subject of this essay. At that time the society was treading slippery ground between the demands of amateur enthusiasts and university professors. Many of the academics felt only a secondary interest in folklore, having been trained in other subject matters. At any rate, our writer of juveniles bounced up and down on the podium flailing at the pedants who squeezed all the juice out of folklore with their dusty monographs while enviously criticizing the successful nonacademic authors whose folklore books sold widely. Seizing on the word "discipline" in the title of the panel's topic, he expressed his astonishment at this thorny term, questioned its meaning in the present context, and asserted that he had queried a number of his friends on its signification to no avail. They were mystified at this esoteric jargon of the pedagogues.

This episode highlights the difficulties faced by the advocate of folklore as a discipline. Part of his audience, who lie outside the university, may not even know what he is talking about. As I employ the term here, I think of discipline in both a pragmatic and a philosophical sense. Pragmatically, the discipline exists if it can reach an intellectual audience with scholarly works, earn a place in the accepted fields of learning of its day, preserve and enlarge its area of knowledge, attract converts and young disciples, and perpetuate itself for another generation. Philosophically, the discipline exists if it can lay claim to distinctive theoretical concepts and empirical data important for man's knowledge about his world. Our title question needs an answer on both counts, for there is little point in seeking to prove the intellectual validity of folklore studies if there are no teachers, students, readers, writers, or followers of such studies, in short no constituency of the folklore-minded. Accordingly, I shall subdivide the question into the power base and the intellectual base.

The Power Base

In discussing the power base first, I reverse my own chronology of interests. My discovery of the subject matter of folklore came long before my awareness of the realpolitik of folklore studies in the academy. Circumstances dictated that, after initially succumbing to the fascination of Andrew Lang and Max Müller, Francis James Child and Cecil Sharp, I have ended up immersed in budget conferences, promotion and tenure decisions, office maintenance, and the thousand and one details and crises of departmental administration. Yet attention to these matters is essential to the survival of folklore as a discipline in the United States, for today the university department provides the chief power base for the would-be folklorist.

By the power base I mean any arena in which the study of folklore can flourish. Throughout the 160-year history of our subject, since the Grimms published the first volume of their *Household Tales,* the isolated collector and independent scholar have registered substantial contributions. We can think of Vincent Stuckey Lean in the British Museum compiling his scrapbooks of proverbial *Collectanea,* published after his death in four volumes; of Hugh Miller writing the traditional history of Cromarty in a corner of Scotland; of the Episcopal clergyman, Harry Middleton Hyatt, by his lonesome amassing and tape-recording thousands of supernatural folk beliefs in Illinois and Negro hoodoo and witchcraft beliefs in the South; and of the enigmatic James Carpenter, who on six years of consecutive Harvard Sheldon Traveling Fellowships collected ballads and other traditional forms in Scotland, slept by his collections every night, without ever publishing any portion, and has just now, when professional folklorists fortuitously established contact with him, deposited his materials in the Library of Congress Folksong Archive. A discipline may well benefit handsomely from these idiosyncratic activities, but without some frame of organization to digest and assimilate them these scattered works would disappear in the bowels of the library or molder in the collector's attic. The classic case in American folklore is the Duke University professor of English, Frank C. Brown, who assiduously collected all manner of North Carolina folk items which saw the light of day only when a team of professional folklorists collaborated to organize, annotate, and interpret them in the seven volumes now known as *The Frank C. Brown Collection of North Carolina Folklore.* A comparable situation in England involves the valuable type indexing of folk narratives in English periodicals undertaken by F. J. Norton, librarian at Cambridge University, as a private pursuit. During my year in Cambridge, 1964-65, Professor Edward M. Wilson, longtime member and former secretary of the Folklore Society, introduced me to Mr. Norton. Astonished at the scope and value of his work, I put Katharine Briggs in touch with him, with the happy consequence that the *Dictionary of British Folktales* incorporated the F. J. Norton collection.

These examples help bear out my contention that folklore, like any field of learning, needs its community of scholars to establish a discipline. There is, I would say, no single formula for that community, which may take the form of an antiquarian or learned society, a professorial chair and seminar, a research institute, a museum or archives with a field staff, a dining club, or a university department. All these options have proved successful, according to the historical circumstances and traditions of a given country. The organization, like the study, of folklore responds to tradition, and traditions change, so that what works in the nineteenth century may well not work in the twentieth in the same country. Being a fringe subject, folklore has veered between private and academic scholarship, and between the conceptions of the performing folk artist and the theoretician. In a number of European nations the professorial chair of folklore provides a nucleus for continuous instruction, fieldwork, and formulation of theory. Hautala's history of the Finnish folklorists clearly reveals how the chair of folklore at the University of Helsinki maintained the momentum and continuity of the illustrious achievements of the Finns: their stellar theorists, not only the Krohns and Aarne but other memorable folklorists such as A. E. Ahlquist, M. A. Castrén, and E. Salmelainen; their fabulous archives and nationwide network of schoolteacher-collectors; their prestigious Folklore Fellows Communications series. But the professorship is buttressed by an urban folklore organization, the Finnish Literature Society, founded in 1831, and by governmental support for its archives and library. Here is a strong power base, the academic chair and the private society closely interlocked and undergirded by a national grant.

Another likely folklore power base can be seen in the research institute, often in Europe divorced from, and seemingly socially inferior to, the teaching university. A handsomely equipped folklore research institute, described in Indiana University's *Journal of the Folklore Institute* in 1972 by Jan Brunvand of the University of Utah, who spent a year there, is the Romanian Institute of Folklore and Ethnography in Bucharest. Its director, Mihai Pop, is also the folklore professor at the University of Bucharest, and so links the teaching and researching sides of folklore. The Romanian institute with its staff of a hundred performs many functions we now consider essential to folklore research: tape transcription and reproduction, film and slide processing, housing of archives and library, initiation of systematic field trips, issuing of journals and monographs. Whether a folklore research institute comprises a community of scholars or a group of technicians, and if the latter, whether it serves a community of scholars, are questions that perhaps will receive different answers in different cases.

Two research institutes with which I have had some acquaintance are the School of Scottish Studies and the Irish Folklore Commission. Neither is called a research institute, and yet until recently, when both became associated with lectures on folklore at the University of Edinburgh and University College, Dublin, that seemed their appropriate designation. The School of Scottish Studies even suppressed the term "folklore" in its title and in that of its journal, *Scottish Studies,* although its work deals entirely with oral traditions, folklife, and place-name and dialect studies. One prominent professor on the committee administering the School of Scottish Studies declared, I was told, that the School should remain a nonteaching unit of the university and amass source materials for scholars to use. Similarly, at Dublin the Irish Folklore Commission did not, until the recent appointment of Bo Almqvist to succeed James Delargy as professor of folklore, actually become involved in teaching. As a consequence, the visitor to Edinburgh and Dublin in the 1950s and 1960s noted an absence of students in these splendid potential centers of folkloric activity, although they welcomed outside scholars most hospitably. Also he observed that little publication issued from them. The full-time fieldworkers of the IFC resident in Irish counties considered themselves collectors, with a mandate to garner the harvest, especially the Gaelic harvest, before the flowers had all withered. In Dublin, Sean O'Sullivan worked prodigiously to archive the mountains of material always pressing in upon the central office. The excellent *Folktales of Ireland* volume which he kindly consented to assemble for my Folktales of the World series represented a rare luxurious excursion into the publishing of the accumulated texts. More of a cadre of folklorists existed at Edinburgh, since the fieldworkers, such as Hamish Henderson, John MacInnes, and Donald MacDonald, resided there in between their protracted field trips. Sitting around the long table in the School's meeting room for morning coffee and afternoon tea, the visitor felt a friendly glow of kindred spirits. Yet the School had not made its impact on the university hierarchy, where only the professors can advance the subject as a discipline. My old mentor Kenneth Jackson, who gave me my only formal instruction in folklore when I was combing the Harvard faculty for guidance, told me that on his return to the University of Edinburgh the responsibilities of Celtic studies had prevented his giving the attention he wished to folklore studies.

There is also the society, of amateurs, professionals, or an uneasy mixture of the two, as a possible power base for folklorists. In the United States at present the large professional organizations often seem to carry more prestige and influence than the universities. A physicist or sociologist, say, will think of himself as a member of his discipline first and of his university faculty second. The American Folklore Society has registered enormous gains over the past quarter of a century, and reached the point in the mid-1960s where it could meet successfully as an independent body. Its growth in numbers and professionalism is directly related to the production of new Ph.D.'s in folklore; yet compared to the major fields in which the Ph.D. is offered by thirty or forty institutions, folklore, with only three universities (Indiana, Pennsylvania, and Texas) offering doctorates is still an upstart. In the context in which I am speaking, the professional society does not generate strength in a discipline so much as respond to and reflect strength already demonstrated. Rather, it is the nonacademic society that on occasion has stimulated folkloric enterprises.

More specifically, the society needs a metropolitan urban setting for maximum results. The French folklore movement gathered momentum in Paris in the 1880s, launched by a monthly dinner first held on February 14, 1882, attended by such dedicated folklorists as Paul Sébillot, Henri Gaidoz, Gaston Paris, Eugène Rolland, and Loys Brueyre. Known as the Dinner of Mother Goose, in honor of Charles Perrault's *Contes de ma Mère l'Oye*, the occasion proved a sturdy and congenial forum, and on February 28, 1895, reached the one hundred mark in a gala celebration, marred by the absence of Gaidoz, who by this time had become a bitter critic and rival of Sébillot. Their intellectual differences—Gaidoz charged Sébillot with superficial, repetitive, and careless scholarship—led to a furious contretemps as to who had originally conceived of the dinner, Gaidoz' close friend Rolland or credit-taking Sébillot. In 1886 Rolland and Gaidoz had departed from the dinner of Mother Goose and initiated their own weekly dinner at the Café Voltaire, where Rolland conducted an informal seminar in folklore. Each leader founded a journal, *Mélusine*, edited by Gaidoz, and *Revue des traditions populaires*, edited by Sébillot, in which the two giants flailed at each other. So in France the power base for the great burst of folklore activity from 1882 to the First World War turned out to be Parisian supper clubs of savants devoted to the study of oral literature.

Although the urban nexus has not satisfied the needs of folklorists in the United States, for short periods it has served their purposes. A Harvard group led by Francis James Child formed a Cambridge Folklore Society, which helped stimulate the founding of the American Folklore Society in 1888. By the quirk of history, Chicago proved to be the city most sympathetic to folkloric enterprise, and briefly, in 1892 and 1893, a Chicago Folk-Lore Society pitted its humanistic and belletristic perspective against the anthropological and scientific mode of the American Folklore Society. This Chicago society owed its existence to the ardor of a retired United States naval officer, Lieutenant Fletcher S. Basset, who published *Legends and Superstitions of the Sea and of Sailors in all Lands and at all Times*, a scrapbook of clippings with little design or method but a testimonial to his amateur zeal. At his instigation and his wife's invitation an organizational meeting was held on December 12, 1891, in the Art Institute Building, and Bassett became the secretary and moving spirit until his death within the year, October 19, 1892. In the less than a year of his tenure Bassett published four numbers of *The Folk-Lorist, Journal of the Chicago Folk-Lore Society* and the first and only number of the Chicago Folk-Lore Society's Publications, *The Folk-Lore Manual*, a collector's guide partly modeled on George Laurence Gomme's and Paul Sébillot's handbooks. In addition he organized an International Folk-Lore Congress, in connection with the Chicago World's Fair of 1893, at which seventy papers were presented and the bulk subsequently published in the proceedings of the congress. Described as The Third International Folk-Lore Congress, the Chicago meeting followed those at Paris in 1889 and London in 1891 in a sequel that Bassett undoubtedly hoped would establish Chicago folkloristically on a par with the other great metropolises. In his imperial schemes he thought of making Chicago the center of American folklore activities and appointed members-at-large as presidents of the Tennessee, Louisiana, and Minnesota branches of the Chicago Folk-Lore Society.

Abroad he claimed correspondents in Latin America, Europe, and Asia. In the United States he corresponded with such figures as Hamlin Garland, Joel Chandler Harris, George Washington Cable, and Mary Hartwell Catherwood. Cable spoke at the second meeting of the society on imagination in folklore, related a folktale of the wind in the forest, and sang the song of the wind in Creole French. Harriet Monroe, founder of *Poetry* magazine in Chicago, belonged to the society. Bassett gathered members from a cross-section of Chicago people— the professions, the business world, the arts, the armed services, the social elite. Mrs. Potter Palmer, whose family owned the Palmer House in Chicago, served as a director of the Society. For one exhilarating year, in their meetings in private homes, at the Newberry Library, or in the Art Institute, Chicagoans read papers, gave talks, watched lantern slides, and avidly discussed Messiah crazes among the Indians, Jewish wedding ceremonies in the Middle Ages, and customs and costumes of Asian peoples. When Basset died the society collapsed and was virtually forgotten until their publications were reprinted in 1973.

Curiously, New York has never witnessed a folklore boom. The New York Folklore Society was founded in 1945 at Cooperstown, where its journal, the *New York Folklore Quarterly*, is edited. State folklore societies have contributed relatively little to the discipline of folklore, lacking any real power base, and have functioned mainly as annual congregation points for the enjoyment of folk performance and the reading of local color papers. These societies, and their journals, bulletins, and newsletters, flourish and wither according to the drive of personalities. Among the most active are those in Tennessee, Kentucky, Texas, New York, California, and Louisiana. Bearing out my thesis of the urban focus of folklore organization, a new society, the Folklore Society of Greater Washington, has recently begun to issue a journal of surprising merit. This group draws on the human and institutional resources of the Washington, D.C., area, which contains the Folksong Archive of the Library of Congress, the University of Maryland with an active folklore program, and the Smithsonian Institution with a few folklore buffs on its staff.

A private institute in Tokyo for a time provided the base for the Japanese folklore movement. One scholar of national eminence, Kunio Yanagita, founded the study of folklore in his country and attracted a coterie of disciples centered in the Minzokugaku Kenkyūshō, the Japanese Folklore Institute. Physically this institute consisted of a large wing of the house of Kunio Yanagita's son, a scientist.

This wing contained Professor Yanagita's extensive library and a number of working desks, to which regularly came various staff members of the institute, some, like Toichi Mabuchi and Keigo Seki, well-known scholars at universities in Tokyo. Venerable Kunio Yanagita, born in 1875, lived in a smaller home next door, and held court with his acolytes when they dropped by to see him. In 1956-57 I spent a year in Japan as Fulbright Visiting Professor at the University of Tokyo, and by good fortune resided in the Seijo district of Tokyo where the Minzokugaku Kenkyūshō was located. In spite of the language barrier I learned something of the institute's activities from manuscripts in English and through personal contacts. For example, Yanagita and his institute sponsored two intensive surveys of *Studies in Mountain Village Life* (1937) and *Studies in Fishing Village Life* (1949) which enlisted the aid of local schoolteachers and village officials in systematically combing the remote farming and fishing communities whose daily life was permeated with magic and ritual. In such enterprises the Tokyo institute reached out into the farthest corners and pockets of Japanese traditional culture. During my year there I conceived the idea of a special volume of research essays by the Yanagita school to be translated into English, and through the benison of Yanagita-*sensei*, who contributed a brief interview, the papers were assembled and, after years of arduous translating and editing, published as *Studies in Japanese Folklore* (1963). Yet, successful as were the conferences, projects, and publications promoted by the institute, it rested on too slender a base, the reputation and personal resources of one famous scholar-diplomat. Possessing no university affiliation, the institute could offer no formal courses in folklore and train no degree-pursuing classes of students, although it encouraged the folklore-minded. In the Japanese family tradition, Yanagita's son-in-law Ichirō Hori engaged in folklore studies, specializing in Japanese folk religion, and his granddaughter Yaeko Yanagita journeyed to America to complete an M.A. degree in folklore at Indiana University. But more than a family inheritance was needed, and the Minzokugaku Kenkyūshō closed its doors in the spring of 1957 for lack of financial and institutional support.

The clearest case of a metropolitan power base for folklore studies would seem to be the Folklore Society itself, which might well have been called the London Folklore Society. Its achievements in the two decades from its founding in 1878 until the end of the century inspire awe: the high excellence of the journal, the number and quality of special publications, the electricity generated by the monthly meetings, the excitement of the international congress of 1891 in London. The great advantage of London, unlike any city in the United States, is its accessibility for the out-of-towner. So Edwin Sidney Hartland could live in Gloucester, a city of which he became mayor, yet regularly participate in the London meetings. George Laurence Gomme, another member of the Great Team of English folklorists, made his livelihood as clerk of the London County Council and wrote on the history of London as well as on folklore as an historical science. Associations of private scholars could flourish in nineteenth-century London, and one thinks of the Royal Society of Antiquaries, the Camden, the Percy, the Shakespeare, and others which furnished models for the Folklore Society. How bankers, solicitors, civil servants, journalists, and publishers could find the time, energy, and means to turn productive author-scholars remains a mystery, but clearly Lang and Gomme and Hartland and Clodd and Nutt and Jacobs acted as catalysts upon each other and upon others whom they attracted into the society. Individuals of breadth and multiple talents, they wrote on various subjects in addition to folklore and mixed in several intellectual circles, as Clodd has revealed in his book of personal vignettes titled *Memories.* Accordingly, they spread the gospel of folklore far more widely than could the conventional academic scholar. Unable themselves, as Londoners with full-time occupations, to engage in fieldwork, they supplied the theoretical frame and the personal encouragement for vicars and country ladies and colonial administrators to collect folklore survivals from "peasants" and "savages."

London's Folklore Society ceased to serve as a power base for the science of folklore in the years following the First World War. With the decline of the private scholar and the rise of the graduate school, the metropolitan society lost much of its constituency and could not reach the new generation. One need only look at the sharply reduced size of the volumes of the society's journal from World War I on to see the diminution of resources. In academic circles the dons sneer openly at the Folklore Society as an antiquarian club; witness the snide comment by the *Times Literary Supplement* reviewer of *The British Folklorists,* a self-admitted social anthropologist, that the Folklore Society might come of age if its officers ever got around to reading Lévi-Strauss! The unequal competition between the university and the urban society in the present century is seen in the demise of the Cambridgeshire Folklore Society, which enjoyed its moments in the 1930s, with the participation of such scholars as Edward M. Wilson and Kenneth Jackson who temporarily left their specialties of Spanish and

Celtic literatures of an evening to converse with East Anglian farmers about olden lore. But the day came when, as the Society's minutes sadly state, the group dissolved itself. Yet members scattered throughout the Cambridge University faculties possessed an active interest in folklore. The anthropologist Reo Fortune even offered lectures on folklore and mythology, attended by only two students, reading in English literature. The head of the anthropology department, Meyer Fortes, made no attempt to conceal his disdain for folklore studies, and told me that a mutual friend had gone into folklore because he had failed as an anthropologist.

Another possible power base for the folklorists is the museum, specifically the ethnographic or outdoor or open-air or folk or historical museum, all somewhat overlapping designations. Two in North America have shown particular partiality to folklorists. The National Museum of Man in Ottawa in 1970 created as one of its five units a Canadian Centre for Folk Culture Studies, an outgrowth of the efforts of the indefatigable Canadian folklorist Marius Barbeau. In the words of the Centre's head, Robert Klymasz, it "functions as the country's leading folklore research center."[1] The Centre employs a permanent staff and also awards contracts to fieldworkers with the understanding that all materials collected will be deposited with the museum. Besides Dr. Klymasz, three Indiana University doctoral candidates in folklore, each with a competence in an ethnic subculture, have held staff positions at the Centre, and a number of other pre- and post-doctoral folklorists, including Linda Dégh and Jan Brunvand, have spent summers in the field in Canada on National Museum of Man grants. It is most unfortunate that in the United States funds for fieldwork are not forthcoming and graduate students must journey to Canada and undertake projects relating to the Canadian rather than the American experience —although, from a broader point of view, the cause of folklore benefits. The main energy of the Centre, reflecting the divisive Anglo-French political situation, is directed toward the forty ethnic groups found over the three million square miles of Canadian soil. Klymasz himself, for instance, specializes in the Ukrainians of western Canada. As small homogeneous countries like Finland and Ireland endeavor through folklore to assert their cultural unity and independence from overweening neighbors, so vast heterogeneous Canada seeks to divert attention from the hostility between two major ethnic blocs by emphasizing cultural pluralism through folklore.

The folklorist at the National Museum of Canada enjoys a free rein to pursue his ethnic area but is expected to undertake educational and research responsibilities through public lectures, popular articles, and substantial monographs. Klymasz reports that priorities in field research are given to artifacts over oral literature, as tangible contributions to the museum's exhibits and displays. How successfully folklorists will operate in this highly attractive but unstructured situation remains to be seen. Without the stimuli and pressures of university life there is always the risk they will channel their forces into public relations.

Parenthetically it should be remarked that the Museum does not replace academic programs in Canadian universities. Departments of folklore exist at Laval University in Quebec and Memorial University in Saint John's, Newfoundland, directed by Luc Lacourcière and Herbert Halpert and devoted respectively to French-Canadian and Anglo-Celtic traditions, while Elli Köngäs Maranda teaches folklore at the University of British Columbia in Vancouver.

A unique and imaginative experiment at Cooperstown, New York, has linked a folk museum to a degree-granting instructional program. Louis C. Jones conceived this plan after he moved from the faculty of the New York State Teachers College at Albany, where he had taught courses in folklore, to the directorship of the New York State Historical Society sixty miles away in Cooperstown. The Society's properties include an outdoor Farmer's Museum reconstructing the buildings, crafts, and milieu of a nineteenth-century agricultural village, and the James Fenimore Cooper House on Lake Otsego, donated by the family of the novelist and housing an extensive folk art collection from the region. These attractions draw many thousands of visiting tourists, but Jones initiated an entirely new function for the museum complex, and devised a master's degree program in museum training and methods of folklife study. The museum staff of curators and librarians formed the nucleus of a teaching faculty, to which he added two folklorists, Bruce Buckley and Roderick Roberts. For accreditation he turned to the nearest unit of the State University of New York, twenty miles away at Oneonta, and worked out an arrangement whereby his instructors received faculty appointments and his students earned their M.A.'s through SUNY at Oneonta. For graduate fellowships he turned to the foundations, and then advertised the fellowships in appropriate media. Over the past dozen years the Cooperstown program has conferred annually twenty master's degrees to students who learn museum management at first hand and undertake folklore and folklife field trips into the surrounding countryside. Most of these M.A. holders take museum positions, New York state abounding in local history museums, but some continue on in doctoral folklore programs.

How far the folk museum can or will go in providing a power base for folklorists remains an open question. Appreciation for folklife studies has led to increasingly close ties between folklore scholars and folk museum directors and curators. In April 1973 I attended a regional folklore conference at the University of Massachusetts in Amherst, at which one panel of folk museum spokesmen dealt with the theme "The Museum is the Message: Open Air Museums and Education." Their reports on Plimouth Plantation and Old Sturbridge Village in Massachusetts and the Farmer's Museum in New York made clear that these outdoor historical museums had become power bases of the museum world, with revenues from hundreds of thousands of visitors a year and large staffs, some of whom were deeply engaged in research and publication on life of the common man in earlier days. In the peak summertime season Old Sturbridge enlarges its staff to seven hundred. These outdoor museum complexes become stages for seminars, workshops, conferences, folk festivals; they sell books; they apply to foundations for research grants. At present their staffs are largely drawn from the ranks of archaeologists, historians, and museologists, but the occasional folklorist turns up in their number and more may be expected to do so.

A related instance of a museum-type operation as a conceivable power base for folklore is the Country Music Foundation in Nashville, Tennessee, center of the music recording industry in the United States, particularly those forms known as country, western, rock, and hillbilly. This Foundation, created by the big recording companies, supports a museum devoted to the history of country music and its celebrities. In 1972 a folklorist, William Ivey, was appointed director of the Country Music Foundation. During his graduate career Ivey presented two weekly programs over the university radio station, one on folk music, "Our Singing Heritage," and one on popular music, "The Sound of Pop," and so possessed excellent qualifications for the Nashville position. He plans to use its resources to develop a teaching and research center in folk and popular music. Already he has initiated a journal of country music; offered research grants for visiting scholars; discussed joint courses with institutions in the area, such as Vanderbilt University; and hosted the 1973 meeting of the American Folklore Society.

Examples of prominent folklore scholars based in museums can be multiplied. We think, for example, of Carl-Herman Tillhagen in the Nordiska Museet in Stockholm, of Robert Wildhaber, longtime director of the Museum für Völkerkunde in Basel, of Iorwerth Peate at the Welsh Folk Museum at St. Fagan's Castle. The Society for Folklife Studies in Great Britain represents in large part a museum-curator constituency. Yet ultimately all these folklore centers—the indoor and outdoor museum, the urban society, the research institute and archives—lack the most essential element for the perpetuation of folklore as a discipline: the formal training of young people. Because this is its primary function, the university department of folklore must be accounted the strongest power base for the discipline of folklore at present. The department holds an advantage over the chair in sponsoring a group of professional folklorists rather than one prima donna.

In saying this I do not elevate the academic scholar over the private scholar, nor the university over the independent museum, society, or institute. No achievement could be grander than that of the English Folklore Society in the 1880s and 1890s. But now the professional training of young folklorists, like the training of physicists and chemists, sociologists and anthropologists, must take place in the university if the discipline is to survive.

Since coming to Indiana University in 1957, as chairman of the committee on folklore, I have received an extended liberal education in the ways and means of establishing, maintaining, and expanding a folklore beachhead in the intensely competitive arena of an American university. Already won by Stith Thompson, who had retired in 1955, were administrative approval of the M.A. and Ph.D degrees in folklore, a separate room of the university library housing a folklore collection of some 15,000 titles, and a folklore monographs series subsidized by $2000 a year. There were no budget lines for a faculty or for student assistantships or fellowships, only a few hundred dollars for a half-time secretary. No funds were earmarked for maintenance of the folklore library, so the room was kept locked and keys circulated among the few users. Books kept disappearing, but the librarian told me it was cheaper to lose a few books each year than pay the salary of an attendant. The physical facilities consisted of one room in the library next to the folklore collection, in which the chairman met with students, the secretary pecked at the typewriter, visitors peeked into the cabinets that housed the folklore archives, and Stith Thompson, professor emeritus, conferred with his research assistant. In 1957 some half-dozen graduate students were seeking higher degrees in folklore. The courses they took originated almost entirely with established departments. That is, the course on the English and Scottish popular ballad belonged to the English department and would be cross-listed under Folklore. In effect, the folklore program simply drew upon the existing faculty and curricular resources of the university. I myself was budgeted full-time in the history department, and all the members of the folklore committee were budgeted in their respective departments of anthropology, English, Spanish, and so on. By such means the university cautiously launched new programs with a minimum of outlay. The programs might grow into departments, remain indefinitely in a limbo status, or wither away. They had to prove their vitality.

The situation in the fall of 1975 contrasted happily with that of the fall of 1957. Under the title of the Folklore Institute, the interdepartmental committee blossomed into an autonomous department with a budget of a quarter of a million dollars, seven full faculty lines and four more (including myself) on joint appointments with other departments, for a total of 9.3 FTE, the university shorthand for full-time equivalent. In addition, six faculty in other departments held the title Fellows of the Folklore Institute and met and voted with the department, in recognition of their commitment to teaching and research in folklore. The physical properties of the Institute include three private houses, two used for offices of faculty, editorial assistants, and two full-time secretaries, and the other for the offices of the teaching associates and the manuscript Folklore Archives. A fourth facility is the Archives of Traditional Music, housed in Maxwell Hall, with its own staff of a director, associate director, librarian, and four graduate assistants. The Institute supports some twenty teaching, editorial, archives, and library assistants. In the bulletins of the College of Arts and Sciences and the Graduate School are listed fifty-four courses originating with the Folklore Department. Over one hundred and fifty graduate students pursue the M.A. and Ph.D degree in Folklore, of whom two-thirds are on campus in Bloomington. Enrollment in undergraduate courses runs about two thousand students, and the new undergraduate major has attracted some fifty students. Folklore courses are also taught in the Evening Division and Independent Study Division of the Bloomington campus, and on regional campuses of Indiana University at Indianapolis, Fort Wayne, Kokomo, and Columbus, staffed by commuting doctoral candidates. According to enrollment figures in a computer printout released by the dean of the college of arts and sciences to departmental chairmen, folklore led every department in number of students per faculty member. So, in 1975-76, when programs and faculties everywhere were shrinking, folklore added a new faculty position and acquired a new building.

Getting from 1957 to 1975 is a chronicle of continual and unrelenting endeavor on a number of fronts: the foundations, the central administration, the space committee, the curriculum committee, the university press, the library staff, the dean's office, the regional campus officials, the Evening Division office, the conference bureau, the housing office, and on and on. Ironically, in the early 1960s we had difficulty finding qualified students for the substantial graduate fellowships made available to us through the National Defense Education Act, Title IV and the Ford Foundation, and in the 1970s excellent student applications pour in when fellowship funds have virtually dried up. High points during this period were the establishment of a separate department in 1963; the appointment of teaching assistants in 1968, when the introductory courses expanded, thanks in good part to a new foreign culture option requirement that included folklore; and the approval of an undergraduate major in 1970.

Over the years, one constant problem has concerned the placement of our Ph.D.'s, and here too we registered striking success. People constantly asked "What will happen to all your Ph.D.'s?" A fair question, since they could not apply for positions in nonexistent departments of folklore. Well, the Ph.D.'s and M.A.'s have found positions, good positions, at the University of California at Berkeley and at Los Angeles, at the Universities of Kansas, Utah, Maine, Massachusetts, Illinois, Pennsylvania, Maryland, Nebraska, Vermont, West Virginia, Houston, at Washington State University, Columbia University, Indiana University, Wayne State University, Pennsylvania State University, The Ohio State University, Louisiana State University, Western Kentucky State University, Temple Universtiy, and in Canada at the University of British Columbia, University of Manitoba, Memorial University, usually in departments of English or anthropology, rarely in history. Foreign students are teaching at universities in Bangladesh, Thailand, Malaysia, Egypt, Nigeria, the Sudan, Uganda, Italy. Alan Dundes attained full professorship at Berkeley when only thirty-three, in the anthropology department, and directs a folklore M.A. program that he initiated. But each position won represents a long dossier of supporting letters and documents, continuous explanation of and justification for the folklorist as a desirable faculty member, and a high caliber of Ph.D. holders. The fortunes of the Folklore

Institute at Indiana University are intimately bound up with the fates of folklore programs and courses elsewhere. A few years ago the graduate department of folklore and folklife at the University of Pennsylvania teetered on the brink of extinction, but the mettle of its chairman, Kenneth Goldstein, won the day and it has rebounded with vigor, abetted by the decision of the well-known linguistic anthropologist at Pennsylvania, Dell Hymes, to move from the anthropology to the folklore department. At the University of California at Los Angeles, where the Center for Folklore and Comparative Mythology has sheltered a strong folklore M.A. program, a long struggle for the Ph.D. in folklore continues, as two dozen holders of the M.A. wait in suspense, or drift to other fields, or even move to Indiana to enter our overcrowded institute. The University of Texas awarded its first folklore doctorate in 1975.

The opportunity to train students in folklore is the great prize which will make possible the continuation of folklore as a discipline. At Indiana University a legion of resident graduate students in folklore make their energies felt in various ways: in a Folklore Student Association with its own meetings and invited speakers; in a journal, the *Folklore Forum*, that although operating on a shoestring, has become one of the established folklore publications in the country; in a gala annual event, now hoary with five years of tradition, the Pig Roast, a two-day campout and cookout signalizing the ritual end of the academic year and rebirth of the new seasonal round. Each new Ph.D. in folklore adds another crusader for the cause, another professional to tilt the balance against the dilettantes. It is the students who will read the books their seniors write on folklore, who will debate the issues, write the new books, and teach the next generation. Without the university department as a power base, where graduate students can learn theory and method and bibliography and convey their contagious enthusiasm to the rest of the world, folklore studies cannot in the twentieth century hope to achieve the status of a professional discipline.

The Intellectual Base

Whatever their power base, folklorists claiming a discipline must justify their existence on intellectual grounds. The well established subjects no longer have to explain their purposes. History attempts to record man's past. Political science studies the process of government. But what does folklore aspire to do? Without some large philosophic purpose the business of folklore becomes a matter of collecting, re-cording, transcribing, archiving, the endless amassing of materials against the day when some creative scholar will interpret them. Or the examiner of folk traditions may be impelled by nostalgic antiquarian interests in the odd customs and notions of a bygone day. In periods of greatest strength, students of folklore have proved to be far more than casual antiquaries or mindless collectors. The Great Team shared a common premise: that surviving folklore—and to them, following Tylor's formulation, all folklore was survivals—mirrored the mind of early man, and through scrupulous inspection of these survivals they could recapture the world view of their prehistoric forebears. Jacob and Wilhelm Grimm looked at the matter differently and considered household tales and peasant supernaturalism as reflecting in frag-mented form an ancient high Germanic culture. No such all-governing hypothesis directs the energies of today's folklorists, who frequently find difficulty in expressing their teleology. But I would say they are concerned with the study of traditional culture, or the unofficial cul-ture, or the folk culture, as opposed to the elite culture, not for the sake of proving a thesis but to learn about the mass of mankind over-looked by the conventional disciplines. Historians write histories of the elite, the successful, the visible; literary scholars study elitist writ-ings; and the critics of the arts confine their attention to the fine arts. Anthropologists venture far off the beaten track, and sociologists look at people statistically. For an instance, I was doing fieldwork in the steelmaking city of Gary, Indiana, and learned that the sociology de-partment had undertaken a project in that city. Eagerly I inquired of the young man on the project what he was up to. He said he knew nothing about the project design, that he was simply paid to knock on doors and fill in a questionnaire. He mailed the results back to Bloom-ington, where presumably some other hireling processed the data in the computer, and eventually the results as to the correlation between criminal propensity and the possession of indoor flush toilets would be published in a learned journal by the major professor. The folklor-ist, almost alone among his scholarly brethren, is talking to the non-elite, the folk. Increasingly his perspective is directed to the contem-poraneity rather than the obsolescence of folklore, to the conception that folklore reflects the ethos of its own day, not of an era long past. Legends in the seventeenth century dealt with witches; in the twentieth century they deal with automobiles. The intellectual problems grow out of the materials; they concern questions of function, aesthetics, origins, transmission, communication, structure, stability, change, symbolic meaning, social value, historical content; there is no dearth of enigmas rooted in the condition of man.

Related to the philosophic view of the discipline is the broad vision of the field as a whole. People come into folklore studies from a variety of special interests, perhaps folksinging or literary uses of myth or African cultures or occultism, but the mark of the professional is his comprehension of the whole domain. Although the members of the Great Team possessed individual specialties, each could and did write generally on the science of folklore. A community of discourse, a common vocabulary, and a set of interior references bind the practitioners of a discipline, who respond with conditioned reflexes to the mention of Child ballad numbers, or the Thompson motif-index code, or Bolte and Polívka's *Anmerkungen,* or the *Internationale Volkskundliche Bibliographie.* Where such communal associations are lacking, a discipline scarcely exists. What unifies the profession of American history above all other factors is the inheritance by the current generation of historians of hallowed predecessors—Frederick Jackson Turner, Charles Beard, Carl Becker, Vernon Louis Parrington— whom they relentlessly pillory in a father-figure love-hate relationship. Familiar outlines of the subject matter also provide a sense of fellowship to members of a discipline. American historians, whatever their specialization, share a series of comfortable landmarks: the colonial period, the Revolution, the westward movement, the early national period, the Civil War, the Gilded Age, America as a world power, the New Deal, the atomic age. What are the familiar zones of the folklorist? Surveys and textbooks indicate the coming of age of a subject; George W. Cox produced an *Introduction to the Science of Comparative Mythology and Folk-Lore* in 1881, based on the solar interpretation of Max Müller; fourteen years later Marian Cox issued *An Introduction to Folklore* redirecting folk studies to the animistic theory of Edward B. Tylor. In *Folklore and Folklife: An Introduction* I enlisted the aid of a number of professional folklorists in charting our province. At one pole the oral genres of folk narrative, folk poetry, and smaller forms seem clearcut; at the other end the categories of material culture, ranged under the relatively new term "folk life," do not so readily fall into place. Folk art, folk crafts, and folk architecture seem to hang together as all involving traditional handiwork, while the performing arts of folk music, folk dance, folk drama, and folk festival appear to form another cluster. Folk costume and folk cuisine belong somewhere in the material culture area, while folk religion and folk medicine, involving belief, ritual, and custom,

spread over the genres and material culture in ways not easily classified. Still the subject has sufficiently established itself so that several
textbooks—the best by Jan Brunvand and Alan Dundes—have found
ready markets in the United States. When Alexander Krappe published *The Science of Folklore* in 1930, he excluded all American examples on the grounds that folklore in the classic sense did not exist in
the United States, and in saying so he simply reflected the state of
scholarship of the time.

Another mark of a discipline is its ability to set and define standards
of worth. In folklore this ability is particularly pressing, because the
subject matter lends itself to dilution, distortion, sentimentalizing, and
commercializing, and because any bystander may pose as an
authority on a topic apparently in the public domain. One sign of a
healthy discipline of folkloristics will be its quickness to dismiss the
scissors-and-paste collections, the jolly children's books, the tourist-
targeted legends, and similar potboilers that swamp publishers' lists.
The excellence of the Victorian folklorists is nowhere more manifest
than in the caliber of their reviews in *Folk-Lore* during the peak years
of the 1880s and 1890s. The Great Team shared a spirit of mounting
excitement as their subject unfolded and viewed additions to the growing shelf of worthy folklore studies and collections as items in which
they held a personal stake. Secure in their society, their journal, and
their science, they gave little heed to the popularizers of their day,
such as Sabine Baring-Gould and Thomas Firminger Thiselton-Dyer,
who were still a cut above the fakelorists of today. In the bibliography
he appended to his pamphlet on *The Fairy Mythology of Shakespeare*
Alfred Nutt summarily dismissed Thiselton-Dyer's *Folk Lore of
Shakespeare*, saying it "cannot be recommended," and wasted no
further words. Here is Sidney Hartland quickly disposing of a six-vol-
ume series of *Folk-lore and Legends* for various countries, issued in
1889 and 1890 for a gullible public that still exists: "It is not easy to
know for what purpose the collection entitled *Folk-lore and Legends*
has been published, beyond that of producing pleasant little books
good in print and paper, and suitable for whiling away an idle hour
. . . It only purports to be 'a selection,' and no hint is afforded as to the
source of any of the tales . . . This precludes all scientific use of the
volumes. And yet the author is evidently impressed with a genuine
love of folktales, and has some knowledge of the subject. He might do
good work, if he would go about it the right way."[2] This voice of
authority sounded throughout the golden two decades at the century's
end, when folklore was demonstrably a discipline, or a science in the

language of the time. It does not sound today. At a meeting of the Folklore Society I once saw the review editor walking up and down the aisle offering books for review to any taker, like a costermonger crying her wares. If the alleged discipline cannot review authoritatively in its own journal, it will likely not control the influential media. The *Times Literary Supplement* review of *The British Folklorists: A History* should have gone to a folklorist; instead it was sent to a social anthropologist, whose opinions were the stereotypic prejudices of British anthropologists toward folklore. The point is not to criticize their inexpertness on folklore, for, generally speaking, no practitioner of one discipline ever understands more than dimly the inner workings of another, but to underscore the weakness of folklore as an established discipline.

In the United States the fakelore issue provided the test, and American folklorists flunked it badly when in the 1940s they praised Ben Botkin's treasuries as lavishly as did the popular press. No folklore Ph.D.'s were around in those years. Now that they exist the standards of reviewing have improved considerably, although soft spots remain, evident in the reception accorded Duncan Emrich's *Folklore on the American Land,* a super-packaged treasury of sentimental filler and flag-waving hoopla, which was lauded in a two-page advertisement in the *Journal of American Folklore* in blurbs from folklorists.

Yet another criterion for the intellectual strength of a discipline is the sense of its own identity, as manifested, in one instance, in the history of its unfolding and the biographies of its luminaries. Stirrings in this direction registered in the past several years include a collective group of biographical sketches of and by Nordic folklorists, and histories of Finnish and British folklorists. At the November 1972 meeting of the American Folklore Society, in Austin, Texas, younger scholars devoted two sessions to the history of folkloristics, and the papers of one session have been published in the *Journal of the Folklore Institute.*[3] Historical and biographical writings about a discipline require more than good will and devotion to the subject and can easily degenerate into lifeless catalogues. A next step forward would be in-depth biographical and critical portraits of the Great Team. The American Folklore Society has under way an oral history of itself based on tape-recorded interviews by younger folklorists of its elder statesmen, turned into informants. Alan Dundes is engaged on a European-wide biographical history of the founding fathers of folklore.

Is Folklore a Discipline?

A further sign of the vitality of a discipline can be seen in its relation with adjacent fields of learning. Does the given subject influence and render an impact upon them or is it a borrower dependent upon their intellectual capital? There is little question about the spinoff from folklore in the 1878-1914 period in England, when the prominence of the stellar folklorists and the national publicity given the 1891 congress made folklore a household word. Andrew Lang in his monthly column "At the Sign of the Ship" in *Longman's Magazine* regularly inserted folkloric items and conducted running dialogues on customs and beliefs with correspondents drawn from the general readership.

Today we see a reversed picture. Two of the most notable scholarly works on folklore since 1970, Keith Thomas's *Religion and the Decline of Magic* and Alan Macfarlane's *Witchcraft in Tudor and Stuart England*, come from historians not folklorists. When they looked to another discipline for assistance, they turned to anthropology. At Oxford, as at Cambridge, there are no folklorists to talk to, but social anthropologists wear the mantle of Tylor and have dealt with witches of a sort, in tribal Africa, so Thomas and Macfarlane attempted, not very successfully, to shed some light on seventeenth-century credence in witchcraft from analogies with contemporary African belief systems. Unfortunately the Africans visited by anthropologists lived in the bush rather than in town, a factor which somewhat skewed the analogy, if it ever really existed at all. On the side of folklore there stands the magnificent *Dictionary of British Folk-Tales* by Katharine Briggs, who determinedly wrested a folklore Ph.D. out of Oxford when none was available, and who maintains the noble tradition of the great Victorians. The *Dictionary*, revealing the unsuspected fecundity of English oral narrative to be ferreted from printed sources, is one of those landmark works produced in one discipline to which other disciplines pay tribute in footnotes. Scholars of English literature, for instance, will have to become friends with the *Dictionary*.

In the United States folklorists are gradually making their presence felt, particularly in newer academic realms that overflow the conventional disciplines. A beachhead was established in 1971 when Yale University appointed William Ferris, a folklore Ph.D. from Pennsylvania, as assistant professor of American Studies and Afro-American Studies, two area programs found on a number of American campuses. A specialist in the oral and material folklore of Mississippi blacks, Ferris has added the motion picture camera to the tape recorder as a field tool. Since arriving at Yale he has taught American folklore to over two hundred undergraduates, he writes in the May 1973 issue of the *Yale Alumni Magazine*. At the University of Texas folklorist Roger Abrahams, who has collected and written perceptively on northern urban black traditions, has served as acting director of their Afro-American Studies Center.

Oral history is another new academic constituency, directed toward historical interviews of living personalities whose taped recollections can serve historians as a complementary source to the printed word and archival document. But the Oral History Association leans strongly to the elitist perspective of conventional history. At the 1971 meeting of the association I chaired a panel on "The Oral Historian and the Folklorist," at which the folklorists endeavored to persuade the audience that the technique of the tape-recorded interview could be extended from the elite to the folk and thereby greatly enrich the source materials of the social historian.[4]

Another booming new enterprise is known as popular culture, and the Popular Culture Association in its third annual meeting, held at Indianapolis in April 1973, displayed 150 papers on topics involving the comics (three sessions), films (half a dozen sessions), television, science fiction, curricula, popular music, the automobile, women in the media, western fiction, the occult, toys, sports, beer cans, popular food, popular architecture, popular culture, and so on. Folklore was plentifully represented in this mélange, in sessions on comparative mythology, folklore and mass media, folklore and popular culture, and American minstrelsy.

Yet another rising tide of academic interest can be identified as urban studies. Folklore has already made a move in this direction, in the symposium on *The Urban Experience and Folk Tradition*, published in 1971 by the American Folklore Society. These trends suggest a series of new groupings within the humanities that seek to overturn the elitist, highbrow, rarefied, and to a large extent stultifying approach of the established disciplines and get closer to the flavor of common life. In this new thrust, folklore studies will play a key role.

Finally we come to the question of methodology. Each discipline has its own methodology. Does folklore? As one who gives a pro-seminar each year to incoming graduate students on folklore theory and techniques, without more than scratching the surface, I find the question vexing. The professional folklorist must master the techniques of fieldwork with oral literature, folk music, and material culture. He must learn a deceptive terminology and a complex multilingual bibliography. He must become familiar with methods of tale-typing and motif-indexing; of comparative annotation; of structural analysis; of archival use; of sifting printed sources; of identifying folk artifacts; of obtaining informant histories; of folk-atlas mapping; of examining literary uses of folklore; of determining historical content in folk tradition; of separating traditional folklore from commercialized and ideological fakelore or *folklorismus*. Each of these techniques could occupy a seminar by itself. Every practicing folklorist has undergone the experience, many times, of having colleagues or acquaintances ask him what the folklorist does, expecting a capsule answer in five minutes, or of reading pronouncements by reviewers and other pundits who think they know what folklore is about, when they have never done more than skim Grimms' Fairy Tales, skipping the notes. An English department chairman once inquired somewhat huffily why I downgraded a job candidate trained in literature who had interested himself in folklore. Would I place all such persons beyond the pale of bona-fide teachers of folklore? Yes, I responded; in today's circumstances, since we have dozens of highly trained Ph.D.'s in folklore available, why choose a well-meaning amateur, especially in a field so plagued by cranks and crackpots? Would he hire a self-taught Milton or Chaucer specialist? Well, folklore has the same standards as literature, or history, or anthropo ogy.

The methodology of folklore is sometimes criticized as soft and anecdotal, a serious charge in this day of the hard social sciences with their strivings to predict human behavior through models, paradigms, and tables of quantified data. Literary scholars receive grants to computerize their intuitions, and a sociologist colleague obtained a handsome three-year stipend to quantify the elements of morale. Yet human nature can never be reduced to statistical graphs, as Charles Sanders Peirce the mathematical philosopher asserted in *Chance, Love and Logic*.[5] Humanists, and especially folklorists, should take their stand on the quirkiness, the idiosyncrasies of man and woman. Tradition does not fetter the individual but provides boundaries for his expression.

Is folklore then a discipline? Pragmatically, it has reached the status of a discipline in various times and places; in England from 1888 to 1901, when the Great Team served as presidents of the Folklore Society; in Finland for the past century; in Germany for even longer; and one could extend the list. At times folklore has sunk to an antiquarian hobby or a storage enterprise. In the United States it qualifies as a discipline at a few university centers and in England only at the University of Leeds. On philosophical grounds folklore is indeed a discipline, as proven by the achievements of illustrious scholars who have written in her name and contributed uniquely to man's knowledge about himself.

The Oral Process

One avid concern of folklore theory today is the nature of oral culture. Folk studies were born in the awareness of oral tradition and its special properties but came to concentrate on written or printed texts, such as Child's great encyclopedia of ballad variants, and tended to treat orally collected texts as literary products. The Grimms kept rewriting and polishing their household tales with conscious intent to alter them from Volksmärchen to Buchmärchen. Archer Taylor studied the proverb as found in literary sources. As the subject matter of folklore expanded, proponents of the material culture or folklife side of folk studies turned to such nonoral concerns as vernacular architecture and ethnic costume. And everywhere one hears the lament that new technological systems have doomed the old word-of-mouth folkways. How can man talk above the roar of the machine?

Yet countertendencies are tilting the balance back toward the spoken word. Sociolinguists such as Dell Hymes and William Labov have influenced younger folklorists to investigate the ethnography of speaking and the modes of verbal behavior. Marshall McLuhan has made familiar the concept of an aural-oral society in the modern world. A rising appreciation for minority cultures has brought respect for the eloquence of native American spokesmen and Afro-American "men-of-words," who with their tongues advance their causes against the dominant white culture oriented toward print and the media. Historians of literature now give attention to the long eras before the advent of written languages. Robert Scholes and Robert Kellogg in *The Nature of Narrative* and Walter J. Ong in *The Presence of the Word* recognize the ethnocentrism of such terms as nonliterate and preliterate in preference to the far more appropriate designations of postoral and nonoral, and acknowledge the spoken heritage behind the Bible, Homer, Beowulf, and the Icelandic sagas.

The recognition that an oral culture exists leads to intriguing questions for the folklorist to ponder. How does oral tradition differ, as presumably it does, between tribal and industrial societies? What aesthetic, psychological, and sociological functions do the modern oral subcultures fulfill? Could they function, for instance, as counter-cultures opposing the values of the established power structure? The essays of this section do not directly face these questions, but they seek to prepare the way for dealing with them. The first considers two approaches to the oral culture, those undertaken by literary and by historical scholars, and attempts to show their points of convergence. The second offers a particular case study of oral historical tradition in one land.

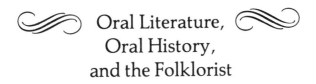 Oral Literature,
Oral History,
and the Folklorist

Literary and historical scholars have suddenly become aware of orality. Trained to scrutinize written words in medieval manuscripts, archival documents, personal papers, and printed volumes, they now confront spoken and sung words and are learning, or learning about, new techniques of interviewing and recording. Oral Literature and Oral History are separate and unrelated growth industries in the universities. The terms flourish and have penetrated the lexicon of educators from top administrators to aspiring graduate students. In response to pioneering by illustrious members of their faculties Harvard has promoted Oral Literature and Columbia has fathered Oral History. Yet the supporters of the movements seem largely unaware that folklorists have engaged in Oral Literature and Oral History for nearly two centuries.

The modern concept of Oral Literature dates from a field trip undertaken by Milman Parry to Yugoslavia in 1934 to record living epic songs. In his dissertation at the Sorbonne, Parry had examined Homer's use of formulaic epithets and concluded that the poet had composed the *Iliad* and the *Odyssey* orally.[1] He then tested his ideas of oral-formulaic composition on South Slavic coffeehouse bards. Parry returned to the Classics department of Harvard University to elaborate his concept but died in 1935; Albert B. Lord, the student who had accompanied him to Yugoslavia and would join Harvard's Slavic department, continued the work. Between 1951 and 1954 Lord published, with Bela Bartók, three volumes of *Serbo-Croatian Folk Songs* and *Serbo-Croatian Heroic Songs* from the Parry collection of traditional poetry sung by the *guslars*, and included not only the song texts but also informative replies of the guslars to questions about their training and techniques.[2] In 1953 another Harvard professor, Francis P. Magoun, connected the oral-formulaic theory to *Beowulf* in an article in *Speculum* that excited controversy for the next decade until consensus decided that Magoun had overextended the hypothesis.[3] The landmark publication appeared in 1960, Lord's *The Singer of Tales*, which developed the thesis of oral improvisation from the "living laboratory of Yugoslav epic" and then applied the thesis to the Homeric epics. A galaxy of doctoral dissertations, articles, and monographs took their point of departure from *The Singer of Tales* to investigate the formulas and themes in dead oral poetries in Ancient Greek, Old French, and Old English, and their living counterparts in eastern Europe, Africa, and Asia. *The Haymes Bibliography of the Oral Theory*, issued at Harvard in 1973, lists several hundred books, articles, and dissertations, the majority written since 1960.

Activities in Oral Literature prospered on several fronts in 1974. Lord perceptively reviewed the accelerating number of oral-literary studies in an essay "Perspectives on Recent Work on Oral Literature."[4] That same year he announced a "major program of instruction in oral literature" at Harvard involving ten courses, thanks to a substantial grant from the National Endowment for the Humanities.[5] His protégé David Bynum, who shared the administration of the new program, published an article in the *Harvard Library Bulletin* contending that oral literary studies had existed continuously at Harvard from 1856, when Francis James Child commenced his great edition of the English and Scottish popular ballads, through the era of Kittredge to Parry and Lord.[6] At the 1974 meeting of the Modern Language Association in New York, Bynum organized a seminar on Oral Literature. And in November 1974 the University of Michigan played host to a conference on "Oral Literature and the Formula" convening classicists, medievalists, linguists, Slavicists, Africanists, Asianists, and a token folklorist (myself) that paid homage to Albert Lord. Ruth Finnegan, author of *Oral Literature in Africa*, flew over from England to present a paper titled "What is Oral Literature Anyway? Comments in the Light of Some African and Other Comparative Material." At the conference one learned of classical and Anglo-Saxon scholars suddenly turning from their library research to seek oral epics among the Ainu and Xhosa.

Oral History is even further along than Oral Literature. Allan Nevins, most prolific of American historians, in 1938 hinted at the movement he was to found when he wrote in *The Gateway to History* of the need to secure from the lips of "living Americans who have led significant lives, a fuller record of their participation in the political, economic, and cultural life of the last sixty years."[7] On May 18, 1948, Nevins conducted his first oral history interview, which would be deposited in the Oral History Research Office of Columbia University, on whose faculty he served with such distinction. The procedures of oral history have been succinctly stated: "With each [interviewee] a series of carefully tape-recorded interviews is conducted. These are then transcribed into typescript, which is checked for accuracy by the interviewer and his respondent, and deposited in the Oral History Collection at Columbia University, subject to such temporary restriction upon use as the donor may wish to impose."[8]

In 1960 and again in 1964 Columbia University issued catalogues of *The Oral History Collection* listing its acquisitions. These were followed in 1965 with a report on *Oral History in the United States* describing the progress in establishing depositories for oral history at other centers besides Columbia. Proof of the widening interest was seen the next year in the First National Colloquium on Oral History sponsored by the University of California at Los Angeles at their Arrowhead conference site. Panel discussants considered "Various Approaches to Techniques in Oral History Interviewing" and "Definitions of Oral History," and Nevins modestly disclaimed having invented oral history.[9] These activities climaxed in an organizational meeting in 1967 at Columbia's conference center, Arden House, at which the Oral History Association was founded. The association promptly began distributing the proceedings of its annual colloquiums, and in 1973 titled this publication the *Oral History Review.*

Within six years after its founding, the association had increased its membership to over a thousand supporters from all parts of the country. By the early seventies the public had come to accept undiluted oral history, in such best-sellers as Merle Miller's *Plain Speaking*, in which Harry Truman recites his own views and recollections, and the interview books of Studs Terkel.[10] Oral history centers, archives, and projects are now commonplace in universities, historical societies, and libraries. Historians of twentieth-century America regularly consult oral history achives, into which the eminent in public life have fed total recall. The third edition of the *Oral History Collection of Columbia University*, published in 1973, cited 360,000 pages of transcripts on deposit, nearly half that of the whole nation. Reviewing the state of the profession in 1974, Charles W. Crawford could say that the names of the 2,697 contributors—"memoirists" and "oral authors" are suggested terms—to Columbia's Oral History Collection "reads like a Who's Who of American leadership and achievement during the last half century.[11]

The folklorist viewing these developments is both delighted and dismayed. He welcomes the opportunity to share with new associates the excitement of the field foray and the personal interview, until he realizes that very few know folklore as a discipline whose chief business is the study of oral matter. Colleagues of mine planning an oral history archive at Indiana University were surprised to learn that the Archives of Traditional Music on campus contained a considerable amount of oral historical traditions on tape, deposited there by folklore collectors. The faculty of the extensive Harvard program in oral literature does not at this time include a holder of the doctorate in folklore. If oral historians and oral literary scholars talk with folklorists about their field experiences and scholarly problems they will find considerable common ground, some of it already well-traversed.

The relation of Oral Literature and Oral History to Folklore can be indicated by the insertion of the term Traditional in both labels. A simple model illustrates the point.

Oral Literature			Oral History	
Nontraditional Oral Literature	Oral Traditional Literature ‖ Oral Literary Tradition	Oral Traditional History ‖ Oral Historical Tradition	Nontraditional Oral History

Oral Tradition
=
Folklore

Oral tradition is a major province of the folklorist, who divides his attention between the verbal and material forms of traditional culture. Both Oral Literature and Oral History involve orally transmitted expressive forms, in the one case Märchen, epics, ballads, proverbs, romances, riddles, topical poems, praise songs, lyrics, and the like, and in the other case reminiscences, recollections, anecdotes, reconstructions, testimonies, sagas, genealogies, myths, memorates, and so on. Some of these forms by definition are traditional, some are not;

some are traditional in form but not necessarily in content; and some have little or no traditional aspects.

Oral Literature is not necessarily traditional. Oral poets who compose new and original songs are contributing to Nontraditional Oral Literature. Only time will tell whether the folk will accept their productions into tradition, and by then numerous singers will have reshaped the piece into a folksong.

Oral bards adept at creating praise songs and topical poems thrive in African societies. An example of an individualistic oral poet is Mamman Shata, a well-known Hausa-Fulani bard in Nigeria who regularly performs throughout the country, accompanying himself with a *kalangu* (a stringed instrument) and being accompanied by a chorus of six singers.[12] Mamman Shata composes praises for wedding couples, chieftains being enstooled, and truck drivers undertaking journeys. His compositions are for the most part confined to his reportoire and are not usually sung by other singers. Each poem addresses itself to a new situation, with new personalities involved, although Mamman Shata knows very well how to develop such a song impromptu.

Mamman Shata's praise songs are directed to the elite of Hausa-Fulani society, to the ruling emirs who govern the people and exemplify their ideals. When the bard composed a song praising a truck driver in Kano named Umaru Danduna, he endowed him with virtues similar to those he had attached to kings and emirs. Since Umaru's grandfather had successfully led the Fulani in battle against their enemy the Gobiwara, a fact mentioned by the poet, Mamman Shata could the more easily shift his eulogistic style from the general to the truck driver. Umaru too is a leader, marked for destiny by a shooting star that appeared at his birth.

> Umar, son of Danduna of Gwandu,
> At first my song was for all the drivers,
> But this song was made to you and you alone,
> I never hear where a coward becomes a leader,
> When it is thrust on him, he will never endure,
> It is only the brave can lead,
> As the shooting star does proclaim.

Textually this praise song about the driver Umaru, who is likened to "a double-humped camel that carries a heavy load," is nontraditional;

131

the poet sings, "this song was made to you and you alone." Yet it involves a number of traditional elements: stock metaphors, a folk belief in the portent of the shooting star, the form itself of the praise song. If people in Kano and elsewhere in the northern states take up the song, and in the course of time collectors report variants that establish its dispersion, it will become traditional, and have crossed the line separating Oral Literature from Oral Traditional Literature.

Folk poets exist in North America too, and three folklorists have inspected in close detail three such poets in *Folksongs and Their Makers*, a splendid multiple study of Oral Literature dipping into tradition.[13] After presenting an informative psychobiography of Dorrance Weir, a construction worker in central New York, and the evolution of his anti-Negro song "Take That Night Train to Selma," composed in the 1960s, Henry Glassie stated that it was no folksong but contained folk ingredients. The deep-rooted folk prejudice at its center, the singing style, the enthusiastic response of the rural blue-collar society whose values the piece reflected—such elements constituted a folkloric frame for Weir's song although it never entered the repertoires of other singers. Similarly John Szwed peered into the ethnographic subsoil from which homesteader Paulie Hall in Newfoundland's Codroy Valley fashioned a plaintive "Bachelor's Song" in the 1930s. This nontraditional song expressed the Valley people's rigid social attitudes, sanctioning marriage and child-rearing and reproving bachelorhood. For his songmaker, Edward Ives chose a woods poet of the Maine-Maritimes area, Joe Scott, deceased in 1918, whose original oral songs had won folk acceptance. Ives concentrated on "The Plain Golden Band," a song Scott composed about his own jilting in the 1890s. In the 1960s Ives located fifty-four versions of the piece, and thereby clearly established its claim to folksong status. Analyzing the ballad's content in its first form, as Scott printed it to hawk around the lumbercamps, Ives found a synthesis of the traditional, the factual, and the creative. After seventy years of oral circulation, with some reinforcement from printed newspaper versions, "The Plain Golden Band" showed a surprising consistency considering its tenuous narrative line.

Folksongs and Their Makers deserves special commendation for its careful empirical studies of three oral poems and cogent theoretical propositions about oral composition. Two of the poems, "Take That Night Train to Selma" and "Bachelor's Song," remain under Oral Literature; "The Plain Golden Band" enters Oral Literary Tradition. All three are similar in many ways, but only one, through the oral process, becomes folk property. Other such studies can be cited, and Ives has written two rich biography-collections of oral poets in Maine and the Maritimes: Larry Gorman the satirist and Edward Doyle the balladist.[14] In these investigations folklorists probe at the boundaries and channels between creativity and tradition.

In terms of oral prose, a discussion now active among folklorists concerns the place of the personal experience story, called a memorate, among the folklore genres.[15] Can the recital of a firsthand encounter with a ghost, or of the single-handed routing of desperadoes, or a comical misadventure qualify as a traditional tale? If the narrative follows a time-honored pattern, the folklorist is inclined to acknowledge its credentials. Often what appears to be a unique nontraditional experience proves on further checking to have traveled widely and to be a personalized rendering of a traditional narration. Sometimes a folk teller will attach to himself tall tales and folk anecdotes which other narrators render in the first person, but again he will develop narratives from his own comical mishaps.[16] In prose as in verse a meaningful line can be drawn between Oral Literature and Oral Traditional Literature.

Distinctions between traditional and nontraditional or between oral and written literature are often shifting and elusive. Appraising the proverbs in *Poor Richard's Almanac*, Stuart Gallacher reported that Franklin had gleaned one part from the floating stock of folk sayings, created a second group which entered American popular usage, and created a third group which never left the printed pages of his almanacs.[17] When Arthur Palmer Hudson investigated the sources of ballads inserted by southern novelists of the 1920s into their fiction, he learned that some writers had used traditional ballads sung in their own families, some recollected only fragments and had completed the texts themselves, and some simply copied them out of Child's compendium![18] An Anglo-Saxon scholar turned Xhosa field collector, Jeff Opland, has categorized four kinds of tribal poets among the Xhosa: those who compose spontaneously, those who memorize traditional poems, those who improvise from a store of traditional themes and phrases, and those who write down their original poems.[19] The repertoires of the memorizers and improvisers belong with Oral Traditional Literature and of the spontaneous poets with Nontraditional Oral Literature. We assume that repeated acts of memorizing an oral poem, or any oral text, will inevitably produce variation. Nontraditional oral compositions remain as unique texts, and in that respect resemble the creations of written literature.

A borderline situation occurs with memorized recitations or monologues based on printed compositions. In 1973 folklorist Kenneth Goldstein recorded a number of humorous monologues recited in English pubs and parlors and compared the original source, say in the poems of Robert W. Service, with the orally performed text.[20] Minor variations had developed between the published and the delivered texts, but would these be enough to allow us to consider the recitations Oral Traditional Literature? One view argues that performance milieu, audience interaction, and oral delivery make the monologue a folkloric phenomenon. Another view, to which I subscribe, holds that the memorized text is much too close to Service's verses to warrant being called folk literature, since it has no independent life in tradition.

The theory of oral-formulaic composition, as applied to the Homeric epics of old and the Yugoslav epics of today by Parry and Lord, is a theory for Oral Traditional Literature. In a recent statement Lord compares the epic singer with the storyteller who reconstructs his narrative at each rendition without concern for exact usage of the same words. This oral process is a kind of limited improvisation, not a "free" or "radical" improvisation, since the reciter remains close to his story line.[21]

The great scholastic feat of Parry and Lord was to join the library study of dead epic poets to the field study of living epic poets. This was a shattering turnaround in the history of humanistic scholarship, and its repercussions are penetrating the universities. Yet the bridge built by Parry and Lord linked only the long ago to the far away. Oral literature remote in time is now being compared with oral literature remote in place. The oral process still seems distant and unconnected with immediate concerns. An enterprising few have turned to the oral literature in their own culture—to ballads, blues, and Negro sermons—and tried out the oral-formulaic theory with surprising success.[22] That oral literature, formulaic or not, thrives on our own doorstep, as in the explosive Afro-American toasts collected in penitentiaries by Bruce Jackson, is yet an unfamiliar notion.[23] Right there in Michigan, where the conference on "Oral Literature and the Formula" was considering oral poetry of the Serbs, the Xhosa, the Ainu, I had collected sagas from Indians, blacks, ethnics, lumberjacks, miners, sailors, in endless profusion.

If the terminological distinctions I have suggested are valid, what difference do they make to scholars working with Oral Literature and

Oral History? Changing the name does not change the thing. My contention is that the things are inherently different and need different labels to make clear the substantive distinctions between folkloric and nonfolkloric materials, and consequently the separate methods and strategies required to gather and study them.

In contrasting Nontraditional Oral Literature and Oral Traditional Literature, we see the issue as individual creativity versus collective traditionality. If an oral poem or recital is the unique production of one mind, it will represent a creative energy and artistic imagination of a different order from the efforts applied to transmitting a piece previously heard and known, in whole or in part. Improvisation involves re-creation, not original creation. Every performance of an oral folklore item—save for the shortest genres like proverbs, riddles, and charms, which also vary—requires some degree of improvisation, in the selecting of words and phrases, the ordering of episodes and stanzas, the choice of names and places. In the last analysis, Oral Literature, created by its own impulses, is much closer to folklore than is Oral History, which is extracted by interviewers. Most of the forms of Oral Literature are folkloric genres, and some critics use oral literature interchangeably with oral traditions—a phrase that is itself often synonymous with folklore. The new deployment of the term Oral Literature consciously avoids the term folklore, much as anthropologists have adopted such euphemisms as "expressive literature," "verbal art," and "oral art" to bypass the word that makes them uncomfortable, because it represents a subject matter and discipline foreign to their training. In spite of Bynum's claims for Oral Literature, no intellectual or philosophical continuity in "oral-literary" studies has existed at Harvard. During my undergraduate and graduate years there, from 1933 to 1943, when I stumbled onto the science of folklore as a result of reading Davy Crockett's tall tales, no one on the Harvard faculty could give me guidance in this arcane area, save Kenneth Jackson, professor of Celtic for a short period before returning to the University of Edinburgh. On any large faculty scholars from one of the humanities or social science departments, or even on occasion from the natural sciences, dip into folkloric matters, but they are not folklorists.[24] The scholar concerned with oral traditions must deal with Oral Traditional History as well as with Oral Traditional Literature, and he should be familiar with partly oral and nonoral forms of cultural traditions, as this table on Folklore and Folklife suggests.

Folklore and Folklife

Oral traditions	Social performing folk arts	Social folk custom	Material culture
Oral traditional literature	Folk drama	Folk religion	Folk crafts
Oral traditional history	Folk dance	Folk healing	Folk architecture
	Festival	Ritual	Folk costume
		Traditional games	Folk cookery

These four divisions overlap at many points. Some folklorists today consider all storytelling and ballad-singing as performance and speak no more of the "informant" or "tradition carrier" but of the performer. He may be the individual reciter or one of a singing, dancing, acting, or instrumental group. From this perspective, the scholar studies epic singers and festival dancers as related expressive forms. Artifacts of material culture, such as traditional musical instruments or dress, are employed by the performer. Folk beliefs will be incorporated in oral traditions and associated with social customs and material culture. For instance, the belief in the evil eye is the subject of memorates and legends; an amulet may be worn to guard against the evil eye; a folk ritual is observed to detect the possessor of the evil eye. And this is the heart of the matter: oral-literary studies cannot be artificially severed from their connection with folklore and folklife studies.

The Homeric question as it is presently phrased suggests the overlap between oral-literary and folkloristic concerns. Classicists now seek to separate the oral poet's personal input from the traditional elements in the epics. Speaking of "The Search for the Real Homer," Grayson Kirk asserts "his poetry can only be adequately understood when we learn how to relate its strictly creative aspect, the imagination and taste of a poetic individual, to the dense background of the inherited tradition."[25] He then conjectures that the *Iliad* consists primarily of traditional themes and typical patterns fleshed out and recombined by the bard. Taking another stance, Joseph Russo has ingeniously attempted to separate Homer's personal poetic contributions from older traditional devices and episodes in the *Iliad*.[26] Here is where the folklorist can apply his techniques. Recurrent themes and patterns are his business.

How a classicist with training in folklore can approach the problem of Homer's debt to tradition is seen in William Hansen's monograph on narrative patterns and inconsistencies in the *Odyssey*.[27] Hansen points out that the inconsistencies that puzzle Homer's critics are a commonplace in oral storytelling. Any student of folktales knows that the narrator occasionally slips and fumbles his narrative line, omits an episode, gets his characters or tales mixed up—but since the story is fluid in any case, not a rigid rote memory piece, such flaws count for less than they would in a written composition. As Hansen observes, the raw oral tale betrays far more inconsistencies than the version usually presented to the reading public, smoothed and polished to give the story a fluency that it never possessed when first delivered. Audiences are much less bothered by false starts, repetition, interjections, and obscure pronouns than are readers. The physical presence of the performer, his gestures, facial expressions, intonations mimicry—his oral style—all contribute to the listener's comprehension of the action. For the same reason a tape recording of the spoken narrative, although faithful to the oral text, conveys much less meaning and satisfaction to auditors than does the human recital. What would be surprising in the Homeric epics, seen as folkloric performances, would be the absence of narrative inconsistencies.

Another insight into the *Odyssey* that Hansen derives from folklore theory concerns the informer or donor, the magic helper who appears fortuitously to succor the hero in time of trouble, alike in European Märchen and in Homer's epic. On the role of the donor Hansen cites Vladimir Propp, whose *Morphology of the Folktale* has so influenced recent folklore scholarship. The old woman in the woods who aids the Märchen hero is a goddess in the *Odyssey*, adviser to Odysseus on one occasion and to Menelaos on another. Yet again, in the scenes where the hero Odysseus consults with the seer Teiresias, and the hero Menelaos with the seer Proteus, while the assistants fade into the background, Hansen alludes to the celebrated exposition by the Danish folklorist Axel Olrik on the laws governing folk epic composition. In Olrik's formulation, borne out regularly in the dramatic tableaux that highlight oral narrative prose and poetry, two characters hold stage center, since the oral bard, unlike novelist or playwright, cannot readily present multiple personalities and conversations in one setting.

The Oral Process

Teiresias' prophecy to Odysseus about difficulties he will encounter on his return journey and the actions he should take includes a sailors' folktale still current. The prophet is telling Odysseus he will find parasites and paramours in his household.

After you slay the suitors, take an oar and travel until you reach men who do not know the sea, use no salt in their food, and know neither ships nor oars. I shall tell you an easily recognizable sign: when another traveler meets you and says that you hold a winnowing-fan on your shoulder, then plant the oar in the ground and sacrifice a ram, bull, and boar to Poseidon. Then return home and sacrifice to all the gods. [28]

On the coast of Maine in 1956 I heard a variant of this episode from a retired lobsterman. Frank Alley told it as a humorous anecdote of a sailor who tired of seafaring and went inland with an oar on his shoulder until he reached a place where the people had never heard of the sea. Eventually he came to a farmhouse where a young girl took his oar for a "pudding stick." He remained there, proposed to the girl, and on their wedding night followed her up to the bedroom.

When he got up, she was in bed flat on her back, with all of her clothes stripped off, and her legs sticking right up in the air. And he says, "What in the world are you doing there?" "Well," she says, "there's been a squall, and I've got everything clewed up. Now I'm scudding on the bare poles." So I guess he found out she knew something about salt water. [29]

Modern Greek sailors also tell this tale. [30] By pointing out the presence of a long-lived folktale in the *Odyssey*, folklorists can enlarge the known elements of oral tradition in Homer's epics.

Oral History, like Oral Literature, is confined to one individual. Oral Traditional History, like Oral Traditional Literature, is shared by a number of tellers and flows from the dead to the living.

The Oral History movement differs from the Oral Literature movement in getting launched from a nontraditional base. Political and business leaders relating their life stories into the tape recorder are producing pure Oral History, although occasionally a family folk anecdote may slip into their stream of recollections. As oral historians broaden their reach and lower their sights to consider the uncelebrated, they move toward traditional history. Folklorists for their part also have been slow to widen their net beyond the conventional oral

138

genres of tale, song, proverb, and riddle and to recognize historical traditions as a legitimate and valuable target.

In its unfolding the Oral History movement has stretched out from elitist history to touch people's history. Folklorists have participated in several of the Oral History Association's annual symposiums and made their plea for attention to the selective and dramatized versions of past events remembered by the folk, regardless of their accuracy.[31] They contend that what the folk choose to remember is itself a historical datum. In this vein some recorders of Afro-American and African oral traditions have addressed the association. Paul Bullock reported how in the ghettos of Watts and the barrios of East Los Angeles he had discovered remarkable verbal skills on the part of youngsters deficient in conventional education. For his survey of their socioeconomic conditions he turned from the usual techniques relying on census data and other statistics to the tape recorder.[32] Courtney Brown, the director of the Kinte Foundation, explained its mission in amassing oral histories of black Americans, "because we have found that the traditions of the written page represented one of the greatest enemies of blacks in describing the black experience in American confines."[33] As he stated, the black lifestyle is an oral lifestyle. Alex Haley, biographer of Malcolm X, related the steps by which he had traced unknown words passed on to him by his grandparents in Henning, Tennessee, to the Malinke language of West Africa. Haley flew to Gambia, made contact with *griots*, the oral traditional historians of French West Africa, and uncovered the roots of his family tree.[34] An academic historian, David W. Cohen, outlined analytic methods being developed by the collector and interpreter of traditional African history, who must weigh variants of a given tradition against biases of family and clan loyalties and factors of migration and dispersal.[35] This sequence of papers shows linkages between the oral cultures of Africa and Afro-America and the necessity for historians studying those cultures to utilize oral traditions.

Historians in a literate society tend to overlook the possibilities of Oral Traditional History, but large subordinate cultures of the American population identify with this kind of chronicle rather than with textbook history. In my field experiences with Native Americans, Afro-Americans, and ethnic Americans I have recorded events of a previous century unreported in print but kept alive by word of mouth. A descendant of slaves told me about the exploits of his grandfather, Romey Howard, in outwitting and outrunning patterollers and bloodhounds on a Georgia plantation. A Sioux Indian related how General

Custer provoked the uprising of the Indian nations by firing when drunk at a squaw and her papoose sitting on an embankment waiting for a train to pull into Fort Bismarck. Two Greek immigrant brothers described how their grandfather Janaikis set an ambush for the Turks when they attacked the town of Bambakou in 1828 and, lacking guns, rolled rocks down on the invaders and gave them their first defeat.[36] In such accounts an aura of legend envelops the core of fact, the heroes become supermen and the enemy villains and monsters.

Oral Traditional History plays a more prominent role in nonliterate than in literate societies, and may be institutionalized through official chroniclers appointed to memorize and transmit the tribal genealogies and chronologies. In African nations today academically trained historians interrogate the tribal historians and record their information as a primary source for the national histories they are now engaged in writing.[37] The work of Jan Vansina entitled *Oral Tradition* deals with the problems of assessing the factual validity in this Oral Traditional History, which varies considerably in perspective depending upon whether a centralized state or decentralized societies maintain the oral records. Not only the sanctioned annalists of the tribe but many of its members may also repeat traditional history in the form of what western ethnologists and folklorists loosely call myths and legends. African proverbs also embody historical traditions in succinct allusion. In the medieval societies of Iceland and Ireland oral family and clan historical traditions flourished in the form of saga, which, when finally written down, have served as source materials for the modern historian.

In between Oral History and Oral Traditional History lies an intermediate form, which can be called personal saga. The teller of personal sagas is a master narrator who portrays himself as a hero of derring-do in bold adventures or a sad-sack in bumbling misadventures that take on mythic outlines, through what appear to be frequent retellings. He creates his own legend. If others in his audiences repeat his narratives, and they endure into a later generation, the personal saga becomes a part of Oral Traditional History. These personal sagas describe a society and its character types, sometimes in vivid detail, as in the narratives of the Fenman W. H. Barrett, a chronicler of both personal experiences and local traditionary events in the boggy country of the Cambridgeshire Fens.[38]

Nontraditional oral history is always elicited by the interviewer. Worried about the inroads on written records caused by the telephone, the oral historian has sought to plug the hole with transcripts from the tape recorder. One consequence is what Barbara Tuchman has cited as "the multiplication of rubbish," the recording of every minutia for fear of its disappearance from the historical record.[39] There is no such danger with Oral Traditional History, for a screening process determines its continued existence. To cross the generations, oral historical traditions must contain sufficient intrinsic appeal to attract new hearers and retellers, for the folk historian transmits only what pleases his elders, his peers, and his juniors. Outsiders may consider Oral Traditional History trivial, as Robert Lowie charged in his celebrated condemnation of American Indian tribal histories, which retained instances of drinking orgies and omitted mention of the white man's technological inventions.[40] But Oral Traditional History is a record of what a people consider important to themselves. Much of the textbook history foisted on American youth is of supreme unimportance to them. While nontraditional oral history is artificially induced, Oral Traditional History lives by its own momentum.

A tradition bearer does not limit his repertoire to Oral Traditional Literature on the one hand or to Oral Traditional History on the other. These distinctions are made in the minds of the scholars. Students of written literatures have reached out to annex oral literature. Historians accustomed to rely on documentary sources have moved into oral history. And once within the oral process both sets of savants have perceived the area of oral traditions from their own vantage points. The folklorist begins from the opposite perspective, with the oral traditions, which he collects, classifies, compares, examines for literary influences and historical residue, and studies from various theoretical premises. Fictional and historical strains blend within the repertoire of the folk narrator. James Douglas Suggs, the animated and prolific black storyteller and folksinger born in Mississippi, who gave me one hundred and seventy tales and twenty songs, narrated not only Brer Rabbit and Old Marster fictions but also vivid and detailed histories of a murderer burned alive by a mob and Ku Klux Klan hired killings of Negro brakemen and firemen.[41] In his rich collection of diverse traditions obtained from the Couch family in Kentucky, Leonard Roberts reports Civil War incidents along with bear and deer hunts and conventional folktales and folksongs.[42]

Among his personal and local sagas Barrett related a historical tradition about the escape of King Charles I past Cromwell's sentries by showing them a split goose feather, the sign by which one Fenman in distress asked another for help.[43] Campbell of Islay, the early Scottish collector who was the first to employ field assistants, published four volumes of Märchen and other fictional tales in the 1860s but considered that the Oral Traditional History of the clans gathered by gamekeeper John Dewar held less interest, and they did not see print till a century later.[44]

Folklorists are equipped to sift out migratory themes and motifs and to recognize mythic patterns and stereotypes in Oral Traditional History. In some of their studies they have extrapolated tradition from history and in others they have recovered history from tradition. Interviewing descendants of slaves in the District of Columbia and adjacent counties in Maryland and Virginia, Gladys Fry kept hearing references to "night doctors." Scanty instances of the term could be found in the vast historical literature on slavery, so Fry decided to concentrate on that line of inquiry. Ultimately she unearthed a vigorous tradition about the night doctors or night riders who allegedly killed runaway slaves and sold their bodies to medical schools for dissection. Fry linked the night doctors to two separate cycles of folk belief. One involved the sale of cadavers and dated back to the ghoulish stories of Burke and Hare, a pair of Irish rascals who robbed graves of corpses to sell to the University of Edinburgh Medical School, the pioneer in anatomy and physiology in the late eighteenth century. The other concerned bogie figures used by the white planters and overseers to terrorize the slaves and thereby inhibit attempted escapes: ghosts, patterollers, night doctors, and, after the war, the Ku Klux Klan.[45]

Folklorist Barbo Klein analyzed a complicated scholarly controversy involving folk history that erupted in Sweden in 1940. Four Swedish scholars asserted in *Carl XII:s död* (The Death of Charles XII), that surviving folk traditions, reinforced by documentary and empirical data, all pointed to King Charles XII's having been shot on November 30, 1718, by a soldier in his own army. The history books had always stated that an enemy Norwegian soldier had killed him. Folk tellers maintained that Charles XII, the great hero-conqueror of Sweden who could straighten out a horseshoe and had killed ten Russians in one battle, was impervious to ordinary bullets. But he met his death when his own soldier, tired of endless war, cut off a button from the king's coat, shot him, and so ended the fighting. The historian Nils Ahnlund attacked the credibility of the folklorist Albert Sandklef in what Klein termed a "conflict between aristocrat and folk that characterizes many of the legends themselves." The verdict remains in suspension, but the vehemence of the debate testified to the shock caused academic historians by information filtered from Oral Traditional History.[46]

A team of anthropologists publishing in the *Journal of American Folklore* has provided a telling illustration of how Oral Traditional History is molded by its carriers to fit their ethnocentric outlook. One half of the team recorded the oral traditional history of a California Indian tribe, the Nomlaki, and the other obtained comparable data from the Yuki, a warring neighbor tribe across the mountains. The anthropologists compared their findings on a war between the two tribes. They discovered agreement on the central facts of the hostilities—a conflict between the tribes had indeed taken place—but almost a complete mirror reversal on the interpretation of the action. Each tribe considered itself the victor and its foe the deceitful aggressor through ambush and treachery properly punished by the heroic stand of its warriors.[47] The Burnt Ranch Massacre of 1853, a conflict between Indians and whites, also recorded in northern California from the oral traditional history of both sides, reveals the same process. In the white version, Indians treacherously murdered white prospectors during the early days of white settlement. According to Tolowa Indian accounts, the whites provoked reprisals by sneaking up on the Indians, and a white officer was alleged to have offered payment for the bodies of Tolowa "outlaws."[48] Such is the patterning that shapes historical traditions retained in folk memory. The extremist position of Lord Raglan holds that after a century and a half mythic patterns have swallowed up all historical kernels.[49]

Following a visit to Indiana University's Folklore Institute and a discussion there about nonliterate folk history, Louis Dupree resolved to explore the same patterning process. He proposed to "test empirically the relationship of folklore to a relatively well-known historic event," specifically the massacre of a British army in Afghanistan in 1842. On his return to Afghanistan, where he was serving on the American Universities Field Staff, Dupree retraced the route of the army's retreat and recorded along the way historical traditions of the event from Afghan villagers. On January 6, 1962, one hundred and twenty-one years to the day after the disastrous retreat which ended in the death and imprisonment of all forty-five hundred English and Indian troops and some twelve thousand camp followers, Dupree and an Afghan associate set out on the same wintry trail from Kabul to Jalalabad. He found that in those villages where a strong father-to-son oral art persisted, folk tellers regaled families and kinfolk with historical and fictional tales and songs, abetted by rhythmic clapping from the listening circle. Because ninety-five percent of Afghan society was illiterate, almost all tribesmen had learned their history orally, though enveloped by a substantial Islamic literature. Dupree soon recognized a patterning and telescoping process in operation; tellers mingled events from three Anglo-Afghan wars, they exalted the heroism and accepted social virtues of their tribal warriors and decried the perfidy and weakness of the British invaders. Folklore touches crept into the sagas: an ineradicable bloodstain on black boulders where the Khugiani killed many English; the alleged fact of the lone survivor of the massacre who escaped to tell the tale; the magical sanctity of the sacred tree at Seh Baba which the British could not fell. Still a substantial core of documentable fact underlay these traditions, and if they were tilted toward the Afghan side, so was the history written by British participants tilted toward Empire.[50]

The methods of the folklorist work equally well with Oral Traditional History and Oral Traditional Literature. And they should, for these are his provinces by right of his own tradition. He does not rigidly accept these scholastic categories. The folk epic contains its historical residue; the historical legend possesses its aesthetic quality. Alike they are fashioned by the oral process of patterning, accretion, stereotyping, repetition, variation, and kindred mechanisms. Oral process is the turf of the folklorist.

Sources
for the Traditional History
of the Scottish Highlands
and Western Islands

History as written by historians usually has little relation to the historical traditions orally preserved by a people. Such traditions are valuable in revealing what episodes of the past endure and what forms they take in popular memory unaided by the crutch of print and the catechism of the schoolmaster. They may also fill in gaps in historical records, although of course historical fact needs to be sifted from folklore tradition.

As an illustration of traditional history, we can look at the Gaelic-speaking Highlands and western islands of Scotland. Folklore and history visibly meet in this romanticized, lonely, and defeated country lying at the westernmost edge of Europe. From this area the great Campbell of Islay collected and published in 1860 his *Popular Tales of the West Highlands,* to be followed by another classic in Alexander Carmichael's *Carmina Gadelica,* a harvest of folk hymns, blessings, charms, and invocations. Historians have never known quite what to do with the feuding warrior culture of the Highlanders that reached its spirited climax in the seventeenth century, only to be crushed by the Hanoverian army at Culloden in 1746 and stamped out by the heartless clearances of the following century. If the history of Scotland is itself a problem, lumped in as it is with its glamorous southern neighbor, what can nationalist historians do with the Highland half of Scotland, set apart from the Lowlands by its clans and Gaelic tongue and tribal feudalism?

The Highlands appeal to the folklorist as a land of traditional culture. Active collectors at the University of Edinburgh's School of Scottish Studies have since 1951 been searching the Highlands and islands for every sort of tradition. They record their interviews on tape, chiefly in Gaelic, and list them in a catalogue to their folklore archives. From these entries I selected items bearing on historical events and personalities, and with the assistance of the School and a grant-in-aid from Indiana University, employed a Gaelic speaker on their staff to transcribe and translate them. This body of material amounts to some one hundred and fifty typed pages.

Also at the disposal of the historically minded folklorist is the handsomely published volume of nineteenth-century Highland local-history traditions, *The Dewar Manuscripts*, volume one, a part of the great collection project of Campbell of Islay that he acquired after his *Popular Tales of the West Highlands* but never published. Campbell's sympathies lay more with magic folktales than with realistic historical stories, although he encouraged the gamekeeper John Dewar to gather such traditions faithfully and employed another associate, the schoolmaster Hector MacLean, to translate them from the Gaelic. This important publication makes possible a comparison between Highland oral history recorded in the 1860s and 1870s with that recorded by the School in the 1950s and 1960s.

Several twentieth-century collections of traditional tales from Outer Isles include historical narratives. Notice should also be taken of a remarkable work by Hugh Miller on the traditional history of Cromarty in the north of Scotland. Three unconventional histories by John Prebble—*Culloden, The Highland Clearances,* and *Glencoe: The Story of the Massacre*—are written with color and dash and a desire to catch the spirit and sentiments of the Highland participants. Prebble is a novelist-turned-historian, who has applied his literary skill to crucial chapters in Highland annals, and most recently has climaxed these specialized works with a general history of Scotland, *Lion of the North.*

Field Texts in the School of Scottish Studies

Traditions of Bonny Prince Charlie

Eight recorded traditions from the archives of the School of Scottish Studies deal with Bonny Prince Charlie and his abortive attempt to lead a Highland army against the Royalist forces. Ever since the Young Pretender landed in the Hebrides from France in 1745 and sailed away the following year after his defeat at Culloden, the whole Highland country, from east coast to the west, has preserved memories of his visit. Here was an episode of high romantic tragedy to delight a novelist or scenario-writer. The '45 brought the Highlanders momentarily into the forefront of British, and even world history, and linked them with the physical presence, in glory and disaster, of the would-be monarch. Folk traditions do not offer any consecutive account of Charles Edward's involvement in the '45, and in their collected form often represent responses to interview questions by Calum MacLean, the late great collector and blithe spirit, who conducted many interviews in South Uist.

In the longest interview-recital, Duncan MacDonald of Peninerine in South Uist relates a series of incidents connected with the sojourn of Bonny Prince Charlie on the islands and mainland (SA 1951/6 B3).[1] The Pretender landed at Eriskay, visited an old friend of his father, MacDonald of Boisdale, who attempted to dissuade him from raising an army. "But the Prince just wanted to have a go at it." He then traveled to Arisaig where MacDonald of Kinlochmoidart raised his sword for him and other chiefs followed suit. "They called him always their own Prince, and they would go anywhere for him and fight for him till the last drop of their blood." When Charles Edward landed at Eriskay he brought with him seeds of flowers that bloom there yet and are known as the Prince's Mult or Muld. (It is actually the Convolvulus.)

Duncan MacDonald briefly switches from tradition to textbook patter. The Highland troops marched south halfway to London but, feeling themselves too far from home, turned back, defeating the Red Army twice in the retreat but finally succumbing at Culloden Moor. Back on home soil, the narrator finds a personal explanation for the defeat of his compatriots, in the treachery of Lord George Murray, who deliberately commenced the battle before all the clans were ready. Murray had requested and received as a bribe from the Royalist commander, the Duke of Cumberland, a full purse of money in return for arranging to lose the battle. When the Duke read Murray's letter he said, "Well, I like the letter, but I don't like the treachery, but you will get that." And he sent the money. Murray not only initiated the battle the day after receiving the money, when half the clans were scattered between Inverness and their own country, but he placed the MacDonalds on the left of his army, a demoralizing act, since Clan Donald has proudly held the right ever since Robert the Bruce had given them that place of honor for their bravery in the battle of Bannockburn in 1314. In their stead Murray placed their archrivals, the Camerons, who held the position for only half an hour, while the MacDonalds refused to fight at all. Hence Culloden was lost and the Prince became a fugitive.

Now the narrator turns to the chapter in folk history arousing most attention: the flight of the Prince through the hills and isles. From Inverness, Charles Edward crossed Badenoch and Glengarry and sought refuge in the west, in Moidart and Arisaig. But when the enemy began to close in he asked his supporters to get him to the Hebrides. After a stormy passage, in which they were battered by a northeast wind, they landed him at Benbecula. From there he made his way to other islands, but not receiving the respect in Lewis that he was tendered in the MacDonalds' country he came south again to Corrod-hale in South Uist, where the Prince's Cave can be seen, east of Howmore Post Office. There were actually two caves, on two sides of a river flowing into the sea, and one, unnamed, was underground; the Prince hid in both of them, being visited by various MacDonalds, including Lady MacDonald. There he was kept fairly comfortable, "until the Government's men of war began to fill up the Minch, and also the Government's army was in the country." A reward of thirty thousand pounds had been set on the Prince's head.

And to show you how well those poor Highlanders was on his side, a very brave Highlander one day—he was just like the Prince himself—and he just led the Redcoats to catch him and they fired at him and now he fell, and he began to shout, "Oho ho, you have killed your Prince. You have killed your Prince." Just to make the search easy for Prince Charles. And when they heard him, at once they took off his head, and went to London with it, and there was a pause in the search, at that time, until they made out it was not the head of the Prince.

Duncan MacDonald next turns to the episode especially appealing to lovers of romance, the appearance of Flora MacDonald as a comely aide to the Prince. At the behest of Lady MacDonald, Flora, a young girl living at Milton, obtained a passport from her stepfather, the commander of the government forces on Uist, ostensibly to enable her to visit her mother at Skye but actually to effect the Prince's escape. Flora took Charles Edward with her dressed as a maidservant, crossed the ford at Benbecula, showed her stepfather the passport, procured a boat at Roisnis, and made for Skye. After landing she took the Prince to Kingsburgh House where he was sheltered for a time. (Flora eventually married Allan of Kingsburgh.) From Skye the Prince reached the mainland and in "September or October" was able to embark for France. (He sailed on September 20.)

Duncan MacDonald's fairly lengthy account can be amplified at certain points by other recorded traditions. John Campbell of South Uist enlarges on the stay of the Prince at Eriskay (SA 1960/7 A5). Charles Edward landed there in a small two-oared boat. Although Eriskay was then completely uninhabited, somehow unassisted he erected a "large and beautiful stone building," obtaining stones which he dressed as beautifully as though the finest mason had worked on them. On the slope of the hill on which he built the house he planted many flowers that still grow; people took away the earth but the flowers would never grow anywhere else.

After some time the Prince began to move about, using the small boat he had carefully preserved. He sailed to Uist, finding it empty of people or highways, and went on to the north until he chanced on a cave in Ben More. To make a fire he struck flint against tall, stout, dry heather, and whatever he could catch he roasted on the fire. A woman called Flora of Airigh Mhuilinn, who lived at Gearrabhailteas, heard of "a man on the mountain and she pitied him greatly—who was he, and how did he live there?" She walked to Ben More and saw smoke coming from the cave. Inside she found Prince Charles, clothed in rags, singeing a lamb. She spoke to him for a while, then returned home and, saying nothing to anyone, returned to the cave with a dress of her own which she made him wear. Then they wandered "hither and thither on the shore" until they spied a small boat with two oars. "Well," said she, "we have had a good chance of running away from here with this boat, wherever we shall land." Eventually they landed at Uig in Skye, also at that time a very bare place. They wandered on until they encountered some natives, who proved very kind and friendly.

The outcome was that they began to hold parties there and these two ladies always went to the ball. But one man was slightly bolder than the rest and he began to say, "That's not a woman," said he, "it's a man, and there was never a woman as good-looking as that man."

"O no!" "No!" "No!"

"But I tell you it is. But the plan will be that we'll have a ball, and all will be gathered there. They'll be there in any case, and we'll get apples, the plan being that we shall throw them to each other. And the lady always, when you throw her something, will spread out her skirt to catch it. The man, on the other hand, tightens his legs together."

There was nothing for it, but the ball went ahead and the song progressed and the dance and at last the time came for them to take [refreshments?]. They had the apples, at least. They began to pitch them to each other. Oh, each one of the ladies would spread out her skirt and catch hold of the apples. When it reached him, however, he put his legs together.

"Well, well," said the man, "I told you so."

Then they realized that they were caught.

Nevertheless, the natives still treated Flora and the Prince generously.

Flora died on Skye and was buried in a cemetery called Kilmaluag. Like the Prince she was a Catholic. John had himself seen the big gray stone with a cross carved on it placed at her head. When sailing past the shore in a fishery cruiser, a lad from Skye pointed it out to him, saying that on a bad night the cross had broken off and the people had tried in vain to tie the pieces together with pins and ropes.

In this last account "prince Charlie" has become a kind of amorous Robinson Crusoe. The incident of a man being discovered in woman's dress when he closes his legs together to catch an object in his skirt also appears in *Huckleberry Finn* (motif H1578.1.4.1, "Woman throws apple to man in woman's dress"). Precise historical details, such as Flora's obtaining a passport from her father-in-law in the previous text, fade into an empty never-never land.

The half-dozen other transcriptions dealing with Prince Charlie are more fragmentary but supply further details. Donald MacMillan of South Glendale in South Uist (SA 1953/37 A10) had seen the house in which the Prince resided for three days, "a big thatched house about fifty feet in length." MacMillan criticized the plays that depicted Charles Edward's experiences in the middle of Scotland but did not dwell on the first six or seven months he spent in the islands. He emphasized how, on landing on Eriskay, the Prince took a seed out of his pocket and threw it on the ground, where the flower can still be plucked in July and August, but will not grow elsewhere. The people of Eriskay called the small yellow flower the Prince's Flower, and the place where it grew the Prince's Bay (Coilleag a' Phrionnsa). Around the patch of white, sandy soil where the Prince had come ashore the people built a kind of wall as a memorial. "And though you would take a large sod of six feet with a spade, put it on a barrow and take it to any part of the island, even, never mind any other country, the flower won't grow anywhere in the world except where it grows out of the ground, by itself."

Some traditions contain forebodings. A curious little episode is recounted by Hugh MacKenzie (SA 1958/81 B6). When the Prince first came ashore on Eriskay, a woman named Isabel MacKay met him with a drink of milk. As he drank the milk, he thought of a warning he had been given, that he would not succeed in his venture if he did not kill the first woman he met. "Oh, I cannot kill that woman," he said, and let her go.

In another anecdote, the Duke of Argyll, a supporter of the realm, offers to change his allegiance if the Prince will change his Catholic faith. According to Duncan Campbell of Oban in Argyllshire, the red-haired Duke said to Charles Edward, "If you walk through the Established Church, with our Bible in your hand, I shall crown you king of Scotland without a blow [being struck] or a shot [being fired]." When the Prince answered "No," the Duke rejoined, "Well, so long as this red head stays on this pale body, you will not be king of Scotland."

Legendary accretions are readily perceived in these recitals of the Prince's wanderings in the isles: the magic flower, the disguise in woman's dress, the self-sacrifice of the soldier who resembled the Prince, and the romance with Flora. These traditions form the main source of knowledge of the Prince's whereabouts after Culloden until he embarked for France never to return.

TRADITIONS OF CULLODEN

The fateful battle of Culloden too has generated its share of traditions, dealing with lucky escapes, savage blows, and sadistic deeds on the part of the Duke of Cumberland. Even in a one-day visit to Inverness and the battlefield of Culloden, I heard traditional stories from my companion and guide, Iain "Rory" MacKay, whose family on both sides had participated at Culloden. In one anecdote, Willie Chisholm, standard-bearer to the Chisholm clan, went hunting the day of the battle and brought home a deer, reaching Culloden Moor the same day.

The most dramatic example in the archives of the School of Scottish Studies of a folktale becoming enmeshed with the '45 is the following account, given in full, of the escape of the Laird of Bernera from Culloden (translation of Gaelic story by Angus MacLellan, Benbecula, on microfilm, as transcribed by Calum I. MacLean; Irish Folklore Commission MS. 1031, pp. 426-429). The island of Bernera can be dimly seen from the east shore of North Uist and is still inhabited by about two hundred people.

As was the case with many others who rallied with the Stuarts to the Prince's cause, the Laird of Bernera was one of the stalwarts, but he managed to flee with his life from Culloden, and it is said that he was magically protected. Bullets pelted him. He threw off his topcoat to make himself lighter, and they say that the coat which he threw off—whether it was big or small —was riddled with bullets, but none of them ever penetrated to his skin. He separated from the others and was coming down—he fled, making for Lochiel [Cameron] country. Night was closing in on him when he noticed a few Hanoverian soldiers in front of him on the road. He didn't know how on earth to get near them, but the group of them left, leaving one, as if to watch. The laird got up to him and killed him. He noticed that the Englishman was wearing a fine pair of boots and tried to pull them off, but come off they would not. Eventually he said he wasn't going to be thwarted in this business, and he cut the man's legs off at the knees, taking with him the legs and the boots.

Then he arrived at a farmer's house, and complained to the woman that he was a fugitive—would she be able to accommodate him? She said to him that the times were dangerous, but that she would do her best, as she did. She hid him in a bundle of straw in the byre. However, I believe the Laird of Bernera's pursuers caught up with him, and what he did was to flee before they got up in the morning. Because the troopers were around when he got up, and he forgot the boots, when the lady of the house got up in the morning and went to the byre, she saw these feet sticking out from around the lintel. She was curious about it and pulled them out. "Oh! Good gracious!" she said. "The cow must have eaten the fellow who was here." And then at last they realized what had happened. They surmised that the Laird of Bernera had left them behind.

The Laird of Bernera got along, reaching Bernera in safety. His name was Donald Campbell. That man, when the Prince was in Bernera on his way to Lewis to find a boat, made him as comfortable as possible in order to save his life, and it's not all that long since a great grandson of his died in Bernera—of this Donald Campbell.

The unfortunate Prince failed to get a boat in Stornoway. He wasn't allowed to get it, because there was a minister in Benbecula who found out that the Prince had left Benbecula with a crew to procure a vessel in Lewis. That minister, a MacAulay, sent word to his father that the Prince had left, and to catch him, because of his faith. But they did not catch him.

Anyway, they were MacAulays, ancestors of Lord MacAulay, a great writer of ours some time ago.

In spite of the factual detail of personal and place names, this incident is an example of type 1281A, "Getting Rid of the Man-eating Calf," known in northern and eastern Europe and carried to North America.[2]

TRADITIONS OF THE GLENCOE MASSACRE
Another event burned deeply in Highland folk memory is the

Glencoe massacre of February 13, 1692. In the words of Donald MacEachan of Arisaig (SA 1954/39.3): "it was said of the Campbells that they came feasting and fasting [sic] and being entertained with the MacDonalds, and that they allowed the MacDonalds to go to sleep, while they themselves stayed up for the massacre. That was how the story went. These people still exist and they keep up their spite for each other . . . They say that Campbell of Glenlyon . . . was the king's agent."

The bitter memories that still set off MacDonalds and Campbells came to view in a boisterous recording session Calum MacLean conducted with Angus MacKay, who strongly criticized the MacDonalds.

I'll say, according to my knowledge of history and to what I heard they used to abuse the Campbells, but I think the Campbells were better than themselves . . . because the MacDonalds were just thieves and murderers. And how much land do they hold today that Clanranald got? What does the Duke of Atholl have today that he got apart from by theft? And all you dukes in Scotland today? Isn't the Duke of Argyll one of them? He wouldn't fight, on any account, on the side of the precious Prince we were to have in Scotland, Prince Charlie. He refused, and opposed him. There now, another of the bad varlets, and plenty of them . . . .

Calum MacLean: But they said about the massacre of Glencoe, that the Campbells they did that, didn't they?"

Angus MacKay: Yes. And they well deserved it! They well deserved it! Didn't the MacDonalds do the same to themselves? Did they not catch them there, out there in some port or other, on the shore! And they killed every single Campbell there on the shore—no, every single MacDonald. [In his ire the speaker confuses the clans.]

Oh, the Campbells are always being abused. I won't abuse them.

Female voice (Mrs. MacKay?): But I won't have the MacDonalds abused at all. My mother was one, and I don't care. But "while there's a twig in the forest, there'll be treachery in a Campbell" [shouting].

Angus MacKay [interrupting]: I don't care what your mother was, or your father, but I'm just telling you the truth. I don't care what you were, or what you are.

This family shouting match bears noisy witness to the vitality of traditional history.

A circumstantial account of the Glencoe massacre is given by John Alexander Stewart Wilson (SA 1959/59 A2,3), as he recalls hearing it when a small lad from Mrs. Donald Vancy, the former Christine

Cameron. As he retells her version, the Campbell regiment of the 21st Royal Scots Fusiliers came from the "Black Fort of Inverlochy" (Fort William), from Blair MacFaoileach, in by Mamore and down the Gairbhleas into Glencoe. Captain Campbell of Glenlyon was sent to command them, since his brother's daughter was married to a MacDonald (John) of Glencoe, and his presence would disarm any suspicions of the MacDonalds. The soldiers were received with hospitality and given the best of food and drink inside the house. Each soldier had been put on oath that he would tell nothing of the plot to any man or woman in the glen. But one soldier, a Campbell, felt a twinge of conscience and asked a young MacDonald to go for a walk with him, on the night of February 13, 1692. The two went down the glen, past the Oir-Fhiodhain, and stood before the big stone, since known as the Soldier's Stone in the Glen. Turning to the stone, the soldier said: "Great stone in the Glen, though you have every right to be there, if you knew what was to happen tonight you would not stay there on any account." The soldier's companion immediately understood the message, and ran back to the house to inform the people inside. They fled, but the massacre had already begun. The MacDonalds who escaped made for Ballachulish where the Stuarts of Ballachulish and the Stewarts of Appin brought them relief.

Mrs. Vancy added another episode concerning a decree of Glenlyon that the soldiers should leave no man or boy alive. The soldiers examined every cave. A sublieutenant hearing a noise said to a soldier standing by, "That's a child's cry over there, and it's not a girl at all, it's a boy. Go up and kill him." The soldier went up and found a MacDonald woman in there with a child at her breast, a wee boy, and a small dog, a terrier, at her feet. He told her his orders and she said, "Save my child. Think of yourself when you were a lad." The soldier plunged his sword into the dog and took the bloody sword to his officer as proof of the killing.

Years afterward, the soldier, having left the army, was on a journey, and he came in to Stoirm of Appin, where there was an inn, and he went inside. And they were saying to him, "You're a soldier?"

"Yes," he said, "I've roamed a good part of the world and I've seen a lot," he said.

"And what's the strangest thing you've ever seen, or the saddest thing you've come across?"

"Well," he said, "the saddest thing I ever encountered was the Massacre of Glencoe."

The innkeeper said, "Were you there?"

"Yes," he said, "I was there." And while he was speaking two men left the table and went outside the house.

"Did anything happen when you were there?"

"Yes," he said, "I did something that I keep remembering. I saved a child's life," he said. And he told the story of how he saved the life of that woman's baby and how he killed the terrier. The man at once leapt across the table and extended his hand. "I am that child," he said, "and you may stay with me as long as you live."

That's how the lady told me the story. [A good variant by John Finlayson has also been recorded (SA 1958/168 B1).]

In this full version two prominent folklore themes are evident: the warning verse recited by the shamed conspirator, a verse that varies in each telling; and the male child saved from death through the killing of a substituted animal. This last incident is motif K512.1.1, "Compassionate executioner: bloody knife (sword) from slain animal substitute."

Calum MacLean elicited from John Wilson other traditions associated with the Glencoe massacre (SA 1959/59 A4,6). He recalled the former site of the village in the middle of the glen whose ruins he had often passed, and the big stone on the left-hand side called the Signal Rock, since a gun had been fired from it the night the massacre began. "You see it mentioned in the story written by Robert Louis Stevenson, when Alan Breck, he and Davie Balfour were there." Wilson, who was a Stewart of Appin, further said that a great secret "was told from father to son, 'handed down' as the Lowland tongue puts it," as to who actually killed Campbell of Glure. The gun that was supposed to have killed him, called "the black gun of misfortune" (*gunna dubh a' mhì-fhortain*) was to be seen in Ballachulish house for a number of years. James of the Glen was hanged for the murder, but the true murderer was said to be a Stuart of Ballachulish. The place where the gibbet was erected has since been known as Poll na Give, "The Gibbet Bog."

Wilson also told of meeting Angus MacDonald in Glasgow, who laid a wreath at the base of the memorial in the Glen every year (SA 1959/59 B2).

He had just come off the train and we went in to an hotel to have a drink and I said, "Angus, how are things going in Glencoe?"

"Oh John," said he, "pretty badly."

"How's that?"

"Do you know that something has happened in Glencoe," he said, "the like of which hasn't occurred since the massacre!"

I said, "What was that?"

"A Campbell has been born in the Glen," he said.

"How was that?" I said.

"Well," he said, "one of the girls in the Glen"—and he named the girl, she was a MacDonald—"went to Edinburgh to work. She married a Campbell and he came home to Glencoe and got a job in Ballachulish store. They lived in Glencoe and they had a son, up in Glencoe, and so," he said, "a Campbell has come to the world in Glencoe."

Narrator Wilson knew too, about the removal of the corpse from the gibbet by a simple-minded fellow named MacPhee, who was able to mix with the soldiers guarding the body. While they were having a dram at the inn, he sneaked the corpse away, threw the gibbet into the bog, and carried the body to the waiting Stewarts who took it to Appin. A further detail is given by an unnamed informant from Ballachulish or Glencoe (SA 1959/112 A3). The hole would never fill in where the gibbet had been set and no grass would grow on the spot. People said it was because the executed man was innocent. "But I saw it myself too, and I often went to see it, and there was no grass at all around, just black earth." The Stuart Society set up a monument in the very hole where the gibbet had stood (cf. motif E422.1.11.5.1, "Ineradicable bloodstain after blood tragedy").

One folk teller after another recounts the tradition of Henry's Stone (Clach Eanruig), the warning and the saving of the child from murder, and the hanging of the innocent man. Texts of the warnings follow:

> Grey stone in the Glen,
> If you knew tonight what was to happen
> You would not be there at all.
> (Duncan Campbell, SA 1953/77 B6)

> If you knew what was to happen this night,
> You would not be here.
> (Duncan MacInnes, SA 1958/82 B7)

> If you knew what was to happen tonight,
> You wouldn't stay here.
> (Sandy Livingstone, SA 1958/81 B8)

You'd better arise.
I arose early
And you certainly needed that.
Women of this glen,
You'd better arise.

(John Finlayson, SA 1958/162 A5)

In Finlayson's telling, the warning is given as a verse played by the piper of the Campbells, actually a MacDonald. A warning verse is also played by a piper in a separate tradition given below, concerning Alasdair MacColl.

Coll, my friend,
Avoid the fort
I am caught.

(Charles MacInnes, SA 1953/110 A4)

The accompanying narrative is fragmentary but explains that MacColl's sail would take three wrong turns when he reached Gocamgo Mill near a fort.

Other narrations amplify episodes of the massacre and its aftermath. According to John MacDonald of Spean Bridge (SA 1953/255), one of the Stewarts of Appin killed Colin of Glenure in 1752 and wished to go to court in Fort William to confess when an innocent man was brought to trial. But other Stewarts locked him in a room and the innocent man was hung at Ballachulish Ferry.

The recorded historical facts of the Glencoe massacre are wilder and grimmer than any legend. Beginning the chain of events, the aged chief of the MacDonald clan, MacIain, swallowed his pride and made a desperate march with his gillies to sign the oath of allegiance to King William of Orange, missing the January 1, 1692, deadline by six days. His delay was in part caused by the absence of the sheriff of Argyll from Inveraray over the holidays. The sheriff finally administered the oath, but a thin line was drawn by enemies through MacIain's name on the list of oath-takers sent to the King in London. Plotters arranged for the extirpation of the marauding clan MacDonald. A wastrel heavily in debt, Robert Campbell of Glenlyon, who had a niece living in Glencoe, was commissioned captain of the Earl of Argyll's Regiment of Foot and instructed to dispatch the MacDonalds. MacIain received him hospitably in the best Highland tradition, quartered his troops throughout the homes in the Glen, and entertained them with food and drink and games, believing all the while that his clan now lay under the protection of the Crown. After thirteen days of comradeship, the King's soldiers, chiefly Campbells, the ancient foe of the MacDonalds, rose against their host at five A.M., shooting MacIain in the back as he was putting on his trews, slaughtering men in the beds or shooting them on dung-heaps, killing some of the women and children and driving others half-naked into the bitter snow and cold. Thirty-eight MacDonalds died in the massacre, but Glenlyon proved less than an expert butcher for most lived to tell the tale—and MacDonalds tell it to the present day.

In *Glencoe: The Story of the Massacre*, Prebble employs oral traditions in greater variety than those I secured from the School of Scottish Studies. For the warning he presents four variations. One was uttered to a child by a Campbell soldier as they watched a game of shinty between the Argyll men and the MacDonalds at MacHenry's [sic] Stone: "Great stone of the glen! Great is your right to be here, but if you knew what will happen this night you would be up and away." A soldier quartered with a family that had treated him well thus addressed their dog, "Grey dog, if I were you grey dog, my bed tonight would be the heather." Another soldier living at the Robertson cottage plucked at a plaid. "This is a good plaid. Were this good plaid mine, I would put it on and go out into the night to look after my cattle. Were this good plaid mine, I would put it on my shoulders and I would take my family out to drive my cattle to a safe place." Also Prebble cites the report that Glenlyon's piper, Hugh Mackenzie, stood on MacHenry's Stone and played "Women of the Glen" in warning.

Prebble discounts as "absurd" the stories of the Glencoe people that the soldiers knew in advance of the massacre, and surmises that one soldier may have guessed at or overheard the order being relayed to his sergeant. Still the tradition of the warning reveals sympathy of the MacDonalds for one of their enemies, a point that strengthens its probability. The fact that the massacre fell far short of total destruction suggests that the news may have leaked out. In another place Prebble supports the view that at the last moment some of the soldiers drew back from the impending slaughter. "Confused and contradictory though the legends became, they do record the truth that some of the Argyll men were revolted by the orders given them, and that within the oath of obedience they had taken they attempted to warn the people."[3]

As another example of the soldiers' clemency, Prebble also gives the incident of the soldier who kills a dog to save the crying child, but with an added twist. The officer who had sent the soldier to dispatch the child recognizes that the blood on the sword is not human blood and sends the soldier back. "Kill the child, or I'll kill you." Thereupon the soldier cuts off the little finger of the child's hand and covers his sword with the blood. Many years later when the ex-soldier stopped at a cottage in Appin, he mentioned having taken part in the massacre of Glencoe. His host resolved to kill him in the morning. But at breakfast the guest told the incident of the child, and his host held up a hand with a little finger missing.

Still another vein of folklore incorporated by Prebble into his stirring history is the oral poetry of the bard Murdoch Matheson. A guest of MacIain and a survivor of the slaughter, Matheson composed a powerful lament on the tragedy, first printed in 1776. "Given equal odds between them and the Lowland band, the feathered birds of the mountains would have screamed from their enemies' corpses."[4]

Other Historical Traditions

Besides the '45 and the Glencoe Massacre, Highlanders and Hebrideans dwell on other historical events and figures known to them through folk remembrance. Deeds of Rob Roy are recalled. Soldiers have surrounded him; he asks them, before he surrenders, to place their hands in a log he has cleft with a wedge, that he may give the wood to his wife for burning. Then he withdraws the wedge, trapping them. After he releases them, they leave him in peace (Angus MacLellan, South Uist, SA 1959/57 B2). This same trick (type 38, "Claw in Split Tree," motifs K551.29* and K1111) is told on American frontier heroes. Rob Roy also pays the rent for a poor widow and then steals the money back from the collector (MacLellan, SA 1959/56 B1), in the same fashion as Jesse James. The story about Robert the Bruce taking heart and renewing his fight after he sees a spider complete his web in a cave on the fourth attempt lives on orally.

A surprising number of traditions concern the ninth-century invasion of the Norsemen, or Norwegians, and sites of battles fought with the clans. One informant remarked, "None of us are against the Norsemen. We would prefer Norsemen to Englishmen." One legend, "How the Caledonian Forest Was Burnt," has become a magical fiction (Miss Munro, Laide, SA 1955/164 B7). The king of Norway wanted to burn the forests of Scotland. His daughter volunteered, telling him to find a witch to turn her into a bird. As a white bird she flew to Scotland and set the trees on fire with a wand she carried under her wing. She turned black from the pine soot and was called Dubh a' Ghiuthais, "The Black of Pine." Finally the farmers lured her to earth by separating baby animals from their mothers. When the bird heard their cries, she flew down to protect them and the farmers shot her. The king sent a ship to fetch her body, but a storm arose every time the crew sought to embark. Finally the princess was buried at Little Loch, where a place is named for her (see motifs A2218.3, "Animal who steals fire scorched: cause of his color"; G211.4, "Witch in form of bird: unspecified"; K2351.1, "Sparrows of Cirencester").

In these instances folklore has fairly eclipsed history, but other, less fanciful accounts in the archives redress the balance.

The Dewar Manuscripts

Turning from twentieth- to nineteenth-century collectors of Scottish historical traditions, we encounter much firmer and fuller materials, only recently made available in a work of unique importance, *The Dewar Manuscripts.*[5] These English texts form an extraordinary body of traditional history. They present in depth and close detail a picture of the cattle-raiding, feuding, warlike clans and lairds of the Highland society finally destroyed at Culloden. Some historical references, such as the battles of the '45 and allusions to the American Revolution and the fighting in Flanders, give a sense of anchorage, but for the most part the raids and fights, pursuits and escapes, killings and reprisals, take place in glens, lochs, and castles remote from the central stage of history. Dates are almost never given, but personal names and genealogies of the actors and place name stories of the stones, braes, hills, and ponds adorn every narrative.

The '45 recitals vary in length from a few hundred to thirteen thousand words. All are clearly intended to describe reality. Because the stories are presented in so straightforward a manner, in clear contrast to the style and supernatural characters of magic tales, their folklore content is not immediately evident. Some feats of strength and acts of brutality inspire awe, but they do not involve gods or demons. Always on the lookout for recurrent tale types and motifs, the folklorist will recognize incidents he has seen before. An account of MacMillan of Glencannel tells of his visiting the homes of his three daughters to determine which was keeping Christmas best (p. 261). At the house of the first, the roast smelled so appetizing that he did not feel the need to venture inside. At the second, husband and wife were in bed as if it were any other day and the hens had scattered the ashes of the fireplace all over the house. At the third house the son-in-law was giving hay to the beasts, but the daughter was abed and the fire unkindled. MacMillan took his Christmas with his first daughter and left his land to her and her husband, Gille-bràigh. (In the first episode MacMillan had fought with Gille-bràigh when he found him secretly consorting with his daughter.) This decision recalls the folktale identified as type 1452, "Bride Test," one of Grimms' *Household Tales*. Two examples from the Pennsylvania Dutch are given in my *Buying the Wind* (pp. 146-148), dealing with the selection of a wife and of a servant by testing three persons. The test for the prospective wife is how well she scrapes her kneading trough and for the servant whether he removes a stone from his shoe before plowing.

On the whole, heroic saga rather than popular folktale seems to have left its mark on Highland traditions. The clan society that reached its height in the seventeenth century exhibits all the characteristics defined by the Chadwicks in their analysis of the Heroic Age. Here is the warring, cattle-raiding, pre-urban culture of which they write. Bards compose songs and laments in praise of their chieftains and of memorable frays; clansmen recite deeds of renowned warriors. When the Duke of Atholl requested Ewen Cameron of Lochiel to meet him alone to discuss their disputed claims to Aird-raineach, Lochiel insisted that his piper accompany him. "Whatever be the affair to which I go, I like always to have someone with me, to listen to what is said that he may remember it and remind me of it again" (p. 89). Besides the piper, who functioned as an oral poet-historian, individual raiders also recalled and related chronicles of their clans. "Gillespie MacCombie" concludes with a passage describing the reliance of the Highlanders on oral knowledge:

When Gillespie MacCombie was young, it was the custom of the people of the country when the long winter nights came, to go to one another's houses and pass the time singing songs and telling stories. Before the year 1800 there was many a one of the Highlanders who could tell the names of his ancestors for many generations back. Also, although they could neither read nor write, they took note of the time, and he who did not always learn the day of the month and the age of the moon, was considered a man void of intelligence. The people who were of old would tell when the new moon would come, when it would be full or in the quarter, as well as though they had an almanac. They trusted much to their memory and when anything remarkable happened, they had a proverb to illustrate it. Gillespie MacCombie remembered many of the stories which he had heard in his youth (p. 259).

This kind of society, paying tribute to the highborn fighting man and dependent on verbal arts, fulfills the precise conditions set forth by the Chadwicks for the formation of heroic legend and saga, and *The Dewar Manuscripts* lives up to expectations. Many of the narratives describe astounding acts of strength, bravery, and heroism performed by prodigious swordsmen and archers. For instance, "Big Auchry was the bravest man and best swordsman in the whole country." Hence the Macfies of Colonsay sought to ambush him, since they came often to Argyll to "lift a prey" and knew that, clad in helmet and shirt of mail, he could dispatch them one after another. To avoid being taken by surprise, Auchry moved from his own house at Baile-ghuirgean to a bothy inside a bank, with a large stone by the door, and took with him his little dog, which he taught not to bark but to scratch his master behind the ear when he saw someone coming. "Someone that was not faithful to Big Auchry informed the Macfies of Auchry's hiding place at Druimban." Three boatloads of Macfies landed at night at the Port of Peats as if they were coming for peat, and they marched in two bands against Auchry, the smaller in advance, knowing that he would scorn to flee from a small band.

The day was hot when they reached Druimban and Auchry's dog was lying at the door of the bothy asleep. He did not observe the Macfies until they were close to him, and he had only time to bark and squeal once, before they killed him. Big Auchry came out and put his back to the large stone at the end of the bothy. There he defended himself with his sword in the best way he could. They surrounded him but he killed them as they closed with him. The chief of the Macfies cried—"Let some strike him above and others in the hams." But before they managed to do this he killed nine of them. At last one of the Macfies succeeded in striking him in the ankle. He was now wounded and another struck him at the knee. He then fell on his knee, but he killed four more of the Macfies before they killed him. When the chief of the Macfies saw Auchry Mor Malcolm lying dead, he said—"It was a great loss and ill deserved that Auchry Mor was a Malcolm. Were he a Macfie, what a champion!" (p. 61).

The death of Big Auchry follows closely the pattern of the hero's fate analyzed by the Chadwicks. Although the greatest warrior of his land, the mighty hero is mortal and must die. It is fitting that he die in battle rather than in bed, but who can kill the champion? Only an army, or a traitor striking from behind. Auchry's death particularly resembles the doom of Grettir the Strong in Icelandic saga. Grettir, also a celebrated fighting man, had similarly retreated to a hideaway in a cave atop an isle, accessible only by a ladder. A faithless thrall left suspended the ladder leading up to the cave. Even though lamed by an axe-stroke that glanced off an enchanted log, Grettir fought the host that surrounded him in his hut, until fatally struck from behind when blinded by two halves of a foe he had severed falling on him. The betrayal, crushing odds, wounding in the knee, and withal the carnage wrought by the champion facing the foe in his retreat, link Grettir and Big Auchry. But other heroes, from Achilles to Davy Crockett, are slain in similar fashion.

One of the longest narratives sets forth adventures of "Big Malcolm MacIlvain" of the clan Ilvain in Strath Eck, "renowned for his strength and exploits, and for being an excellent swordsman" (p. 125). Among his feats Malcolm fights a black bull in Lock Eck and cuts off its ears. He wrestles and fells the notorious robber Nial na Gainne, and then asks the Earl of Argyll to set him free, offering to stand security that Nial will rob no more. He steals another man's wife and conceals her for seven years in a cave that he blocks with a stone seven men can not lift. Caught in a bog by a band of pursuers, he fights them off until his sword breaks, then defends himself with a piece of the sword until he has sunk to his hips, and kills the commander of his enemies with a blow on the forehead with the fragment of sword. Captured and imprisoned, he escapes with a key his sister makes for him from an impression of the jailer's key she obtained in barley dough; he lowers himself down a rope blanket and walks to a waiting boat, carrying seven stones of iron on him, each weighing twenty and a half pounds. In a subsequent episode he toys with and finally slays a champion Irish swordsman at Skipness. In his old age, dirty, ragged, and bearded, Malcolm still throws strength-stones further than any of a group of caterans (cattle thieves) and by felling their captain seizes their cattle spoil.

While the heroic death by treachery or against tremendous odds is not present here, most of the episodes in heroic saga make their appearance: the single combats with beasts and men, with the hero always victorious; the lifting of enormous weights; the code of chivalry. Tales were also told about Big Malcolm's grandson, Big John, who squeezed an arrogant fencer by the hand so hard the blood squirted from his finger tips and then threw him out of a window; as an old man Big John wrestled his son and a servant to the ground, lifted them one under each arm, and tied them back to back with a horse's halter (p. 143).

A number of strong-hero motifs can be identified in the saga of Big Auchry, under the general category F610, "Remarkably strong man." They include F624, "Mighty lifter"; F624.0.1, "Strong man slays monster"; F628.2, "Strong man throws enormous stone"; F639.9, "Strong man crushes ribs of person he embraces."

One hero-tale of a single combat takes place on the battlefield of Culloden and involves well-known historical personalities. The day after the battle the victorious Duke of Cumberland, along with Generals Wolfe and John Campbell of Mamore, who commanded the Highland regiments on the King's side, was examining his prisoners in their pens. The Duke paused to sneer at fifteen Highland lads and the Prince who would use them for soldiers. General John Campbell spoke up for his countrymen, even though he had fought against them, and concluded a wager with the Duke: to buy him fifteen bottles of wine if one Highlander lost in a duel with a picked English swordsman, while the prisoners would all go free if the Highlander won. An accomplished English fencer was picked, who bragged he would take the prisoners on one after the other. Each of the Highlanders volunteered, including Fierce John who had lost a hand and was staunching the blood with a sword heated in a fire and held in his good hand. In the end, the brother of Fierce John was chosen and brought against the English champion. "They did not resemble each other in appearance. The Englishman was a big, stalwart man and seemingly very strong. The Highlander was but a chip of a slender, sallow stripling, very bare of flesh, but tough and brawny, and slightly under middle size" (p. 235). At first the Highlander only defended himself, but when urged on by General Campbell, speedily dispatched the Englishman. "Go home now," said Campbell to him, "and thank your mother, because she gave you such good milk." In wrath, Cumberland ordered all other prisoners and all the wounded found on the battlefield to be put to death.

Documentary support does not appear for this gripping scene, which follows an honored tradition of single combats harking back to David and Goliath. But the narrative reveals known Highland attitudes and sentiments: the bonds among the clansmen, both within their own clan and for fellow Highlanders even when divided by war; the hatred for the bloody Duke of Cumberland; and pride in Highland valor.

Besides heroic saga, another vein of folklore permeates *The Dewar Manuscripts* in the form of supernatural belief. Key junctures in the narratives turn on prophecies, dreams, and warnings from witches and the second-sighted. "The laird of Glendariel dreamed that he looked at his hand and that his small finger had taken the place of his thumb" (p. 67). An old woman who could foretell the future explained this as a sign that his youngest son would be laird in place of the oldest. The laird was angry, since he had five sons, and he disputed the woman. But so it happened, and the speaker recounts how the older brothers died without legitimate heirs, and the despised youngest son became laird of Glendariel.

When the Campbells marched against the Lamonts, a raven croaked thrice, and Mannach of the Big Boots cried, "Ha! Ha! Boys! That is a good sign! You shall draw blood before you return!" (p. 76). The Campbells secured the high ground and drove the Lamonts into the sea, where those first in the boats left their kinsmen behind to drown or be destroyed.

Few clans were as loving among themselves as Clan Nail who once possessed Strath Eck. One day they went fishing together on the river Echaig, nine nines in number, and a stranger woman passing by remarked to a forester, "If there are many of them fishing on the river today, there will not be so many of them tomorrow. You will not see so many of Clan Nail together fishing on the river Echaig again" (p. 122). The woman went away and when the forester looked again at Strath Eck he saw Clan Nail madly fighting one another. An eldest brother attacked his youngest brother with a sword, because his wife had falsely accused the youngest brother of attempting to violate her. Those nearby ran to the aid of one or the other person, and in the end the fishing party turned into a slaughter from which Clan Nail never recovered. So the proverb is confirmed, "There is no forest without withered branches."

When Ewen Cameron of Lochiel set out to meet the Duke of Atholl to discuss disputed land, an old hag named Gormla, known as a witch, met him on the way. Lochiel cursed her as a bad omen, until she advised him not to meet the Duke alone but to return for his men and hide them behind a hill within call. He heeded her advice, and wisely, for Atholl had secretly brought his own men, whom Lochiel was able to defeat. Thereafter he esteemed Gormla (pp. 89-91). So too did the "One-Eyed Ferryman," Archibald MacInnes, credited with the second sight, warn Colin of Glenure not to go home by the side of Loch Leven. Colin did not take his advice and was fatally ambushed (p. 203).

A ludicrous episode in a lengthy narrative about Big Archibald MacPhail shows the strong hero cowed by a spirit. Big Archibald of Glencoe was strong and fearless, an expert swordsman and a successful cattle-lifter, but he had his foolish side. Once going to Ballachulish he met a Lowland gentleman with a gun on his shoulder, whom he saluted in Gaelic with "God's blessing to you, Sir." When the gentleman, knowing no Gaelic, replied "This is a fine day," Archibald slew him for despising the word of God and took his gun, shoes, and a gold guinea he found in his pocket. But he missed sixty gold guineas later found by men of the laird of Ballachulish. Ever after Big Archibald was afraid of meeting the spirit of this gentleman. He did not fear Highland spirits, because he could converse with them. One night he went to see his son in Glen Creran and at the top of a pass met a soldier's wife who had lost her way and was smoking a pipe while resting. Never having seen a pipe-smoker, Big Archibald was taken aback, especially when the woman puffed smoke out of her mouth. She spoke to him in English, and he exclaimed, "O! God of the Elements! have I met a Lowland spirit?" He turned and fled, but the soldier's wife followed him hoping he would lead her to a house. Big Archibald ran to his daughter's house with all the breath out of him, crying that a Lowland spirit was pursuing him. When he learned that she was a real woman he pulled out his dirk and would have killed her if not prevented.

While the spirit in this narration proved to be a living person, Big Archibald's belief in the reality of spirits could not be more convincingly illustrated. In a note (p. 362), the editor, John MacKechnie, emphasizes the Highlander's dread of meeting a spirit unable to converse with him in Gaelic. MacKechnie gives a "well-authenticated" tale of a highly respectable, elderly lady on her way home from a religious affair, encountering a stranger who talked with her in Gaelic, chiefly about the Jacobites. At the end of their walk he said that she seemed apprehensive of the road, and she replied she was indeed apprehensive, since Alasdair MacMhaighstir Alasdair, a wild sort of man, used to live there. The stranger introduced himself as Alasdair and vanished. For the whole two-mile walk the lady had felt no fear or uneasiness and was struck only by the musical quality of her companion's Gaelic. Alasdair was the famous Gaelic poet and "poet laureate" to Prince Charles.

Belief in spirits also appears in the narrative "Sir Neil Campbell's Promise." While in Holland, Sir Neil had promised a brave soldier to care for his wife and family should he be slain. The soldier was killed in battle with the French but Sir Neil forgot his promise. One night the shade of the soldier appeared to Sir Neil and said, "I do not find rest in the grave; the cries of my wife and family reach me there. Remember your promise." Sir Neil did thereafter take care of the widow and her children. The narrator concludes: "It is difficult to believe this story, but many of the people of Cowal believe it to be true" (p. 81; cf. motif E363, "Ghost returns to aid living"). Curiously, this is the only instance in the volume where the narrator is described. "From Mr. Archibald MacLean, Glaic near South Hall. He is an old man of eighty-five years of age, and can tell a tale punctually, without stopping or hesitating. He lives in an old-fashioned house, with a Lothian brace in the kitchen instead of a vent, which lets the heat of a fire out through the house better than a vent does."

The idea of weapons becoming accursed appears in the story of "Donald Stewart" (No. 32). An altercation had arisen between Donald, who had shot a deer at a great distance with a Spanish gun called the "Slinneanach," and Alexander Campbell, who said that his brother Colin had been shot in the same manner as the deer and by the same gun. "The people of Ballachulish after this gave a bad report of the gun called the Slinneanach; that any house in which it was should take fire" (p. 216). For a while they kept it in an outhouse, and at last sent the gun to the north, since the North Country men did not share their fears about the "Slinneanach." MacKechnie comments (p. 354) that a gun fired upward at a deer and downward at a man could hardly have left the same marks; but he documents the belief in accursed weapons and missiles from ancient Greece to an Act of 1846 revoking *deodan,* or the surrendering of lethal instruments to the king, in order to protect railway engines from surrender.

Folk humor is conspicuously absent from the Dewar texts, although other traditions or narrators or collectors might well have emphasized comic elements. A straighforward beginning to one relation informs us, "There was a gentleman of the MacKellars called MacKellar of Cruachan dwelling in Cruachan at the side of Loch Awe opposite to Inishconnel"—a typical, low-keyed, matter-of-fact start, but followed by a sensational development—"and he held a right from the Pope that when any pair was married between Cruachan and Kilchrenan, he might claim the first night of the bride" (p. 273). The teller goes on to explain how strong the authority of the Pope was in those times, confirmed by the law of the kingdom. Instead of a Boccaccio-like bedroom romp, however, we are given a sober clan fight between MacKellar and his four sons with MacArthur, father of the bride, and MacArthur's four sons, with morality triumphing over popery. In a note the editor documents this *ius primae noctis,* mentioned in a number of Celtic myth-stories that allude to royal and semi-divine persons with a ritual access to another's marriage-bed, such as King Conchobar, who could enjoy the first wedding night with the bride of every Ulsterman.[6]

The loutish strong hero, Big Archibald MacPhail, could easily be presented as a buffoon, but his humorous prayers are obscured in a serious saga. Seeing a large band of armed men coming in pursuit of cattle he and fellow caterans have just stolen, Big Archibald got down on his knees for his first prayer:

"O! God of the Elements! Thou knowest Thyself that I have never troubled Thee hitherto with any request. And thou knowest Thyself that there are many of them come against us and that there is but a small number of us; I pray thee render us aid at this time. Be with us—be among us to rout them—and it may be that I shall not trouble Thee with another request for a long time hereafter" (p. 238).

Apparently the Lord heard Big Archibald, for he and the Glencoe raiders escaped on this occasion, but at a later time he found himself again in troubles as the Campbells swarmed around the MacDonalds. Down again he went on his knees and looked to the sky:

"O! God of the Elements! Thou knowest Thyself that I did not propose to Thee so much as this all my life but once before. . . . It is now five years since I troubled Thee with a request. I pray Thee that Thou wilt be with us today in the battle; that Thou wilt be among us to give us direction; and if Thou wilt not be with us, be not against us, but just let it be between ourselves and the earls" (p. 242).

In a note MacKechnie quotes Campbell of Islay, who recognized an American folk parallel: "this is exactly like the Yankee hunter's prayer which is in some modern funny book: Lord help me! But don't help the bear. If you will stand aside and help neither, you will see the darndest fight you ever saw" (p. 360). An outstanding black American informant, James Douglas Suggs, sang and recited to me a version of "The Preacher and the Grizzly Bear" with the celebrated punch line, "Oh Lord, if you don't help me, don't help that grizzly bear."[7]

For the social historian and the folklife scholar *The Dewar Manuscripts* is rich in descriptions of customs and behavior of the old Highland culture. The narratives refer to methods of preparing food, techniques of sword-play, and codes of honor and social etiquette. Several recitals contain details on roasting meat. In the days of the Feinn, their great chieftain Fionn MacCumhail would give a feast after winning a battle. A deep hole was dug on the plain and fuel burned until the hole was half full of hot coals; then it was covered with flat stones, deer meat placed on the stones, more stones placed on the meat, and a layer of sods on top of all (p. 154). MacKechnie adds that the cooking pit was filled with water brought to a boil by the hot stones (p. 321). In another story, the robber Nial na Gainne and his gillie kill a wedder (yearling ram), take out and clean the paunch, put a hoop in the mouth of the paunch and place a withe across it for a pot-hook, and hang the paunch, filled with a piece of flesh and with water, like a pot over the fire to cook (p. 130; cf. pp. 139-140). Feudal customs are explained, such as the taking of the so-called "door-post horse," the best horse on the farm, by the laird when a farmer died, but in return the laird must help the widow and children until the latter are grown (p. 257). One narrative opens with a detailed picture of a dwelling-house owned by a Highland laird in the period of James VI (1567-1625). The teller comments that a farmer of the present (1865) with less than a thousand sheep would scorn this house of the laird of Arrochar.

> The house was but thirty-four feet long and thirteen broad, inside. It contained but three rooms: a kitchen, a sitting-room and a pantry, and the pantry was in the middle of the house. The kitchen-fire was on the middle of the floor and a hole right over it in the roof allowed the smoke to escape. The fire of the sitting-room was near the gable and a stone with a smooth surface behind it. A chimney-top made of twigs and daubed with clay was above the fire of the chamber to let out the smoke. The rafters of the house were about three feet asunder. Beams of cleft oak placed close together and covered with sods formed a loft above the laird of Arrochar. There was but a single window with six panes in the chamber. There was one window with four panes in the kitchen, on the front of the house, and there was a window-hole at the back,

which was shut with boards when the wind blew through it. There was another window-hole in the pantry shut with boards which was opened when anything was to be done there. The house was thatched with bracken (p. 115).

John Dewar had seen this house and the Dukes of Argyll used it as an inn. The narration concerns an affair between the wife of MacFarlane, laird of Arrochar, with the laird of Luss, who met clandestinely at a weaver's house. Accordingly the narrator explains that in "those olden times" gentlewomen spun wool and flax and did not consider it demeaning to go to the weaver's house and give directions how the web was to be woven. A tale begun with these neutral facts about house-style and clothmaking leads into another grisly Highland report of clan slaughter, with the MacFarlanes storming the castle of the laird of Luss and bringing his private parts to MacFarlane's faithless lady.

There are other connections between history and folklore in John Dewar's collection. Nearly every narrative contains a scatter of incidents giving rise to place-names. For instance, in the one text dealing with the legendary Feinn (No. 23, "The Great Strait of the Feinn"), a whole series of place-name origins is given in a single passage. The King of Lochlann prepared a great fleet to conquer the Feinn and it set sail for the Isles. One ship was named the *Iubhrach*. MacKechnie's note (p. 321) explains that this word, meaning "made of yew wood," denotes a magical ship in many Gaelic tales, yew being a sacred wood. The *Iubhrach's* skipper Paruig, unfamiliar with the strait, let his ship strike a rock, thereafter called Glach Pharuig (Paruig's Stone), while the strait was called Caolas Mhic Pharuig (MacPharuig's Sound). As the rock damaged the *Iubhrach* and she began to fill with water, the crew sailed her to an island, since named after the ship, where she was abandoned and carried by the flood tide to a bay where she rotted, and the bay is named after the *Iubhrach* (pp. 155-156). Such instances could be many times multiplied, and afford challenges for the historian-cum-folklorist to determine whether a legend has grown from or given rise to a place-name.

The previous comments have faintly suggested the wealth of tradition, belief, and custom in *The Dewar Manuscripts*. But the presence of folklore does not invalidate the content of history. In his appended notes MacKechnie identifies and documents many of the personalities and events mentioned in the texts. A case in point is the lengthy account of "Colin of Glenure" (pp. 194-206), and its sequel, "James Stewart of the Glen" (pp. 207-213). James Stewart was tried and sentenced for the murder of Colin of Glenure, September 21-25, 1752, although Allan Breck Stewart later confessed to the murder. MacKechnie is able to compare transcripts of the trial proceedings with the traditions collected by Dewar over a century later and finds them coinciding at many points, although there occur folklore intrusions such as the one-eyed ferryman.

Conversely, there are traditional texts for which documentary support is hard to find, and yet these may be all the more valuable since they provide the sole record. The startling account of "The Family of Ardsheil" gives information on relations between Highlanders and Americans at the time of the American Revolution. After losing the estate of Ardsheil, Duncan of Ardsheil went to America, became Town Chamberlain and Chief Collector of taxes in Boston, and married Ann Irvine, daughter of the governor of Boston. The narrative then has General John Campbell and Charles Campbell of Inverary, both British officers, apprehended while traveling in America, imprisoned in Boston, and sentenced to be burned as spies. From their prison cell they heard called the name "Mistress Stewart of Ardsheil." Getting word to her, they asked that she bring her husband to them. In the end he engineered a hairbreadth escape for them, his wife stealing her father's keys to the prison. When the prisoners were missed, Duncan Stewart himself had to leave secretly for England. There he ran fortuitously into the Campbells, who interceded with the Duke of Argyll to have Ardsheil restored to him. After some complicated land transactions, Duncan regained Ardsheil and settled his family upon the estate (pp. 218-224). Such episodes in Highland-American relations rarely appear in conventional history, although thousands of Highlanders emigrated to America before 1776.

Twentieth-Century Folktale Collections

To supplement *The Dewar Manuscripts* we can add three twentieth-century collections of traditional tales from the Highlands and the Hebrides which include, as any representative and faithful collection from that area must, local historical traditions. They are *The Peat-Fire Flame: Folk-Tales and Traditions of the Highlands and Islands* by Alasdair Alpin MacGregor; *Tales of Barra Told by the Coddy (John MacPherson, Northbay Barra, 1876-1955)* with Foreword by Compton MacKenzie and Introduction and Notes by John Lorne Campbell; and *Stories from South Uist*, told by Angus MacLellan, translated by John Lorne Campbell.

These volumes, in contrast to *The Dewar Manuscripts,* cover the range of Scottish Gaelic oral traditions. The latter two collections are especially meritorious, preserving the repertoire of two Gaelic-speaking master narrators of the Hebrides and buttressing the texts with valuable historical notes and glosses. John Lorne Campbell, himself laird of the isle of Canna, has followed modern folklore methods; he presents literal texts, recorded on wire or tape; translates them directly from the recording into natural and equivalent English, avoiding the "pseudo-archaic" and misty "Celtic Twilight" styles; groups them into families of stories by subject matter; prominently introduces and describes the narrator; and appends notes to correct, amplify, and substantiate statements in the tales and to indicate folklore comparisons. These are indeed model volumes. MacGregor's work offers none of these contributions and the author avowedly eschews the "science of Folk-tales." Informants and printed sources are rarely or loosely identified, and traditions are recounted in colorless paraphrase. Still the work has some value, for MacGregor knows the Hebrides as a native, referring to cousins on the isle of Lewis who believe the seventh son can cure the king's evil, and he has brought together many scattered materials.

A homogeneous body of oral narratives emerges from these collections, with traditional history one of the main storytelling genres. Where Campbell of Islay has emphasized the international folktale, only six of the forty-two tales told by Angus MacLellan and none of the sixty-seven told by the Coddy or the more than two hundred summarized by MacGregor fall under this rubric. The strength of the tradition lies in the believed rather than the imaginary story. Believed narrations themselves cover a wide spectrum, from two-thousand-year-old legends of the warlike Feinn or Fingalians, to clan feuds and the '45 and the evictions taking place from the fourteenth to the nineteenth centuries, swelled by numerous memorates dealing with fairies, spirits, water-monsters, witches, treasure searches, and second-sighted prophecies.

Several chapters in *The Peat-Fire Flame* involve local and general history, particularly those on "Rievers' and Caterans' Tales," "Folk-Tales of Doughty Men and Doughty Deeds," "Norse and Viking Folk-Tales," and "Folk-Tales of the '15 and '45." In his introductory comment to this last chapter, MacGregor declares that the Jacobite uprisings of 1715 and 1745 constitute "the only outstanding phase of Scottish history since the arrival of Columba."

The Scottish War of Independence with all its adventures of Wallace and Bruce, the Cromwellian activities north of the Tweed, the Union of the Crowns and, later, of the Parliaments, were all important in their way; but not one of them raised Scotland out of the drab, monotonous succession of minor battles and political intrigues and skirmishes. Bannockburn, it is true, has its peculiar significance for every Scot the world over; but the rout of Edward was of less consequence even to Scotland than Culloden—the last and greatest outburst of Highland chivalry. [8]

Folk tradition in this case accurately reflects historical significance, and the '45 is still being fought and reenacted by Scots. MacGregor met many Highlanders and Islanders who spoke as if they had known Prince Charlie personally. One tradition contradicts the usual version that the Prince landed at Eriskay, and instead assigns his initial landing to Colonsay, with considerable details on his vain attempt to store kegs of gold on the island and to win the support of the MacNeills of Colonsay. (Apparently the Prince believed he could confidently leave his treasure with any people living where heather grew.) MacGregor also gives a variant of a tradition, known to the older people of Glen Moriston, that a peddler passing through the glen was shot by English soldiers mistaking him for the Prince, whom he closely resembled. The officer in charge cut off the peddler's head and took it to the Duke of Cumberland at Fort Augustus. Jacobite prisoners, hoping to give their fugitive leader a respite, assured the Duke that it was indeed the head of the Young Pretender. In the version given earlier, a follower of the Prince deliberately pretended to the soldiers that he was Charles Edward.

Another novel tradition about the Prince, from Skye, ascribes the beauty of a lass born to the Beatons in Bracadale to their encountering the Prince incognito, with Flora MacDonald and a guide. The Beatons offered the three strangers milk, and noticed that one drank from a gold cup and the other two from an ordinary Highland *cuman* (wooden drinking dish). When, shortly after, goodwife Beaton gave birth, her awe of the noble stranger left its mark on her beautiful daughter. Here the wandering of Prince Charles has become fused with the folk belief that a woman may transmit to her babe any powerful impression she received during pregnancy.

Thanks to their notes documenting or revising facts in the texts, the two collections by John Lorne Campbell demonstrate the usefulness to the historian of specific traditions. Campbell appreciates local-history stories as a distinct genre, and comments, in his Introduction to *Stories from South Uist*, that Angus MacLellan related many about the MacDonalds of Clanranald, who formerly owned South Uist, and their hereditary poet-historians, the MacVurichs. "There is, or was, a wealth of such stories extant in South Uist, and a whole volume could easily be devoted to them and nothing else, but as far as I know, they have never been brought together." He makes similar remarks about the Coddy and the atmosphere of Barra in which memories of men stretched back to comprehend events in their past as if they were still near at hand, events known from the telling and not from printed books or English-school education.

Material events, such as the evictions, the potato famine, the departure of the last of the old race of lairds in the direct line, the Napoleonic wars and the oppression of the pressgang, none of which happened later than 1851, seemed to be matters of yesterday. The Jacobite risings of 1745 and 1715 felt only a little farther back, and the events of the seventeenth century, the wars between Royalists and Covenanters, and the visits to Barra of the Irish Franciscans (1624-40) and the Vincentians (1652-57), of whom Fr. Dermid Dugan was particularly well remembered, seemed only a very little earlier. Behind all this lay memories of the exploits of the old MacNeils of Barra, of the Lords of the Isles, and of the Viking invaders of Scotland and Ireland, who started coming in the ninth century [9]

As an illustration of how a historical tradition may be checked and found reliable in good part, we may consider the Barra story of "The Weaver of the Castle" and its sequel, "The Life Story of the Little Weaver."[10] This long narration contains an improbable Hollywood thriller plot of banishment, murder, and revenge. The Weaver was banished from Barra to the Stack Islands, where he built a castle and practiced piracy. Aided by his wife and sons, he cut ships' hawsers so that they would drift to shore and be wrecked. A cutter was sent to dispatch the Weaver and his sons. The commander hunted them to Eriskay, slew them, and left the blood of the Weaver on his sword to dry. The story now shifts to the youngest son, John MacNeil, who had escaped the fate of his father and brothers. John eventually made his way to Greenock and shipped aboard a cargo vessel bound from Scotland to Vancouver around Cape Horn. The Little Weaver rose to command of his own ship and one day was in a club in London with old tars drinking whisky and telling stories. One told of killing a raider and his three sons on a western isle of Scotland. John MacNeil made his acquaintance, was invited to his house for tea, beheld the sword stained with his father's blood, and killed the veteran with a blow of his fist.

John Lorne Campbell is able to compare two other recorded versions. An elaborate variant, probably recorded in 1893, was written down by Father Allan McDonald, the priest-collector of Eriskay, and survives among his papers. This text follows in the main the above outline, but after John's revenge veers into a typical Gaelic heroic-magical fiction. John encounters a princess transformed into a deer, follows her to the Kingdom of the Great World with the aid of a griffin, and finally finds and weds the princess. An inferior and poorly annotated version of this latter part was collected for Campbell of Islay in 1859 and printed in *More West Highland Tales*.[11] A reader of the 1859 variant unfamiliar with the other two would never suspect that a historical basis underlies the original narration. Campbell sees no reason to doubt the accuracy of the Coddy's tale. He visited the Stack Islands in 1951 and observed landmarks and remains of the castle mentioned by the Coddy. The practice of piracy in the manner ascribed to the Weaver is documented for the late sixteenth and early seventeenth centuries by references in the Privy Council of Scotland. "So that the activities of the Weaver and his sons, his death and the revenge exacted by his younger son, are perfectly probable. The folkloric elements are likely to have been tacked on to the story of young John by later storytellers in order to entertain their audiences."[12]

A striking confirmation of one of the Coddy's historical tales is offered in printed testimony given to a royal Commission of Inquiry. The narrative concerns the infamous clearances of 1851 that followed the potato famine of 1846. Ground Officers offered meal to families who would sign up to emigrate to Canada. When the ship came to Lochboisdale to take them away, men and women ran to the hills to escape. The Coddy says, "Now I am going to describe the scenes that took place while the emigrants were put aboard and the brutality shown to human beings was beyond description." And he gives details. A deposition given to the Crofters Commission by John McKay, crofter, of Kilphedir, South Uist on May 28, 1883, elicited this testimony:

Chairman (Lord Napier): You make a very serious charge in this paper which requires a little explanation. You say, "Others were driven and compelled to emigrate to America, some of whom had been tied before our eyes, others

hiding themselves in caves and crevices, for fear of being caught by authorized officers." Will you explain these words?
McKay: I heard and saw portions of it.
Lord Napier: Will you relate what you heard and saw?

McKay then proceeded to relate instances of a policeman and a dog chasing Lachlan MacDonald and Angus Johnston and tying them upon the pier of Lochboisdale before they were taken aboard ship.[13] Thus, after the lapse of a century, the Coddy's tradition is well substantiated.

In a number of cases John Lorne Campbell points to chronological inaccuracies and impossibilities. Also one can observe how favorite motifs in Highland traditional history reappear. The South Uist narrative of "The Widow's Son's Revenge on Clanranald" contains the episode found in the Glencoe massacre of the substituted animal: officers save a boy from the death being meted out to all male members of his clan by bringing Clanranald the heart and lungs of a dog (motif K512.2, "Compassionate executioner: substituted heart"). The two officers also calculated that they would escape reprisal if the child sought revenge.[14] Even for the Hebrides this is a particularly gruesome chronicle: Clanranald ordered Farquhar and his family to be killed to avoid vengeance for his killing Farquhar's brother, a plowman; Farquhar killed the plowman for eating a blade of dulse he found in the seaweed, and so shaming his master for feeding his farm servants so poorly. There also recur a prison escape, this time from France, the intercession of a Gaelic-speaking gaoler, and the incident of the strong hero squeezing blood from the fingertips of a man whose hand he shook.[15] The folklorist-historian will need to identify and make allowance for conventional formulas and elements that drift from one annal to another.

The well-stocked repertoires of Angus MacLellan and John MacPherson suggest a change in the narrative materials employed by twentieth-century raconteurs of the Western Isles. While the grim clan histories are still heard, although not in the profusion and density of John Dewar's time, newer and lighter themes have entered tradition. Alongside the laird and the invincible swordsman now appears the public house wag. Often the anecdotes related about eccentric characters are traveling folktales. "The Holiday of Donald and Maggie," describing the visit to Oban of a Highland couple who had never left their croft, matches American jocular tales, often in dialect, of the countryman's first visit to the big city.[16] "The Story of the Thrush," telling how Iain mistook a thrush's call for advice to take a drink, recalls the Irishman's similar misunderstanding on hearing a frog's croak.[17] A rollicking series of comic stories has grown out of the actual wreck near Eriskay in 1941 of the *Politician*, whose cargo of splendid whiskeys never reached America but brought good cheer to the Outer Isles. The wreck and its aftermath form the plot of Compton Mackenzie's novel and film, *Whisky Galore*, retitled *Tight Little Island* in the United States. In other anecdotes a crofter mistakes a balloon for a flying cow; Mary of the Stream is deceived into thinking a galvanic battery is a fishing tackle; and a second-sighted man in Uist sees a weaving loom in the sky, moving at high speed, and years later when the first airplane flies over Uist recognizes the loom. These modern story themes suggest that current history is still contributing to the formation of local tradition in the Outer Isles.

A final word must be devoted to the unusual and unique book by Hugh Miller, *Scenes and Legends of the North of Scotland*, with the revealing and accurate subtitle, *or The Traditional History of Cromarty*. Between 1829 and 1832, as a young man, Miller wrote down most of the sketches that comprised the book. He hoped to gain a literary reputaton by capturing the personality and biography of the coastal town where he had been born in 1802. Although the book enjoyed success, Miller expanding its first edition of 1835 in 1850, and the 1850 edition being often reprinted, it is forgotten today, and Hugh Miller is remembered primarily as geologist, religious editor, and Scottish nationalist.

The *Scenes and Legends*, and portions of its related work, Miller's splendid autobiography, *My Schools and Schoolmasters*, complement the sources for Highland folk history already described. In place of clan chronicles and heroic exploits of feudal warriors, we find the annals of a town and its odd characters and its occupational groups of farmers, fishermen, sailors, and stonemasons. Though north of Inverness, Cromarty represents a Sassenach enclave within the Gaelic-speaking Highlands. The clans lived in glens, not towns, and they depended on cattle-raiding and warring, not trade and industry. In *Scenes and Legends* Miller assembled all the communal traditions of the townsfolk, embracing the kirk and the school, the sea and the hills, smuggling and marketing, plague and famine, town politics and town literati. Nineteenth-century Cromarty, a hardy, isolated community of some fifteen hundred souls, abounded in oral history of many layers and veins. In the early decades of the nineteenth century an enterprising small proprietor named George Ross sought to industrialize and modernize Cromarty with a cloth factory, a brewery, an enlarged port, a trade in pork, up-to-date methods of agriculture, a factory for nails and spades, and a lace-making industry. He imported so many laborers from the Western isles that he built for them a Gaelic chapel and they for themselves a Gaelic cemetery. His handsome stone house and attractive gardens and walks gave Cromarty some elegance. Yet this valiant effort to effect a bustling metropolis in northern Scotland utterly failed, in part because of the antipathy of the townspeople, in part because of economic difficulties inherent in the town's location. Today Cromarty is a ghost-town, shrunk to five hundred dispirited people, with the fishery gone, the brewery and factories empty, the magnificent bay empty of vessels. Only briefly during the last two World Wars has the bay come back to life as a harbor for the Royal Navy. No one now would care to write, or find materials for, its history. Yet Cromarty is heir to an instructive and significant history, preserved by Hugh Miller in 1835.

Miller did not record literal texts, as did John Dewar, but rather wove traditions into the fabric of his chronicle. The folklorist recognizes a number of circulating motifs in *Scenes and Legends*, involving such matters as the prophecies of Kenneth Ore the Brahan seer, the curse that drove the herring away, the foundation sacrifice in Craighouse Castle.[18] Cromarty is a different world from the Highland glen and Western isle, and traditions reflect the difference. For an example: the '45 and Culloden made their impact in Cromarty, as elsewhere in the Highlands, but in place of epic accounts of mighty feats of arms, sadistic cruelties, and hairbreadth escapes, we receive lugubrious anecdotes of scavenging and discomfiture. When Highland supporters of Bonny Prince Charlie entered town, a lone Jacobite rushed out to greet them crying, "you're welcome." "Welcome or not, give me your shoes," replied a Highlander. When two clansmen tried to rob Nannie Miller after the Cromarty men had fled, she ducked one in a meal barrel. The obtuse, simple-minded local character attracts legends in Cromarty much as did the strapping swordsman among the clans. A favorite Cromarty tale, presented by Miller, which I found still current in 1967, concerns Sandy Wood, a small crofter who in moments of excitement sputtered helplessly. Sandy discovered his neighbor stealthily shifting their boundary stones and thereby reducing the size of Sandy's farm. When Sandy accused his neighbor before the townspeople, his neighbor accused Sandy of the same misdeed, and in his ire Sandy choked over his words. He took to his bed and shortly died. On his deathbed he left instructions that he should be buried outside the iron railing bounding the church cemetery, so that he could get a headstart on Judgment Day toward Navity Moor, where in popular Cromarty belief God would interrogate the risen. Sandy's grave can still be seen outside the cemetery fence on the South Sutor overlooking the town. Here in these Cromarty legends is the other half of the coin, the traditional history of farming and fishing folk to supplement the raids of the lairds.

The points suggested in this paper can be summarized as follows. Historian and folklorist can find common ground in the area of traditional history. Such history may include personal, family, neighborhood, and township historical traditions. In countries where literacy, formal schooling, and printed publications dominate the culture, traditional history is slighted or scorned by professional historians. Yet in these societies large numbers and groups of people still possess oral traditions that differ markedly from conventional written history. The black and the immigrant in the United States comprise such groups.

To support this thesis I have examined oral sources available to the historian of the Highlands and western islands of Scotland. This culture area meets the requirements that appear necessary for the preservation of traditional history. The extended families of the resident population maintain a deep interest and pride in their ancestral prowess. Bards and oral historians are institutionalized figures. The clans have inhabited the same lands continuously over an extended period of time and the surrounding landmarks and place-names reinforce memories of historical episodes. Books and book-learning have played little part in Highland culture.

As always occurs when oral narrations last across the·generations, folklore themes intrude into the mass of saga. The folklorist can identify these themes and the historian can corroborate the factual residue. There remains the question of judging the value of individual traditions for the final history written by the folklorist-historian. Some traditions will provide local detail, some will indicate popular bias and emotional commitment, some will cast new light on controversial events. The record left by traditional history shows a few brightly lighted spots and many dark areas as contrasted with the record of written history. For the Highlands, three episodes in particular have caught the folk imagination: the bloody battle of Culloden; the escape and wanderings of Bonny Prince Charlie after his defeat at Culloden; and the Glencoe massacre. High and desperate drama has made its impact in folk history, but of mundane matters there is little recollection.

Elsewhere I have suggested certain criteria for evaluating the historical validity of oral traditions.[19] These criteria may be applied to the present materials.

Identifying folklore themes grafted onto historical settings. The folktale attached to the escape of the Laird of Bernera from the castle of Culloden is a case in point.

Allowance for personal and emotional bias slanting a tradition. The animus behind a MacDonald or a Campbell version of the Glencoe massacre illustrates this factor.

Crosschecks of multiple traditions. The plethora of oral accounts surrounding the escape and wanderings of Bonny Prince Charlie does not present a unified story, but beneath the vagaries of oral tradition is seen a common thread. Charles Edward did go into hiding, and make his way from one isle to another.

Corroboration of a tradition from printed records. This kind of check is seen in the deposition of a crofter given in 1883 determining an event of 1851 described by the Coddy from oral traditon a century later in much the same fashion.

Corroboration of a tradition from geographical landmarks. An example is offered in the Coddy's account of the Little Weaver whose father was slain on Stack Island. In its physical situation the island lent itself to the piracy practiced by the Weaver. The Coddy himself had seen the remains of the Weaver's castle.

Corroboration of a tradition from material culture. Physical objects used in the daily life of an earlier period may also assist in confirming an episode of traditional history. Thus, the detailed description of a laird's dwelling in the reign of James VI was verified two and a half centuries later when collector John Dewar observed the structure.

Knowledge of the character of an informant. Modern collectors have changed the practice of presenting anonymous texts and now offer full reports on the careers and personalities of tradition bearers. In the cases of Angus MacLellan and John MacPherson, we can judge their texts the more confidently because we are given illuminating information on their lives and attitudes.

With guidelines such as these, the historian may handle oral historical traditions with some assurance. Nowhere in the western world will he find greater resources on which to draw than in the Highlands and Outer Isles.

In the Field

Theoretical pronouncements command far more respect nowadays among folklorists than the reports of field collectors, a situation that holds true for other disciplines as well. Historians rank analysis and revisionism above straightforward narrative, as C. Vann Woodward has lately deplored.[1] The contextualist school of younger folklore scholars insists on a complete description of scene and setting for each "storytelling event," and denigrates mere accumulation of texts without explication of their meaning, function, and message. These are valid points, but they can be carried too far, until the text of folk-song or folktale is shunted to an appendix and hidden behind a mountain of commentary. Also the boosters of theory tend to overlook two vital matters: that the battle for accurate recording and publication of oral texts, with their variants, is far from won; and that the collecting, selecting, and printing of field materials may, indeed should, involve theoretical issues.

The presumed discovery of a new genre in the course of fieldwork requires an intellectual process beyond the mere writing down or taping of sung and narrated items. One of the essays in this section is called, "Dialect Stories of the Upper Peninsula: A New Form of American Folklore." The title advances a theoretical argument chiefly supported by the evidence from the article's eighty-four tale texts. A new genre must by defined against the spectrum of the known genres. The eighty-four texts did not drop serially into the collector's net, but turned up randomly in the midst of many other oral narrative forms. Once the collector has identified the genre he can of course seek it actively, and this I did, not only in the Upper Peninsula but elsewhere. The Jewish dialect story, for instance, enjoys a near national popularity.[2] In one subcycle of Jewish dialect jokes the Jewish storyteller makes fun at Jewish oversensitivity to anti-Semitism. Local character anecdotes of J. Golden Kimball, the Mormon elder who has entered legend, are often told in a Scandinavian dialect.[3] Throughout the southwest Mexican dialect stories are told about Juan and Pedro, although folklorists have not yet collected them.[4] Fieldwork can thus document the theoretical formulation of a folklore genre.

Folklorists currently devote much attention to individual styles of traditional singers and storytellers. "Tales of Two Lobstermen" describes the contrasting styles of two talented folk narrators from the same subculture and matches texts each has told of the same tale type to illustrate their divergences. Field materials assembled in this way can illuminate the large question that haunts all students of folklore, the relation of individual creativity to the traditional corpus.

Sometimes a given collection carries its own message. "Collecting Legends in Country Kerry" describes my observations on a three-day visit with a fieldworker for Ireland's famed Irish Folklore Commission, and presents the oral narratives garnered on that trip. The main purpose of that paper was to report on the sophisticated, government-supported system for collecting and archiving folklore in the Republic of Ireland. Yet theoretical implications can be perceived from the report. County Kerry oral narrators in the 1950s told me only legends—no magical fictions, no mythical tales, so renowned in the Irish repertoire. These legends incorporated magical elements, but within a framework of belief. Only in the past decade have international folktale scholars devoted much attention to the legend as opposed to the Märchen, stimulated by lessons from the field. In his flights of speculation no folklorist should ever venture too far from the terra firma of the field. In the field he finds his sustenance and inspiration and puts to the empirical test his—and others'—armchair hypotheses.

Collecting
in County Kerry

The magnificent work of the Irish Folklore Commission[1] takes on increased excitement when viewed against the slow growth of folklore over the past hundred and fifty years. From its beginnings in the "popular antiquities" of Brand and the fumbling efforts of the first collectors, T. Crofton Croker and Mrs. Bray and Jacob Allies, who refer only vaguely to informants and improve stories for their readers, the science of folklore has marched ahead to the formidable collecting program directed from 82 St. Stephen's Green in Dublin. There in a neat four-story building the Irish Folklore Commission accumulates and digests the oral traditions of a six-thousand-year-old heritage.

In the basement Kevin Danaher has set up his recording equipment and records cabinet, and when the occasion arises he packs it into the Commission's van and drives into the field to record some special storyteller or folk singer. Next to the recording room a large microfilm machine transfers to celluloid the notebook material in the archives. On the first floor the secretary's office receives the daily packages of manuscript sent in by full-time and part-time field collectors, and stencils the questionnaires on selected topics that go out periodically to the Commission's helpers.* In a separate room at the rear rests a

---

*They are sent to about four hundred persons, chiefly primary schoolteachers. "Each questionnaire is in effect a complete survey of the distribution of one aspect of oral tradition over the whole country. It is then possible . . . to mark on a blank map of Ireland, by means of symbols, the distribution of the tradition . . . This may reveal surprising differences of custom from one area to another, or show that a tradition which is commonplace in one part of the country is entirely unknown in another." Caoimhín Ó Danachair, "The Questionnaire System," *Béaloideas* 15 (1945): 204.

new prize, the library of the great von Sydow. The office of the Director, Professor James H. Delargy, whose vision and devotion created the Commission, occupies the second floor, together with the general library of standard folklore dictionaries, studies, and journals being continually expanded by librarian Thomas Wall. Kevin Danaher's office and photographs of material culture, with the lecture room, take up the floor above. And on top of all lies the precious archives, with its thousands of notebooks of Gaelic tales directly written down from the words of the storytellers. In the next room archivist Seán O'Sullivan steadily catalogues the materials according to the Swedish classification system adapted by him in the *Handbook of Irish Folklore.* The activities of the whole building, financed by the Irish Government on a present annual budget of eleven thousand pounds, testify dramatically to the scientific possibilities of folklore collecting.

[*On April 1, 1971, the Irish Government reassigned the activities of the Irish Folklore Commission to a Department of Irish Folklore located within University College, Dublin. Professor Bo Almqvist succeeded Professor Delargy, who retired on that date, to the Chair of Irish Folklore at the college and assumed the headship of the new department. All the collections and library holdings of the Commission were transferred from 82 St. Stephen's Green, where they had been housed since 1950, to the new quarters in the Arts Building of University College. They included 1,735 bound volumes of field collections running to 900,000 pages; 20,000 books, periodicals, and papers; and 25,000 photographs and other pictorial items.*

The chief effect of the change is to move the base of folklore work in Ireland from a state institute located within the Department of Education, financed by an annual grant-in-aid from the government and devoted to collecting and archiving, to a university teaching program. A professor and two lecturers in the Department of Irish Folklore teach degree-level courses in Irish and comparative folklore and ethnology. Fieldwork continues, but the department will encourage research and publication on the collected material and train students to become folklorists.]

To see the other end of operations, the fieldwork, I took, on November 28, 1951, a train straight across Ireland from Dublin to County Kerry, until the ocean loomed up at Waterville. Three elegant tourist hotels and a cable station bring the modern world to this village of four hundred people, but in winter it looks bleak enough for the hardiest folklorist. Tadhg Murphy lives here, and ever since the

Irish Folklore Commission set up shop, in 1935, he has collected for them, day and night, winter and summer, cycling into the countryside with his Ediphone machine packed in a box over the handlebars. (Tadhg bought a car shortly before I arrived, but forgot to release the emergency brake on a trial spin and when I came the car was in the repair shop.) He has just begun his *ninety-first* diary—the notebook describing the storytellers and the experiences of the collector, which accompanies the copybook of texts when they are transmitted to the archives.

Literally Tadhg has grown gray collecting folklore. Immensely relishing his work, sprung directly from the people he visits but well read and previously a teacher of modern Irish, he superbly fits the requirements of the professional field collector. Tadhg was born in 1896 on a farm twelve miles southeast of Waterville, spoke Gaelic as his first language, and grew up steeped in the folktales of his father. He had only the ordinary national schooling, plus a summer's course for the teaching certificate, and then spent ten years, from 1925 to 1935, as an itinerant teacher to adult night classes. When Delargy came to the Ballinskelligs district in 1927, on his own linguistic researches, he met Tadhg, and recognized his merit. That year the Irish Folklore Society was formed, and Tadhg contributed Gaelic tales to its journal, *Béaloideas*, until eight years later when the Vocational Education Committee of Kerry loaned him—permanently it seems—to the newly formed Irish Folklore Commission.

Prominent people have beaten a path to Tadhg's remote door. Walt Disney came by for a day, on the trail of leprechauns, and later sent over his writer Larry Watkins to work on a script that never blossomed. John McNulty of *The New Yorker*, visiting his ancestral land, paused long enough to get material for a pungent article. An editor of the *Providence Journal*, George W. Potter, spent a day watching Tadhg at work, and wrote about the experience for his newspaper and a book reprinted from its articles. Potter went over, interestingly enough, on a memorial visit for a former editor of the paper, Alfred Williams, who in the 1880s and 1890s had shown keen interest in Irish culture and tradition.[2] Professors have come from various countries, Stith Thompson from the United States, Sigurd Erixon from Sweden, Ingrid Boberg from Denmark, to observe his field methods. I was only one of a procession. Tadhg can meet the literati as genially as the folk, for he brims with good humor and bursts with stories. More than any single old time shanachie (accomplished Irish storyteller) he knows the repertory of the Dingle Peninsula, for Tadhg has visited them all and absorbed their tales and can outmatch any storyteller in the field. When I asked about a particular motif or theme, Tadhg invariably countered, "We have a fund of such stories in Irish folklore" (save only in the case of the tall tale). When an informant knows only a fragment of a tradition, as frequently happens, Tadhg can immediately connect the missing parts. Yet for all his years in the field he keeps hearing fresh items.

If you want picturesqueness with your folklore, the thatched stone farmhouses lying among the hills and peat bogs of County Kerry provide an unbeatable setting. Driving into the hills our first afternoon together, Tadhg casually pointed to a little yellow house set like a fly-speck in the midst of empty stretching bogs and high ranges. "That's the schoolhouse," he said. Not another sign of life met the eye as far as one could see. But in the morning barefooted children trooped from lonely farmhouses for miles to converge at that building. Nine miles over a dirt road brought us to the mountainside dwelling where William Stack has lived since he was born, eighty years ago. Liam stood in front of a hayrick cutting plug tobacco for his pipe, with the mountain slope rising dizzily on one side and a blue lough lying at its foot on the other. The mountain mists curled up the valley as we spoke but Liam and Tadhg talked on, although my frozen fingers could scarcely hold the notebook. Old Liam in his torn clothes, the white stubble of his beard covering the sharp clean features of the Irish farmer folk, and thickset, genial Tadhg, with a felt hat tipped a bit rakishly over one ear, both puffing away at their pipes across the wooden gate, blended naturally into the rugged scenery. External appearances can of course be entirely deceptive. Liam, the countryman full of folk belief, had never seen the fairies; but two days before, lunching at the faculty dining room in University College, I had heard a graduate doctor tell Seán, Kevin, and myself with the utmost intensity how at the age of two he had seen the fairies dancing on the green close by a fairy fort, which was shortly after desecrated by a workman who died within the year. The afternoon following our visit to Liam we called on blind, bedridden Michael Sugrue across the bay, and in that equally isolated farmhouse, with barefooted children scrambling over the stone floor, his daughter mentioned having spent five years in New York City as second cook in the staff of twenty-three serving steel millionaire George F. Baker. By and large the omens read correctly, however, and in this medieval corner of western Ireland a richly aged tradition pours from the tongues of the old men.

The observer notices curiously how the rural families now take for granted the visits of the field collector. He has become an institution, like the priest and the postman, and receives a friendly welcome and often a high tea when he arrives. The old men respond eagerly to his coming, both from social pleasure and from a vague appreciation of the significance of the work. Here is collecting streamlined indeed: the bonds of a fading language and a country kinship, the sanction of the government, and the backlog of many congenial interviews, all facilitate Tadhg Murphy's task. He even tells (in a recent article in *Béaloideas* surveying his fifteen years of experience in collecting) how one shanachie whose neighbor he had called on felt deeply slighted that Tadhg had not come to collect from him! Still the demands on the collector's patience, tact, good humor, and insight remain enormous.

One wonders whether Tadhg, working all these years within the limited radius of his bicycle, has not exhausted the supply of folk tradition. In one respect he has, for he now rarely obtains the long narratives for which the shanachies are celebrated, and in consequence he has discarded his Ediphone machine and substitutes pencil and notebook. He finds this method more satisfactory, in that the storyteller never feels completely at ease talking into a microphone, while the collector still faces the arduous task of transcribing the record. However, Tadhg continues to uncover manifold traditions in other categories, such as the shorter anecdotal stories, or descriptions of the customs and observances classified in O'Sullivan's *Handbook*, which he uses on occasion to steer the speaker's recollections. Going through the handbook item by item with a well-stocked informant may take two years or more. Then again the field-worker can never be sure he has exhausted the folk knowledge of even his most visited informants. Liam Stack told us only one complete tradition (when I asked him about Stephen O'Shea the charmer), but Tadhg had never heard it, and he kept shaking his head in amazement at this new local *Sage*. Gradually, however, Tadhg is enlarging his area, through field trips away from home in the summer, and now by means of his newly acquired automobile. The archivists in Dublin believe they can estimate the number of years required to gather the tradition in a given county, and they do not envisage the end of their collecting program for many years yet.

The valiant work being done in Ireland can well serve as a model and a stimulus to other countries. Professor Delargy has long asserted the need for intensive collecting in the Gaelic-speaking islands and Highlands of Scotland, and results are now appearing. The recent Report of the Advisory Council on Education in Scotland, *Libraries, Museums, and Art Galleries* (Edinburgh: His Majesty's Stationery Office, 1951), devotes an entire chapter to developing Delargy's recommendation for a National Folk Museum, to be administered through a National Folk Lore Commission for Scotland, with financial support from the government. In 1952 the University of Edinburgh embarked on a collecting program, directed by Professor Kenneth H. Jackson, with one of Delargy's fieldworkers, Calum Maclean, as a fulltime collector; Maclean went to Sweden to learn the language and the Swedish classification system as a preparatory step. An unusual feature of the University of Edinburgh plan lies in the coordinated activity of several departments, those of Linguistics, Phonetics, Music, and Celtic, in the collecting and recording; one record may provide dialect words, tonal stresses, a ballad tune, and a ballad text valuable for study in each field. As one result the budget for recording equipment amounts to fourfold the regular outlay for such apparatus, and the elaborate recording room with its own staff engineer demonstrates the benefits of this policy.

From two days with Tadhg Murphy I brought back the following local tales, told by him and by two storytellers we visited.* They testify to the dispatch with which the visitor may acquaint himself with living Irish tradition, to further some special problem that engages him, perhaps after first investigating the archives in Dublin. For instance, an American folklorist might well desire to correlate Irish and Irish-American tradition. In spite of the vast Irish emigration to the United States over the past hundred years, we have no collections from these transplanted Irishmen. Here he can quickly and

---

*Douglas Hyde has described very well this narrative type. "Irish folk-stories may roughly be divided into two classes, those which I believe never had any *conscious* genesis inside the shore of Ireland, and those which had . . . To this second class belong also that numerous body of traditions rather than tales, of conversational anecdotes rather than set stories, about appearances of fairies, or 'good people,' or Tuatha De Danann, as they are also called; of pookas, leprechauns, ghosts, apparitions, water-horses, etc. These creations of folk-fancy seldom appear, as far as I have observed, in the folk-tale proper, or at least they only appear as adjuncts, for in almost all cases the interest of these regular tales centres round a human hero. Stories about leprechauns, fairies, etc., are very brief, and generally have local names and scenery attached to them, and are told conversationally as any other occurrence might be told, whereas there is a certain solemnity about the representation of a folk-tale proper." *Beside the Fire: A Collection of Gaelic Folk Stories*, ed., trans., and annotated by Douglas Hyde; with additional notes by Alfred Nutt (London: David Nutt, 1890), pp. xxxiv-xxxvi.

accurately ascertain, in a few days of directed fieldwork, what kind of narratives the emigrants are likely to have brought over with them; what changes the American experience has wrought in the exported sagas; how awareness of the United States (in a country where every family has "Yank" relatives) has affected the folk tradition at home. The marvelous adventures of Seán Palmer, whom the fairies transported to New York, a saga collected by Tadhg in 1933, illustrates this American impact. On the transfer of tradition, the long master-tales probably have not crossed over and stayed alive, because, as Seán O'Sullivan points out, the professional shanachie delivers them in Gaelic; and similarly the vigorous fairy tradition fails to relocalize in the United States simply because the necessary fairy rings and fairy forts which the small folk inhabit are lacking in the New World. On the other hand, the tenacious beliefs in "overlooking" with the evil eye, in the return of the unquiet dead, and in such otherworldly beings as the luricaun, the pooka, and "spirits," could very easily blend into the New World scene.

With respect to western Kerry, I soon learned from Tadhg its regional storytelling habits. The tall tale does not appear in local folk humor, but the noodle tale does—and he pointed out a hillside village in the distance named Kill Mhic Kiarainn, whose people are known as "iron fools," and told me some Gothamite tales about them. "Spirits," the souls of women violated by priests, are well known; the Devil is not. My inquiries about charming led rapidly into the local cycle about Stephen O'Shea, a noted curer of "overlooked" cattle a generation ago; and Tadhg took me past his house, a lonely, windswept cottage fronting the bay. The set formulas connected with overlooking soon fell into place: the cause—failure to say "God bless you" when praising some person or creature; the cure—spitting on the object and saying a prayer to place the evil elsewhere; the source—an evil power lodged in different parts of the body that may operate unconsciously as well as deliberately. Michael Sugrue explained: "The overlooking is hereditary in families. It is either in the tongue or in the hand or in the leg or in the eye. Some people have it who are unaware of its possession. Old Conway had it, and his four sons had it, in the hand. Anything they touched, man or beast, was liable to suffer." And he placed my hand emphatically on his own leg while he spoke, to indicate where the malign force might reside.

Three of the stories in this sheaf match the fairy legends first collected by T. Crofton Croker in 1825, a proof of Croker's basic trustworthiness. Pondering over the remarkable achievement of the Irish Folklore Commission in raising the technique of collecting and classifying to such high standards, a century after Croker made the first pioneer collection, one realizes the direct line of continuity that runs through this evolution. The IFC represents no sudden, unique eruption of folklore interest but the fruition of a solid, century-long British development of folklore science. English and Scottish folklorists reached their climax just before the First World War (although Edward Clodd lived till 1920 and Hartland till 1928), when the Irish enthusiasts picked up the gauntlet, establishing the Folklore Society of Ireland in 1927 and the Irish Folklore Commission in 1935. Different emphases are apparent of course, in the Irish stress on Gaelic tradition, on fieldwork, on Märchen, but they build on the English foundation. The pioneer group of English folklorists included two Dubliners, Croker and Keightley, one a collector and the other a comparer of fairy narratives. It was Hartland who made the classic study of the laws of fairy behavior, so conspicuous in Ireland, in *The Science of Fairy Tales.* The chief connecting figure between English and Irish folklorists is of course Alfred Nutt, who combined his scholarly studies of Celtic romance with a lively interest in Gaelic folktales, and asserted their folkloric kinship. He provided comparative notes to the Scottish Gaelic collection of MacInnes, an introduction to Jeremiah Curtin's *Tales of the Fairies and the Ghost World*, and both annotations and commentary to Douglas Hyde's *Beside the Fire.* The latter volume well symbolizes the confluence of the two groups, with the champion of scientific collecting in Gaelic lore teaming with one of the foremost English enthusiasts. Hyde's successor, James Delargy, was inspired by the example of Campbell of Islay to employ trained fieldworkers, the core idea of the Irish Folklore Commission. O'Sullivan's splendid *Handbook of Irish Folklore*, articulating the sphere of the Commission's work, adapts categories devised by the Swedish ethnologists, but the Swedes themselves have produced no handbook; George Laurence Gomme issued the original *Handbook of Folklore.* The Swedes and the Irish have arrived at their present rapprochement from quite different routes, and their biases still reflect their traditions: material culture as against oral literature. The science of British folklore, first stimulated by Brand's *Popular Antiquities*, culminates in the skilled Irish collecting.

Collecting in County Kerry

The Evil Eye

Stephen O'Shea and the Mad Dog
(William Stack)

Oh, I knew Stephen O'Shea—he was a herdsman in Derrinan, down in the next township, when I was about twenty. One Saturday night they had a big party at the house—there were doctors from France there and all. (Derrinan used to be a center for smuggling woolens to the French for brandy and tobacco.) Stephen was tending the cows, when a mad dog bit one of them, and then bit Stephen when he tried to drive it away. Well, they killed the cow and they were going to kill Stephen, by smothering him between two ticks, as they used to do then. (There was a man in that district who was bitten by his own cat—he beat the cat, and it jumped on his horse and bit him in the neck —and they smothered him between two ticks.) But the doctor from France said not to kill him, but to put him to bed and have him look into a bowl of water in the morning, for three mornings. They asked Stephen what he saw in the bowl, and he said he only saw his own face. If he had seen the mad dog that would have been bad. So the doctor said Stephen was all right, and the cow was all right too and he would eat it, if nine leaves of ribleaf were put in a boiling pot with the first flesh, and then the ninth leaf thrown away. And they did that, and ate up the whole cow.

I head that from Stephen himself sixty years ago. That was before he became known as a charmer.*

Stephen O'Shea and the Overlooked Cow
(collected by Tadhg Murphy from Pat Fitzgerald)

There was a man of the surname of Curnain [who was my wife's grandfather] and the first name of Timothy, who lived in Cluan Eachlann [the

---

*In old times, in Ireland, people afflicted with canine madness were put to death by smothering between two feather beds; the near relatives standing round until asphyxia was produced, and death followed"; Lady Wilde, *Ancient Cures, Charms, and Usages of Ireland* (London: 1890), p. 47. Apuleius in ass's form was bitten by a mad dog; he had a bowl of water placed before him; if he drank it he was healthy, if he backed away he had rabies; Lucius Apuleius, *The Golden Ass*, tr. Robert Graves (Harmondsworth, England: Penguin, 1950), p. 206. Tadhg later explained that ribleaf was locally known as the "healing herb," and was actually ribwort or grass plantain; the efficacy of the herb was lost if its true name were mentioned. It is surprising that the people of Derrinan knew no folk remedy for hydrophobia. Black reports such treatments as applying stones, wolf skin, churchyard grass, the hair of the dog that bit you; drinking rue boiled in ale; passing between a priest's legs; walking nine times around town on the Sabbath praying; William G. Black, *Folk-Medicine* (London, 1833), pp. 50, 69, 120, 144, 149, 154, 200. This tradition does not refer to Stephen O'Shea as a charmer, but suggests his possession of unusual power.

meadow of the steeds] about sixty years ago. He was driving home his cows one morning to be milked, and met a man on the way. The man singled out one of the cows which had the appearance of being a good milker. "Timothy," said the man, "does that cow yield milk from her four paps?" "She does undoubtedly," replied Timothy. He was scarcely twenty yards from the house at that time. When the cow reached the farmyard, her head and legs were struck together [i.e. she fell]. Timothy could not account for the happening. His hands and legs trembled. The people said one to the other that the cow must have been overlooked, so the horse was saddled, and they set off hurriedly. They went towards a man whose name was Stephen O'Shea, who lived at Muirbhuibhch (sand dunes), and the story was told to him. They asked him if he could come along, that they had a sick cow.

"I will, my dear," Stephen replied, and away they went, and they reached Cluan Eachlann, and they examined the cow. "This cow has been overlooked," said Stephen. "Some evil eye lay on her." Stephen had some sort of charm which he used to set for a sick animal, and he knew from the words he repeated whether the cow had been overlooked or not. "Do you know," he said, "if any stranger passed this way since morning?" "There did," replied Timothy Courtney. "There was nothing wrong with the cow when I brought her home to be milked, until I met this man, and he asked me if that cow yielded milk from her four paps." "That was the same man who overlooked this cow," Stephen told him. "Spit three times on that cow." He did so, and the complaint stopped. The cow was all right from that time on.

This is a story that actually happened, as sure as you are writing it.

(Mrs. Murphy: "My mother told us that many times. It was in her home it happened. She said it was a man named Shea who overlooked the cow.")[3]

Shaun Sigerson's Cow Story
(Tadhg Murphy)

This was told me by Shaun Sigerson of Rineen (the little peninsula). He was a very young lad at the time. A woman, his neighbor, had a sick cow, and sent for Stephen O'Shea, who lived about four miles away. When he came he said the charm, and could tell that it was a woman who had overlooked the cow. "Are there any women in town who are jealous of you?" he asked. "There is Mary ——." "No one named Mary ever overlooked," he rebuked her sharply.

The form of the charm was to say the secret prayers with his back to the fire, using unsalted butter—perhaps to banish the complaint into the stones. The overlooker has to come and spit on the animal and say "God bless you" three times.

Collecting in County Kerry

A Doubter Convinced
(Michael Sugrue)

An uncle of mine lived in Corrach (between Waterville and Ballinskelligs). He didn't believe in overlooking.

He was herding his cows near the roadside on a Sunday morning. He had four cows. A neighbor happened to come along on his way to Mass, and spent some time chatting with him. "These are four fine cows you have," he said. He didn't say "God bless the cows." When he had made those remarks he continued on his way to Mass. The man had not gone very far when one of the cows got a seizure and fell. My uncle called him back, and then the neighbor repeated the prayer, and the cow got on his legs again. After that my uncle no longer disbelieved in the evil eye. [4]

The Priest who Overlooked his own Horse
(Michael Sugrue)

This man, named Casey, lived in the glen near Ballinskelligs—Bealach Nagcúl. He used to set charms. The clergy of the parish denounced him, and refused him the sacraments unless he promised to give up charm-setting. He used to make a little money out of it.

One Sunday the curate at Ballinskelligs went to the glen on horseback on a young spirited horse to celebrate Mass. And when Mass was over the congregation as was the custom at the time loitered on the road outside the church. And Casey happened to be in the congregation. The priest mounted his horse and started off at a brisk canter on his way back to Ballinskelligs. He had not gone very far, when suddenly his horse stumbled and fell underneath him and lay on the road as if it were dead. The priest tried every means to get the horse on its legs again, but failed. In the meantime the congregation rushed towards him, and did their best to help him to get the horse up. But all their efforts failed.

Suddenly a member of the congregation said, "If Dennis Casey were here, he would probably do some good for the horse." The priest overheard the remark and he told him to fetch Casey along. Casey came along and repeated the words of the charm over the stricken horse, and the horse immediately got on its legs again, shook herself three times, and was as well as ever. The priest thanked him and said, "I'd rather than the price of the horse that I'd know who did her harm." "You yourself did her harm," replied Casey. "How?" "I will tell you," said Casey. "When you got on the horse's back, you said in your own mind that it was grand to have the horse to ride on. But you didn't say 'God bless her.' "

The clergy never interfered with Casey afterward. [5]

In the Field

The Pig
(Michael Sugrue)

This old woman lived in Sosa. She was his sister's mother-in-law. She was fattening a pig for the fair. There was a neighbor living next door and he had a little garden. Matches were not as numerous at that time, and the custom was when you'd light your pipe you'd call at the neighbor's house for a light. So this old man did that, and the pig happened to be eating a mess on the floor out of a wooden trough, and he started to praise the pig. "That's a fine pig you have," he said, without saying "God bless you." She said, "It's hard for the pig to be good, he isn't getting enough food." So immediately the pig took its head from the mess and staggered and reeled around two or three times and fell on the kitchen floor. When the man saw the pig falling, he ran towards her and started spitting on her. It was of no avail.

The old woman said, "Stop that now, and repeat these words after me. 'If it is I did you harm or overlooked you, may God and His Blessed Mother bless you.'" And immediately that he repeated those words, the pig raised her head and got up. In the course of a few days the pig came out of it all right.[6]

The Evil Eye of Brennan
(Michael Sugrue)

There was a Brennan man living at the cross at Kinaird. He had it in the eye. He made his living fishing. He was out on the sea one night fishing with his crew and he saw a pollock jumping in the sea. He looked in the direction in which the pollock jumped, and when the pollock struck the surface of the water, it remained dead on top of the water. The crew rowed towards the pollock, and found that its backbone was broken in two halves.

His name was John Brennan—a very pious man, Shaun of the prayers—an itinerant, a poor traveling man. He was reputed to have an evil eye. It was the custom of the priests to visit at each house, say Mass, collect dues. John Brennan used to follow the priests on those occasions (to get a free meal). And the curate he knew that John was possessed of the evil eye.

After the "station" was over the curate started to come along on horseback. There was an old gentleman, Sigerson (a middleman, a petty landlord), lived down near the sea [where Delargy later stayed], who was taking his usual morning walk. He met the priest, and they chatted awhile. So as they were engaged in the conversation, the curate glanced towards the east, and he saw a horse and carriage approaching, with a parson who lived in Waterville. He was on his way to the Coast Guard station at Ballinskelligs to conduct a service for the crew. But he was driving at a very quick rate, and the curate drew John's attention to him. "Now, John," he said, "there's a good opportunity of trying out the power of that eye of yours."

John turned around and looked to the east, and immediately he did so the

194

horse plunged forward and dropped on the road, upsetting the carriage and throwing the parson onto a clump of briars on the roadside. When the curate saw what had happened, he was shocked. "Oh, John," he said, "run at once and restore the horse." "No, Father," said John, "you go, because you've got the power." "Oh, no, John," he said, "you go, because it was you did the harm." So John went, and repeated the words of the prayer over the stricken horse [cf. "The Pig"], and the horse jumped up immediately, and the parson resumed his journey.[7]

Demonic Beings[8]

The Spirit of the Tobacco
(collected by Tadhg Murphy from Seán O'Sullivan)

We heard there was an old woman long ago who used to be seen underneath a little bridge each night smoking a pipe. People used to see her there at an unusual hour at night. Well, there was a poor man (we don't know whether he was young or old) who lived near the place, and it so happened that he had no tobacco. He said to himself as night came on, "I will go to this old woman who is underneath the bridge. Perhaps she will give me a smoke." He did, and when he approached her, she handed him the pipe. When he had smoked of the pipe to his satisfaction, he handed it back to her, and he prayed for her. He said, "May the Lord have mercy on your soul, and on the souls of your dead, and on all the souls of the world combined." She herself smoked the pipe again, and handed it to him a second time. He drew another blast from the pipe, and he handed it back to her again and prayed for her as he had already prayed. She handed him the pipe a third time, and he drew another pull from it. He gave her the same prayer again a third time.

She then told him that that was the duration of her purgatory, that she was now all right, that her purgatory was finished. That was the purgatory placed on her, until somebody would come along, take the pipe from her, pray for her soul, and for all the souls of the faithful departed.

They say that is how the custom of smoking tobacco at wakes originated.[9]

How the Guerins Got Their Name
(heard by Tadhg Murphy from several informants)

There was a fisherman in Ballinskelligs, just across the bay, who was coming home one night late, and on his way home he met the pooka. He took it to be a horse. He stared at the pooka, and suddenly the pooka addressed him and said, "Get on my back, and I'll give you a ride to my home." He got on the pooka's back. The pooka started to jump and rear, and after a while he set off in full gallop, along by the cliffs of the sea and through briars and brambles and every type of crosscountry. And the poor fisherman was almost scared to death. The pooka kept going at full gallop until the cock crew. (All spirits and ghosts and fairies were laid at first cockcrow.) He landed the fisherman at the first spot he met him and left him there. So the poor man ambled home as best he could, exhausted and weary and terrified after his experience with the pooka.

The next day he met a blacksmith who lived in the vicinity, and he told him what had happened the previous night. "And I've got to go fishing tonight again," he said, "and I'm afraid of meeting the pooka." "Don't worry," said the smith, "I'll give you a remedy by which you'll turn the tables on the pooka. Come along with me to the forge." They both went to the forge, and the smith made him a pair of iron anklets or spurs with sharp spikes sticking out. "Now," said the smith, "take those along with you tonight, and if you happen to meet the pooka, and he suggests taking you for a ride, accept his invitation, get on his back, and don't hesitate to use the spurs freely on his flanks."

So he did. He went fishing again that night, and on his way home he met the pooka on the same spot where he had met him the previous night. "Well," said the pooka, "would you like a ride tonight?" "Oh, certainly, I'd be very pleased." "Get on my back." He jumped on his back, and immediately the pooka started his pranks again, to jump and rear, and the fisherman started to use his spurs mercilessly on the pooka'a flanks. So the pooka didn't take him very far on this occasion. He was very glad to get rid of him. His flanks and sides were punctuated and torn and lacerated from the spurs. So he brought him back after a short while and let him down where he found him. "Now," said the fisherman, "although tonight's ride was very short, I enjoyed it immensely, and I should very much like to ride on you tomorrow night." "You'll be very welcome," said the pooka, "but don't bring those sharp points along with you."

The fisherman went fishing again the next night, but he didn't meet the pooka, and that is how the surname Guerin ("the people with the sharp points") originated.

The pooka looks like a pony with a long shaggy mane; he sticks his head between a person's legs and throws him on his back. [10]

The Luharacán
(Michael Sugrue)

The luharacán was a shoemaker, a little man about three feet. A man happened to come on him one day and snapped his purse. The luharacán told him, "Look behind you and see the crowd." The man said, "Never mind the crowd, but hand out the purse." He gave him the purse, and the following wish also: "A white house on a height to you, a fine-looking woman to you, and the praise of the neighbors to you." The man thought he had cursed him. "Oh, here is your purse," he said, handing him back the purse. The luharacán then changed the wish and said, "A small low house to you in a hollow, a rusty woman to you, and the face of the neighbors to you."

The house on the height would attract attention, the good-looking woman would arouse jealousy, and the neighbors' praise would bring the evil eye.

A man in Port Magee caught a luharacán. This happened as late as thirty years ago. The man was looking for wreckage, and he came on him in a cave by the seashore making shoes. He ran towards him and caught him with both hands, and told him to hand over his purse. "Oh," said the luharacán, "look behind you and see all those people. They're going to throw you over the cliff." The man suddenly looked around him, and saw nobody. When he looked back again, the luharacán had disappeared. He held only two blades of hay in his hands. [11]

A Funeral from the Other World
(collected by Tadhg Murphy from Jerry Shea)

I happened to be south in Kill Mac Eoin; there's a daughter of mine married there, Nora. Well, the old man, Nora's father-in-law, was telling me a story that happened to a neighbor.

He was a carman named O'Shea, who used to take butter and eggs to Cork from Kill Mac Eoin. Late one night he was returning from Cork, after disposing of his groceries in the shops in Eyres, about four miles from his home. And as he was coming home he met a funeral coming against him, going to the north. So he pulled in his horse at the roadside, to let the funeral pass by. It was a bright night, and he saw a man at the extreme end of the funeral procession. And as he passed he attempted to kick the carman. "Shame, shame for ever," a woman spoke. "Don't ever strike the father of the children." (O'Shea had a large young family.)

And who should that woman happen to be but Mary Murphy who lived in Eyres. She told him the whole story afterwards. "Ah," said Mary to him, "you should have come out of the cart, and walked a few steps in the funeral procession. (That was according to old tradition, to walk three paces of mercy.) The funeral came from the East Indies to the cemetery west of Eyres, Kill Katharne, with the corpse either of a woman or a man, and I was with them."

Glory be to God, wasn't it far away they came! [12]

In the Field

The Cattle Buyer
(Tadhg Murphy)

At a fair in Castletown Beare this man saw a stranger buy quite a number of
cattle. The stranger bought from him also. Then he drove the cattle down to
the pier and out into the sea, on top of the water. At a certain distance they
disappeared. A number of years afterward he saw the same buyer, and stared
at him. "Are you the cattle jobber who drove the cattle into the sea?" he
asked. The jobber came over to him and blew a puff of breath under his eyes,
so he lost his sight immediately. "You'll never see me again, nor anything
else," he said. [13]

The Return of my Uncle from the Dead
(Michael Sugrue)

My uncle, Dan Dennahy, from my mother's side, lived in Tooreen in the
glen. His father was a widower and had six in the family, of whom Dan was
the eldest. There was a widow living in the village also with three in family,
and Dan's father wanted to make a match with the widow. Dan was very
much opposed, and made some reference to the woman's character. The
remark reached the widow, who said, "May God not forgive him until I
forgive him." The marriage fell through.

When Dan grew up he got married in Toreen and had four in family. He
went down to the sea looking for wreckage on a Sunday morning. It happened
to be the last day of the Old Year, the thirty-first of December. Next day was
New Year's Day. He had no coat on when he was drowned in attempting to
take some wreckage. He was swept away by a wave, and all he had on was a
frieze pants and waistcoat. The sea was so violent at the place where he was
drowned that he was dashed to pieces immediately. In about half an hour's
time a leg of the pants and half the waistcoat were cast ashore. His body was
never found.

Well, this woman, the widow, lived in a bothan (a little hut) with her three
children. And the next night, New Year's night, the three children had gone to
bed, and she remained up by the kitchen fire. She used to smoke a pipe, and
she wanted to have a smoke before retiring. There was no light in the kitchen
(at that time there were no lamps), only the glow thrown out by the fire. She
had the pipe lighted, when suddenly it fell out of her mouth into her dress.
She started to look for the pipe. She searched her dress and couldn't find it.
She was wondering where it could have gone to. Suddenly she raised her head
and saw Dan sitting on the rack with the pipe in his mouth.

"Are you Dan?" she said.

"I am," said he. "Don't be in the least bit afraid of me. It isn't to do you any
harm I have come. I come to ask you to forgive myself and my sister Mary
that is in America, to take the curse off us."

"Oh, I am forgiving everyone dead and alive," she said. Then she asked him where were his bones.

"Yerra, Peg," he said, "it doesn't matter where the bones are as long as the soul is all right." She then asked him how were things on the other side, and the answer he made her was, "Those who deserve it have a good time, but those who do not, have not." She then asked him where was his purgatory. He said it was in his father's house, and he made an appointment with her to meet him at his father's house on a certain night.

She went to the house and met him there, and started a chat with him in the presence of the members of his family. The family did not see him, nor were they able to hear his part of the conversation. But they heard hers. They heard all the questions which she put to him, but they were unable to hear his answers. The members of the family used to get his sign on the floor. When lighting his pipe, when alive, his method was to pull out a coal from the fire, turn the mouth of the pipe over the coal, and press it down into the bowl, which therefore bruised the spark against the floor. [Tadhg demonstrated this procedure to me.] Next morning the family used to find the sign of the spark on the flag of the fire.

Tadhg: "That was quite an experience!"

Michael: "He had others!"

This woman Peg happened on some occasion to go down to the glen in the month of March. And when she reached the Bealach Cun (mountain pass), she met a crowd of people on the northern side of the Bealach. And she thought that all that ever left the world were in the glen. All the glen was full of people. She continued on her journey, and when she got halfway through the crowd this man, Dan, stepped out of the crowd and spoke to her. He told her to turn back. "And when you go down to my aunt's house" (in the direction she had come), "go in there, and when you'll be inside the threshold, a shower of hailstones will come, and that will scatter us. And go home and have some other day to come on your journey."

So she went back, and had only put her foot inside the threshold when the heavy shower of hail fell. [14]

Local Traditions

Poor Jack of the Thorn
(Tadhg Murphy)

This man, a small farmer with a small patch of land in Kerry, derived his name from a whitethorn bush which grew at the back of his house. He was a poor simple man, illiterate, who believed in dreams. He dreamt on three occasions that if he went to the Bald Bridge of Limerick he would come into the possession of a large treasure, on condition that he remained on the bridge

In the Field

for three days. He told his wife about the dream, and that he intended going to the Bald Bridge of Limerick to see if his dream would come true. "Ah, you silly old man," said the wife, "your dreams are all nonsense. Stay at home." "No," said Shaun, "I'll start off tomorrow morning and try my fortune."

So he set off, on foot of course, and never stopped until he came to the Bald Bridge of Limerick. And he started his vigil on the bridge. He walked up and down all day, and still no treasure came. He took lodgings in a little house beside the bridge at night, and resumed his vigil early next morning, and spent the day on the bridge again. And still no treasure appeared. He took lodgings again in a little house at night. And on the third day about midday, as he was standing on the bridge, a man came up to him and addressed him. "Pardon me, stranger," he said, "I don't want to be curious," he said, "but I have noticed you on this bridge during the past two days, and I'm curious to know what is your business." So Shaun told him the story about his dream and the treasure. "Ah, poor silly man," he said. "Go back home to Kerry, and don't be wasting your time here. I also dreamt of a treasure which was supposed to be hidden in a little farm in Kerry at the back of the house of a man named Poor Jack of the Thorn, under a whitethorn bush. And I suppose the man does not exist."

So Shaun returned home very well pleased with the result of the information which he gleaned from the stranger. And when he got home he got a spade and digged under the whitethorn bush. And he had not digged very deep when he came on a large iron pot, with the lid on. He lifted the pot, and it was rather heavy. He removed the lid, and the pot was full of gold. He bore the pot into the house and removed the treasure, and hid it carefully in some corner of the house. His wife took possession of the empty pot, and used it for cooking purposes in the kitchen.

Some time afterwards a poor scholar happened to come on that way, and asked for a night's lodgings. And Jack said he was quite welcome. So they sat by the kitchen fire at night, and Shaun's wife put a pot of potatoes to boil on the fire for supper. The glow of the fire lighted up the side of the pot, and the poor scholar noticed some writing or characters on the side of the pot, and he was able to decipher the writings. "Where did you get that pot?" he asked. "To tell you the truth," he said, "I don't know where it came from. It has been in the house since my grandfather's time." "Well," said the poor scholar, "wherever it came from, I have deciphered the writing on the pot, and it states that there is twice as much on the other side."

Next morning the poor scholar went on his way, and when he had left, Jack (Shaun) got a spade again and went and digged at the other side of the farm bush, and found two pots of gold. So Shaun was then the richest man in the county of Kerry, as the result of his dream.

("That was one of the first stories I heard from my father—he used to tell it often. He died in 1928, at the age of 84. That was in Skehanagh in the parish of Cahardaniel, twelve miles south of Waterville.")

Mrs. Murphy: "I used to believe those stories till after I was married. If your father and mother believed it you believed it.")[15]

Oliver Cromwell and the Wall
(Tadhg Murphy, heard from his father)

When Oliver Cromwell had become master of England he was naturally very interested in securing the country against invasion, and he thought it would be a good plan to build a stout stone wall along the coast. He always kept a Black Bible, which was usually carried about by his footman. So when he got the idea of building the wall he acted on it immediately, and set out for the nearest coast accompanied by his footman to start building the wall. It was a very warm day in midsummer, and he and the footman were on foot. When he reached the coast he felt very tired and sleepy. He told his footman that he would lay down for a while and rest before starting the wall. "And you take charge of that Bible," he said, "while I'm asleep. And on no account open it."

Cromwell lay down and fell into a sound sleep, and was soon snoring loudly. And when the footman found his master asleep, curiosity seized him. "I'll see for myself," he said, "what is in this Bible that my master is so particular about." He opened the Bible, and suddenly a crowd of little men issued forth and swarmed on the shore like ants on an anthill. And they all started shouting loudly, "Give me work, give me work, give me work." The poor footman looked at them terror-stricken, fearing their shouting would wake his master. "I got no work for you," he said, "but if you wish you can start making ropes out of the sand." So they got to work immediately and tried making ropes out of the sand. But of course the task was an impossible one. "We can't do the job," they said. "Well, if you can't," said the footman, "get right back here again into the Bible." So they trooped back. And when the footman found the last man within he slammed the Bible.

After a while Cromwell awoke, and he told the footman to hand him the Bible. The footman did so, and he opened it. But if he did, no man came forth from the Bible. "Ah, my good man," he said to the footman, "I'm afraid you opened the Bible while I was asleep. And that will leave England forever without a protective wall.[16]

The People of Kill Mhic Kiarainn
(Tadhg Murphy)

[A village in the parish of Dromaid about eight miles northeast of Waterville. Its inhabitants were referred to in Gaelic as the "iron fools."]

In the Field

The Story of the Bridge

At that time, about one hundred and twenty years ago, the principal butter market for Munster was in Cork city, and the farmers took their butter in firkins to Cork on horseback, a hundred weight in each firkin. The horse had a straddle on its back and two firkins were suspended on each side of the straddle, with another firkin on top. They usually set out for the market in fairly large parties, on an appointed day.

So the people of Kill Mhic Kiarainn set out for Cork city one day with their horses and packs. At that time bridges were unknown in that part of the country. Rivers and streams were usually forded in shallow places. So on their way through the county of Cork they came upon a bridge, and they gazed at it in wonder and astonishment. They halted their horses and held a consultation. One of the men said that this was surely some trap which was set for their destruction. "And I think," he said, "it would be a very grave risk to cross it with our valuable horses." They all in turn expressed their opinion about the safety of crossing the bridge. Finally one of the men who had the reputation of being the wisest of the party volunteered to step on the bridge and test it with his feet to see if it would hold up a man. He stepped on the bridge, assuming a very brave air, and marched backwards and forwards about a dozen times. He then called out to the party, "Drive over the brown mare. I think this ford has a solid foundation." So the whole party crossed the bridge.

The Story of the Clock

On another occasion they were going to Cork with butter, and they came on a clock which happened to be in the middle of the road. Clocks were then unknown in their district and they had never seen a clock before. Somebody had lost this clock. They stopped their horses, and fear seized them. They were afraid to approach the clock fearing that it might be some infernal machine. They kept at a safe distance, and each in turn expressed his opinion about the clock. Finally they came to the conclusion that it was a serpent. And there and then one of the party was told off to destroy the serpent.

He walked over to the roadside fence and took a large stone from off the fence, and placed it on his shoulder. He walked very cautiously out on to the center of the road, fearing he should disturb the serpent. He threw the stone with a crash on the body of the serpent, and broke the clock in smithereens. And as a result the clock was disemboweled, and the wheels and works were scattered all over the road. He stood over the wreckage, very proud of his feat. "Ah boys," he said, "it is a good job that we destroyed this serpent, because if she had lived she would have filled the countryside with young serpents." [17]

Collecting in County Kerry

(I can remember when it was a rare sight to see a clock in the house. The time was usually told by the sun in the morning, when it shone on the kitchen door.)

America in Irish Lore

Seán Palmer's Voyage with the Fairies
(collected by Tadhg Murphy from William Bradley)

The extraordinary story which follows represents a grafting of twentieth-century Irish experience onto the sanctioned themes of Irish fairy lore. The Irish migration to the United States in the last century has established a network of kinships across the Atlantic that embraces virtually every Irish family. Both Mr. and Mrs. Murphy, for example, asked me to look up their brother and sister living in New York and Boston on my return. Seán Palmer's wish to see his well-to-do relatives, friends, and old sweetheart in America could properly be satisfied by the traditional transporters of Irish folk to remote, exotic places—the fairies.

Tadhg told me this story just as I was leaving Waterville. He had collected it in Gaelic from William Bradley, who had heard Seán Palmer tell it, in June, 1933, when Mr. Bradley was seventy-five. Rineen Bán, Seán's home, is a little village four miles from Waterville on the southwest side of Ballingskelligs Bay. Tadhg describes Liam Bradley as "a small farmer and water-keeper, a grand step-dancer, gay, light-hearted, and possessing an inexhaustible fund of Gaelic stories, anecdotes, and songs."

I attempted to secure the original text of the narrative from the archives in Dublin, but it proved to be missing. Tadhg looked through his old notebooks, and by luck found the tale as he had originally taken it down in his field notes. Below is his translation, faithful to the Gaelic idiom.

Seán Palmer, he lived in Rinneen Bán. He had a small farm, and owned a fishing boat—he fished during the summer season. He was married and had three children growing up. Now, Seán was very fond of tobacco—he was a very hard smoker—and would prefer to go without his meals any day than to go without a smoke of his clay pipe, and at that time shops were few and far between. The country folk had to depend on huckstering egg-women who

In the Field

visited them once a month perhaps, to buy their eggs, to supply their various household needs—tobacco, soap, needles, pins, etc., which they exchanged for the housewives' eggs. They sold tobacco for a penny a finger—the middle finger of the right hand from the top to the knuckle—that was the measure. It was called "a finger of tobacco."

Now it so happened that on this certain occasion to which our story refers, the egg-woman who used to visit Rinneen Bán was not as punctual as was customary with her, and Seán Palmer had to go without his usual smoke; and as with all heavy tobacco smokers, this enforced abstention from the nerve-soothing weed had a very serious affect on Seán's usually active and industrious disposition. For two days he sat on the hob by the kitchen fire, grumbling and grousing, and cursing the egg-woman roundly for her delay in supplying him with his favorite weed.

On the evening of the third day, after he had made about the twentieth trip from the hob to the kitchen door, in the hope that the egg-woman would sooner or later make her appearance, he spoke thus to his wife: "Mary," said he, "I can't stand it any longer! The end of my patience is exhausted. I think I'll set off to Seán [Murphy] The Locks for a finger of tobacco. There will be no living in this house with me if I have to spend the night without a smoke of tobacco!"

Seán The Locks kept a little shop about a quarter of a mile to the south of the present village of Waterville—there was no village then—and sold tobacco and groceries.

"The potatoes are boiled, Seán," said the wife, "and you may as well sit over to the table and eat your supper before you start off."

"Yerrah, woman," said Seán, "I cannot see the table, nor can I see the potatoes—I am stark blind for the want of a smoke! I will start off this very minute for Seán The Locks' shop, and the potatoes can wait until I come back."

He arose from his seat on the hob, grasped his blackthorn stick, and set off for Seán The Locks' shop, dressed only in his sleeve-waistcoat and flannel drawers—he had neither shoes nor stockings on his feet, as men wore shoes only when going to Mass, or to the local town on a fair or market day, at that time. As he approached the quay—there is a little quay on the roadside at the bottom of Rinneen Bán, where fishing boats came to shore and landed their catches of fish—it is how there were two men on the road before him, standing, and as he was making towards them: "That is Seán Palmer," said one of the men to the other. "I know what is the matter with him, and where he is going. He has no tobacco," said he, in Seán's hearing—they knew Seán was listening to them. When Seán came within speaking distance of the two men, he saluted them, and they returned his salutation.

"I presume you have got no tobacco, Seán," said one of the men, "and do you see those two men down there? Go down to them and you will get your fill of tobacco from them." There was a little boat pulled up alongside the quay below, and two men in her. Seán hesitated for a moment. "I suppose it is rather late to go to Seán The Locks' shop, now," he said, "and my supper is on the table, awaiting my return. Even if I only got one pipeful from them, sufficient to satisfy my craving 'til morning, I'd be very well pleased." "Go on down," said one of the men, "and you'll get plenty tobacco."

Seán went down to the quay and stood on the pier—the boat was pulled close in beside the quay—there were two men in her. Seán addressed them very politely, and said he would be ever so grateful if they would kindly give him a smoke of tobacco. "That you shall get, and plenty, and to spare," said one of the men. "Step into the boat and be seated—come in," said he.

As Seán was stepping into the boat, he chuckled with delight at the idea of having had such good luck. "By gor," said he to himself, "isn't it I that have struck the good luck! It is an old saying—and a true one—that a hound let loose is better than a hound on the leash." "Here you are, Seán," said one of the men who was in the boat, "take that and smoke to your satisfaction," handing him his own pipe, which was red [i.e. lighted], and in full steam. Seán took the pipe from him, thanked him, and sat on the center thwart of the little boat, puffing great blasts of smoke from his pipe—he was almost enveloped in tobacco smoke. He sat there puffing eagerly at the pipe, oblivious of his surroundings, and oblivious of everything, like a man in a trance. "Oh, man alive!" said he to himself. "Isn't it the oil of the heart! 'Tis the grandest pipe of tobacco I have ever smoked in my life!"

It was not very long until the two men in the boat made a sign to their two companions who were still standing on the roadway, bidding them to come down and get into the boat at once, and so they did, and no sooner had they stepped aboard than the sails were raised close to Seán's ear, and the order was given: "To sea with you boys!" and the little boat shot out from the quayside and away to sea with her! "By gor," said Seán to himself, "you have high notions like the poor man's cabbage (an old saying or cant-word), whatever destination you are bound for!"

Neither Seán nor any of the four boatmen spoke a word for some time, nor interfered with one another in any way, and in the meantime the boat was racing along, skimming over the surface of the sea like a shot from a gun, and it was not very long until Seán saw lights—the lights of houses he presumed. "Yerrah," said Seán to one of the men, "are not those the lights of Lóhar houses?"

"Och! God help you," replied one of the men. "Wait awhile and you shall see much finer houses than your Lóhar houses!" "By the cross of the ass," said Seán, "surely they are the Lóhar houses, and there is Rinneen Bán to the west!" "Och! God help you," said another of the men. "Do you not know where you are now—you are beside New York Quay!" said he. "See the ships and the people and the grand houses. Step ashore now, Seán," said he.

Seán stared in confusion at the sight that met his eyes, and it took him some time to regain his usual composure. However, he stepped ashore, as he was bade to do by the man in the boat, and he mixed with the crowds of people on the quay, but they were all complete strangers to him—he knew none of them, and he imagined they were all staring at him. "Oh, good heavens," said he to himself, "no wonder they are all staring at me, with nothing on me but my sleeve-waistcoat and my flannel drawers, and without a shoe or a stocking on my feet! Why did I not put on my frieze coat when I was leaving the house!"

A man passed close by him as he stood there on the quay, gazing at the crowds. "Upon my conscience," said the man, as he passed him by, "but that fellow bears a very close resemblance to Seán Palmer of Rinneen Bán!" "By heaven," said Seán to himself, "that fellow certainly is in America—Andy Pickett from Rinneen Bán! Sure I knew him well before he came over here—and if he is in America, I am in América also! I suppose he did not recognize me." "Make no mistake about it," said one of the men who brought him over in the boat. "You really are in America. Now, Seán," said he, "you have a brother here in New York, have you not?" "I have," said Seán, "but New York is a big place, and how could a poor greenhorn like me find out where he lives." "Never mind," said the man, "come along and we shall find him."

Two of the men accompanied Seán, and the other two men remained in charge of the boat. They walked along through the main streets of New York, Seán and his two companions, until they came to one of the side streets. The two men suddenly stopped in front of a tenement. "Your brother Paddy lives in this house," said one of them to Seán. "Knock at the door and tell the people of the house that you want to see Paddy Palmer." Seán did as he was bade—he knocked at the door, and one of the servants came in response to his knock. "Does Paddy Palmer from Rinneen Bán live here?" Seán asked the servant. "Yes, he does," the servant replied. "Come right in to his room." Seán followed the servant upstairs to an upper room. "This is his room, now," said the servant. "You can step right in," and left him.

Seán stepped into the room, and when Paddy saw him, dressed in a sleeve-waistcoat, flannel drawers, and without shoes nor stockings on his feet, he thought he belonged to the other world—that he was dead, and that this was his spirit which had come to visit him.

"Good heavens, Seán!" he exclaimed. "Was it how you died?" "No, faith," replied Seán, "but I am very much alive!" "And when did you come to America?" asked Paddy. "I landed on the quay about a quarter of an hour ago," Seán replied. "And when did you leave home?" asked Paddy. "I left Rinneen Bán about a half hour ago," said Seán. "And what brought you over, or were there many people on the boat coming over?" asked Paddy.

"Wait a minute until I tell you my story," said Seán. "I ran short of tobacco, and I started off just after nightfall for Seán The Locks' shop to get some tobacco, and when I reached Rinneen Bán Quay [repeats his experience]. As I stood there on the quay, gaping at the crowds as they passed to and fro, Andy Pigott from Rinneen happened to pass by. 'My soul from the devil!' said he, as he passed along. 'That fellow resembles Seán Palmer from Rinneen Bán very closely!'

"Well, one of the men asked me if I had a brother here in New York. I said, yes, I have. So they brought me along here." "Sit down just for a moment until I order some supper for you," said Paddy, "and while you are eating, I'll go out to the store next door and fetch you some tobacco, and when I come back I shall give you my best suit of clothes—you look terrible in those old duds you are wearing. I can buy myself another new suit tomorrow."

Seán sat down when the supper came and started eating, and he had just finished as Paddy came back, carrying a fairly large box of tobacco under his arm.

"Now Seán," said he, "you have a half-year's supply of tobacco in this box," putting his hand in his trousers' pocket at the same time and producing a bundle of dollars. "And here are a few dollars for you," said he, "which I intended sending you at Christmas, but as you happen to be on the spot now, you will save me the trouble of sending it along to you."

'Pon my word, he gave him a very good present, Paddy did. "Well," said Seán, "you have given me a very decent present, Paddy, and I am very thankful to you, and now I must be going—the two men are out there on the street waiting for me, so I cannot delay any further."

Paddy wrapped up his best suit in a sheet of brown paper, together with the box of tobacco, and handed the parcel to Seán. "Goodbye now, Seán," said he, "and God speed you." Seán stepped out into the street. His two companions of the boat were standing there waiting for him.

"My word, Seán," said one of them, "you have not fared too badly by your visit!"

"By my soul!" replied Seán, "you bet I haven't! I have a bundle of dollars to the value of seven pounds, together with a large box of tobacco, and a fine suit of clothes!"

"Give me the bundle now, Seán," said the man, "and I will put it on the boat." Seán handed him the parcel and the man set off towards the boat with it; and said the other man, addressing Seán: "Seán," said he, "haven't you got a sister up in Boston?" "I have, by gor!" said Seán. "I have a sister somewhere in the States—probably in Boston." "Yes, she is in Boston," replied the man, "I know the house where she lives, and if you wish to visit her, I will accompany you there, and we shall find her out. The other man will catch up with us—come right along," said he. "By my soul," said Seán, "I'd like very much to see my sister Cáit—why shouldn't I?"

They started off and reached Boston in less than no time. As they were going through the city of Boston, Seán's companion stopped suddenly in front of one of the houses in the main street, in front of the door. "Well, Seán," said he, "here we are in Boston, and your sister Cáit lives here in this house. Go over and knock at the door and enquire if she is in, that you want to see her." Seán went over and knocked at the door. The door was opened by a middle-aged woman, in answer to Seán's knock. "Whom do you want to see?" the woman asked. "I want to see Cáit Palmer," said Seán. "I am Cáit Palmer," said she. "Good God, Cáit," said he, "do you not know your brother Seán from Rinneen Bán!"

"Yerrah, Seán," said she, "and when did you die?" She thought that it was from the other world he had come, when she saw the sleeve-waistcoat and the flannel drawers on him, and he barefooted.

"By my soul!" said Seán, "I am not dead—I am very much alive," said he. "I have come all the way from Rinneen Bán to see you. I have been down in New York with Paddy since I arrived in the States, and he will tell you the whole story when you meet him."

"Wisha, Seán," said she, "and when did you leave Rinneen Bán?"

"I left there about suppertime tonight," said he. "I started off for Seán The Locks' shop to get some tobacco; but it would take too long to tell you the whole story now—Paddy will tell you all about it when you see him. I had supper with him down in New York. God bless poor Paddy! He was very kind to me. He gave me a big box of tobacco, a grand new suit of his own clothes, and a bundle of dollars to take home with me."

Cáit opened her purse and handed him a twenty-dollar bill. "Here, Seán," said she, "take that—it is all the money which I have got on me at present; but I shall not forget you at Christmas time—I will send you a cheque at Christmas." Seán bade his sister goodbye and stepped out into the street, where his two companions were still standing, waiting for his return. "Well, Seán," said one of the men to him, "how did you get on with your sister Cáit?" "By my soul!" replied Seán, "I did very well! She gave me a twenty-dollar bill." The three then set off again for New York, and as they were approaching the city, Seán stopped suddenly. "Good heavens!" he exclaimed. "Where is my pipe! It must have fallen from my mouth, or I must have left it behind in Boston! I should have handed it back to the man who gave it to me, and now it is lost—and what a fine pipe it was!" "Never mind about the pipe," said one of his companions. "Don't worry about it, we shall get another pipe."

As they were going through New York: "By the way, Seán," said one of the men, "I suppose you knew Cáit 'Strockaire' O'Shea from the top of Lóhar?" "I did indeed," said Seán. "We were very close friends before she emigrated to America. As a matter of fact, I had a great notion to marry her at one time." "Would you like to see her?" asked the man. "She lives here in this lane—I know the house where she lives." "Ah, I don't think I should," said Seán. "My clothes are very shabby, and I would feel ashamed to meet her in this rig-out."

"Don't let that prevent you from seeing her," said the man who asked the question. "I'll run down and fetch your new suit from the boat, and you can exchange it for your old duds. We are in no hurry—we have got plenty of time." The man started off for the boat, and was back again with the new suit to Seán in less than no time. "Come along now, Seán," said he, "and peel off every stitch of your old clothes from the skin out, and put this suit on you."

He handed Seán the suit, and the other companion took Seán aside—he took him into a dark corner of the alley—and Seán put the new suit on.

His two companions then directed Seán to the house in the lane where Cáit "Strockaire" O'Shea lived. Seán knocked at the door and was admitted by Cáit, who recognized her old neighbor as soon as she laid eyes upon him. She gave him a *céad mílle fáilte*, and asked him how long was he in America, and when he came over. "I have been here during the past few years," replied Seán—he did not want to let her know that he had only just come over that night—"and I am going back to Ireland again," said he, "so I decided to call to see you before I go back."

"That was very kind of you indeed, Seán," said she, "and when are you sailing for Ireland?" "I am sailing this very night," replied Seán. "I shall be leaving in a few hours time." "Ah, Seán," said she, "had I known in time that you were going back to Ireland, I would have booked my passage on that boat along with you!" She opened her purse and handed Seán a fifteen-dollar bill. "Take this little present to my brother Con," said she—her brother Con "Strockaire" O'Shea, who lived in the top of Lóhar—"and here is a little gift for yourself," said she, handing him a five-dollar bill. "You can drink my health on the boat when you are crossing." "By the way, Seán," said she, "did you marry ever since?" "I say marry to you!" replied Seán—he gave her no direct answer. "Perhaps, Seán," said she, "we may both splice it up yet." "You could never tell," replied Seán, as he bade her goodbye, "stranger things might happen!"

Seán stepped out into the street, where his two companions were still standing waiting for him. "Well, Seán," said they, "how did you get on with Cáit 'Strockaire'?" "We got on fine," replied Seán. "We had a very pleasant chat and she gave me fifteen dollars to take home to her brother Con, who lives in the top of Lóhar, and five dollars for myself, to drink her health going over on the boat."

"Come along now, Seán," said his two companions, "our time is running short—we must make off the boat." They started off for the quay—New York Quay—and they made off the boat, and the other two men were waiting for them at the boat, where they had left her. They told Seán to come aboard, and he did. They spread their sails by the quay-side, and loosed the mooring rope. One of the men spoke in a low tone to the fourth man, who was at the steer, "There is no time to spare now. Give her all the canvas which she can take!" And the little boat bounded out from New York Quay like a falling star.

They were not very far out to sea when Seán felt the missing pipe being shoved between his teeth. "My soul from the devil!" he exclaimed, "is not this the missing pipe!" "Never mind," said one of the men, "but see if it is still red, and if it is, puff away at it to your heart's content!" The pipe was still red, and when Seán saw the puffs of smoke coming out of his mouth, "Ah," he exclaimed, "it is an old saying and a true one that a lucky man only needs to be born!"

In the Field

That was well and good, and it was not very long until Seán saw land appearing in the distance, and very soon he was able to distinguish the houses on the mainland. "Bless my soul!" said he to one of the men. "Are they the Lóhar houses which I can see in the distance?" "Yes, they are," replied the man. "Well, I give this little boat the lead for good speed," said Seán. "I thought we were only a few miles out from New York, and here we are now within a few oars' length of Rinneen Bán quay!" The boat swept in towards the quay like a rushing wave, her forward part resting on dry sand. "Step out of the boat, Seán," commanded one of the men, "you are landed safe and sound on Rinneen quay!" Seán took up his parcel and stepped ashore, and as he turned 'round to thank the crew, there was no trace or tidings of the crew or of their boat to be seen anywhere, as if the sea had swallowed them up.

As Seán walked up to the road from the pier, he heard the cocks crowing in the houses above. When he reached home, he knocked loudly at the kitchen door. "Get up and open the door for that rascal of a father of yours!" said Seán's wife to her eldest daughter—they had retired long since and were sound asleep. "He has spent the night card-playing in Seán The Locks' shop, I presume." The little girl got up and opened the door, and when she saw the strange man dressed in an elegant Yankee suit, the likes of which she had never before seen, complete with panama hat, and wearing a pair of well-shined glacé kid shoes, she shrank back in fear before the stranger, and rushed back to the bedroom, screaming and calling her mammy that there was a strange man in the kitchen. Her mother got out of bed, dressed, and came up in the kitchen. She knew Seán at once, of course—Seán had thrown some bog deal on the fire in the meantime, and it lighted up the kitchen. The wife looked at Seán for some time, and surveyed him from head to foot, and when she recovered her composure, "Good lord, Seán," said she, "where have you been all this night, or where did you get that fine suit of clothes which you have on your bones?"

"I did," replied Seán, "I got it over in New York from my brother Paddy!" She looked at him again more closely—she thought he had lost his reason. "And see here again," said he, "as proof that I have been in New York, see this fine box of tobacco which I got from Paddy—a full half-year's supply!" said he. "And see here again," said he, putting his hand in his trousers' pocket, and pulling up a fistful of dollars. "There's some money which he gave me to take home with me. I was up in Boston also, and I visited my sister Cáit and she gave me some more money; and on our way back to New York I visited our old neighbor Cáit 'Strockaire' O'Shea from the top of Lóhar—and 'tis she that is looking fine and strong—and she gave me a twenty-dollar bill to bring home with me to her brother Con, and a five-dollar bill for myself, to drink her health coming over on the boat." Seán's wife took up the tobacco box and examined it—she had a little education and was able to read and write—and she saw the words "New York" in large characters on the lid, and the date of the month on which the tobacco was packed. "By gor, Seán," said she, "your

story is a true one. This box came from New York sure enough, but how in the name of heaven did you manage to get there and back again, and in such a short time too?"

So Seán told her the whole story, as I have already told it to you, and next morning when Seán got up out of bed—he didn't get up too early, I suppose, as he felt tired after the voyage of the previous night—he ate his breakfast and dressed himself up in his grand new suit of clothes, shoes, and panama hat, and strolled out around the little farm. And when the neighbors saw the well-dressed stranger, they were wondering who he was—nobody knew Seán when he was dressed up in the suit of fine clothes—and after awhile they approached closer to Seán to find out who he was. It was only then that they recognized Seán.

In the course of time letters came from America to Seán's neighbors in Rinneen Bán and the top of Lóhar—from Andy Pickett and Cáit "Strockaire" O'Shea, telling them that they had seen Seán Palmer in America and that they had spoken to him.

So that is now the story of Seán Palmer for you, and the tobacco, and his voyage to America with the fairies.[18]

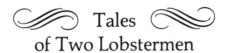

Tales
of Two Lobstermen

United States folktales differ from the traditional narratives of Europe. The animal tale, the Märchen, the origin myth, the saint's legend, the novelle are not native American growth. Anecdotes and yarns, tall tales, and supernatural experiences, though worldwide, seem especially characteristic of the American storytelling that has developed since the seventeenth century. However, the repertoires of individual narrators employing these forms have not yet been closely examined. Two fertile raconteurs, whom I encountered during a field trip to the coast of Maine in July 1956, illustrate personal variations in style and content within American anecdotal folk narrative.

The high coast of Maine was settled in the early nineteenth century from communities further south, which in turn had spawned from Massachusetts maritime towns in the late eighteenth century. These settlers were of English stock, from fishing villages in East Anglia. In the numerous offshore islands and the mainland harbors of coastal Maine they gained their livelihood from coastwise trade and the products of the sea. During the bustle of mid-nineteenth-century commerce and shipbuilding, the Maine harbor towns presented a lively appearance, but with the decline of the American merchant marine and the disappearance of the sailing ship, they decayed. Especially in the northern third of the indented coastline, above the summer tourist colonies culminating in the glitter of Bar Harbor, have these marine villages languished.

Here, in neighboring townships in Washington County, I met James Alley and Curt Morse, both retired lobstermen who had passed their lives (Alley was seventy-six and Morse seventy in 1956) on this coast. Alley was born on Head Harbor Island, among the cluster of islets ten miles deep between Jonesport and the open sea, but the colony of his kinfolk moved to the mainland early in the present century, and a number of the Head Harbor families, all densely interrelated, now live in Jonesport along a little dead-end road known as Alley's Lane. There Jim Alley mends nets and shucks clams. Curt Morse resides at the end of a country road overlooking a scenic bay in Kennebec, twelve miles from Jonesport and five miles from the county seat of Machias. After clamming in the morning, he spends each afternoon sauntering up and down the main street of Machias greeting friends and cracking jokes. He is popularly known as "Uncle Curt," and does in fact possess a string of relatives all along the road from Kennebec into Machias.

The two men know each other, and I met them both for the first time in the same group gathered at a home on Alley's Lane. Their personalities are extremely unlike, a fact reflected in their repertoires. Curt enjoys considerable local reputation as a wag and humorist, and lives up to his role with great glee. Curiously the community had no knowledge of Jim's narrative talents, and regarded him suspiciously because of alleged immoralities. Jim was moody, sensitive, and bitter, never smiling even in the midst of his humorous stories, while Curt was continually grinning and chuckling.

In three sessions with Curt Morse I tape-recorded 61 of his stories, and on eight different occasions I recorded 151 texts from James Alley. Their repertoires reveal common elements characteristic of American storytelling in general, and of the Maine Yankee coast in particular. But they also reveal striking dissimilarities.

Common Features

The tales of Alley and Morse all follow certain well-established patterns of American folk narrative. They are brief, single-episode jokes, anecdotes, tales, local legends, and supernatural experiences. The longest narrative does not exceed seven hundred words, and frequently an abbreviated jest or gag will be compressed into fifty words. Lengthy fictional pieces are conspicuously absent. Yet in the back country of Kentucky, Virginia, and North Carolina, Märchen have survived in abundance among Americans of Anglo-Saxon descent, as Leonard Roberts, Marie Campbell, and Richard Chase have demonstrated.[1]

Both Alley and Morse related comic anecdotes about local characters. Morse told six such tales, and Alley twenty-four. These characters are named, and actually lived, usually in the preceding generation. In the numerous town histories printed in New England, the odd sayings and doings of the village eccentrics are frequently noted. Anecdotes tend to cluster in little cycles around particularly colorful individuals. Thus an errant old sea-captain, Horace Smith, played the fool in a trio of Curt's narratives: Captain Smith stole a pair of pants from a one-legged man, inadvertently; hailed into court in Machias for stealing a black suit, he denied the charge, saying the suit was "dark blue"; when mischievous boys tied up clumps of herds' grass, he tripped over the tufts and finally exclaimed, "By jesus, chum, I seen a good many fields of grass, but I never saw a field where the grass all growed in staples." Jim Alley had still a different little anecdote, about a Christmas breakfast Captain Smith ate with his brother, only to find that the holiday repast provided "Same old thing, bread and butter."[2] Jim Alley told three anecdotes apiece about Art Church of Indian River, John McGee of Jonesport, and Frank Addison of Mason's Bay, and two about Enoch Smith and Leighton of Milbridge. Often migrant folktales become attached to the local character. Jim Alley ascribes to Art Church, who was reputed to be quite a liar, the trick told on various American local characters, and indexed by Baughman and Thompson as motif X905.4, "The liar; 'I have no time to lie today'; lies nevertheless." A story he relates about Frank Addison also has traveled widely. "Uncle Frank" Addison lived at Mason's Bay on the outskirts of Jonesport, drawing a veteran's pension. He possessed a "ripe wit," in Alley's phrase.

Well, he went in the war, drafted, he went in the war. (Which war?) World War. Old Revolution. And he got his ramrod out and got a string on it and doubled up a pin for the hook and went fishing in a pond of water over there. And the sergeant come along and says, "What are you doing there?" And he says, "I'm fishing." He says, "You come to the office." And he went up and he give him his discharge. He says, "Just what I was fishing for."

During the last war a popular GI folktale described the goldbricker who wandered around the barracks looking for invisible pieces of paper. Finally he was handed a medical discharge, and said, "That's the paper I was looking for."[3]

Jim Alley also related how John Fleet finally broke his long-standing silence and feud with Timothy Walters.

John married Timothy Walters' sister, you know, on the island. And they got mad at one another and hadn't spoke for six, seven years. And Mary Walters, she felt bad with John mad at her brother and wouldn't speak to him. She kept coaxing him to make up with him. So one day they were workin' on the road down on Beal's Island. And he said, "Well, Mary, I've got some good news for you." And she said, "What is it?" He says, "I spoke to Timothy today." She said, "You did? Well now, that's good, John. What did you say?" He said, "I told him to kick my uncle right plumb to hell."

A similar anecdote is reported by the discursive chronicler of local traditions in South County, Rhode Island, reminiscent Thomas R. Hazard. In *The Jonny-Cake Letters* (1882) he records how John Hazard broke a ten-year silence with his brother Sylvester by shouting at him across the street, "When are you going to return that iron bar you stole from me, you thief?"

Another form of local tradition common to the two narrators is the supernatural legend. This grouping includes maritime experiences and witch and birthmark stories. One sea legend widely told around Jonesport deals with the buying of wind in a becalmed boat by a blasphemous sailor, who swears a mighty oath as he throws a quarter into the ocean. A gale comes up and nearly wrecks the vessel. Half of the versions I obtained from twelve informants ascribed this feat to Paris Kaler, and Jim Alley's account was among these, but five other impious souls were named in further texts, Nick Bryant being the offender in Curt Morse's variant. These wind-buyers were all captains of small boats in the area, and belonged to an older generation.[4]

Both Jim and Curt recalled notorious local witches. Jim spoke of Mother Hicks, who bewitched a cow on Beals Island, and received her deadly retribution when the owner killed the cow and burned its "innards," thus causing the death by fire of Mother Hicks. Alley also talked of Liz Beal, who caused a well to dry up after its owner had refused her water; and the dry stones in the well can still be seen at Mason's Bay. The witch in Kennebec of whom Curt Morse knew was named Sal Joe, and she had cursed the district with a disastrous fire in spite against the people for calling her a witch. Both Mother Hicks and Sal Joe had the power to tip tables, a spiritualistic practice in wide vogue on the Maine coast.

Curt told of a woman on Beals Island marked by a seal, whose baby had a perfect seal's head, and smelled and sounded like a seal; and of a man in Machiasport who bore the mark of a hog, and was fed on swill. Jim too mentioned the "hog man," Will Lowe, during a conversation at Kilton's store, remarking how he could stick his tongue out and lick his hair back; and another time he related how Herb Pinkham of Milbridge was marked by a dying cow, so that his eyes rolled back in his head, and yet without sight he picked his way unerringly through a snowstorm in the woods, while all the other pulp-cutters failed to make camp.

Both Morse and Alley indulged in tall tales. Curt spun nineteen of his twenty-five around himself and his kinfolk, while Alley told seven fairly stock "windies." Also both narrators spouted forth jokes, Curt telling eight and Jim twenty. Each related a story in French dialect, reflecting the presence of French Canadians in the Maine woods, and each knew talking-parrot jokes (Morse two, Alley one) from the cycle, largely scatological, so popular all over both urban and rural America.

Here are some common elements in the tale repertoires of these two lobstermen. There is no surprise in the similarities in forms and themes of tales told by two storytellers who have passed their entire lives in the same isolated subculture. What is surprising are the considerable differences in the repertoires that a closer inspection reveals.

Individual Differences

Although both storytellers employ the briefer forms of folk narrative, they vary widely in their choice of subforms. Curt Morse leaned heavily to the peronal tall tale; he made himself the central figure in exaggerative fictions, or hung them on his wife and relatives in a kind of family saga. Nineteen of his "whoppers" take this guise, but not a single example appears among Jim Alley's stories. This genre perfectly suited the personality and public role Curt Morse had assumed in Washington County. He was a "character" in his own right, known for the witticisms and sallies with which he greeted storekeepers, loungers, and shoppers on his daily parade through Machias. Social and gregarious, Curt liked nothing better than to be the center of a laugh-rocked circle egging him on for more sidesplitters. In conformance with his "persona" of gagster and clown, he projected himself into his narratives at every possible point. These personal tall tales can be still further subdivided. They include three clearcut groups: short descriptive "lies" Curt wove around his wife and relatives; standard fictions into which he intruded; and actual incidents from his own life which he had selected and colored for storytelling purposes.

Curt familiarly refers to his wife as "Dynamite," saying, "She blows me up so often." He continued: "And I bought her a radio. You know, it couldn't get nothing but barn-dancing. I called the feller up and he come and find out I had the aerial hooked to the barn!" Another little gag on "Dynamite" came from Jim Alley, obviously as he heard it from Morse; Curt told a friend he could get anything on his radio, and in fact had turned it on once in the middle of the night and got—hell. Employing the theme of the errant husband, Curt related how one night he had been out drinking with the boys and tiptoed home late, but had the misfortune to catch his toe and trip over a chair. "Dynamite" awoke and said, "Is that you, Skippy?" thinking it was their dog. Curt said, "I sneaked along, lapped her hand, and she went along to sleep again." Curt also alluded to an aunt of his, "So thin, that in the fall of the year we always give her a spoonful of cranberry sauce and used her for a thermometer," and an uncle so thin, "when they come in from hunting we'd tie a grease rag 'round his head and send a shotgun out with him. We used to have to tape his Adam's apple so when he swallowed it wouldn't cut his necktie off" (motif X924 "Lie: remarkably thin persons"). These last exaggerations are proverbial comparisons rather than tales, and in his conversation Curt continually tosses off such extravagances.

Into his family saga and crestfallen autobiography Curt weaves common lying tales usually told in the third person. Curt alleged that his uncle had sheep's intestines substituted for his own in the hospital, an operation that worked very well, except that "every spring they had to shear the old devil" (motif X1721.2 "Lie: man's organs replaced with animal's"). Curt also attached a folktale to his hunting dog Skippy, who, he claimed, would run to the river looking for birds when Curt picked up his shotgun, then shift and run across the road and start looking for deer when Curt stood the shotgun in the corner and picked up a rifle. One time Curt thought to fool Skippy, so he rigged up a fishing line and walked down to a little brook, Snow Brook, under a hill. Skippy never appeared, and Curt mused, "Well, I guess I've overestimated his knowledge." But when he went back to the house, there behind the shed was Skippy, digging for worms! (motif X1215.8 "Lie: intelligent dog"). A close variant of this tale was told me in northern Michigan by the Finnish humorist Herman Maki.[5] Curt even employed for comic personal effect the divination motif of looking in a mirror at midnight to see the reflection of one's future mate; but a big black tomcat jumped on the potato bin and the cat is what he saw—another dig at poor "Dynamite." In the popular American tall tale of the frightened hunter who claims he is bringing a live bear back to camp (motif X1133 "Lie: the hunter in danger"), Morse makes himself the hero.

Now you see, I was up river about 19—oh 1940. And there was a party I went with up there, oh, everybody wanted to shoot a bear. So I never seen a bear in the woods and I was kind of nervous. So the door was open in the morning, to let the heat out of the camp while they was washing the dishes, I thought I'd go out. So I went out and I walked just a little ways when I met an old regular bear, and I looked at him a minute and I started to camp and he after me. Just before I got to the door I looked back to see if he was gaining on me, and I caught my toe and fell down and he went over me and went right into the camp. Well, I jumped up and pulled the door to and run round to the window and I says, "That's one, boys. Skin him out and I'll go run in another one."

However Alley tells the tale impersonally on a greenhorn from "Down East."

Dorson: What's that other one about the fellow went out hunting the bear?
James Alley: Oh, he was up to west'ard there, and he belonged down east, and the fellow asked him, said, "Any bears down in your country?" And he said, "Yes." So he said, "Well I'd like to see one." Well, he says, "All right. Come down," he says. "I got a camp up the river, and we'll go in."
So they went down, and he went up at night—afternoon, went up to camp. After supper he said, "I'll take a run out and look around, to see if I can't locate them bears." And he got a little way from the camp and a bear tackled him and he run for the camp. Well, the bear was right on to him and he stubbed his toe when he got to the door and he fell in the door and the door come open and the bear was right after him—and the bear went right in ahead of him into the camp, and he shut the door. He says, "You take this one, and I'll go get another one."

Some of Curt's seemingly improvised and elaborated personal experiences turn out to be folktales after all, such as the story of a Bangor mental hospital patient who rushed up with a scythe to "tag" him. The *Hoosier Folklore Bulletin* reports the same incident from Morganfield, Kentucky.[6]

A third group of yarns Curt has evidently constructed from incidents that befell him. His longest narrative deals with a trip he took to Aroostook County to dig potatoes. Lobster fishing was slow, and

Curt accepted a friend's invitation to drive inland and pick up a little cash during the potato harvest season. The humor of this adventure, for Curt's audience, lies in the lobsterman's discomfiture and comical mishaps in an alien subculture. The potato farms of Aroostook County represent another world from the coastal fisheries, and Curt encounters a series of cultural shocks: he is unfamiliar with automobiles, and puts so much free air in the tires they all blow up; a small French-Canadian beats him at potato digging and takes his last cent. Clearly Curt has often retold this adventure; the yarn is structured into a series of episodes, and certain high points are well known to his circle. (In the recording I made, his daughter recalled to his mind one humorous commentary Curt had omitted.) In other ludicrous stories, Curt tells how he played in a baseball game with the team from the next village, and was hit in the Adam's apple by the croquet ball they were using in place of their wornout yarn balls; Curt passed out cold, and never did learn how the game came out. Another time Curt thought he had found ambergris while lobstering and made his fortune, but the final laboratory test proved the sticky substance to be cocoa butter.

In contrast to these tales of woe, Curt did relate one personal experience in which he fooled some city fellows from New York, who saw him lugging a corroded seventy-five-pound anchor on his shoulder, which they imagined weighed eight to ten tons. Curt padded out this yarn with characteristic tall tale motifs. When one city chap inquired how the lobsterman could tote home an anchor with so much heft, Curt replied nonchalantly, "The heft don't mount to much. When I see a heavy storm coming up, I always take my boat under the other arm" (motif X941 "Remarkable lifter"). Then he had one New Yorker say to the other, "If that land hadn't been dry and hard, he'd never got up there because he'd sunk in to his knees with that much heft on his back" (motif X1733.1 "Lie: man lifts heavy load, sinks into solid rock").[7]

These autobiographical exploits and misadventures make no appearance in the extensive repertoire of Jim Alley, who possessed his own specialties. Twenty-five of his tales concerned Irishmen, but Curt told not one Pat and Mike jest. The extraordinary popularity of these Irishmen noodle jokes in remote corners of the United States has attracted the attention of collectors in the New Jersey piney woods, the Kentucky mountains, and the Afro-American South.[8] Another point of difference lay in Alley's taste for the supernatural. When humorist Curt did occasionally utter a birthmark tale, he must perforce add a comic twist, as in saying that the hog-faced man was fed swill. But James related with solemnity and conviction the occult tradition shared by his kinsfolk from Head Harbor Island. As Morse personalized the tall tale, so did Alley personalize these legends of witchcrafts, table-tipping, and divining for buried treasure. Jim had been present at some of the table-tipping sessions on Head Harbor Island, when the folks sat around a table and called up the spirits to answer their questions through the rappings of the table. A seasoned spirit-caller could make the table perform wonders, and Jim told how Uncle Allen Alley had made the table shoot a pair of scissors at Harmy Alley as he entered the door, the scissors grazing Harmy's head and sticking in the door. "I was there and I seed that when they done that, by gorry. It scairt me," confessed Jim. Even when Jim retold his father's tale of how Mother Hicks bewitched a cow, he provided a personal note of verification. A gulch down on the cape shore is named Mother Hicks' Gulch. "I been down there and looked at it. It's a big long gulch, some wide too, and she straddled across there with a apron full of cranberries."[9]

Another feature of Alley's repertoire is his inclusion of European humorous tale-types, camouflaged by their American anecdotal style. He related examples of types 726, 750 A (two variants), 1159, 1365 B, 1456, 1626, 1700, and 1739. Morse told only one tale of European origin (type 726), "The Oldest on the Farm." Comparison of the Alley and Morse texts again reveals Curt's penchant for wrapping the tale around himself and Jim's adherence to an impersonal, almost formulistic delivery.

Old Man Crying
(James Alley)

Well, a fella went into a house, and fella settin' there on the doorstep there, oh he was an awful old man. He says, "Can I go in the house?"
And he says, "Yes, my son's in there."
And he went in and says, "That your father out there?"
And he said, "Yes."
"What are you crying for?"
And he says, "Why he give me a licking."
He said, "What for?"
He said, "Sassing my grandfather."
So he went out and he looked. "Your son said you give him a licking for sassing his grandfather."
And he says, "I did."

And he says, "Where is your grandfather."
And he says, "In the next house."
And he said, "I went over, and he was old, he had four inches of moss right on his back."
He said his boy was over a hundred.

Old Man Crying
(Curt Morse)

One day I started for town and there was an old fellow up in our district setting alongside the road, long chin whiskers, and he's crying. I says, "What are you crying about, Uncle?"
"Well," he says, "my father just gave me an awful basting."
I says, "What in the devil the old man lick you for?"
He says, " 'Cause I was throwing some potatoes at grandpaw."

Although Alley does not personalize his stories, he does localize imported narratives. American local color permeates his European tales, as in this comic account of "The Indian's Three Wishes" with its coastal place names (type 750, motif J2071, "Three Foolish Wishes").

Why the Indian wished a first wish, he wished all the Bay of Fundy was rum. Well they said, "What's your next?" He said, "Mount Desert Hills was a lump of sugar." "Well," he said, "What's your next?" He says, "A little more rum."

Alley also knew the traditional obscene form of the tale (motif J2075, "The transferred wish").

An old man and an old woman going to have their wishes, so whatever they wished, they could have. So the old man wanted to wish and the old woman says, "No, let me wish." He says, "All right." So she says (they had this poor sick baby), says, "I wish I had a barrel of rags." Made the old man mad, and he said, "I wish they was up your ass." Well, then he had to take another wish and wish them out, and they got nothin'.

The compression of Alley's style is apparent in these texts, whose brevity and slightness might well conceal the fact that they are trans-atlantic importations.

In the Field

Old Gram Shaw
(James Alley)

A fellow was in a place where he couldn't understand what they said nor nothing. So he got hungry and he went to a house and knocked on the door. Says, "Can I get some dinner here?" All they'd say, "Old Gram Shaw." Well, he'd leave. And he'd go to another house and ask them. It was "Old Gram Shaw," and he was about starved to death. At last he walked and fell into a funeral procession. Somebody was dead. And he said, "Who's dead?" They said, "Old Gram Shaw." He said, "I darned glad of it, I'll get some dinner now."

Here is a faithful if terse rendering of type 1700, motif J2496, "The man thinks 'I don't know' is a person's name," reported from Europe, West Africa, and in the United States among southern blacks. "Old Gram Shaw" is a Yankeefied phrase adapted to the Down-East environment. Curt Morse too supplies local color for the international theme, but as usual brings himself into the story, and gives it a comic turn (motif G303.16.14, "The devil exorcised").

The Devil Crying in Machias
(Curt Morse)

You know one time a fellow was goin' out by 'Riah's garage here in Machias, that was off of the road that leads out to Kennebec where I live. And he said when he got out there by just this side of 'Riah's garage, the Devil was setting on the rock crying. And the fellow says to him, "What are you crying about?"

"Well," he says, "I'll tell you. I started for Curt Morse, but I don't dare go down through Kennebec."

So much religion here.

Further instances of Alley's varied repertoire could be given. He narrated half a dozen "infidelity" tales, without counterpart in Morse's stock. These are not dirty jokes but subtler, racy, Boccacio-like pieces, revolving around domestic duplicities, with clever twist endings. However the evidence already presented demonstrates the wide variation in style and theme of two folktale narrators from the same culture, region, and occupation.

Dialect Stories
of the Upper Peninsula:
A New Form
of American Folklore

In the folklore-laden north peninsula of Michigan, modern and native-born jostle antique and imported story traditions, and one may hear Old County fairy tales from one raconteur and twentieth-century dialect jokes from the next. That such unlike genres are found in juxtaposition is no accident, for the European folk who bring over the olden tales become the burlesqued subject matter of dialect recitals. These dialecticians perform throughout the Upper Peninsula, formally before lodges, conventions, clubs, and church socials, and informally in yarn-spinning circles; no town, from the Soo to Ironwood, lacks one or several well-known dialect humorists, and the urge and the talent for this mimicry extend to the rank and file storytellers.

The strictly regional popularity of the dialect yarn results from conditions of Upper Peninsula life and society. In this self-contained country washed on the north by Lake Superior and on the south by Lake Michigan, immigration has planted a remarkably diverse ethnic mixture, and remoteness has bred a free and easy social interplay not to be found in the giant cities where impersonality and segregation are the dominant attitudes. As the land has affected its people and welded them into a regional in-group, so too the people have affected the land, stamping it with the cultural hues of the Chippewa, the French Canadian, the Cornishman, the Finn, and a dozen smaller strains. Consequently, to the Peninsularite these peoples, or the types that have come to symbolize them, strike imaginative reflexes that outsiders cannot appreciate.

Because the newcomer groups have made a deep impression on the overall population, they have aroused a reaction within the popular mind, often a humorous reaction, and this has produced the dialect story. The second generation relishes the mishandling of American English that continuously surrounds them; and gifted mimes reproduce the phonological and grammatical errors, the special intonations and interpolations, that are irresistibly funny to any American-educated listener. Because the Canadian French, the Cornish, and the Finnish have played the most active historical and economic role in the Peninsula, and because they represent rural and peasant stocks (all of whom are rich in their own inherited tradition and lore), they have stimulated the greatest number of stories, and specialists for all three have emerged. Less prominent and less peculiar to the area are Swedish, Italian, and Irish dialect tales, although they too frequently swell the repertory of the local dialectician. Of the major ethnic stocks in the population, only the Germans and the Poles are wanting in dialect imitators.

Although these English-crucifying stories may begin as simple repetitions of overheard prize mistakes, they tend to assume anecdotal and narrative form almost immediately. The individual word-mangler becomes the folk-hero in an expanding cycle that incorporates outside stories; or the stories gravitate to the stock comedy characters—the Finnish Eino and Weino, the Cornish Jan and Bill, the Swedish Ole and Yon, the Irish Pat and Mike. All the generic characters in the various dialects in turn tend toward a common genus—the fool, the dolt, the immigrant bumpkin. The humor of ignorant speech converges on humor of situation; while the brief anecdotes may deal solely with language misuse, the lengthy narratives which burgeon forth in the genre confront the immigrant with strange and baffling American mores. He visits Chicago, and is nonplussed by trains, streetcars, and hotels; he marks his door with a penknife so he can distinguish it from the others in the apartment; then he hangs a paper bag on the tree outside so he can tell his rooming house from all the others—but the bag blows away. Actually the narrative scenes portray the immigrant as accurately as do his bumbled words for they too are grounded in observation and personal experience. For the substance of his famous adventure at the carnival, Burt Mayotte drew upon his own youthful visit, as described in Canuck English by his grandfather; Walter Gries says he heard the Italian boy deliver his misinformed masterpiece about Columbus in a Keweenaw County grade school; the Detroit ball game classic is founded upon a ceremonial visit by a Canadien to see those Tigers of whom his sons spoke so fervently; yarns about racial hostility between the Cornish and the Finns or the Swedes and Norwegians are only too historically authentic. Other themes and plots besides those derived from immediate fact enter the dialects, often by the deliberate redaction of the dialectician; these include a host of dirty stories and the tall tales and traveling jokes that form so much American floating storylore.

The first question which a consideration of the dialect story prob-ably will inspire is, Is it folklore? By all the standard criteria, this type fits the definitions of folk narrative. Dialect tales enjoy an almost completely oral life. Because they are a new growth they depend for their chief comic effects on sounds, and print tends to resist dialect. In their oral flights they undergo all the characteristic permutations of folk material: textual variation, assimilation of familiar plots, dispersion of original compositions, and even crossovers from one dialect into another. Burt Mayotte told me that he had heard "The Carnival," ten years after he had composed it at Sault Ste. Marie, recited by another raconteur at Manistique with differing details but the same punch line, and that it is now current throughout the Upper Peninsula. In commenting on the Detroit ball game, which he told me in the French, he said he heard a sailor on the Lakes give it in Swedish and seen it in Italian on cards printed in Chicago's Italian district; and subsequently I collected Finnish versions. Some stories, like the Cornish plot about the miner who steps on the plank that wasn't there, or the Finnish GI who proves immune to cannibal parboiling, or the Frenchman lost in the woods who answers the hooting owl, are virtually common property. But even with the unusual and unique tales, the generic motif of the fool character and his absurd antics remains to wed the genre firmly to universal folklore patterns.

Who tells dialect stories? Men—seldom women—from all the occupations and nationalities of the Upper Peninsula, men of business, not of the woods and mines. Burt Mayotte at the Soo is an auto mechanic, and the raconteur for the local French Canadian group, the Allouette Singers. His grandfather was a Keweenaw pioneer, whose broken dialect always intrigued Burt. Mayotte assumes, seemingly by instinct, the quick, expressive Gallic gestures, glances, grimaces, and the rhythmic cadences that distinguish Canadien talk. Walter Gries, of German descent, and known all over the state for his Cornish and other dialect renditions, is personnel supervisor of the Cleveland Cliffs Iron Company at Ishpeming, and was formerly warden of the Marquette prison. As a schoolteacher in the Copper Country he heard and retained the Cousin Jack, French, and Italian missayings which formed the basis of his present extensive collection. John Laitala of Ironwood works in and partially owns a tavern, and is frequently called on to give "lingoes"; he is one of the few American Finns to practice the Finnish dialect. If he hears a good story, he will render it into the idiom, for his repertory. Howard Springer, who possesses a superb Swedish style, developed it from hearing Scandinavian housemaids and dockworkers at Gladstone and Escanaba; although now in business in Minneapolis, he still entertains friends with his "Yumping Yimminy" anecdotes. And so it goes; the dialecticians may be undertakers, like Jimmer Thomas of Laurium, John Chappell of Ironwood, and Mort Plowe at Houghton, or a mason like Bambi Hoffman of Hancock, or a company superintendent like Dan Harrington at Manistique, or a county treasurer like Bob Pryal of Escanaba, or a ticket agent like Frank Ahlich in St. Ignace, or owner of a bottling works, like John Johnson at Besemer—but all have the same keen ear for word sounds and aptitude for reproducing them in a fluent, rapid, easy, and sometimes singsong delivery. Because the dialecticians are continually called on to entertain large audiences, their stories travel readily. Persons in many towns have repeated to me prize anecdotes by Walter Gries, for example, while conversely the friends and listeners of the performers send or give them choice yarns. All the narrators seem to have their yarns at the top of their heads and dictated them to me seriatim without so much as pausing for breath.

What are the characteristics of the dialects? They of course differ for each dialect, but the general principle holds: that they derive from the inapplicability of grammar and alphabet structure in the mother tongue to American English forms. For instance, the Finnish omission of extra consonants before the initial vowel in English words results from the fact that no Finnish word begins with more than one consonant. The constant misuse of the Canadien "she" comes from the lack of a neuter gender in French. Common dialect traits are: in the Finnish, the transposition of *b*'s and *p*'s, *d*'s and *t*'s, the substitution of *w* for *f*, *v* for *w*, and *g* or *s* for *c* (there is no *c* in Finnish), and the frequent use of the present participle for regular conjugations; in the French, the substitution of *d* for *th*, the addition of aspirate *h*'s to words beginning with vowels, the employment of double *e* or *ay* endings for *y* or *ie*, and of the double *e* sound for short *i*; in the Cornish, the incorrect omission and addition of beginning *h*'s, and the use of the third-personal pronoun for the second; in the Swedish, the substitution of *y* for *j* and *v* for *w*, and frequently short *a* for short *i* or *e* before a double consonant.

Another element in the dialect lies in syntactical malformations, which often are repeated independently as choice comic morsels. Some examples are: in the Finnish, "Urho, go out in te parn and trow te horse out te window some hay"; in the Swedish, "Et's notting coming laft" (There is no change coming to you); in the Cornish, " 'Er ed'n calling ta we, us don't b'long ta she"; in the French, "Take dis horse here, she's de mos' wore out" (best broken in). A further coloring lies in conventional expletives and expressions: the Canadien *Maudjit* and *sapré*, the Finnish *Satana* and *Sesus 'Rist*, the Cornish *bloody*. Words like "sauna" (steam bath), and "pasty" (meat pie), are now generally diffused through the Upper Peninsula, but have occasioned special Finnish and Cornish folklore tales. An important aspect of the dialect rendering is the rhythmic cadences into which the stories tend to fall; in fact, the jump from prose to verse is easily accomplished, as the habitant poems of William Henry Drummond indicate, and I have a Finnish song which was improvised on the spot by listeners when a Finnish lumberjack complainingly asked the barman for his axe and saw. Mayotte almost chants his recitations, and all the Canadiens employ an upward intonation that invites metrical repetition. The singsong quality of the higher pitched Swedish speech makes mimicry practically irresistible, and I have heard a dozen men and boys in a L'Anse boardinghouse all telling anecdotes involving Big Eric Ericson, a local lumber jobber, in an identical tearful whine.

One final question deserves to be raised about the dialect story. I have called it "A New Form of American Folklore," but is it actually without precedent? The closest approach would appear to be the Yankee yarns that liberally strew the mid-nineteenth-century press, in which the rustic speech of backcountry New Englanders is phonetically reproduced and the plots turn consistently on bumpkin gaucheries. Many of these yarns were orally delivered, on the lecture platform or the stage, by Yankee comedians like Dan Marble and George H. Hill or the monologuist Dr. Valentine—set pieces based on observed eccentricities of character. Jewish, Italian, Irish, and Negro dialect stories are widespread in United States tradition and have appeared in print. But in their geographic concentration, wide dispersion, multiplicity, and extreme oral popularity, the Upper Peninsula dialect tales represent a novel folklore phenomenon.

In the Field

French

LOCAL CHARACTERS

Fred Felteau
(Walter F. Gries, Ishpeming, May 14, 1946)

There is a lot of French-Canadian stuff I've run into myself in the iron and copper regions. Joe Bedore is a famous character talked about below the Straits. Up here there are characters like Fred Felteau, Louis Bizette, and Captain Jack Lamerand, who was my neighbor at Eagle Harbor.

Fred Felteau was a great big fellow who weighed about two hundred and fifty pounds. He ran away from Canada and came to the Upper Peninsula as a boy of fourteen or fifteen. He originally studied for the priesthood, but he gave it up and worked in the woods till he was fifty, when he got rheumatiz. Fred used to shack on Gratiot Lake, Keweenaw County, in a little cabin. I used to go fishing there with my pal. He had a shack with a door and a window on each side. The hind seat of an old automobile was his front porch—he picked it off a dump. He would sit there and look at the beautiful lake. As we walked in from the road, this very hot day in July, we couldn't see Fred; he wasn't on his front porch. And I remarked to my partner, "Fred must be out on the lake." "No, I ain't on de lake," he said. We stepped into the cabin; he was lying on the bunk with his stag shirt and woolen pants and rubber swampers, stretched full length. I said, "What's the matter, Fred, are you sick?" "Jesus, no, I ain't sick, I'm only tired sitting down."

(Walter F. Gries, Ishpeming, May 14, 1946)

This is another story at Gratiot Lake. He's sitting there on a little homemade boat dock—couple boards out in the water. A mother and her children from nearby came down to go in swimming. "Oh, mother, it's nice, it's warm, it's hot," said one of the children. Fred says, "Jeesus pwell, I'm living roun' here feefty years, an' I don't see nobody burn himself on dat water yet."

(Walter F. Gries, Ishpeming, May 14, 1946)

Pea-soup 'n jelly cake
Dey make de Frenchman's belly ache.

That's an old rhyme. Pork pie and pea soup are the favorite dishes of the French Canadians.

In the fall when I left the camp I would take up to Fred any little food I had left over. This time I took up some dried navy beans because I knew they'd get

228

wormy. I saw him in the spring, and asked him how he was doing. "It wasn't veree bad," he says. "You know, I got a leetle rheumatiz on my leg, an' my back is sore, but I'll get a leetle help from de welfare, so I'll get t'rough de wintaire. By gar," he says, "you remember dem little bean you bring me. Well, 'Im gonna tole you, she don't make veree good pea-*soup*."

(Walter F. Gries, Ishpeming, May 14, 1946)

A township caucus is still held to nominate officers at Eagle Harbor. There are just enough year-round residents so everybody can serve on the school or county board. The boys come down at caucus time, gather round the store, talk things over, and see who is going to run for office. Electioneering, tanking up at the bar, are in order. They had what they called a poorbox—nothing more than an open drawer back of the bar with a pound package of Peerless chewing tobacco. A customer having purchased a beverage could take a free chew. All availed themselves of the privilege before retiring downstreet to the schoolhouse for the caucus.

After the gathering of the gang, Fred, the leader, switched his chew from the left to the right side of his mouth, and got up on the little rostrum. "Well I guess we better start da meeting." He switches the chew back. "First ting we gotta 'ave is nomeenashun for superwisor. I tink I'm da bes' one for dat, I'll take dat myself." Switches the chew again. "Nex' ting we gotta have is nomeenashun for townsheep clerk." Somebody got up and says, "I nomeenate Camille Rielle for townsheep clerk." Fred replies, "Well, Camille, he can't read and he can't write, but he can make hees cross, and we ain't got very much beezness anyway, so I tink Camille be all right for dat." Switches chew back, looks around. "By gar, I tink de nex' ting we gotta have is cuspeedor." A French-Canadian friend gets up and says, "I nomeenate Joe Bellack for cuspeedor."

(Walter F. Gries, Ishpeming, May 14, 1946)

It was rumored around the Keweenaw Point that Fred was going to get married, and he had already reached his fifty-fifth birthday. His friend Camille came down from the Bluff mighty excited, came into Fred's cabin and said, "Jeesus pwell, Fred, everybodee on de countee's talkin'." Fred answered, "Well, wat's de matter wid dat?" "Well, dey're talkin' about you." "Talkin' about me? What are dey talkin' about me?" "Well, everybodee she say you're gonna get marree wid Rosee Plouff." Fred says, "Well, wat's de matter wid dat? I'm feefty-five years old. I'm old enough to get married, ain't I?" Camille says, "Well, sure, but wid Rosee, she ain't veree nice girl. Everybodee on de countee knows about Rosee." Fred says, "Well, dat don't bodder me, because it ain't veree big countee."

229

In the Field

Joe Reno
(Tom Beaton, Escanaba, August 13, 1946)

My father, Tom Beaton, Sr., used to lumber all through this area, Big Bay de Noc, drove on the Salmon Trout River for Pittsburgh and Lake Superior Company (later the National Pole Company). He had charge of the river drive. As a kid, I kept time in the woods. I am a forester by profession.

Joe Reno, who died up at the poor farm, was an actual eccentric Canadian Frenchman, at old Camp One of the Stephenson Company, in back of Ralph. He knew the alphabet with difficulty, learned to recite it, A-B-C. He'd study a word out painfully, might get the word right or be way off. He had a little logging camp outside the main camp, making his living cutting cedar by the piece and "batching."

So this morning he was cooking with hot grease on the stove, and he gave me a cup of coffee, and with it one of these concoctions he had made. I said, "What is this?" It was small, very dark, no zest to it. Joe said, "I dunno. I follow direcshun, and she come like dat." I said, "Let me see the directions." So he handed me a package of pancake flour, and I said, "Where do you see anything about doughnuts here?" And he said, "See dem black word." I said, "Joe, that says nothing about doughnuts. That says, 'Do not use anything but water.'" Joe had thought "Do not" meant "Doughnuts."

(Tom Beaton, Escanaba, August 13, 1946)

There was a group of Kentuckians imported by the company to cut cordwood, about 1917. Joe Reno was invited to go hunting with this Kentuckian, at night. It developed into a miserable, cold, rainy night, in the fall of the year. They were out all night, found their way back by the cookshanty horn blowing for breakfast. I said, "You're a good woodsman, Joe. How come you were out all night and couldn't find your way back?" He was wet and miserable. He said, "Dat feller he point way off and say, 'Joe, raccoon dat way.' And we *travel* and *travel* and *travel*. And by'n by he point in a different direction and say, 'Joe, raccoon dat way.' And we travel after dat raccoon. By'n by I want to go home, me, but I'm all mix up and I don't know which way to go, until de horn she's blow.

"Den I come to de camp, and it's a good ting de horn she's blow, odderwise dat Kentuckian she still look for dat goddamn raccoon."

(Tom Beaton, Escanaba, August 13, 1946)

One night Joe Reno was going from Main Camp Number One to his own little shack—no road, had to follow a trail through the woods, pitch dark. I said, "Joe, take a lantern with you." "Bah gosh, I can' do dat, because de ghos' she see de lantern a long way."

Dialect Stories of the Upper Peninsula

Joe Bedore
(Pete Vigeant, Sault Ste. Marie, April 21, 1946)

Joe Bedore ran a lodging- and beer-place at St. Clair's Flats. He spoke habitant French, and was quite a character. His place was the headquarters for fishermen and yachtsmen. Bums, roughnecks, civilized people hung out there.

A bunch of fellows was sitting around there leaning with their chairs tilted against the wall, when a smart aleck came in. "Come on, boys, have a drink," he said. After a while he looked around and said, "Joe, I bet you one dollar there's five doors in this room."

Joe looks and sees only four, so he says, "Bah gosh, I take you on dat. Show me."

The smart aleck counts, "There's one door, two doors, three doors, four doors, cuspidor. That's five doors."

So Joe says, "All right, Hi'll buy the drinks." But the next day he says to the bunch. "That aleck weel come again, and dis time I get heem." The aleck comes in with his lunch pail and says, "Give me a schouper of beer." But this time he doesn't offer to treat the crowd.

Joe says, "Hi'll bet you dere's fi' door in dees room." The aleck looks around and sees only four. "Aleck, Hi bet you de drinks for heverybodee in de house."

"All right, I'll take it," says the aleck. "Show me."

Joe counts, "Won door, two door, tree door, four door, spittoon."

[I heard this story also told by E. P. Sawyer in Escanaba, August 14, 1946. "At Pete Lemmer's saloon a young fellow came in and said, 'Pete, how many doors in this room?' 'Three.' 'I'll bet you drinks on the house there's four.' So he counts, 'Front door, back door, cellar, cuspidor.' Pete says, 'That's pretty good, I'm going to try that on the whiskey salesman.' He bet drinks on the house with him and counts, 'Front door, back door, cellar door, shpittoon.'"]

Jeandel Paquin
(Frank Ahlich, St. Ignace, April 17, 1946)

(This one's true.)

Jim Miller, supervisor from Hendrix township in Mackinac County (used to run a store at Rexton), on his way back to Detroit from a meeting stopped in to see some of his customers. He stopped off at Jeandel Paquin's, who was out in the garden. Jeandel had about twenty children, one in Guadalcanal. "Who dat, Chimmy Miller?" And he begins crying, "What's the matter, Jeandel, don't you feel good?" asks Miller. "Yes, Chimmy, I feel good, but you know my boy Will*ard*. He's in California on hospitale," he says. "He got shot in the got on God-canal with some sharp nail. He was git along good all right and the doctor write and he say Will*ard* coming along fine, and just last night we get a letter from Will*ard,* and he say, 'Papa, I got Purple Heart'. And you know damn well, Chimmy, he can't live long wid dat."

Albert Dufours
(Dr. Alfred La Bine, Houghton, August 26, 1946)

Albert Dufours at Hubbell was having his eyes examined. He couldn't read the cards, so the doctor gave him a chart with figures pointing up and down. He asks, "How many of these columns point up and how many point down?" But Albert can't tell. The doctor gets exasperated. "Don't get mad, docteur. I wanna pair a glass like Joseph LeBeau from Hubbell. He was pass his foot on my house last week, and I was tole him about my trouble with my heye. And LeBeau he took hoff his glass, and he put him right on top of my nose, and by golly, docteur, Boo' Jack (Boot Jack, on the other side of Portage River) jump over on dis side just like dat. Dat's de kinda glass I want."

Henry Lequin
(Tom Beaton, Escanaba, August 13, 1946)

A French-Canadian jobber, Henry Lequin, was working out from Camp Number One. One day he was scrubbing his floor with what he thought was washing flour. All the windows of the shack were open, as it was a hot summer day, and I heard him using much profanity—"Sacré Moujit." "What's the trouble, Henry?" I asked. "Look at dat," he said. "Bought dat washing powdaire hon Ralph, and dat feller had dat powdaire for de last fortee year. She's all dry out, de strengt' is all gone, she's just like flowaire. Can't do nodding wid it to wash de floors. She's no good. De gold dus' is all gone." I said, "Let me see that powder." He handed me a package of pancake flour.

Adelore LeBlanc
(Tom Beaton, Escanaba, August 13, 1946)

An illiterate Frenchman, Adelore LeBlanc, worked for my father at piecework. He was just paid off—on his time slip was itemized what he had cut as a piece-maker, so many posts, poles, ties, logs, pieces of pulpwood, including eleven six-inch thirty-five-foot cedar poles. He walks nine miles to the tracks, and meets an educated Frenchman, Big Joe. "Let me look at your slip, I'll tell you what you got," says Big Joe. "You got two six-inch thirty-five-foot." Adelore says, "Dat must be wrong, I know I got eleven." So he walks nine miles back, and says to dad, "You made a mistake, you. You know I got *eleven*." "That's right, I gave you eleven." "Can't *be*, you only got two marks."

Dialect Stories of the Upper Peninsula

Alec Destramps
(Dr. Alfred LaBine, Houghton, August 26, 1946)

Alec Destramps from Chassel went to Chicago for a visit. He registered at the Morrison Hotel. In the morning he came down at four-thirty and asked the clerk for the key to his room, 426. The clerk looked in the pigeonhole and said, "I'm sorry, sir, but this room is taken." "It is? What's his name?" The clerk tried to pronounce it—Alec Destramps from Chassel, Michigan. "Cripes dat's me, gimme de key. I just fall outa de win*dow*."

Munizippe Perron
(Tom Beaton, Escanaba, August 13, 1946)

In the early days of Escanaba there was much French-Irish rivalry. A French mayor had been elected, Munizippe Perron. The whole town was celebrating St. Batiste day. He was asked to make a speech. He got up on top of the bandstand and said, "Ladies and gentle*men*. You can talk about your St. Pat*rick*, but Saint Batchees is de boy."

STRANGE AMERICA

The Carnivalle
(Burt Mayotte, Sault Ste. Marie, April 28, 1946)

Hi get up very very hear*ly* and walk four, five, nine mile, till Hi pass hon de cittay where is de carni*val*. Before time is come for djiné, Hi have fin' de place, and Hi hear de musik, and Hi see all de pipple pay de fi' cents and pass in de carni*val*. Before long time some feller Hi know is come dere too and pay de fi' cents for Paree to pass in de carni*valle*, an' Hi see de most beautiful ting Hi never have see before. Dere is much musik an' manee strannge ting wich you never believe have been make an' put hall in won place for fi' cents. Hi see won of de most wonder*ful* ting is called de merry-go-horse. She have many horse wat galloop roun' and roun,' and make one hell of a hurree, to get no place fast. Hi would like veree much for galloop hon dem horse but Hi don't have de fi' cents.

So Hi pass over hon annudder strannge ting which is call de hup-go-weel. Hi don' know from w're she's get hall de buggee seat, or who have a buggee w'at can spare such big w'eels, but Hi see dat wid my hown eye. Great big w'eel wich roll all de time in one place, an' manee manee buggee seat is hook on de run. De pipple is sit on de seat—de w'eel is go roun,' an' heveryone get a chance to pass hon de sky an' pass down to go hup some more. Hi would love for to do, such a wonnerful ting, but hagain Hi don' have de fi' cents. Seem like heveryting, from de time Hi have buy my tickette, she's want fi' cents.

You know Hi have see so many ting, de sun is go down, an' de first ting Hi know, is time for suppay. Hi ham veree much hongry, as Hi don' have no djiné eider. But dat's because Hi still don' got fi' cents. So Hi listen on de beautiful musik, an' Hi pass around in de carnivalle to manee odder beautiful tings until is pass on my nose a grande beeg butiful smell. Hi foller dat smell an' wat do you tink Hi fin'? A nice beeg place wid manee tings for heat, an' nothing is cost more dan fi' cents. Hot puppay, you should see dat! She's a ground up meat, all squeeze in a swim suit, an' wrap hup in a bun wit' leetle bit moustarde hon de top. Honlee fi' cents! Et Maudit! De popnuts, de pea-corn, de hass-crim, some more honlee fi' cents. An' Paree is have no monee. Dat make me feel too hemptee on de bellay, so Hi pass hoff dat place.

An' den Hi hear de most butiful musik wat have never pass on de hear of man. Some crazee buggaire, he's holler hout loud, so heverybodee hear, "Twenty-fi' dollaire for ten minoots." Et Maudit, Hi fin' dat place fas'. Dat's too mooch monee for ten minoots. You should see wat Hi fin', small square floor midout a roof an' a rope all haround for a wall. Manee manee peeple is dere an' can see dere is four *coin* hon dat floor. An' won dam' fool hon de meedle is try for tell heverybodee h'it h'is a reeng. Moost a be, Hi'm crazee, han heverybodee helse his right, she look more like ha square dan a reeng, but Hi'm get away from de main ting, Hi don' come dere for argument, Hi come dere for de twenty-fi' dollaire. Hi got lots of minoots. She's tol' me, eef Hi stay ten minoots hon dees reeng square, wit' nudder man who is sit dere, he pay me de twenty-fi' dollaire. Maudit hell, Hi ham mos' happy man hon de hirt'. Wid twenty-fi' dollaire Hi can buy dat sapré merry-go-horse, Hi can ride on dee hup-go-weel, Hi can h'eat heveryting wat please my heye. Twenty-fi' dollaire, she's ha lots of monee for ten minoots. So Hi clim' hover dee rope and says, "Hi'll stay dee ten minoots."

She's have hanudder man hon dat reeng square. He seet hon dee cornaire, wid his head hang down, han he is all wrap up in a carpette. She don' look like much of a man. Sapré! Wat a commosseeion. Heverybodee she's commense to hollaire. Some h'is hollaire "Hooray," some h'is hollaire for raspberray, wich hain't veree funnee, h'as Hi don't see henny raspberray dere. But heverybodee hollaire hennyway. An' den de man wat make beeg noise hon de first place, h'is make dem stop, and commense to spik on de pipple, "Ladees an' gentlemans: Hover hon dis cornaire, we have dee man for wich we pay twenty-fi' dollaire hon hennybody wat stay wid him for ten minoots. Stan' up, Tigaire." Han dees man is trow away de bat'robe, han raise hup hees head, han stan' hon dee meedle wid two hans hover de head. Et Maudjit—heverybodee tink, she's look prettee dam tough dis man. She's got hon de small shoes, an' de small boy's pants. He have much hair on dee bellee, han he look like dee Tigaire for w'ich he is call. Den he go back and sid down. Han dee beeg noise, wat hollaire so much, he's look hover h'at me, han holler some more, "Han hon dees cornaire, ladees an' gentlemans, we have dee man wat wants twenty-fi' dollaire."

So Hi trow away my jackette, Hi pull hoff my chemise, Hi stan' hon dee meedle, han Hi look prettee dam tough too. We shake dee hand, de bell is ring, an' Hi commense to see dat twenty-fi' dollaire. Dat's gonna be prettee heezay. But vait a min*oot*. Dis Maudjit tigaire, she's grab won han', han den first teeng you know, halmost Hi don't be there hatall. But you know, a good French*man*, he don't stan' for dat. Han Hi poosh heem hoff, Hi heet heem hon dee floor, an' teenk for myself, maybee she don't come back alive in ten min*oot* for pay me my monee. So Hi ben' down for shake heem hup, han' dat Maudjit two-time cross buggaire, is ketch won foot, han' hudder harm, han' tie hon greet beeg knot. Maudjit hell, dat hurt. Before Hi can undo dat, she's have dee hudder h'arm 'n foot, han make some more knot, han' Hi ham all in won piece on dee floor. Before Hi can roll ovaire, she make more knot hon my hair. Han den she find someting helse, han tie anudder knot too. Paree, Paree, Hi cry like ba*bee*. Oh, dat hurt. De wataire pass hoff my heye, han almost Hi teenk Hi don' leave for ten min*oots*.

But Hi don' give hup. Wid hall dee cries han dee knots, Hi see my chanse. Oh Paree does see his chanse. Wen dis man is try for tie more knots, Hi have see my chanse. Hi see won great big red behin'. Hi see won great beeg brown harsehole. Oh, Paree is see his chanse. Oh, Paree bite dat harsehole. Et Maudjit, Paree. You know, twenty-fi' dollaire is too much monee for ten min*oots*. Hi have bite my hown harsehole!

(It must be told with motions. One can describe sideshows, and so on. I told this all over the Green Bay zone with Standard Oil, told it at service men's clubs, at the Coronation Banquet for King George on his visit to Canada at the Windsor Hotel.

The dialect is my own grandfather's. He razzed me, said if I wanted to bite the wrestler back I would have to bite my own behin'. Lots of fellows lay claim to it. I heard a fellow tell it in Manistique ten years after I made it up, with the same punch ending.)

The Ball Game
(Burt Mayotte, Sault Ste. Marie, April 28, 1946)

(It's been told all over the state. It's told as an Italian, as a Finn story. In the Upper Peninsula the older people stick close to home, while the younger boys adopt pleasures of American boys, become great baseball fans, particularly of the Detroit Tigers. After they acquire a job and an automobile, it is considered quite an adventure to see the Tigers play a World Series game. Older folks didn't like to see the boys spend their money for such foolishness, on transportation, expenses, as well as the taking the time off. Getting the parents' consent was the biggest obstacle to making the trip.

One old Frenchman, a little more modern than the rest, never objected to his boys going down. The boys figured it would be good strategy to take him down to the game, and describe it to him so that he would influence other boys' parents to remove the obstacle in the future. Being a most modern

In the Field

father, he had permitted his boy to own a car. The boy in company with friends took the old man to see a World Series game—supposedly during the time Schoolboy Lynwood Rowe was in the limelight. The old fellow had never witnessed a ball game of any kind. He was from L'Anse supposedly. During the trip they told the old man to influence parents to this annual vacation. When he returned, he endeavored to relate what occurred.

This is supposed to be the original baseball story. Since that time it has been retold in different dialects and claimed by them. It was put on little cards to pick up in bars, as a novelty on beer ads. It was published in Cicero, the Chicago Italian District. It was told around Duluth as a Swede; I heard a sailor tell it on the Lakes in Swedish.)

"You know, Hi see dee beeg ball game wid my boy Batiste. We go by hauto for long tam unteel we pass on dee citee which is more beeg dan Quebec or Moreal (Montreal). My boy she is pretty smart feller, an' she's find dees place where is play de ball game. She is called De Worl' Serie, an' Hi believe she spik de troot' for by Gar, hit look like dee whol' worl' is gathered dere. Dee place is about two arpents beeg, an' have great beeg step all aroun', an' by Cris', she is cost much monee for sit on dem step. On dee meedle of dees beeg cow-pastur' is nice rabbit-pat' w'ich is have some mark on hevery *coin*. On de meedle, she's got piece of rubbaire on dee ground, w'ich is called dee box. Heverybody is spik someting an' holler for play ball.

"An' den Hi see mos' funnee ting. Ha great beeg bonch of grownup mans is run out on dees pat' an' to me she look pretty much crazee. Dey is going to commense dee ball game, an' my boy Batiste is tell me wat all dees men is do. One feller at de start of dee pat' he don't look so bad like dee rest. All dem hudder ballmen is dress up in small boys' pants han dat look like hell in front hof all dees pipple. Dees man at dee start of dee pat' she is call de catch, an she try for hide dem small boys' pants. She's put some kind of a mattresse over dee bellee an' a pillow on won han', she's put his cap on back first an' den a bird-cage hover dee head. She's put some piece mattresse hon hees leg, go hover hon dee side, han come back wid tree, four nice new ball. She's trow dem hout hin dee fiel', han trow won hover hon dee meedle. Hon dee meedle she's have great beeg tall mans. She's call dees man Schoolboy. Hi tink dat beeg meestake, for great beeg mans, hee make to go hon dee school wit' small boys' pants. If she can't be make to learn someting before she grow dat beeg she should put on dee farm an' teach for make hay an' pail dee cow. But dee schoolboy is don' make no anyhow, han play wid dee ball an' trow to de catch han speet his tabac like he have no hudder care in dee worl'.

"Hall dee people is holler much for play ball, han Hi commense to teenk is beeg meestake for come dees long long way to see such a sight. Some hof dees ballman is go way hout in dee back of dee pastur' behin' de rabbit-pat' han Batiste is tol' me, 'Watch close dees man. Dey is pretty good an' dey is call de fly catch.' Everybodee is get more excite w'en dees man run hout, han dey call for hanudder feller wat is call de hump. De hump is stan' behin' dee peetch, hon she's dee man w'at ran dee game. W'en she say Play ball, de mos' crazee ting is commense you nevaire did see. Dees tall man call dee peetch is much skinnee, han look like she's got de consumpsion. She's do someting Hi don't tink veree nice, she's speet hon dees nice new ball, han rub two tree time hon hees behin', wind haround hees head, han make two tree pass hon dee catch. She's good ting dee catch have pillow un mattresse un birdcage, for Hi'm tol' you dees ball she's go pretty damn fas'. Un den won more crazee buggaire is walk hover hon dee side hon peek up nice piece of canthook stock, hov w'ich dere is manee hon dee groun'. She's stan' hon dee front hov dee catch, han make won hell hov a swing to frappe dee leetle ball. Han dee hump hees hollaire, 'Strike won!'

"Now dat's won hell hov a beeg lie, for tol' him fronts hov h'all dem pipple. Hi see wit' my hown heye, dees man have not strike dee ball. Han manee hudder people is see dee same ting, han hollaire bad name hon dee hump. Dee peetch is joost laugh, speet some more consumpsion hon dee ball, wipe hon hees hass, wind hon hees head, han trow wonce more hon dee catch. Dee people hon dee front hov me is say he honly got won ball, w'ich is bad ting for say, w'en somebodee can hear. Hi'm feel veree much sorree for man like dat, but dee peetch is trow again, hand de hump is hollaire, two ball. Hi tink dee man myself, he's joost like anybody helse, han is good ting de hump can tell dee trut' has well h'as dee lie. But w'en dee peetch trow wonce more han de man is swing so hard she helmet make dee sitdown. Dee hump is tell hanudder lie, for he call 'Strike two,' han Hi steel don't see heem heet dee ball. Dee peetch is don't believe dee hump needaire, for she's stan' by straight long time han look hon dee catch, han give dee man wid de stock de bad heye. Den hall hov a suddink, widout no speet, no wind, no rub, she's trow dee ball like lightning. He have make a won hell hov a mistake to give dees man de bad heye. For dees man is heet dee ball so hard she almost fly hout hov de pastur'. Dee fly catch is run like hell for catch dee sapré ball before she get los'. Han dee man wat heet dee ball is run like hell too, right down dee rabit pat'. Heverybodee is jump hup hon hollaire, 'Home run, Casey!' But dee crazee buggaire she don't run home. She's come all way roun' dees pat' han look like she's pretty mad hon dee catch. De fly catch is trow de ball for de catch. Must be she tink dees man goin' hurt dee catch who hol' hees groun'. De catch is small man, han she don' need no ball for stop dees crazee buggaire. She steel have manee canthook stock for which to defend himself. Dee peetch is run dere too, han w'en dee runner man is see all dem fellaire gang up halong wid dee hump, she fall hon hees hass, han go feet firs'. Dee catch is fall hon top, han dee hump is look prettee close, han heverybodee is h'all excite. Han den dee hump is hollaire, 'He's hout!'

"Hi get prettee mad w'en she say dis. Dis man is no hout hatall. He's stan' right hup hon hees feet han walk hover hon dee bench. Hi ham tol' you my frans, Hi hav' seen heenough. Heverybodee hon dee ballgame must be crazee, for pay dee good monee, to see such crazee ting, han see such sapré lie. Hi have make Batiste take me home, han nevaire more will Hi make such long voyage to see such sapré Maudjit ting."

In the Field

Burying Oley
(Dan Harrington, Manistique, August 9, 1946)

Although ascribed to a local character, this is a widely told tale.

At Green Schoolhouse location (on U.S. 2 between Gulliver and Blaney Park), old LaCrosse at LaCrosse's tavern tells about a Swede who died at McCakren's camp. And one of the crew was taking up a collection to bury him, asking a dollar apiece from every lumberjack he met. When he came to LaCrosse's tavern he asked LaCrosse for a dollar. Then he started for the cookshanty where old Joe the French cook was. So LaCrosse says, "I'm gonna watch dis, for Joe he's tight as hell, and he hates Swedes anyway." So when he asked Joe for a dollar to bury Oley, Joe pulls out a pocketbook as big as a suitcase, and takes out a dollar and says, "Whan." (Gesture of licking.) The fellow started to go away, and Joe says, "Here's two. Here's tree. Here's four." "Well," he says, "Joe, I only wanted one dollar to bury Oley." "Dat's all right," he says, "bury four of 'em."

Dave Spencer of Ishpeming told it (May 17, 1946) on an Irishman who, asked to give a dollar to bury a dead Swede, said, "Gladly—here's five dollars—bury five of the buggers." To Wayland D. Hand I am indebted for a Salt Lake City variant, involving a banker who gave twice the amount asked for to bury a saxophone player, with the instruction, "Here's a hundred dollars. Bury two of 'em."]

The Apology
(Dr. Alfred LaBine, Houghton, August 26, 1946)

This apology at the dance hall is told in different ways and on different nationalities. Generally the insult is unprintable. Dr. LaBine said he picked up these stories from French patients in the hospital.

A Frenchman from Boot Jack comes to Lake Linden for a dance, all alone, looks around for a partner. The ticket seller said, "You can go up and ask anyone." He said, "But I don't know nobo*dee.*" "That's all right." He goes up to this pretty schoolteacher sitting with her legs crossed and says, "How do you do, mamselle. Will you pass your leg wit' me hon top of de floor for de next number?" She answers, "I'm sorry sir, but you're a stranger to me." "Well, what's the diffayrance? Come on, pass your leg once or twice." She still refused him, and the Frenchman said, "Well, if you don't want to pass your leg for any nomber, you can go to hell." She reported that to her brother. He got five or six other friends and they walked back of the hall to interview this Frenchman, and told him he had to apologize. He didn't know what that meant. They told him he had to say he was sorry, or else. "How many are you?" "We're seven." "That's five too manee." He goes over to the girl. "Are you the young ladee I tole to go to hell little wile ago when I ask you to pass your leg on de floor wit' me?" "I am, sir." "Well, you don't have to go now. I've made different arrangements with your big brother."

The Duck Hunt
(Burt Mayotte, Sault Ste. Marie, April 23, 1946)

The incident of the Frenchman on the raft or boat who says in the morning, "Bah gosh, we ain't here, we seven mile from here," is widely told as an independent anecdote. The rest of the tale belongs to the American tall tale tradition of marvelous hunting.

Two old Frenchmen decided to get an early start to Munoscong. They wanted to get down early, so they tied up at Brady Pier here night before. Buck season opened the next day. Curley was the first one to waken—the boat had broken loose from its moorings and drifted down to Hay Lake. "Woke up, Joe, woke up, we're not here at all, we're twelve miles from here." "What's de difference?" said Joe. "It's too dark to hunt anyting."

It was getting gray in the east. Curley said, "I see one duck myself two mile off—dee ducks he come pretty quick." So Joe said, "Get your thirty-eight feefty-five and take dee first won." No, it was too far for Curley. Then Joe said, "Hit's not too far for me. Hi'll take my two pipe shoot gun han show you how to get dat duck. Hi'll raise my gun hup high, and Hi'm take pretty good haim." He said, "Bang, bang, Hi'll shoot. Maudit, what you tink? De duck he's fall, and when Hi'll pick heem hup, he have been hit on de behin'. You know, Curley, Hi'll have haim for his neck."

The fellows told him he'd scared all the ducks away, so they might as well start cooking their breakfast before the flocks came in. So they went into the shankyay, but there was no kindling. So Joe came out to get some kindling and spied more ducks but they were way up high, too high for his trusty two pipe shoot gun. He said to himself, "Joe halso have de pretty good heye, but not good henough for duck dat high." He called Curley with his thirty-eight feefty-five. Curley looked at the height of the ducks, with grave aplomb. "Dis time Curley take de hell of a good haim. Bang, bang, he shoot. Two times he shoot some more, bang, bang, and nobody see some more ducks. So we all go hinside, han Joe cook de pancake, han heverybody h'eat. W'en all of a suddink, she's come one hell of a noise on dee roof. Joe he's don' fineesh wid dee dish. So he says, 'Curley, you go see who's make all dat rakette.' Curley she's come back in, she's have dee great beeg smile on hees face. He said, 'Wat de hell do you know, Joe. Dem Maudit sapré duck was high.' "

The Bear on Sugar Island
(Burt Mayotte, Sault Ste. Marie, April 28, 1946)

John Laitala of Ironwood told me this story in Finnish dialect. Dr. Stuart Gallacher of Michigan State University heard it as a straight story from an old sheep herder in Henefer, Weber County, Utah.

This happened at Sugar Island. At first there was plenty of game there. Still quite a few deer are taken in the regular season. It was supposed to have happened to a Frenchman named Doe Bissonette, commonly known as Doe Beeznots. Doe was awfully afraid of bear. He lived on the mainland here in the city (Sault Ste. Marie); he had brother clearing himself a homestead on the island. His brother had been injured that day by a falling tree, so he sent for Doe to bring him supplies, and take care of his horses; his needs were urgent. Doe was confronted with making a trip down to the island at night with no means of transportation except a footpath. Deathly afraid of encountering a bear, he sought advice from another friend of his, very familiar with the island and bears, and reputedly a brave man. He was advised by this friend in the event of encountering a bear to mimic the bear and he need have no fear of getting past any bear he might find in his path. He made his trip and was gone several weeks, after which he came back to his friend, and related the experience he had had.

He says, "You know, Hi'm start late on de night for de hisland. De night is have no moon. Maudit hell," he says, "she's black like de hinside on a cow, and Hi must feel my way for every step on de pat'." He says, "Hi do dis for two, tree, four, mile, and all of a suddink Hi feel one great big handful of hair. De moon is come out from behin' de cloud, an' Hi see on de front of me one great big she-bear. Hi'm tell you, Hi'm pretty much scare, but Hi remember everything you tole me, and Hi'm watch dat bear pretty close. She stan' right up on her teet' an' snap her behin' on me. Hi tell you Hi have one hell of a time for do dat, but Hi mimic de bear hennyhow." He says, "Den de bear commense to danse, but dat's heezay. Hi'm pretty good man for de danse myself. An' den de bear is stoop over. An' Hi stoop over too. She's wiggle his behin'—sapré, you should see me wiggle my behin'. Hi make de mimic perfectment. Den dat sapré bear, he stop da wiggle, make some grunt, an' do a little job, right on de pat'. By de Maudit hell, Hi have no more 'fraid. Hi pat dat ol' bear on de back, and Hi says to him, "Bear, now you gotta let me pass. Hi'm way ahead of you. Hi'm have a pants full like dat w'en Hi see you de first time."

Dialect Stories of the Upper Peninsula

Directions
(Frank Ahlich, St. Ignace, April 17, 1946)

A city guy sees a Frenchman fishing. "How did you get such a nice fish?"
"I ketch him down de river."
"How do you get to this river?"
"Are you 'quaint about here?"
"No."
"Well, you go down de road a little ways, you go down t'rough de fields, you come to some woods, you go between two trees. There's lots of trees dere, but just go between two of dem. You'll come to a fence den, crawl under de fence and you'll come to a creek. But dat ain't de creek. You go quite a ways furder and you'll come to a lot of stumps. Just go between two of dem. Den you turn left for quite a ways."
"How far, a mile, two miles, couple of hundred feet, or how far?"
"No use telling you, you're lost already."

Directions
(Tom Beaton, Escanaba, August 13, 1946)

One Frenchman made an inquiry from another how to get to old Camp One. "You take dat road, and you go about a mile and a half. By'n by you come to a blacksmith shop, de store, de church, and de saloon. When you fin' dat, you come back. You gone too far. You fin' an ol' road, which twis' on de lef', and you go down dat road about one, two mile, and you fin' a trail an' she twis' on de lef', an' you took dat trail. By'n by you'll come to de river. She was a river one time, she's all dry up now. You pass de river, and by'n by you'll come to an ol' rail fence. She was a fence one time, but she's all burn now. An' by'n by you'll come to tree trail and you'll take de middle one. An' you'll turn on de trail one, two, tree, four, five mile maybe, 'n by'n by you'll come to five trail. An' when you come to dem five trail, take any one, because by dat time you'll be los' anyway."

Finnish

STRANGE AMERICA

Vorty-two Wifty Harrison
(Bob Kotila, L'Anse, May 22, 1946)

An old Finn lumberjack worked in the woods for years. He spent all his money for whiskey every spring. The boys in camp talked him into taking a trip to Chicago to broaden himself. "I yust going to do that." He buys a suit. Then he goes to the depot, and asks the ticket agent. "I want de best ticket you got for de Sicago." At the depot the fellows say, "You better change your

241

name, Eino Yloheiki is too hard to pronounce." So he changed it to Eino
Harrison. He got on the train, said, "Jesus Rist, I'se da gedding on da Bullman
gar. A big black nigger taking hold my suitcase. 'What the hell place you go
wid dat?' Anyhow I'se da follow him to mine bert'. And Jesus Rist dat's a nice
bert'. De white s'eets an' everyding. I'se da going to bed, taking off mine
sooses, and I go to sleep. Pretty soon dat nigger he's da pushing me, say
'Getting up, dat's Sicago.' I gedding up, and Jesus Rist, my soose is all bolished
up, and de borter ista laughing and holding out his hand. I don't know what
he holding out his hand for, but I reaching in my pocket and I take fi' cents
and I give it him. I getting off dat union depot. Jesus Rist, da beeg building.
Lotsa people. I gotta go da doilets. I look for dat Informatson Boot'. Dere's de
nice girl, I ask her what blace dat doilet. She showing me and I going in dat
blace. Jesus putt dat's a pig blace, wid pig marble billars. I boot in nickel.
Jesus, I never have to bay before to go doilets. I sidding down, and I see
bocketbooks. Bicking up forty-two wifty ($42.50) bocketbook. Jesus Rist, I
going to have good time now. I gedding oud dat blace and nigger say, 'Wash
your hands?' And he's de handing me towel, and den he say, 'Ten cents
blease.' Gosting lotsa money for doilets. I never baying dat up in de Lay
Anse. I gedding oud dat blace, and I take de street car, and I go see de sights.

"Dat conducktor on de street car, he's de knowing everypody. He say,
Jefferson, and Mr. Jefferson he's de gedding off. He say, Washington, and
Mr. Washington he's de gedding off. I laugh to myself. He not knowing me.
Preddy soon he say Harrison. Jesus Rist, how de hell he know my name? So I
gedding off dat blace. I walking down de street, and Jesus Rist I see de nice
girl. She's got de nice red s'eeks, and nice s'ape, and she's saying, 'Where's
vorty-two wifty Harrison?' And I'm taking out da bocketbook and giving it
her, and I'm saying, 'Jesus Rist, de people in Sicago too smart for me. I'm
guess I go back to Lay Anse.' "

The Baseball Game
(John Laitala, Ironwood, August 23, 1946)

Matti goes to pasepall came in Deetroit. He goes to one kind of a weendow.
De feller says, "Dollar wifty cents." He gives him dollar wifty cents and de
feller give him little ticket. Ten he start to go inside and one wellow start to
take dat ticket away. He says, "No, I bay dollar wifty cents for dat." Ten one
man say, "You gotta give it dat ticket for gome inside here."

"Ten I go where everypody's going, look like pig jiggen goop, pig jiggen
wence and den blaces where de jiggens roosting, and lots of beeple sidding
dere. Ten I go vay up high and sit town too. Ten I sit down and I look around
and see in dat pig field dere pig fellows wid short bants, wool socks, and it
look like wool suits too. And so hodt out tere. Ten bretty soon I see one
wellow out tere in de meedle, he'sta go and bick up a white rock, and he trow
dat one wellow who has a pig pandage on one hand. And you know, tat

Dialect Stories of the Upper Peninsula

wellow catch it tat rock wit tat sore hand, and he's never get mad. He's te take tat white rock and trow it pack easy to tat man. So tat wellow again he trow it pack, he's really mad, tat man. Ten I see tat one wellow wit clubbee. He'ste mad at tat man for trowing tat white rock at tat man wid de sore hand. So he goes right town py tat man wid te sore hand, and he'ste s'ake tat clubbee at tat man. Ten tat man gets mad, and he sweeng and he sweeng and he sweeng, and he trow tat white rock at tat wellow again. And tat fellow try to hit tat white rock wit tat clubbee again. And tere was one fellow stanting right in pack of tat fellow wit te sore hant, wit mattress on his pellee, and bird cage over his head. He'stoo holler, "Strike vun." Ten tat man wit tat sore hand, he'sta catch it easy and trow it pack again, never get mad. Ten tat wellow out tere in de center again he's sweengeeng, he's really mad. And he's trow tat white rock at tat wellow again. And tat fellow wit te clubbee he's miss tat rock again. And te fellow catch it wid te sore hand again. And tat fellow wit te mattress on his pellee holler "Strike two." And ten he'sta trow tat pall pack easy again. Now t'is man is really mad, out tere in de center. Even look as if he's trying to kick tat man from tere, he's trowing his legs so high and sweenging his arm. And tat fellow wid de clubbee his miss again. And tat fellow wid de mattress on his bellee holler, "Strike tree. You're oudt." Yesus dat's fonny. In de Gopper Gountry where I gome from, one strike and everypody out."

[This refers to the 1913 strike of the copper miners in the Keweenaw Peninsula, which is locally regarded as the reason for the economic decline of the area.]

Gerko's Baseball Experience
(Bambi Hoffman, Hancock, May 26, 1946)

I live in koompany poarding-house, de number six seven nutting, by de boor-rock pile. Eino in my poarding-house is going blay pall. Eino's purty good fellow so I'se figger I hafta go in de pall game, buta myself never be in da pall game pefore. One fellow in my poarding-house he wanta go in game too, and he's got de kinda car wid de bubbaloon tires and de running-poards and start wid a P—it's Puick, no Pilly-Knight. We're gomin' to high poard fence look like cow-pastur'. Vun feller say dats wifty-fi' cents. So I bay in my own bocket wifty-fi' cents. Vun feller say, "Gimme de ticket." I say, "No, not py damn sight, I bay my own bocket dat ticket." Den somebody say, "Randstand"—got de benkees (benches) like in a sauna, and a big shicken-wire, and dere was many fellers running around in de short-pants like de kids vear, and was nodder bunch in de roothouse. [Gerko calls the clubhouse a roothouse, in which Finns store potatoes and turnips during the winter.] Purty soon fellow come out of de roothouse wid a pird-cage and a mattress, and Jesus, he's look him funny. And he say, "Sittay, say Alco."

243

In the Field

(Play ball.) And he say, "One pall." Sure I see vun pall. But ven he say two palls, tree palls, I know he's crazee. He even tell it to one feller, "He's got four palls, take your pase." I say, "Any feller who's got four palls he can take anything."

Dat fence is busted coupla two tree places anda cows come in on de week days. And one feller slide he tought dat was tird pase but he maka meestake, it was cowflop. Looks purry bad. Den Eino my poarding house come up. And he hita de pall outa de cow pastur', and everybody say, "Run home, Eino, run home." And I say, "What de hell Eino run home for, he got money, he buy new pall."

UTTERANCES

Kumala
(Charlie Larsen, L'Anse, Ermart Cafe, September 5, 1946)

Give it te ax, give it te saw,
Ise te gonna work for de Kumala—
Sahoo, wahoo, s-a-a-hoo.

He gotta 'wamp, and a big 'wamp,
And he got te 'ruce and de palsam too—
Sahoo, wahoo, s-a-a-hoo.

He got te wide open 'laces,
Sesus Rist, I don' know,
What te hell should I do?
Sesus Rist, gimme my ax, gimme my saw
Ise te gonna work for de Kumala—anyhow.
Sahoo, wahoo, s-a-a-hoo.

A Finn fellow came in to the saloon and he was asking me for his tools: a cedar saw, an ax and a packsack. Jacks often leave their stuff with a bartender when they're traveling. He took the bus in from Ishpeming, and was going to Houghton with Kumala, a lumber jobber. Big, strapping fellow—two hundred, two twenty-five pounds. He was traveling all over, cutting pulp. A friend of mine, Dick Trimbach, who used to be engineer for the State Highway, later for Ford, took down what he said in shorthand. It sounded like a song in his long draggy voice. He started swinging his arms and asking for his tools. So we made up a song about it. We had more goddamn fun with that, couple three years ago. Sometimes they say Hutala for Kumala—he's another jobber around here.

That was about 1941.

[The song has traveled; I recorded a variant text from John Laitala in Ironwood, September 2, 1947. He did not know the circumstances of its origin.]

Dialect Stories of the Upper Peninsula

Sermon for Aylius
(John Laitala, Ironwood, August 23, 1946)

Aylius Mattson and me get yobbee Matti Hekla's gamp Nort' Ironwood. Aylius he's ta pull it one side de saw, I'sta pull it nudder side. We'sta worka in de gontract, and make it ta goodt monee. One day Aylius and I bulling on de saw, and we'sta sawing town tis big tree. Tree valling vrong vay, and he'sta valling on de boor Aylius. So den ve have to get anudder mans getting dat tree off dat boor Aylius. Boor Aylius he'sta tie. Poss he's goming to me, he says, "Matti, I gifve you half te holitay, you be te minister." I say, "All right, poss, I pe minister." So we take de Aylius back to gamp. We make pox, boot Aylius in tat pox. We boot Aylius on de lumber vaggon, and trive deam town road about half mile. We dig ta hole, and boot Aylius in tat hole. Ten I bick up tirt, and trow it on Aylius, and bray.

"Aylius Mattson, he's too tie on te Nort' Ironwood, Matti Hekla's gamp. He'sta bull it one side te saw, I'sta bull it on de nudder side. Tree he'sta falling down on tat boor Aylius. He'sta tie. He'sta tead. He's gonna be tead long, long time. Yesterday he was vort' tousands and tousands of tollars. Today he's not vort' one ten-cent biece on a sit-bile. As'es to as'es and tust to tust, if Yesus don't get you, Satana must.

[Bambi Hoffman told me the sermon as an independent item (Hancock, May 28, 1946):

> Ashes to ashes and dust to dust,
> If Yesus don't get you, Satana must.
> Yesterday he's wort' tousands and tousands of dollars,
> Now he's not wort' a fi' cent piece.]

Letter of Protest
(Rod McDonald, Dollar Bay, May 29, 1946)

Nels Nordstrom tells about a trout creek on his farm which the Conservation Department posted because of a beaver dam on it. When he found a city fellow fishing in the creek, and couldn't make him stop, he dictated this letter to his wife.

"Mister Gonversation Depot, Lansing. Hello. I got de big warm on Leminga Road. And I got de good wishing dat warm. But de liddle beaverses is making dam on my 'reek. So Gonversation Depot posted dose 'No Wishing.' But de udder day goming along one a dem big s'ots, and he's got pinsy nose 'lasses and de s'iny pole, and he's wearing rubber-brook bants and de raincoat poots. So I going up to him and I speaking to him very nice and I say, 'Hey, you bugger, ain't you never look for dat sign reading?' So he say, 'Ah you go to hell.' So I giving him a goupla gicks in de bants seat, and when he goming outa de hospital you better wix dat guy."

Vood for Sollie
(Walter F. Gries, Ishpeming, May 15, 1946)

Coming out of the bank, in Iron County, I met a Finnish friend, Weino. I asked him, "How're things going?" "Vell, I yust make de last bayment on my varm. Now I going to build a sauna, yust like my pardner, Sollie (Charlie) Salo. He buy de varm, and he gots sauna, and he buy de new Savrolette trucks. He's going to sell da wood from de varm."

Just then Salo's big truck goes by with a sign, "Wood for Sale." And Weino said, "Look, dat's de Sollie now. Py gaas, Sollie iss going for de bolitics." "How do you figure that out?" I asked. "Vell, look de sign he's got his truck. Vood for Sollie." (Wood for Sale he interpreted as Vote for Charlie, or Salo.)

FLOATING TALES

Home Brew
(Dan Harrington, Manistique, August 9, 1946)

Finnish fellow talking about farms. So he said, "My prutter, he's got de best warm what you ever see. He's got gows, sickens, and biggs. But do one ting what he's got on his warm is dat flowing well. Dat's de kind of well what he gome out de top and run all over. And de gows and biggs and sickens dey's all drinkin' dat water. So I say for him one day, 'How's dat you're never making any of dat home prew wid dat nice water you got it ?' 'Well, I never have de wormula.' So I said, 'I'm all ready for you. I'se got all de malt and hops and soogar and tynamite 'east cake right here in de gar.' So he said, 'I get some of dat flowing well water and boot on de stove for gookin'. Den when dey iss chust right I put on de stove de malt and hops. Den when s'e's gooked just right, I put in de rock. Den when s'e's gooling chust right I boot de tynamite 'east cake in.' Den I say, 'You leaf dat dere for ten tays and you boot it in de bottles. Den I gonna gome up and help you drink a little bit.'

"So apout ten days after, I start for his warm. And I meet his neighbor warmer coming on de road. And he say, 'You going on your prutter Yohn's warm?' And I say, 'Yes.' And he say, 'Petter you never go there. You know dat home prewing peer dat you making. Well, he chust get it put in de pottles, and he call all de neighpors arund for have a drink; and after dey drink a couple pottles day fight and 'cratch and raise lotsa hell around dere. And his wife s'e get mad. And s'e preak all dem bottles. All put one. So next day your prutter John he wind dat pottle. And he say for himself, 'I like to wind out how much power dere pe in dat peer.' So he sent dat pottle down to Lansing, Misigan, to wind out how much bower dere pe in dat peer. But he warget to

246

tell de 'Tate chemist wat peen inside dat pottle. And today he's mad as hell. Cause he get letter pack from Lansing, Misigan, and in dat letter dat guy say, 'It's petter you s'oot dat horse you got it, cause he got a pad case a diapetes.' "

[This is a widely circulated non-dialect story. I heard it in Munising told on two local brewers (Cal Kirk, May 5, 1946). "An old story about town is that Blongie and Burns were arguing about who had the best beer. Each is a beer distributor. They placed a wager and sent samples to Lansing for analysis. The report came back, 'Both horses are in good condition.' I've heard that fifty times, in the beer gardens, and I still get a kick out of it."]

Accidents to Aylius
(John Laitala, Ironwood, August 23, 1946)

Aylius Maki he's ta goming from da old gountree, and he go for poarding house first to see his friend Matti Mattila. Matti and he's vas talking many hours bout da old gountree. Den winally I ask Matti, "How's de gances in dis gountree get a yobbee in de mine?" Matti say, "Oh, iss goot chance now." So next morning I'se to go and see de bossee for mine. I aska him for yobbee. And he give me yobbee vork for timber gang. Vell, I start to vork, and I working bretty hard, and trying to show poss I goot man for vork. Den bretty soon dose lokkees start to rolling down, and I'se ta trying get out of de vay, and my tummee gets gaught between de lokkees. I see de nudder lokkees goming down de pile. And I pulling hard and de tummee goming oudt. Ten I have no tummee. Ten ve get de ganthooks oudt and rolling de lokkees around and winally winding dat tummee. I boot it in my pocket. So ten I have to go for mining gompany toctor.

Toctor say, "Ello Aylius, what trouble you today?" And I say, "Toctor, I losing my tummee between de lokks." Toctor say, "What blace your tummee?" "Toctor, I got it in my bocket." (Business of looking through pockets, finally finds it in the last pocket.) "Oh, here's dat tummee, toctor." Toctor he say, "Vat's de trouble, Aylius, you never boot dat tummee on? Now you never have tummee." Aylius say, "I never go 'cool very muts, and I never knowing dat. But next dime I remember dat." So Aylius say, "Tank you toctor."

Ten Aylius have date wit his girl Hilda from de poarding house. And he's to have to shafe de face cause he's ta have long viskers. He take his shoes and sogks off, and stand dere only in his underwear, and he's gonna shafe. He boot de looging glass on de vindow, sun going to shine in, good blace to shafe. De sidevalk yust outside vindow. And he's to start to shafing. Bretty soon nice kirl iss going py on de sidevalk. Vell, Aylius looking de girl but is keep on shafing. (He was using straight razor.) Aylius shafing and shafing and bretty soon dat same girl is goming pack and is looking Aylius, and Aylius iss looking her, and what you know, Aylius iss gut de nose off. Aylius remember vat toctor say, boot on right away, he's ta get pig egsited, trop de razor, gut de toe off. Ten he get so pig egsited he make pig mistake. He boot de nose on de toe and de toe on de nose. Now every time he sneezing he plow de shoe off.

[Charles Follo told me this as a Paul Bunyan story (Blaney Park, September 20, 1946). "Paul Bunyan dug out Little Bay de Noc and threw up the dirt to form the Gladstone bluff. He didn't want to take time to shave, so he told them to throw down his razor. It cut off his nose and his toe. He put them back on again but the wrong way. Every time after that when he sneezed he had to take his shoe off."]

Prized Parts of the Body
(John Laitala, Ironwood, August 23, 1946)

Eino and Matti and Hermani wass valking town te road, and tey wass talking and winally Matti says (softly), "What part te pody you hate to lose te most?" Eino says, "I would hate to lose my eyes, pecause I gouldn't see de peautiful 'lowers and trees and pirds, 'specially on a vindy day ven de ladies gedding on a street gar." Ten Matti says, "Sesus yess, dat's bretty bad, losing de eyes." Ten Matti says he hate te losing te ears. He says, "I gouldn't hear te music, te pirds, and 'specially when Lempi from te poarding house say, I love you Matti." Eino says, "Tat's bretty pad too." Ten Hermani, he's te last one. Dey say, "What you hate to lose, Hermani?" Hermani says, "I hate to lose my pelly putton." Matti and Eino say, "Well how's tat you hate to lose your pelly putton?" Hermani says, "Zometimes when I gome home from vork late, I like to read de newsbaper, and eat celery in ped. And ten I vould have no blace to boot de salt."

An Example for the Bull
(John Laitala, Ironwood, August 23, 1946)

A cattle salesman was trying to sell a big bull, but none of the farmers wanted him. Finally one said, "Why don't you go see Matti Mattila, he's a rich farmer." They told Matti, "You can make a lot of money with that fine bull, people will bring their cows." So Matti buys it, but nobody brings their cows to see the bull.

But lotsa beeple goming to see dat pull, from Ironwood, Wakefield, Bessemer, Hurley, Saxon, Iron Belt, Marenisco. So his neighbor tell Matti, "Vat's te matter Matti, you never puild pig fence round tat pig pull? and boot zign, 'Ten Cents Abiece Looking de Pull.'" So Matti tinks dat's all good idea. So Matti build a fence around de pull, boot de zign, "Ten Cents Abiece Looking

248

de Pull." Lotsa beeple come to zee dat pull, Matti start to make good money. Erkki Matteson's son has pig family, and all his gids iss crying every tay, tay wanna go and see te pull too. So Erkki Matteson boot all his tirteen gids in his second-hand Puick seven-bassenger touring car, wit no top, and his missus tere too. Well he's ta triving over to Matti Mattila's warm to see dat pig pull. He's winally get tere, and he 'top de gar by tat big wence. Ten te kids start yumping ouda te car. Erkki start to look at de zign, "Ten Cents Abiece Looking de Pull." So he start te gounting, Lempi, Eino, Taisto, Urko, Weino, Hilma—and he gounts up to tirteen gids. Missus fourteen, me fifteen. Fifteen times te ten cents, dollar wifty cents te looging de pull. And he says, "No sirree, I no gonna bay tat, I no gonna bay dollar wifty cents looging no pull." Matti Mattila says, "Hol' on. Tese all your gids? Every one of tese? Yusta minute. You ton't haveta bay notting. I going get tat pull. He's going take a looking you."

[In a somewhat similar story, a Finn running for sheriff in Baraga County resists the advances of his hostess. In the morning a neighbor farmer brings over his cow to her bull, who acts indifferent. She berates the bull, "Wat's de matter you pull son-of-a-pitch, are you running for s'eriff too?" (Dan Harrington, Manistique, August 9, 1946).]

Officer of the Law
(Burt Mayotte, Sault Ste. Marie, April 17, 1946)

This story is widely told throughout the Upper Peninsula, usually in the form of a brief anecdote.

The Finns in the Iron Country never traveled around much. Most Finns thought below the straits was another state. There were few educational requirements for citizenship. They believed they were citizens if they had first papers. They knew just Wisconsin and Canada.

In the Hoover depression the sheriff of Ishpeming was an illiterate Finn. He was a pretty good law enforcing officer but getting too old to manhandle fellows. The village council decided to deputize a few men at New Year's Eve to take over, and as they had no desire to offend the old sheriff, they let him use a county car to be a traffic enforcement officer for the occasion. They sent him out to the village limits with instructions to arrest any drunken drivers or speeders ignoring traffic laws. He sat shivering there for several hours—no violators or speeders—getting kind of disgusted. Finally saw pair of headlights bobbing toward him at three A.M. at high rate of speed. Waited till the fellow passed city limits speed sign, then he took after him. Motorist stopped on only light in town, at intersection of town's main street formed by a main highway passing through it. Pulled up alongside of offender, opened his coat, displayed his badge, addressed the man this way. "I wave it Hello on you. Me s'eriff in Iron County. Who de hell you tink it you is? Speeding for feefty mile a hour on main street, I tink I goin' arrest you." Pulled out his book and pencil—acted very officiously—opening it up to the right place—while the motorists looked him over, figured he was just a hick cop they could have some fun with. Sheriff says, "Wat's your name, you." Poised his pencil. Guy says, "John Smith." Old fellow says, "Yon Smit', I look your lizense for number." Then he says to him, "Where are you from, you." "Detroit." Old fellow got kind of huffy at that, says to him, "Say you, don't try give it me no bullsit. You got da Misigan lizense."

Cornish

For two collections of Wisconsin and Colorado Cousin Jack tales, see the eight-page booklet by Charles E. Brown, *"Cousin Jack" Stories: Short Stories of the Cornish Lead Miners of Southwestern Wisconsin* (Madison: Wisconsin Folklore Society, 1940); and Caroline Bancroft, "Cousin Jack Stories from Central City," *The Colorado Magazine* 21 (March 1944): 51-56.

COUSIN JACK CHARACTERS

Patience and Perseverance
(Jimmer Thomas, Laurium, May 24, 1946, also told by Reuben Rowe, Munising, May 6, 1946)

Jack and Bill were having hard luck in their drift. (Every once in a while miners strike hardpan in the rock.) The Captain comes along, asks them, "How are ye, Bill and Jack?" Jack says, "Not very good, Cap." "What's the matter?" Bill says, "We'll starve this month." The Captain visits a little while, and when he is leaving says, "Never mind, Bill and Jack, Patience and Perseverance will put it through all right." Then he went out to the shaft. Bill asks Jack, "Who in the 'ell is this Patience and Perseverance?" "I don't know, unless it be them two bloody Finlanders workin' across the shaft."

Fire! Fire!
(Walter F. Gries, Ishpeming, May 15, 1946)

This story took place in the little town of Central in Keweenaw County. Most of the social life centered around the church and the morning after one of the socials at the Methodist Church, Captain Sam Bennetts, who was the captain of the mine, said to Willie as they were going down in the cage: "Well, Willie, I seed you over to the social last night with Mary Jane," "Yes, Cap'n." "Well, Willie, I guess that's all right. But I'm going to tell 'ee something. Mary Jane is a pretty maid all right but she esn't very workish. She don't know 'ow to bake a pasty or pudden skins or things like that." "That's all right Cap'n, I aren't worried about that." Captain Bennetts then said, "I've seed you together many times and I'm a h'older man than you. I knaw 'ow they things go." "That's all right, Cap'n," said Willie.

In the fall Willie and Mary Jane were married. They had a company house —four rooms (half of a double house). The water supply came from deep wells that were dug down into the rock. One day in the middle of winter, a very cold morning, as the night shift came off duty all the chimneys in the location poured forth smoke—all but Willie's. Captain Bennetts, being a kind of fatherly man to all of his workers, was quite concerned and said to Willie: "See, Willie, that's what I do mean. Damme, it ed'n right—a man working all the bloody night and 'ave to go 'ome to no fire or breakfast or nawthen. I tell 'ee, I wouldn't 'ave it in my 'ouse!" Willie was embarrassed. "That's all right, Cap'n, I'll take care of that."

So he went home, opened the back shed door and reached in and got a twelve-quart pail. He lowered the pail in the well and got it full of ice cold water. He went into the house and into the bedroom where his wife was still sleeping. He then threw the pail of water right into her face and yelled, "Fire, fire, fire, Mary Jane!" Mary Jane, of course, awakened with a start. "Where to, my love, where to?" "In every bloody 'ouse in the location but yours."

Fooling the Captain
(Walter F. Gries, Ishpeming, May 17, 1946)

I heard this from a friend, E. Garfield Gifford of Cleveland, Ohio, told on two factory workers. Cf. Caroline Bancroft, "Folklore of the Central City District, Colorado," *California Folklore Quarterly* 4 (1945): 332; Wayland D. Hand, "The Folklore, Customs, and Traditions of the Butte Miner," *ibid.* 5 (1946): 18-19, esp. n. 52.

The iron miners used to use lard-oil lamps—medium thick oil made a big flame in the wick. The superstition was that if the miner's lamp went out, trouble was brewing and he'd better get out and go home. Alfred Penpraze's lamp went out so he climbed up to the surface and went home. He noticed a light in the kitchen and the bedroom, peeked in the window, and saw his wife had company—the captain of the mine. Alfred immediately returned to work, and reported to the boys, "Well, I fooled Captain Dick tonight. He doesn't know that I saw 'im 'ome there with my missus." [16]

In the Field

Talented Canaries
(Walter F. Gries, Ishpeming, May 17, 1946; also told by Jimmer Thomas, Laurium, May 24, 1946)

Two Cornishmen were riding on Keweenaw Central, hunting rabbits. They see some wild canaries. Sammie said, "See there pardner, see the pretty birds, wild canaries they are. My mother got one they birds 'ome, and my mother's bird is a grand singer. 'E does sing' 'Ome Sweet 'Ome' so bloody natural you'd a think you were sitting 'ome on the front porch in Cornwall." Whereupon Harry said, "My mother got one they birds 'ome too." "Do 'e sing?" "Ess, my mother's bird is a powerful singer. 'E do sing 'The Village Blacksmith,' and 'e do sing it so bloody natural that thees can see the sparks flying outa his hinder."

Hanging an Innocent Man
(Walter F. Gries, Ishpeming, May 17, 1946)

A Cousin Jack named William Jan was terribly worried in the slack days of depression because he had no job. He lived at the edge of the location on a little farm, with a family of five children, a cow, chickens, rabbits, and a rabbit-hound. He said to his wife one day after he started to spend savings, "Mary Jane, I'm hawfully wearied." "My love, what are you wearied for?" "Well, 'ere we are, with our children, I aren't workin', and nawthen is comin' in." To which his wife said, "There ain't nawthen to be wearied for at all. With our little 'ouse and farm 'ere, we'll get along grand." "Well anyhow I'm wearied, for if we 'ad another child I couldn't take care of it." Mary Jane reassures him. In the fall another son was born. And William Jan really was concerned. Again he said to wife, "Mary Jane, I'm turribly wearied. I'm so wearied about our children and this 'ere new son that I'm feared I'm going to 'ang myself." "O my 'ansome, dostn't thee do nawthen like that." However, one day William Jan went out in the barn, put the noose of rope around his neck, threw the rope up over the rafters. He stood on a box, and then he hesitated, and said to himself, " 'Old fast, 'ere pardner, maybe thee art 'angin' of a hinnocent man 'ere."

Big Bagies
(John B. Chappell, Ironwood, August 24, 1946)

See motif X1024.1, "The great cabbage," in Stith Thompson, *Motif Index of Folk-Literature.*

A Cornishman from Davenport, near Plymouth, was invited to his cousin's ranch in Montana. He was amazed at the great open land. "What does 'ee do with so much land?" "Well, we need that because we grow things so large

252

here. Now take this piece of land here, it's two hundred and fifty acres; it takes that much for five bagies, four in each corner and one in the middle, and they grow so large they touch each other." Next summer the American cousin visits in England and is taken to see the dockyards in Plymouth. (The only place in the world where you can hear the music and see the sound.) He tells his American cousin, "See 'ere, we're making a tank, and there's two thousand men working in it, and they're so far apart they can't 'ear the sound of each hother's 'ammer." "What on earth are they going to do with a tank that size?" "That's to cook your bagies in."

Self-Swallowing Snake
(Dave Spencer, Ishpeming, May 15, 1946)

All Cousin Jack stories are true, and this one's true too. A Cousin Jack was going to work in a mine in Africa one morning and he seen a snake ahead of him on the path. And the snake started to swallow himself. He started at his tail and swallowed everything till there was nothing left. So the fellow he was telling it to said, "I don't believe it. What did he do when he came to his head?" "Well he was a tight one, but damn 'im he done 'im."

Gondolas
(James E. Fisher, Houghton, August 26, 1946)

This same error is ascribed to the locally celebrated Pat Casey of Central City, Colorado; see Levette J. Davidson, " 'Gassy' Thompson and Others: Stories of Local Characters," *California Folklore Quarterly* 5 (1946): 348.

The Marquette County Board of Supervisors was discussing equipment for Champion Beach Park. One man suggested having five gondolas instead of rowboats. A Cousin Jack amended the motion. "I don't want to be too heconomical, but I suggest we start out with two and let Nature take its course."

Rendezvous
(John B. Chappell, Ironwood, August 24, 1946)

Two single men in the Copper Country during the strike had saved money, being thrifty, and had nothing to worry about except killing time. They decided to go hunting, walked up a path, came to a wind. Jan says to Bill, "Know w'ere we are, do 'ee?" Bill says, "No, I don't know, I was never 'ere before." "Well then we're lost." "I guess so." Jan says, "We'd better sit down 'ere a bit and try and figger out w'ere we are. According to my calkelations, there must be a railroad track out here ahead of us someweres. I'll take this road to the right, and you take the road to the left. If I get to the track first, I'll stank (step) around and make a lot of tracks in the snow. And if you get there first, you rub 'em out."

Driblets
(Walter F. Gries, Ishpeming, May 17, 1946)

A Cornishman, Jimmer, came to work one morning, and said to his partner in his underground team, "Well pardner, we had a great thing at our 'ouse last night." "Well what was et 'en?" "We 'ad driblets." His partner asked "Driblets? What sort of thing is driblets?" "Well we had three babies come to once." "I can't believe it—I don't believe 'tis possible." The proud father said, "Well, we ab in at our 'ouse, and 'gens we finish our shift, I'll take ye over to my 'ouse an' I'll show them to ye."

After the shift they went to Dick's home, where he showed his partner the three fine babies. His partner said, "Edn't that grand, my son. I never seed nawthen like it before." Pointing to the middle one, he said, "Damme pardner if it was me, I'd keep this 'ere one."

Plank Wadn't There
(Frank Ahlich, St. Ignace, April 17, 1946)

The tale of the Cousin Jack miner who stepped on the plank that wasn't there is the best-known Cornish story in the Upper Peninsula.

Jim Watts at Norway was on the sick committee for the Sons of St. George. So when they had their meeting the president said to Jim, "Anything that the sick committee has to say? Jonesy got hurt, you know." And Jim Watts spoke up, "I called on 'im at the 'ospital last night." "What did 'e 'ave to say?" "Well, 'e said 'e didn't know much about it. So I said, 'You must know something about it. I've got to put in a report.' So he says, 'Well, I was going down in the driftway, an' I come to the shaft, and I stubbed my toe on a bloody plank, an' the plank wadn't there, an' down I went, down the shaftway, plank an' all, and as I fell, I fell head afore, and when I come to I was unconscious. So therefore I don't remember much about it.' "

Appreciating a Pasty
(Mrs. Howard Anderson, Ironwood, August 24, 1946)

On one trip to Hurley a big Swede named Axel bought a drink for a Cousin Jack miner who had already drunk more than he could handle. The two became very friendly and the Cousin Jack said, " 'Ave a drink on me, Haxel." The obliging Swede did, although he was anxious to be getting on to Hurley. While he was drinking this second drink the Cousin Jack left by the back door to visit the outhouse. He returned and excitedly explained, "Hi've lost my jacket, hit's dropped down hin. My good worsted jacket, Hi've gotta get hit out. Will'ee 'elp me, Haxel?"

The Swede swung off his stool and went out to the outhouse, where he tried his best to reach the jacket while the Cousin Jack kept moaning over his loss. "Val, vy do yu vant to fish it ut for nu? It's slimy and von't smell gude," said the Swede, anxious to be on his way.

"Jenny will be very hangry. Hit's my best jacket."

"Val, ve can get it ut vit a long pole, maybe," said the Swede. Together they cut a pole and went back to try again to get the jacket but with no better luck. Finally Axel threw the pole down in disgust and said, "Vy the hell you vant to get a rotten smelling jacket ut of the uthouse?"

"Hit's not the jacket so much, but hit's got a bloody good pasty in the pocket."

Using the Telephone
(Walter F. Gries, Ishpeming, May 15, 1946)

Another story is told about the first telephone line which was installed in National Mine, about three or four miles from Ishpeming. This happened years ago and when the line was extended a phone was installed in the store, in the doctor's office, in the mine office, and in the captain's home. The captain, as you know of course, is the man in charge of actual operations at a mine. Next door to the captain lived a miner by the name of Johnnie Rowe. He had a large family. They were grown up and all away from home and one of the daughters lived in Ishpeming.

Mrs. Rowe went into Ishpeming one day to visit her daughter. It was a nice day and she hung the carpets and the drapes out to air while she was away. Some time after she arrived in Ishpeming it started to rain and thunder and lightning and she said to her daughter, "Mary Jane, I shall 'ave to go 'ome." And the daughter asked, "Ow, mother?" "Well," said mother, "I got they carpets and they curtains 'anging on the line. Your father wan't knaw enough to put them in." "Well, mother," the daughter said, "You don't 'ave to go 'ome. We got one they new telyphones. You can call up Captain Broad, 'e have a telyphone and 'e can go over and tell faather and faather can come to the phone and you can tell 'im what to do." So they called up Captain Broad and he went over to Mr. Rowe and said, "Johnnie, comez on over to my 'ouse. Your missus want to talk to 'ee." "Why, my missus is down Ishpeming," said Johnnie. Captain Broad said, "That's all right, but we got one they new telyphones. You come along with me and I'll tell 'ee what to do." So Mr. Rowe went over to Captain Broad's house where there was one of the old-type phones hanging on the wall. Captain Broad said, "Now, Johnnie, stand up against that greaat h'instrument, put your mouth again that pipe and put that 'orn against you ear and say 'Ello!" Johnnie did as directed, stood before the phone and said, " 'Ello!" Just then the lightning struck the line and knocked him down. He looked at Captain Broad and said, "My glory, that's the old lady, shore 'nuff!"

UTTERANCES

Describing a Drill-boy
(Jimmer Thomas, Laurium, May 24, 1946)

We were walking in looking for steel (miners' tools), Harry Williams and I. We were going in the level and met Mr. White coming out. His drill-boy Ed Hicks was never around very much. He'd make his clayrolls and snofs (piece of candle wrapped in clay for to snof the fuse—clayroll to tamp the powder) and beat it. The boys were supposed to bring in sharp drills, or a pail of water, or tend the machine for the miner. We recognized Mr. White at a distance when the light shined on his whiskers—he had a full beard. "Hello, Mr. White," "Aarh, aarh." Then he said, "Did 'ee see the boy?" I said, "No." White said, "That boy haven't got nothin', can't do nothin', haven't got nothin' to do nothin' with, and nothin' else."

We never memorized our prayers, but we memorized that. We peddled that all over the mine and thirty-five drill-boys repeated it.

Cornish Grammar
(Walter F. Gries, Ishpeming, May 15, 1946)

At a conference in Ironwood a good Cornish friend of mine came to hear me. After the meeting was over we went down to the hotel and sat around, exchanging stories. During the course of the conversation he asked me if I knew Harry Soady (a very well-known and clever storyteller). I replied, "Why, yes, I know Harry very well." "Well," my friend said, " 'Arry was 'ere the other day and when 'e do come we do certainly 'ave a good time. We sit around a spin a few plods and we do 'ave a pasty dinner." I said that I would imagine that Harry would enjoy that. "Yes, 'e do. The last time he was 'ere 'e said to me, 'Jimmer, 'ow long 'ave I knawed you?' I said, 'Well, 'Arry, I'd say you've knawed me forty years.' And then Harry said, 'I dearly love to visit with you, Jimmer. I love the Cornish people. I love them 'cause they are quaint people and good people. But there's one thing that 'as always bothered me.' And I said, 'What is it, 'Arry?' And 'e said, 'Hit's the way you Cornish use your pronouns and verbs. You don't seem to 'ave any rhyme or reasons, any rules or regulations for the way you use them.' I said, 'I tell 'ee, 'Arry, 'ere's 'ow it's about they pronouns; we got a rule for they.' 'You 'ave?,' said 'Arry. 'Yes, we 'ave,' I said. 'What is it?' said 'Arry. 'Well, we do call everything she excepting a tomcat and we call 'er 'e!' "

Dialect Stories of the Upper Peninsula

Analysis
(Walter F. Gries, Ishpeming, May 15, 1946)

Here's a story I got when I taught night school. We had a night school here years ago. We had signs around town announcing "Free Night School," explaining where to go, etc. Two Cornish lads saw the sign and Jim said to Dick, "Look see, 'Free Night School'; that's the place for us to go." So they went to night school. They attended classes for non-English speaking people who were getting ready to get citizenship papers. They attended several times. Finally, Jim told Dick that he wasn't going any more. "All that bloody teacher do is talk English and I can do that." So Jim dropped out of the class but Dick continued throughout the winter. One day in spring they were sitting at the boarding house and Jim picked up a paper and he saw the word "category." "H'mm, I never seed that word before. Look 'ere, Dick, you been going to night school all the bloody winter—'ere's a new word. What do 'e mean?" "Let me look upon it a minute," said Dick. So he looked at the new word and said to Jim, "Naow, my teacher do say when you 'ave a new word like that you must h'analyze it an' naow I'll h'analyze it for 'ee. Cat—anybody knaw what a bloody cat is. 'E'—that's a 'e cat. Gory—that do mean bloody—why it's a bloody tom cat, that what 'e is!"

Swedish

Vich Yohnson?
(Dan Harrington, Manistique, August 9, 1946)

A Swede comes to Minnesota from Sweden, stays there a few weeks, then goes to Kentucky. Later he comes back to visit his cousin at Echo Bay, Minnesota. And he says, "Minnesota is notting like Gentucky. Das are do country. You shall go into one of dose caves, and hold your hand up to your mout' and holler, 'Hullo, Yohnson.' You wait fafteen or twenty minutes and comes back a voice and says (low), 'Hullo, Yohnson.' " "Oh," his cousin said, "dass are nutting. You go up on top of Echo Pay on a nice day, looking over Lake Superior, and you hold your hand up to your mout' and holler, 'Hullo Yohnson.' You might wait fafteen or twenty minutes and comes back a voice and says, 'Vich Yohnson?' "

The Midnight Ride of Paul Revere
(John Laitala, Ironwood, August 23, 1946)

Lissen my shildren and you shall hair
The midnighth ride of a dern gude Svede, Paul Revair.
He's ta steal da horse from de neighbor's barn,
And he ride like hell from farm to farm

In the Field

He yumped in de boat and trew de oars away
And svim like hell for anudder shore.
And yust as te mune wass rising ofer de pay,
Paul, he trow de snuse avay.
He says "Come on poys, bull up your guns,
Every time you pull a trigger back.
You soot de Cousin Yack."

Courtship
(Walter F. Gries, Ishpeming, May 17, 1946)

The Swedish janitor asked advice from me. He and Steena had been going together fifteen or sixteen years, he was fifty-four and thought it time to get married. I told him when I had felt that way I had taken the Cliffs drive in a new Franklin in the moonlight, and proposed successfully. He said, "That don't sound werry bad." Couple weeks after he told me, "Vell, ve are going to get married all right, and I do yust like you told me to. Ve been driving around de Cliffs drive, and ve stopped at Cedar Lake, and right away I said, 'Steena, will you be my wife?' and she said, 'Sure, Lars.' "

I asked him, "What then?" "Then we went home." "Wasn't there anything else said?" "Vell ven we got downtown Steena said, 'Vy don't you say someding, Lars?' And I say, 'Py gosh, I tink I say too much already.' "

Easy Come, Easy Go
(George T. Springer, Gladstone, August 12, 1946)

Yon met Ole on the street, and the following conversation took place.
Yon: "Mey gudeness Ole min (but) jur luking fine. Vat iss ju doing now?"
Ole: "Ay have gude yob wit da Soo Line."
Yon: "Vat kind yob ju gat?"
Ole: "Ets gude yob. All day ay load steel rails; gude pay, fifty cents a day. Avery night ay buy beer wit' et. Eassy come, eassy go."

Something Must Have Happened to Ole

Yumpin' Yimminy: Scandinavian Dialect Selections, by and compiled by George T. Springer (Long Prairie, Minn.: Hart Publications, 1932), p. 68. When I met Mr. Springer in Gladstone, August 12, 1946, he gave me a copy of this little yellow paper-backed book, read me selections from it in his superb Swedish dialect, and then, at my request, indicated those he had heard as traditional in Upper Michigan, as distinct from the majority of stories which were reprinted from books and periodicals.

258

Dialect Stories of the Upper Peninsula

I heard this joke as an Irish Pat and Mike story, told by Norm Thompson at L'Anse, May 20, 1946. Mr. Springer referred to it as an old Swede story.

Ole and Yon were walking along the railroad track. A fast train came along. Yon stepped off the track, but Ole was not so fortunate. Yon was later asked by the company's claim agent how the accident happened. He answered: "Ole en Ay ban valking on track en Ay har train coming. Ay jump off track en train go by lak hal. Ven ets passed Ay see von arm on track, Ay go furder en Ay see leg, purty sune Ay see noder arm en den man's head. Den Ay tenk, bae yimminy, someteng must a happened to Ole."

Fifteen Gallons to the Acre

Springer, *Yumpin' Yimminy*, pp. 53-54. Mr. Springer commented, "Glenn W. Jackson, prosecuting attorney in Gladstone, told me this one as having actually happened during Prohibition days."

A Swede farmer in Delta County, Michigan, was arrested for a violation of the prohibition act and upon pleading guilty the judge said: "Ole Oleson, you are hereby sentenced to pay a fine of $200.00 and in default thereof, ninety days in the county jail."

Oleson paid the fine and went back to the farm where some of his patrons called on him. After indulging in several drinks Ole became confidential and exclaimed: "Dis har Yudge ant such bad fallar. Ay tenk hae ban farmer some time himsalf. Hae give me time to put mey crop in."

Asked how he arrived at that conclusion, he replied, "Vell hae fine me two hundra dawlers in cash now en in da fall ay go ninety days in yail."

Using His Head

Springer, *Yumpin' Yimminy*, pp. 61-62. Mr. Springer commented "This is one of the oldest Scandinavian wheezes."

A Swede was being pursued by an officer for a theft. He rushed into a grocery store where a friend of his concealed him in a gunny sack under the counter. The officer came rushing in.

"Did you see anything of that Swede? Where did he go?"

Already the arm of the law was on a tour of inspection behind the counter. Finally, coming upon the gunny sack in which the Swede was hiding, he inquired: "What's in this sack?"

"Oh nothing but an old harness and some sleigh bells."

Whereupon the officer gave the sack a vigorous kick.

From within the sack was heard: "Yingle, yingle, yingle."

In the Field

Yump, Ole, Yump

Springer, *Yumpin' Yimminy*, pp. 32-33.

In Escanaba, Michigan, they tell the story of Ole and Yon who agreed to meet at the dock to take the ferry to the Eagles' picnic at Maywood. As the time of departure drew near, Yon became uneasy at the failure of Ole to appear and boarded the ferry. The gangplank was pulled in and the ferry was slowly leaving when Ole, all out of breath, approached the edge of the dock. Yon, excited and anxious that Ole get aboard, cried out: "Yump, Ole, yump. Ay tank ju can mak et in two yumps."

Italian

Columbus Day
(Walter F. Gries, Ishpeming, May 15, 1946)

Columbus Day is still observed in the northern U.P. by Italian fraternal groups. In schools the teachers give special attention to the day, read again of the discovery, have the students recite poems, write themes. In my grade this theme was given. Tony had come from Italy the summer before and learned English as we taught it to him but writing the theme was beyond him. So at the suggestion of some of the kids, he told the story.

"Christopho Colombo was greata man. Dis time wen he was small kid, he live Genoa, Italy. An' he sailed de liddle boat on de big ocean. One days he getta big idea. An' he say, "I tink I gonna fin' America.' So whad you tink? He'll gone see de queen, because de queen you know was a good fren' for him. An he's say, 'Queen old kid, you pretty good fren' to me ain't you? Howsa chance you catch for me two, tree boat, I gonna fin' America?' And de queen is say, 'Don't you maka so much noise; de king is playa de check, he no wanta so much noise.' So whad you tink, de queen is sell his broach, his earring, his wristwatch, and is buy tree new boat, Nina, Pinta, Santa Maria." An' one days he sail on de big ocean. An' he's a saila for tree, four months. An' one day de big osh is getta pretty rough. Everybody was getta sick. He's a comin' one boy from up de hole, an' he say, 'Chris I tink de whole idea is cockeye. Is better we turn around an' go home.' An' Chris was getta pretty mad. An' he say, 'No sirree. Don't you give uppa da ship till you see his whita eye.' So he's sail again for two, tree months. An' is come one udder boy. An' he's say, 'Chris, I tink I see de tree.' An' Colombo is say, 'Never min' de tree, is land we wanta see.' So he's a saila tree or four monts some more. An' ona day is come annudder boy from de hole, an' he's a-say, 'Colombo, I tink I see de land.' An' Colombo's a-say, 'Dat's a good boy, old kid, datsa whad we wanta see.' So whad you tink, he's put his foot on land. An' he's come one Indian chief. An' Indian chief he's say, 'Hollo, Mister Colombo, it's you, ain't it? An' Colombo

Dialect Stories of the Upper Peninsula

say, 'Hollo, hollo, you Indian fella too, ain't you?' And Indian chief is turn around say to his pals, 'Boys, jig is hup, now we're discover.' "

Dominick in Church
(Walter F. Gries, Ishpeming, May 15, 1946)

Dr. Christian of the Isle Royale mine in the Copper Country tells this. Tony, the janitor of the church, was given a vacation. The priest realizes next Sunday he has no one to take up the collection, so he sends the altar boy for Dominick and asks him to substitute. "I don' know disa bizness." "Well, follow me and watch my directions, you'll get along all right," the priest tells him. Then he resumes the mass, and Dominick makes a round—the priest hears coins drop, but had given him no directions to collect. This happens a second and a third time. He talks with Dominick after, "I appreciate your helping out, but you didn't wait for me to give a signal." "I do justa like you say." "What do you mean, what did I say?" "Well, lotsa time you say, 'Dominick, go frissk 'em.' "

Stuck in the Mud
(Dan Harrington, Manistique, August 9, 1946)

Some Italians were working on a construction job where they were using dynamite, blasting. After the blast was set off, one of the Italians come running down the road hollering, "Tony, Angelo, Joe. Come queek. Bringa da shovel, bringa da two pick. Pete she stuck in de mud." "How deep she stuck in de mud?" "Up to his knee." "Well, tell heem to walk out." He said, "No, no can he walk out. He de wronga way up."

Don't Pincha de Oranga
(Bambi Hoffman, Hancock, May 26, 1946)

The Italian fruit store proprietor on the corner said to a lady pinching fruit, "Looka lady, don't pincha de oranga, don't pincha de banana, don't pincha de pomadoree (tomato). You gotta pincha something, pincha de coconuts."

Dialect Jokes

BIRACIAL

(Tom Ristell, Houghton, May 25, 1946)

The Finns and Irish always used to feud in early days. Finns called the Irish "Irish booger," as a term of contempt. A Finn went into a Chinese laundry and asked for his laundry. The Chinaman said, "No leady yet." "Vassa matter, I bring dis laundry one veek ago, and no ready yet." "No can help, he come next week." "I vant laundry now, not next veek, you Irish booger."

261

In the Field

(Tom Ristell, Houghton, May 25, 1946)

An Irishman out hunting came across a Finn farmhouse and asked the housewife for a glass of water. She says, "What natchional you be anyhow?" "I'm Irish." She says, "Plenty water in de 'wamp for you, Irish booger."

(Wallace Cameron, Gladstone, August 12, 1946)

The Scandinavians are very proud of their native heritage—the Norwegians the Swedes, the Finns. A Swede does not like to be called a Norwegian and so on. A Swedish farmer at Ensign staggers home from a Grange meeting—his wife had left him because of his drinking—and falls asleep in a neighbor's pig-pen. In the morning cool breezes wake him up, he blinks and finds his arm wrapped around a pig. "Ar du Svensk?" he asks. The pig rustles a little bit, grunts, "Norsk, Norsk."

The Frenchman, in a similar position, says, "Good morning, mistaire, what time is eet?" Pig says, "Neuf, neuf." "Jesus Chris'! That late alreadee." The little pig alongside says, "Oui, oui." Frenchman says, "Tank you, mistaire."

(Reuben Rowe, Munising, May 7, 1947)

Judge P. H. O'Brien, now in Detroit, tells this one.

About forty years ago there was a saloon halfway between Houghton and Calumet. A fight took place between a couple of Finns and some Irishmen. The Finns were killed and the Irishmen brought to trial—Verdict: Not Guilty. Three years later a couple of Finlanders rented a single horse and rig from Old Pat Shea to go to a sporting house. Going at breakneck speed over the bloody hill, the horse stumbled and broke his neck. Pat brought them to trial before Judge O'Brien. They were fined two hundred dollars.

The two Finns said, "Sesus Christ! Dat's funny damn ting. Two Irishmen kill two Finlanders, get it nutting. Two Finlanders kill Irishman's horse, get fined two hundred dollars."

[The comic anecdote of racial discrimination is a common pattern. One story has a Norwegian killing a Swede and hastening to a Norwegian lawyer, who after consulting many law books says he cannot find any law giving a bounty on Swedes. George Lyman Kittredge quotes the first American dialect poet, Benjamin Thompson, on an Indian complaint: "We drink, we so big whipt; but English they—Go sneep, no more, or else a little pay"; *The Old Farmer and His Almanack* (Cambridge, Mass.: Harvard University Press, 1924), p. 358.]

Dialect Stories of the Upper Peninsula

Cornish

(Rod McDonald, Dollar Bay, May 29, 1946)

Two Cousin Jacks met on Quincy Hill. "Hello, Jan, where going?" "Going down to see the doctor about my wife—she don't look so good." "I'll turn around and go with you. I 'ate the bloody sight o' mine."

(James E. Fisher, Houghton, August 26, 1946)

A cross-eyed Cousin Jack at the Quincy saw some large grapefruit in the window and thought they were oranges. He said, "It wouldn't take many of they to make a dozen."

(William Palmatier, Calumet, May 29, 1946; also told by Jim Hodge, Munising, May 6, 1946, and Jimmer Thomas, Laurium, May 24, 1946)

This is a true one, it happened up at 5th St. "I going up 5th St., I looked up by 'arper and Thomas' and I see father coming down the street, and father seed I too. Damme when we got up to each other, 'twasn't neither one of us."

(Jimmer Thomas, Laurium, May 24, 1946)

Two Cousin Jacks meet on the street each leading a dog. The machinist brags about his, "Mine is a machinist's breed." "Ow do 'ee make that out?" "I give 'im a kick and he makes a bolt for the door." The carpenter says, "Mine is a carpenter breed. 'E does little odd jobs around the house."

(Dr. A. C. Roche, Laurium, May 27, 1946)

It's been told around here for a number of years in different ways and different shapes. A Cousin Jack in the mine says, "Bet you can't guess what I 'ave in my dinner pail—it begins with an H too." "Horanges?" "Naw." "Happles?" "Naw." "Honions?" "That's right."

(Mrs. Paul Eickmayer, Lansing, December 16, 1946)

When I was going to college in Marquette a friend of mine whose brother-in-law was postmaster told me this.

A Cornish woman in Marquette moved to Harrison Street, a good substantial section of town. She tells the postmaster of her change of address. "I've moved to 'Arrison." He asks, "Where's that?" She repeats it, so he asks her to spell it. She spells, "A haitch, and a hay, two hars and a heye, a heff, a ho, and a hen."

In the Field

(Jim Vivian, Ishpeming, May 14, 1946)

An Irishman had a brother in the Old Country and wrote him to come to America. "You can pick up money in the strait." The brother comes over. Walking along the street, he picks up a piece of tin, it looked like money to him. So he went into a saloon, and says to the bartender, "Give me a beer." So he drank the beer, and put the tin up on the bar. The bartender says, "That's tin." He says, "Excuse me, I thought it was five. Give me another one."

[Also told by O. S. Winther at Blaney Park, September 21, 1946; the Irishman picks up a tobacco tag in the street.]

(Walter F. Gries, Ishpeming, May 17, 1946)

It is customary to close a mine when somebody died and to inform the widow of the death. So Mike was selected to break the news gently to Bridget. Mike talked with her over the back fence quite a while. Finally he thought it time to discharge his duty, and said, "Well, Bridgee, I suppose by this time Pat's shtrikin' harrps with the angels." "No, Mike, yez don't know Pat. He's probably shtrikin' angels with the harrps."

(Archie Megenuph, Hannahville, August 18, 1946)

I was considerably startled to hear my Potawatomi Indian story-teller suddenly interrupt his Nanabush tales and bearwalk experiences to tell Pat and Mike stories.

Pat and Mike came over from the Old Country. They lost all their money, so they decided to fly back. So Mike took some big chicken feathers and plastered them on Pat with sticky stuff. So Pat says, "Be jabers, Mike, I'll try." So Pat sails down the street, and he falls and kills himself and breaks his collarbone. (There was all horses in the street then.) So Mike waits and after a while he says, "Be jabers, Pat, don't turn into a sparrow and start flicking dat horse manure."

(Archie Megenuph, Hannahville, August 18, 1946)

Pat and Mike came over from the Old Country—they must have come over lots of times—and they had lots of money. So Pat bet Mike that he couldn't whistle before he reached the ground. Pat had a big wad. Mike got up on a limb, and tied the rope around his neck, and jumped. It tightened before he could whistle. "Well, Mike, you didn't whistle, I'll take your money." So he goes off looking for a lumberjack job, and comes back about a week later, and Mike is still hanging there. Just then two trees scrape against each other. "Be jabers Mike," Pat says, "you did whistle, I'll take you down."

FRENCH

(Mrs. Paul Eickmayer, Lansing, December 16, 1946)

Everybody around St. Ignace knows this. When anyone wants to try a dialect story it's the first one they learn.

Two Frenchmen meet each other. One says, "Hello Joe, what you got in de bag?" The other says, "You tell me how many rab*bit*, Hi'll give you all two." "You got two rabbits." "Oh, somebodee tole you."

(Joe Beach, Newberry, April 29, 1946)

This is told on a local French Canadian character in several Upper Peninsula towns.

Bill Obey was lost in the woods. The owl goes Hoo-hoo-hoo. He answers, "You don't know Bill Obey? Make de cedar for Underwood" (the local undertaker).

FINNISH

(Irving Edwards, Hancock, May 28, 1946)
Finnish No Trespass Sign

Whos the Hell Give It You Promis for Huntit
My Land. Better You Get It Out My Land or I
Get It My Two Pipe Sotgun. And Dats To be No Pullsit

(Everybody seems to know that in Upper Michigan.)

(Dan Harrington, Manistique, August 9, 1946)

Finnish fellow running for coroner was told by the candidate for sheriff, who was also a Finn, that he should have a campaign slogan. So after working on it for several days he met the candidate for sheriff on the street and said, "Well Toivo, I got it. My gampaign slogan is, 'A new suit of glothes for every gorpse, wid two bair of bants.'"

265

In the Field

(Walter F. Gries, Ishpeming, May 15, 1946)

Dave in the consular service in Chicago tells this on himself. In a bus he stares at a blond girl with beautiful hair, very fair, and fair complexion and thinks she's Scandinavian. She realizes he is staring. He stands in the aisle, gets closer to her seat until at a curve he loses his balance and falls in her lap, then clumsily tries to get up. She exclaims, "You big Swede." "Vell, I guess I fool you dat time all right. It look like I am a Laplander."

(E. P. Sawyer, Escanaba, August 14, 1946)

A bunch of loggers cutting timber were driving home in the wagon. One Swede said, "Pass the yig." Another Swede answered, "Yesus Chris', Ola, you bin here two year and you can't say yug yet."

(Heino Korpela, Ironwood, August 23, 1946)

A Swede goes back to the Old Country and is asked how he liked America. "Py Yesus, it take me twenty year to learn to say yelly and den dey call it yam."

IV

Folk Heroes
of the Media

The preface to the second section posed the question of what happens to oral tradition and the folk process within a print-saturated society, and the third section has shown the folklorist collecting oral narratives in our literate society. But the folklorist must also make his peace with printed and media sources, these do not damp the folk spirit, as generally supposed, but rather extend and reinforce it. A query invariably put to the collector who publishes his songs and tales is: Are you not destroying the tradition by imprisoning it in type? As if the singer or teller will cease to cater to his particular audiences of listeners because a scholarly press—or even a commercial publisher—has issued a book which will reach a far different audience of readers! Newspapers, magazines, radio, television, and paperbacks naturally will affect today's oral tradition, as in an earlier day did chapbooks, almanacs, broadsides, jokebooks, and dreambooks. But they do not dry up the oral sources. Rather, they draw from and feed into the floating oral lore. Local legends are sustained and reinforced by lurid Sunday supplement features. Ethnic jokes keep traveling from lips to print to the airwaves— if they are bland enough—and back again to lips. Recording artists sing folk ballads which may or may not affect the continuing folksong stream. There also are literary and journalistic legends and ballads that live almost entirely on the level of print and the mass media, although they are lumped with oral folklore.

So the folklorist learns to work with printed and media sources as well as to record in the field. In the vast repositories of print he may uncover traditional texts unavailable to field collectors. He can chart the histories of popularized and pseudo-folk heroes in the library stacks. And he must develop research strategies for finding these miscellaneous and widely scattered publications.

Folk Heroes of the Media

These essays draw profiles of American comic-heroic folk types as they appear in printed sources. The first deals with the folk Indian, overlooked by anthropologists and folklorists, who nevertheless left a trail of humorous anecdotes in a variety of printed records from colonial chronicles to nineteenth- and twentieth-century memoirs and travelers' narrations. They show his development into a comic folk figure, a hero of sorts, who cuts down the white man with sly retorts rather than with arrows or bullets. The second traces the expansion of the John Henry tradition from the first ballad reporters to the writers of children's books who have designated him as a national folk hero of black Americans. Yet the books, and the shifting interpretations about the Negro steel-driving man, build upon one broadside-influenced ballad and not upon oral legends. Finally, the greatest mock-hero of them all, Paul Bunyan, comes forth in a new light, as a manufactured folk hero created largely by journalists, admen, and resort promoters. A news clipping service supplied the evidence. These articles are not intended to debunk John Henry and Paul Bunyan and their kin—Pecos Bill, Tony Beaver, Febold Feboldson, Old Stormalong, Annie Christmas—but to examine the conceptions of folk heroes formed by the media. If the Paul Bunyan "legend" contains little folk basis, it does convey symbolic meanings to many Americans through newspaper stories and other avenues of popular culture.

268

Comic
Indian Anecdotes

In conventional view, the bequest of the North American Indian to United States literary culture takes two forms: his modeling for the fictional portraits of the Noble Savage, the forest barbarian, and the Vanishing American; and his stores of tribal myth and tale. Neither of these legacies conveys much human impression of Indians as people with whom white settlers had personal relations. In the romantic stereotype employed in novels, drama, and poetry from Cooper to Neihardt, the Native American has little more life than the woods and plains scenery through which he moves. And his mythology, even in a Longfellow transcription, has not more pertinence to United States civilization than the *Mabinogion* or the *Kalevala*.

The literary treatment of the American Indian has been fully reviewed by Albert Keiser. Stith Thompson in *Tales of the North American Indians* assembles traditional Indian stories. The gulf between these approaches—the white man's literary conception of the Indian, and the Indian's traditional conception of himself—would seem to be unbridgable. Yet Constance Rourke has already indicated one point of racial literary fusion, in the many printed colonial treaties reproducing their ceremonial pageantry in which both races participated and which, she feels, foreshadow native drama.[1]

Some more realistic, more intimate literary record of Indian individuality logically should exist, considering the easy assimilation of other racial and ethnic types into the portfolio of American folk characters. Arguments that Indians were somber and humorless nomads, or that they enjoyed little contact with their white neighbors except in violence, do not explain away the links of a common humanity—and anyway can quickly be refuted.

Some traces do exist, in a corpus of American folk anecdote, of personal relationships between the races. This body of story seems to derive from a double source: the play of Yankee humor on racial mingling, and the Indian's own sense of wit and shrewdness. That red men possessed humorous faculties, Catlin emphatically documents for the Mandans of Missouri, and for all the tribes he has observed, pointing out their continuous indulgence in laughter and mirthful small talk. Ingenious fabricators, the natives deluded the first visitors to the Americas with wondrous reports set down by their interviewers: Peter Martyr, "repeating the tales of a wily Indian," describes a fish-eating race of man with tails a meter long of solid bone, requiring them to sit on seats with open bottoms, or otherwise to dig holes a cubit deep; Waterton relays the fantasy of the ferocious water-manna, which swallows canoes, Indians and all, and dives to the bottom to devour them leisurely; Lawson tells how Indians straddle whales at sea and kill them by plugging up their spouts. Even when the Puritan invaders had settled on the land, an ingenious redskin could amaze the palefaces: witness the tributes to Sam Hyde, called the Baron Münchausen of the red men, and the prince of Indian liars, and honored in the compliment, "he lies like Sam Hide."[2] In the legends attached to Manshop or Maushop, by the Gayhead Indians of Martha's Vineyard, appear suggestions of Paul Bunyan storytelling. This giant created the offshore islets when he threw his moccasins into the water, and they filled with sand from the dunes; Nantucket sprung into being when he flicked off ashes from his pipe; when fogs rolled over the bay, Indian children cried out, "Old Maushop's smoking." An eyewitness to an aboriginal practical joke describes the stolid amusement of one "Big Bear," who captured a snake, tied a sack of powder to its tail, attached a slow match, and sent him off among his serpentine fellows, who exploded in all directions. A Cape Cod local legend testifies either to Indian playful imagination or resourcefulness in the case of Deacon Nauhaught, a respectable Christian Indian of Yarmouth; surrounded and literally embraced by black snakes, he calmly waited until the leader reached his face, whereupon opening his mouth he bit off the creature's head, to the vast consternation of the pack which immediately retreated.[3]

Besides the Indian's own ability to contribute to American humor, biracial anecdotes profited from opportunities available to the white man for laughing scrutiny of the native people. Some tribes lingered on the fringes of towns, as did the Narragansetts in Rhode Island and the Creeks in Georgia. During the colonial wars, Indian allies among the Six Nations lived in close association with the foes of New France. Treaty negotiations required elaborate and protracted social intercourse; fur-trading posts formed nuclei for gregarious activity; even in their later reservation stage, Indians continually dealt with white agents, Western neighbors, and curious visitors. If the literature of Indian oratory, captivities, and stately treaties grew from such contacts, so might a common folklore with Indian actors and white recorders. Interest in Indian traits, manners, and personalities displayed itself in early tribal and biographical annals by Colden, Heckewelder, Thatcher, and Drake, based on colonial race relations. When ethnology and scientific history dehumanized the Indian, anecdotal chaff dispersed into obscure channels; it reemerges today in jokebooks and humor omnibuses.

In the humorous observations on Indian character registered by white people, the picture of a degenerate race hopelessly addicted to drink took shape. In toasts and eulogies to liquor, the savage admitted his lack of self-control in the face of this alluring vice. Thus, during the Treaty of Greenville, an unabashed young chief, when asked by General Wayne to propose a toast, filled his tumbler with wine, gave "The Great Spirit," and after a pause, placing his hand on his breast, explained why: "Because he put it into the heart of man to make such good liquor." In still more eloquent vein, an Ottawa chief named Whitejohn, a great drunkard, asked by the Count de Frontenac what he thought brandy made of, replied, "Hearts and tongues; for when I have drunk plentifully of it, my heart is a thousand strong, and I can talk, too, with astonishing freedom and rapidity." Impudently the alcoholic native dodged a ministerial reproof. "You should love your enemies," concluded the parson after a long admonition, "and preserve an affection for those that hurt you." "I do love my enemies," asserted the culprit, "and have a great affection for them that hurt me." "Who are the enemies you love?" "Rum and cider." But the bibulous native was not undiscriminating in his praise; old Metallak, last of the Coo-ash-aukes, asked to comment on a bottle of rum he had received, answered, "Very good, only a little too much brook." Rightfully could he complain; for the inquest of an Indian jury over the corpse of a tribesman who had drunk freely in cold weather, resulted in the verdict: "That the said John Tutson's death was occasioned by the freezing of a large quantity of water in his body, that had imprudently been mixed with the rum he drank."[4]

Indians cunningly employed various devices and expedients to secure the coveted firewater. Two thirsty Podunks lingering on the environs of East Hartford, realizing that Squire Hills distributed rum only at funerals, arranged that John should report the death of Sam to the Squire and procure the rum. Afterward the Squire saw Sam alive and soggy with drink; upon next encountering John, he inquired wrathfully, "Look here, you rascal! Why did you lie to me? Sam is not dead." "Me not lie," responded John; "me thought him dead; he say so himself."[5] (This compares with the widely printed nineteenth-century tale of the soldier carrying a wounded comrade to surgery, unaware that his head has meanwhile been blown off; when the doctor points out that the man has had his head shot away, the soldier exclaims in surprise, "Why, he told me it was his leg.") Another trickster obtained drink by a literal fulfillment of contract. Governor Jenks of Rhode Island offered a mug of flip as a reward to one Indian acquaintance for information about any strange Indians to visit his wigwam. One day the informant turned up. "Well, Mr. Gubernor, strange Indian come to my house last night." "Ah," said Jenks, "What did he say?" "He no speak at all." "That looks suspicious," said his excellency. On being told that the stranger had not left, he ordered the flip. The Indian drained it and said, "Mr. Gubernor, my squaw have child last night." When French *coureurs du bois* established a trading post at Grand Rapids, Michigan, Indians of the Grand River Valley observed that on New Year's Day the traders called upon their lady friends and planted a kiss upon each cheek. This custom the Indians eagerly adopted and improved; the squaws without waiting to be approached called upon all accessible white men, on the festal day, volunteered the kiss, and at once demanded as *quid pro quo* a drink of whiskey. Did any resist, the charmer called upon her sisters for aid, who threw the victim down and kissed him in turn. Drinking led to more kissing and more drinking. Pride and honor rapidly evaporated before the lure of alcohol; a noted Potawatomi warrior presented himself to the Indian agent at Chicago, explaining that, as a high chief in his village, a very good man, and a friend to the Americans, he would appreciate a dram of whiskey. The agent thereupon replied that good men never asked for whiskey and refused to drink it when offered. "Then," rejoined the warrior hastily, *"Me one great rascal."* Equally unabashed was the Indian of Portland, Michigan, whipped by his chief for stabbing a trader who refused to sell him more liquor. Crawling from his cabin after a week in pain, he accosted the trader with a demand for more whiskey, saying he had been whipped two quarts too much.[6]

According to tradition, their passion for intoxicating beverages led Indians to practice deceit and guile, while maintaining dignity. In its upper reaches in the Cohos country, the Connecticut River contracts to violent narrows, whose compressed rushing waters support the weight of iron as if it were cork and whose rocky sides shiver the tallest trees into splinters—according to the dubious history of Samuel Peters. Only one living creature ever passed through safely, an Indian woman whose canoe came within the force of the current as she attempted to cross the river above the narrow. Stoically she drank off a whole bottle of rum she had with her, then lay down in the bottom of the canoe to await her destiny. Somehow she passed through without injury, and was found some miles below, quite drunk, by several Englishmen. Asked how she could commit so imprudent an act in the face of such danger, the squaw replied, thickly but heroically, "Yes, it was too much rum for once, to be sure; but I was not willing to lose a drop of it; so I drank it, and you see I have saved all." In quite a different scene, a tattered Sagamore emerged with a similarly unshaken poise. Picture the dilapidated Nonnewaug, last chief of the clan that bore his name, former owner of rich lands he had sorrowfully deeded to the town of Woodbury, Connecticut, now in court, like any ordinary vagrant, answering to a charge of drunkenness. So drunk had been the state of Nonnewaug, that his trial had to be postponed for a day of sobering off, and the magistrate informed him that his only response to previous interrogations had been, "Your Honor's very wise, very wise." "Is that so," temporized the fallen sachem, Yankee-like, and we may visualize him adjusting his tawdry headdress, and regally contemplating the crowded courtroom; *"Then I must have been drunk, very drunk!"*[7]

Other anecdotes reemphasized Indian naiveté and ignorance of white man's customs. They told of the Pima boy in Arizona's Gila Valley who fled to the brush for two foodless days because his mother warned the white strangers would douse him in boiling water and peel him white; of the disappointed savage who attempted to scalp a bewigged foe, and exclaimed in chagrin, when the hair came off without effort, "A d--d lie!"; of the fiercely painted member of Buffalo Bill's Wild West Show who entered a drug store and demanded "Heap Smell" until the trembling clerk handed him a bottle of perfume.[8]

Difference in attitudes toward the law emerges in a tradition of the

273

Saginaw chief Kiskauko. At a council meeting between relatives of a slain Indian and of his slayer, Kiskauko stepped up to the murderer and dispatched him with one blow of his tomahawk. Since the parties had agreed upon the payment of compensating presents, they angrily questioned his violation of their customary law; he coolly answered, *"The law is now* ALTERED!" In this instance Kiskauko behaved like a white vigilante, by taking the law into his own hands.

Difference in styles of dress gives point to the ancient folktale, variously attributed, of the unclad native who discomfits his white inquisitor. The white man asks how the red man can endure winters with no clothing. "Is your face cold?" "No." "Well, me all face." This riposte is attached to individual Indians from Maine to Texas, and had earlier been imputed to beggars in England and France by Thomas Fuller and Montaigne, and to a Scythian in a Roman history of the third century.

Difference in notions of work ethic appears in the tale about a slatternly chief living in shiftless bliss in Michigan's Upper Peninsula. Offered lucrative work during a manpower shortage, he demanded to know why he should take a job. "Well," explained the hopeful employer, "you can make good money, lay it aside, and never have to work again." "Huh, me no work now."[9]

In these brief scenes the ignoble savage has sometimes scored the telling hit, and in time he triumphs over his conquerors, not by brutish strength but through Yankee cunning. Even in the matter of strong drink, an Ottawa chief under reproof could point out, "Ah, yes, we Indians *use* a great deal of whiskey, but we do not *make* it." And one outspoken warrior, Silver Heels, seeing a British soldier about to be lashed for intoxication, declared, "Then provide another set of halberts and tie up your chief, for he gets drunk twice a day."[10] But if white traders successfully sold rum to Indians, white missionaries dismally failed to sell them theology, and the attempt received subtle rebukes. In a Boston newspaper of 1736, Lord Lovelace, fresh from England, interrogates a Christian Indian on the principles of true religion and divine revelation. He asks, "Well, tell me then, how came this World, and how came Man at first?" In reply the Indian gives this synopsis of Genesis:

Well—now me tell you what me tink: When first Time God make dis World, he make one Man and one Woman, den he make one clebber Orchard, den he tell 'em dat Man and dat Woman,—see, me gib you dis

Orchard, best way you lib here and eat Apples, only dat one Tree grow dere dat side, be sure you no eat, cause so big Poison, if you eat dat sure you poisoned, you run mad and turn Rogue presently, therefore sure you no eat; he say no,—so when go it away God, dat Man his squaw she look dat Tree, see, 'tis clebber Apples, all red one side, and smell sweet, she good mind taste, she taste, O clebber sweet, den she speak dat Man her Sannup, here you—you nebber taste all one such sweet Apples, best way you taste too; see den he taste too,—den presently both on 'em turn Rogue, quite Rogue, and ebber since all his Children Rogue too; now ebbery body Rogue, now I Rogue, and you Rogue, too, and ebbery body Rogue.[11]

In his literal acceptance of white man's religion, the Indian revealed not his own simplicity but the absurdities of medieval Christianity which the Enlightenment had already begun to puncture. One of a party of Indians visiting the Academy of Natural Sciences at Philadelphia was observed to examine a human skeleton very attentively, then turn away with a "wagh" of disgust; to an inquisitive bystander he confessed his pain that the blackcoats (clergymen) had deceived him. "They tell us," he said, "that their Great Spirit took from man's side a rib, and made of it a woman. But in the skeleton, no rib is wanting—there are the same number on each side." Upon a Swedish missionary's delivering an eloquent exegesis of Genesis to some Susquehanna Indians, one grave Sachem stood up and proffered thanks: "What you have told us is all good—very good. It is, indeed, bad to eat green apples—much better make them all into cider. We Indians are much obliged by your kindness, in coming so far over the Big Lake to tell us these things—which you *learnt from your grandmother.*" When in return he recounted Indian myths, which disgusted the missionary, the Sachem expressed regrets that faith in each other's stories was not mutually accorded. One repeated tribute to Indian cleverness at Biblical exegesis describes the verbal encounter between an old native and a patronizing traveler at a New York inn. The traveler inquired who was the first man circumsized, to which the Indian promptly replied, "Father Abraham." Then he propounded the question who was the first Quaker, and upon receiving an admission of ignorance, indicated his surprise and pointed out that obviously it was Mordecai, since he would not pull off his hat to Haman. These rebukes to supercilious Christians employ what Percy G. Adams has called the Adario motif in his study of seventeenth-century travel liars. Adario is one of the names given a philosophic Indian in the travel literature, who indirectly criticizes the white man's religion and government in a colloquy that actually reflects the ideas of the writer. Such bemused natives appear in the Upanishads and Pausanias.[12]

This shift in anecdotal emphasis from white- to red-man victory in the incessant race-battle of wits clearly emerges in popular accounts of bargains and revenges. In the very first legendary transaction between the two peoples, the European invaders cheat the aborigines out of their inheritance. According to the tradition, friendly Micmacs permitted the white settlers to share a corner of their land, until one day a white man came forward asking to buy a piece, a very small piece, the size merely of a cow's hide. The Indians agreed, having seen the strangers living in the narrow confines of a ship. As soon as the bargain was agreed to, the white man killed his largest bull, and instead of stretching the skin over the ground, cut it into tiny strips and measured out a huge piece of land. In another telling, the white visitors ask the Lenapees if they can place a chair on the shore; thereupon they pulled out the lacing from the bottom and carried it inland across the continent. Hence the tribes repeat the sorrowful saying: "So it was, and so shall it always be! The white man will cheat the Indian until he has everything."[13] Told as true, these accounts of the deceptive land purchase have entered the chronicles of many scattered peoples, who recall devious ways in which a smiling intruder tricked them through an innocuous offer (type 2400, "The Ground Is Measured with a Horse's Skin," and motif K185.1).

Later negotiations seemed to bear out the prophecy of the white man's duplicity. The sale of Manhattan Island for twenty-four dollars gave factual support to the dismal legend. One oft-recounted tale pictures Sir William Johnson, British superintendent of Indian affairs in America, outsmarting Hendrick, chief of the Mohawks, in a dream contest. During a council meeting Hendrick remarked to Sir William that he had dreamed the previous night that the Englishman had given him a fine laced coat. Knowing the Indian veneration for dreams, Johnson immediately pulled off his rich garment and gave it to the delighted chief, who departed crying out "who-ah" in great good humor. At the next council meeting Sir William informed the Mohawk that he too had dreamed, namely that the chieftain had given him a fertile five-thousand-acre tract along the banks of the Mohawk River. Hendrick accordingly deeded over the land, but remarked ruefully: "Now, Sir William, I will never dream with you again; you dream too hard for me."[14] A relished pioneer legend, variously attached to Daniel Malcolm of Brunswick, Maine, and John Lovel of Washington, New Hampshire, illustrates the mental resourcefulness of the white man. Surprised by half a dozen Indians while splitting rails alone in the forest, the stout-hearted woodsman admits his capture without protest; he promises to throw away his axe if his captors help him open the log he is splitting. Agreeing, they place their fingers in the cleft as he instructs them, in order to pull the log open, whereupon he suddenly struck out the wedge inserted into the cleft, the elastic wood snapped back, and tightly bound the Indians' hands. On one occasion a Yankee traveling across the western plains found himself confronted with hostile Indians. Approaching the warriors under a flag of truce, he announced himself a great medicine man, and in the face of their derision pulled out his false teeth and unstrapped his cork leg. The terrified Indians still standing their ground, the desperate Yankee took his head in both hands and made a move as if to unscrew it and lay it on the ground with the other parts of his body, at the same time informing his beholders that he could serve them in like manner. At this they fled in dismay, leaving the field to the medicine-man Yankee.[15]

Most frequently the anecdotal literature pictured the Indian not as a credulous booby but as a sagacious and cunning rascal, quick to adopt the business ethics of his conquerors, as expert at the literal contract as any Yankee. One narrative describes how an idle Indian named Joseph outsmarted Governor Dudley of Massachusetts. When Joseph presumes to ask the Governor how he had procured so many fine things without working, he is informed that the key to the matter lies in headwork, a mystery too thick for the Indian's skull. At a later date Joseph agreed to "kill a calf" for the Governor for two shillings. After waiting overlong for his dressed veal, Dudley went to the stable to find his calf still lying there with its throat cut; Joseph when summoned and reprimanded declared himself ready to dress the calf for two shillings more, and asked if that was not something like "headwork?" In the incident of the Gunpowder Harvest, the defrauded Indian scores in the final accounting. Sold gunpowder grains by a trader who extolled the "seed" as productive of a fine wheatlike grain, the gullible savage planted and sowed the powder with great care, but no results. Some time later the trader demanded of his victim payment of a large credit he had accumulated. Responded the savage, "Me pay you when my powder grow." In some cases the wily Indian duped white customers on his own initiative. An Ouiattanon had received favors from Lieutenant Bird of the Vincennes garrison upon promise of venison; after a long delay the officer pressed for his meat, whereupon the native replied he had in readiness some forty hams. "Where are they?" "All in the woods."[16] Sam Hide's much-bruited trick of securing cider, with his ingenious apologia, follows the manner of Yankee knavery. Thirsty Sam (sometimes Tom) Hide promises a gentleman to reveal the location of a deer he had just shot, in return for half a crown and a mug of cider; Sam describes the meadow, and the ash tree by the brook, under which lies the deer. When upon a subsequent encounter the gentleman indignantly demands an explanation for the lie, Sam in injured vein inquires: "Why, would you find fault if Indian told truth half the time?" "No." "Well, you find him meadow?" "Yes." "You find him tree?" "Yes." "What for then you find fault Sam Hide, when he told you two truth to one lie?"[17]

So prevalent did the tradition of the crafty redskin become, that in one tale in a collection gathered from Indian students, the white man deliberately asks the red man to cheat him—much as Southern and Western people were wont, to their sorrow, to ask the wandering Down-Easter to show them a Yankee trick. Sane-day demurred, protesting to the white man that he could not cheat without his cheating medicine, which lay beyond the third hill. So the white man lent him his horse, but Sane-day slyly pulled on the rein, causing the animal to balk; thereupon he explained that the horse did not recognize his new rider, and requested from the white man first his hat, then his coat and shirt, to deceive the animal. Dressed in the white man's clothes, straddling his horse, Sane-day turned to the importunate one and said, "Mr. White Man, see without my medicine I cheated you just the same." And he rode off.[18]

Like the Old World fools and simpletons who turned the tables on their tormentors, the underdog Indian perpetrated successful upsets and reprisals. Hailed before a justice of the peace for trespass and sabbath-breaking, the accused Indian was compelled to pay a fine, whereupon he demanded a receipt. The justice, surprised, agreed to furnish the receipt if the guilty one could show its need. Naively the Indian explained. " 'Tis best to have things sure; for perhaps by and by, you die; an Indian being a little tougher, perhaps, I live a little longer; then I die, and go up to God's house and knock. 'Ah! who comes there?' I must tell, it won't do to tell lies dere. 'Well, have you settled for cutting the tree on the sabbath day?' Yes, sir. 'Where is your receipt?' I haven't any.—Then I must go away, along down from God's house, to HELL, to get a receipt of you, sir; but if you will give me one now, sir, it will save me all dat trouble." In subtler style, a weary but penniless Indian, denied with abusive words the supper he requests from the Litchfield tavern hostess, exacts revenge. A charitable bystander volunteers to pay for his meal, and the Indian proffers a partial recompense with a story of Genesis, which he delivers in the presence of the hostess. "Well, the Bible says, God made the world; and then he took him, and looked on him, and say, 'It's all very good.' Then he made dry land, and water, and sun, and moon, and grass, and trees, and took him and say, 'It's all very good.' Then he made beasts, and birds, and fishes, and took him and looked on him and say, 'It's all very good.' Then he made *woman*, and took him and looked on him, and he no dare say one such word."[19]

In one unusual encounter, representatives of the two American subject races meet, and the Indian finds himself outmaneuvered by a strange kinky-haired African. Black Horse, a Comanche chief, while scouting in Texas, chanced upon the ragged "black white man" astride an old mule pony, who begged in terror, "Please, massa Injun, don't kill poor nigger!" Amused, Black Horse led the shaking and quavering Negro back to camp. Coming to a deep waterhole, the Comanche stretched on the sloping bank for a drink. Suddenly the black white man seized Black Horse by his hair and belt and pitched him head foremost into the middle of the waterhole. When the bedraggled chief rose to the surface, he saw his prisoner riding off on his pony, kicking with both feet and whipping with his hat. The Comanche rode the old mule pony back to camp, "and all the Indians heap laugh at Black Horse."[20]

In the comic stereotype outlined in the anecdotal tales a new American folk figure emerges, sharply in contrast with the wooden warrior of literary romance. This Indian folk type is a jester and wit, shrewd, sagacious and impudent, chained to a white man's civilization but cynically aware of his racial plight and still mentally competitive. Especially in the latest jokebooks, which articulate popular views about social and racial types, does this personality take form, although the jokelore merely crystallizes a long-established legend.

As his clever retorts to and sly revenges on the white man indicate, this folk Indian is waggish, even slightly impish. When the itinerant bishop asks the Indian chief if he can safely leave his effects inside the lodge, the chief promptly reassures him: "There is no white man within a hundred miles of here."[21] (I have heard this orally from John Lufkins, an Ojibwa, at Brimley, Michigan, who tells it as having happened at his reservation.) Behind the expression "talk turkey" lies a bit of native wisdom. Out in the woods hunting, a white man and an Indian shoot a fat wild turkey and a scrawny black crow. Discussing a means of equable division, the white hunter offers the proposal, "I'll take the turkey and you can take the crow; or you take the crow and I'll take the turkey." "Ugh," exclaims the Indian, "you no talk turkey."[22]

Placed in an embarrassing dilemma when Theodore Roosevelt advises him to cut down his menage from five squaws to one, the Comanche chief Quanah Parker provisionally consents. "You are my great white father, and I will do as you wish—on one condition." "What's the condition?" asked Roosevelt. "You pick out the one I am to live with and then you go kill the other four."[23]

When ridiculed for his pagan superstitions, the caustic redskin dealt a lethal rejoinder. To puncture the aboriginal myth that Manitou would cause to sink like a stone any offender who shouted while crossing Saratoga Lake, in western New York, a lady being paddled across by an Indian boatman deliberately screamed several times. Upon reaching the other shore she confronted her grim ferryman with the fact of her safety. Dispassionately he explained: "The Great Spirit is very patient and all wise. He knows white squaws can't keep their mouths shut."[24]

Coupled with his edged wit lay a realistic sagacity that enabled the folk Indian to deal with disturbing situations. This wisdom plausibly evinced itself in forest lore. One popular narrative describes how, in good Sherlock Holmes fashion, an Indian detected the unseen thief who had stolen venison from his cabin as a little old white man, with a short gun, and accompanied by a small dog with a bob-tail. To the curious travelers who had actually seen such a person, he revealed his occult divination. "The thief, I know, is a *little* man, by his having made a pile of stones to stand upon, in order to reach the venison . . . that he is an *old* man, I know by his *short* steps,—which I have traced over the dead leaves in the woods; and that he is a *white* man, I know by his turning out his toes when he walks—which an Indian never does. His gun I know to be *short*, from the mark which the muzzle made, by rubbing the bark of the tree against which it had leaned; that his dog is *small*, I know by his track; and that he had a *bob-tail*, I discovered by the mark it made in the dust, where he was sitting, while his master was busied about my meat."[25]

Indian astuteness extended into other fields besides that of woodcraft, even into the white man's own game of high-pressure diplomacy. A special agent from Washington met the Ojibwa chiefs in solemn council to persuade them to relinquish their excellent holdings, guaranteed by the government, for a tract of the most worthless land in Minnesota. The government agent delivered an impassioned address in behalf of the new treaty and his own integrity. "My red brothers, your Great Father at Washington said he was determined to send an honest man to treat with his red children. He looked toward the North, the East, the South and West to find this honest man. When he saw me he said, 'This is the honest man whom I will send to treat with my red children.' Brothers, as your friend and as an honest man, I ask you to sign this treaty." After the customary meditative pause Old Shah-Bah-Skong, the head chief of Mille Lac, arose and answered briefly: "The winds of more than fifty-five years have blown over my head and silvered my hair, but they have not *blown away my brains.*" This ended the council.[26]

And so the native American fixed himself in white folk memory as an untutored but brainy rascal, ever plying his wits to save his life, his property, his traditions. Captured by the enemy, Captain Johnny stuffed bullets into his mouth preparing for a getaway, and when the man at his side noticed the motion, calmly remarked, "Me chaw heap tobac." Two Chickasaw Indians intrude upon a party of travelers, and inquire which has lost a dollar; one claims the loss, whereupon the red men pronounce him a rogue, since the dollar is actually theirs.[27] (This recalls Quiroga's trick of detecting a culprit among Argentine gauchos by handing out sticks of equal length, and announcing that in the morning the wand of the guilty one will have grown longer than the others. In the morning the thief is discovered by possessing the shortest stick; he has cut it in fear.)[28] When the land shark finds his deed faulty, he secures the promise of the Indian heir, Chokun, that he and his wife will sign the deed for twenty-five dollars. Chokun signs, but then explains, "My wife she want twenty-five dollars, too." And no browbeating by the indignant white would change his answer or budge the adamant squaw, until the second sum was paid. As crushing proof of superior Indian sense, the native points out to whites his inestimably more efficient technique of courtship and matrimony. Where the white man courted for a year or two, and then exposed himself to endless nagging with no hope of relief, the red man took no risks. He picks out a likely squaw, goes up to her with two fingers held close together, sees her smile and takes her home. If she acts cross, he throws her away and takes another. Squaws love meat; no husband, no meat; so squaws do everything to please husbands, and they, gratified, do everything to please squaws. But the squaw, too, could match her aboriginal guile against the tyrant male. One jilted young maiden brought her case to trial; the defendant ungallantly alleged that his visits to her wigwam were intended merely to pass away time during the slack hunting season. During the hearing the unwanted squaw fainted. Sentence was pronounced awarding her a yellow feather, a brooch dangling from the defendant's nose, and a dozen coonskins. At once she jumped to her feet, clapped her hands, and exclaimed joyfully, "Now me ready to be courted again."[29]

In biracial anecdotes the Indian plays more than a passive part; he is a creative element. His telling word-blows and incisive comments give barb to the scene. And Indian humorists undeniably exist—for example the Oklahoman Alex Posey, editor of the *Eufaula Journal*, "a philosopher who applied the legendary Indian fables to current issues and drove home a point much in the style of the late Will Rogers."[30] Even when the red man served as the butt and dolt of derisive tales, his very human traits and frailties furnished substance for amusing anecdotes much as poor whites and village eccentrics serviced the professional humorists. These tales give at least some reflection of live Indians, mingling in a normal way with white people.

The Career
of John Henry

For thirty-seven years after the completion of the Big Bend Tunnel in West Virginia, where John Henry presumably defeated the steam drill, his ballad escaped attention. Then in 1909 it received a short and cryptic note in the pages of the *Journal of American Folklore*. A collector of folksongs from the North Carolina mountains, Louise Rand Bascom, coveted a ballad on "Johnie Henry," of which she possessed only the first two lines:

> Johnie Henry was a hard-workin' man,
> He died with his hammer in his hand.

Her informant declared the ballad to be sad, tearful and sweet, and hoped to secure the rest, "when Tobe sees Tom, an' gits him to larn him what he ain't forgot of hit from Muck's pickin'." Apparently, Tobe never did see Tom, but the key stanza was enough to guide other collectors. In the next decade, five contributors to the *Journal* expanded knowledge of the work song and the ballad carrying the name of John Henry. In 1913 the pioneer collector of Southern folk rhymes and folksongs, E. C. Perrow, printed four snatches of the hammer song and the first full ballad text, though from a manuscript. Perrow noted that workmen on southern railroads knew a considerable body of verse about the famous steel-driving man, John Henry. A then little-known collector, John Lomax, printed a splendid text of eleven stanzas in 1915, saying this was the ballad sung along the Chesapeake and Ohio Railroad in Kentucky and West Virginia, but he provided no source at all, nor the tune.[1]

John H. Cox, another active folksong collector, published an article on "John Hardy" in the *Journal* in 1919 mixing John Henry with John Hardy, a black desperado hung in West Virginia in 1894, and repeated this view in his standard collection of 1925, *Folk-Songs of the South.*[2] The confusion between the two folksong characters became apparent to Newman I. White, who separated their texts in his *American Negro Folk-Songs* of 1928.[3]

Meanwhile two scholars had dedicated themselves to the task of recovering and weighing every last scrap of evidence surrounding John Henry. Guy B. Johnson, a professor of sociology at the University of North Carolina, included a chapter of texts on "John Henry: Epic of the Negro Workingman," in *Negro Workaday Songs*, a collection he made in 1926 with Howard W. Odum.[4] At this time Johnson believed the song hero to be a "myth," but he changed his mind during the next three years and ended up accepting Big Bend Tunnel as the factual basis for the ballad. He interviewed many blacks and advertised his quest in black newspapers in five states, even staging John Henry contests to secure song texts and information. The resulting harvest of letters and statements revealed a pervasive and widespread tradition, deeply enough rooted to manifest all the vagaries and inconsistencies of popular legend. Nearly every state in the south, and several in the north, claimed John Henry as their offspring. One particularly circumstantial account placed the steam-drill contest in Alabama in 1882—but no documentary support could be found. However, struck by the relative stability of the ballad as compared with the fluctuations in narrative accounts, Johnson searched for and uncovered an undated printed broadside by one W. T. Blankenship, which presumably both drew upon and contributed to the singing of the ballad. Johnson presented his book-length study in 1929—*John Henry: Tracking Down a Negro Legend.*

The second sleuth pursuing John Henry had trailed him to Big Bend Tunnel before Johnson. Louis W. Chappell, an associate professor of English in West Virginia University, published *John Henry: A Folklore Study* in 1933. It took the form of a minutely detailed critique of Johnson's methods and interpretation, mainly because they preceded, and derived from, his own. Chappell accused Johnson of using without acknowledgment a preliminary report he had made in 1925 on his findings at Big Bend Tunnel. The evidence, painstakingly gathered and skillfully evaluated by Chappell, builds a powerful case for the historicity of John Henry at Big Bend.[5]

With Chappell's exhaustive monograph, the scholarly probe into John Henry virtually ceased, and the two main questions—the relation of John Henry to John Hardy and the factual basis for the steam-drilling contest—were laid to rest. Popular interest, however, continued to grow.

In his inquiry into the John Henry tradition, Johnson had anticipated its potential for the creative arts. "I marvel," he wrote, "that some of the 'new' Negroes with an artistic bent do not exploit the wealth of John Henry lore. Here is material for an epic poem, for a play, for an opera, for a Negro symphony. What more tragic theme than the theme of John Henry's martyrdom?"[6] A response was not long in coming. Within two years, a book entitled *John Henry* had been published by the Literary Guild. Its author, Roark Bradford, although not a "new Negro," had grown up on a plantation near the Mississippi River and observed Negroes closely. Exploring their culture for literary themes, he struck a profitable formula with fictional works depicting the childlike Negro conception of the world based on Scripture. Bradford had achieved his greatest success with *Ol' Man Adam an' His Chillun* (1928), rendered by Marc Connolly into the Broadway hit, *The Green Pastures*. The revelation of a tragic Negro folk legend seemed timed to assist his career. In Bradford's *John Henry*, the contest with the machine occupies only 5 out of 223 pages, but it serves as the dramatic climax for such structure as the book possesses. A cotton-rolling steam winch on the levee replaces the rock-boring steam drill, and New Orleans and the Mississippi River form the locale. John Henry is a cotton-loading roustabout, when he is working; much of the time he is loving and leaving his girl Julie Anne, who follows him into death after his fatal contest with the new machine. At other times, he performs great feats of lifting, eating, and brawling. The whole narrative is written in a repetitious, rhythmic stage dialect, interspersed with plaintive little songs and centering around Negro literary stereotypes. The sporting man, the hell-busting preacher, the woman of easy acquaintance, the old conjure mammy are all present. John Henry is a new stereotype for the Negro gallery, but a well-established one in American lore—the frontier boaster —and he reiterates his tall-tale outcries on nearly every page.

In 1939 an adaptation of *John Henry*, billed as a play with music, appeared on the Broadway stage. Co-author with Roark Bradford was Jacques Wolfe, who also supplied the musical scores. The Broadway production, starring Paul Robeson, closed after a short run.[7]

The book and the play of Roark Bradford, with attendant newspaper reviews and magazine articles, popularized the name of John Henry and fixed him in the public mind as a black Paul Bunyan.[8] In many ways the growth of the John Henry legend and pseudo-legend parallels that of the giant logger, who was well established as a national property by the 1930s. Bradford's *John Henry* resembles James Stevens' *Paul Bunyan* of 1925 as a fictional portrayal of an American "folk" hero based on a slender thread of oral tradition—in one case a few northwoods anecdotes, in the other a single ballad. Bradford, like Stevens, created the picture of a giant strong man, although with a somber rather than a rollicking mien, as befit a Negro hero. In 1926 Odum and Johnson called John Henry the "black Paul Bunyan of the Negro workingman." Carl Sandburg made the comparison the following year in *The American Songbag*, saying both heroes were myths. Newspapers referred to John Henry as the "Paul Bunyan of Negroes," "the Paul Bunyan of his race, a gigantic river roustabout whose Herculean feats of work and living are part of America's folklore."[9]

The parallelism persists in the later history of the two traditions. Writers, poets, and artists attempted to wrest some deeper meaning from the Paul Bunyan and John Henry legends and failed. But both figures lived on triumphantly in children's books of American folk heroes and in popular treasuries of American folklore.

The first presentation of John Henry as a folk hero came in 1930 in a chapter of *Here's Audacity! American Legendary Heroes*, by Frank Shay, who had published books of drinking songs. His account of "John Henry, the Steel Driving Man," followed Guy B. Johnson's preliminary essay of 1927 on "John Henry—A Negro Legend." Shay's formula was repeated by a number of other writers for the juvenile market, all of whom inevitably included the story of John Henry and his contest with the steam drill in their pantheon of American comic demigods.[10]

Other authors of children's books found it rewarding to deal individually and serially with Paul Bunyan and his kin. Consequences were *John Henry, the Rambling Black Ulysses*, by James Cloyd Bowman (1942), *John Henry and the Double-Jointed Steam Drill* by Irwin Shapiro (1945), and *John Henry and His Hammer*, by Harold W. Felton (1950). Of these, Bowman's nearly three hundred pages went far beyond the ballad story to give a full-length improvisation of John Henry's career, from a slave boy on the old plantation through the Civil War to freedom times. John Henry encourages unruly freedmen to mine coal, cut corn, pick cotton, and drive railroad ties. He outsmarts confidence men and gamblers, stokes the *Robert E. Lee* to victory over the *Natchez*, and at long last dies with his hammer in his hand at the Big Bend Tunnel. But a final chapter presents an alternate report, that John Henry recovered from overwork and resumed his ramblin' around. In Shapiro's much briefer story, John Henry never dies at all, but after beating the steam drill pines away to a ghost, until his old pal John Hardy convinces him that he should learn to use the machine he conquered, and the tale ends with John Henry drilling through the mountain, and the steam drill shivering to pieces in his hands! So for American children John Henry unites the blacks in faithful service to their white employers and accepts the machine. [At this writing (August 1975) there has just appeared *A Man Ain't Nothin' But a Man* by the black novelist John Oliver Killens, a fiction for children that chronicles a six-foot-seven-inch John Henry from slavery to freedom times, and gives him supporting characters. Killens attempts to read the theme of black liberation into the tradition.] In these children's books the full-page illustrations of a sad-faced Negro giant swinging a hammer contributed as much as the printed words to fixing the image of John Henry.[11] In the 1930s, Palmer Hayden completed twelve oil paintings, which now hang in the Harmon Foundation in New York, on the life story of John Henry.

Folklore treasuries and folksong collections also continued to keep John Henry before the public. In his best-selling *A Treasury of American Folklore* (1944), currently in its thirtieth printing, B. A. Botkin reprinted accounts of John Henry in oral hearsay, balladry, and fiction; he gave him further notice in *A Treasury of Southern Folklore* (1949) and *A Treasury of Railroad Folklore*, done with Alvin C. Harlow (1953). The lavishly illustrated *Life Treasury of American Folklore* (1961) offered a picture of John Henry spiking ties on a railroad track rather than driving steel in a tunnel, and in a skimpy headnote to the retelling of the ballad story revived the discredited hypothesis that the contest might have occurred in Alabama in 1882.[12] John A. and Alan Lomax, naturally sympathetic to the ballad hero first presented in a full text by the elder Lomax in 1915, always included John Henry ballads, some adapted and arranged, some recorded in the field in their popular folksong compilations: *American Ballads and Folk Songs* (1934) *Our Singing Country* (1941), *Folksong U.S.A.* (1947), and *The Folk Songs of North America* (1960). "John Henry" was the opening song in their first book, and in *Our Singing Country* they called it "probably America's greatest single piece of folklore. Alan Lomax, more recently, having shifted from a Marxian to a Freudian analysis, found John Henry equally receptive to his altered insights. The steel-driver shaking the mountain is a phallic image; singers know that John Henry died from lovemaking, not overwork:

> This old hammer—WHAM!
> Killed John Henry—WHAM!
> Can't kill me—WHAM!
> Can't kill me—WHAM!

Thus, the hammer song vaunted the sexual virility of the pounder. Lomax had returned full cycle to the psychoanalytic views of Chappell. The steel-driver also appealed to social reformers. In *American Folksongs of Protest* (1953) John Greenway called "John Henry" the "best-known (and best) Negro ballad, the best-known Negro work song, the best song of protest against imminent technological unemployment."[13]

While collected folksongs and literary retellings of the John Henry theme poured into print, only one or two folktales landed in the net of collectors. A curious folk narrative, mixing tall-tale elements of the Wonderful Hunt, the Great Eater, and Schlaraffenland with heroic and erotic legends, was told to Howard Odum in 1926 by a black construction camp worker in Chapel Hill. Yet subsequent Negro tale collections added only one substantial text to the John Henry tradition, while a whole cycle of trickster John tales dating from slavery times were being uncovered.[14] A folktale volume of 1943, prepared by the Federal Writers' Project in North Carolina, contained a graphic and fantastic prose tradition of John Henry's birth, deeds, and death in the contest with the steam drill on the Santa Fe Railroad. Data are given on the informant, an aged Negro of Lillington, North Carolina, who asserted that John Henry was born north of him on the Cape Fear River and worked with him on the Santa Fe, but the text is obviously edited. The talented black novelist and folklorist, Zora Neale Hurston, asserted in *Mules and Men* (1935) that the ballad was the only folklore item connected with John Henry.[15]

The greatest impact of John Henry on American culture has come through commercial recordings. In 1962 the most widely recorded folksong sold was "John Henry." That year the Phonolog Record Index listed some fifty current renditions of the ballad "John Henry" and fifteen of the work song "Nine Pound Hammer." As many popular singers have made recordings for the general public as have folk singers for collectors in the field. The Library of Congress Copyright Catalogue reveals over one hundred song titles devoted to John Henry from 1916 on, embracing all kinds of musical arrangements from simple melodic line and text to full orchestral composition. Arrangers staking claims include: composer Aaron Copland; song-compiler John W. Work; musicologist Charles Seeger; folksinger Huddie Ledbetter (Lead Belly); bluesman W. C. Handy; concert arranger Elie Siegmeister; and popular singer Bob Gibson. Chronologically, only ten copyrights are registered before 1937, ten in the period 1938-1945, twenty from 1946 to 1954, and eighty from 1955 to 1963. Although the popularity of "John Henry" has climbed dramatically in the past decade, fresh field texts are rarely reported. Still the commercial recordings are frequently traditional or semitraditional in source.[16]

Popular singers and recording artists have altered the formless sequence of independent stanzas which comprised the folk ballad into a swift-moving, tightly knit song story. John Henry has shifted from the sphere of Negro laborers and white mountaineers into the center of the urban folksong revival and the entertainment world of jukebox and hootenanny, radio and television. The earlier texts from tradition show the usual variation characteristic of folklore. John Henry drives steel chiefly on the C&O, but once it is located in Brinton, New Jersey, and he also drives on the AC and L, the Air Line Road, the L and N, and the Georgia Southern Road. He comes from Tennessee most often, but also from East Virginia, Louisiana, and Mobile, Alabama. His hammer weighs nine, ten, twelve, sixteen, twenty, and thirty pounds; sometimes he carries a hammer in each hand. His girl is named Julie Ann, Polly Ann, Mary Ann, Martha Ann, Nellie Ann, Lizzie Ann, and Mary Magdalene. In one unique text, John Henry's partner kills him with the hammer. Among the visitors to his grave are, in one instance, Queen Elizabeth.

Yet the shifts and twists of tradition are perhaps less surprising than the tenacity and recurrence of key phrases, lines, and stanzas. Analyzing his thirty-odd texts, Guy Johnson determined that the three most frequent stanzas, and therefore probably the earliest, were the opening stanza of John Henry sitting on his papa's (or mama's) knee, the declaration to his captain, "A man ain't nothin' but a man," and the verse about his gal dressed in red, Polly Ann. Otherwise, the story line varied considerably, and Johnson observed, "The stanza, not the song, is the unit," a conclusion later supported by Alan Lomax. Phonograph and radio have given the episodic stanzas of the ballad a structure and symmetry; by 1929 Johnson could list eleven examples of "John Henry" on commercial records, and in 1933 Chappell added eleven more. One of the most astute folksong scholars in America, Phillips Barry, believed that mountain white song tradition, perhaps in the person of John Henry's white woman, helped stabilize the ballad. He pointed to its parallelism with the opening stanza of the old English ballad "Mary Hamilton":

> When I was a babe and a very little babe,
> And stood at my mither's knee,
> Nae witch nor warlock did unfauld
> The death I was to dree.

"Mary Hamilton" and other English and Scottish ballads lingered in the southern mountains and could easily have influenced the new ballad.[17]

Today the ballad of John Henry lives on in remarkably stable form for an anonymous oral composition. It has been refashioned into a national property, shared by singers and composers, writers and artists, listeners and readers. The ballad commemorates an obscure event in which several lines of American history converged—the growth of the railroads, the rise of the blacks, the struggle of labor. Various interpreters have read in the shadowy figure of John Henry symbols of racial, national, and sexual strivings. The tragic tension and simple poetry of "John Henry" have attracted black and white, teenager and tot, professor and performer, who all draw nourishment from one unforgettable American ballad.[18]

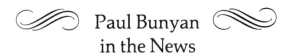

Paul Bunyan
in the News

Folklorists may well wonder why Paul Bunyan, with so little oral tradition behind him, has captured the public mind. Because the average American thinks Paul is his country's leading folk hero does not of course make Bunyan a folk hero; still one would like to know why so many people have that idea. The answer dawned on me after I subscribed to a news clipping bureau from January 1939 to March 1940, and from February 1941 to September 1941, for items in the nation's newspapers mentioning Paul Bunyan. Hundreds of clippings poured in to testify that Paul's name was constantly flourished before readers. They learned nothing more than that Bunyan was a giant lumberjack folk-hero of the north woods, who possessed a giant blue ox. But that lesson, by virtue of incessant repetition, they learned well.

Why should the name of Paul Bunyan make news? Before the Civil War, when newspapers served their communities with matters of local interest and amusement, they printed many sketches and jests, but the modern metropolitan dailies rely heavily on national news services and canned columnists, and local folklore rarely creeps into print. Paul Bunyan suits contemporary journalism since he represents a syndicated colossus useful for promotional stunts and feature copy. Were he more truly folkloric, he would be less newsworthy. Different groups find Bunyan useful for their purposes and keep his name before the public.

These groups include tourist and resort promoters, writers and lecturers, professional artists, and feature-minded journalists. Once the name of Paul Bunyan became sufficiently familiar, various entrepreneurs attached it to their enterprises and made his name still better known. Vacation areas in the north-woods states linked the timber god with their domain, to provide a colorful association; festivals, contests, and pageants styled themselves Paul Bunyan affairs. Individuals promoted causes and catered to public demand by telling Paul Bunyan stories, and notices of these lectures appeared in the papers. Artistic elaborations of the Paul Bunyan theme, in a variety of forms, further increased the amount of newsprint consumed by the timber deity. Each new book (and every publishing season offered at least one Bunyan) and any play or painting or statue about Old Paul brought fresh publicity. The majority of references, however, were purely journalistic. A provocative headline or lead-off sentence or verbal image could easily be gained by invoking Paul Bunyan, to emphasize any sort of mammoth event. Many clippings contain pictures, an added attraction from the feature writer's standpoint; they show Paul, fashioned from concrete or snow or aluminum, or a human representative, or a stunt of Paul Bunyan proportions, or a vista of lumber woods, or a scene at a Bunyan carnival.

The following excerpts and reprints taken from my file of clippings document the journalistic development of the Paul Bunyan legend.

Paul Bunyan Celebrations

By 1939 the tradition of a Paul Bunyan winter-sports festival seems to have become well established. An earlier clipping of 1937 shows a full-length photograph in blue and white of the concrete and steel statue of Paul at Bemidji, Minnesota. The caption reads:

> Not since the winter of the Blue Snow has there been such a rallying around as in Paul Bunyan's Playground where the townsfolk of Bemidji are staging their Paul Bunyan Winter Carnival. Center of activities is the colossal figure of the legendary hero of lumbercamp whoppers (pictured herewith) which stands on the shore of Lake Bemidji and roars out invitation to the fun. [1]

From St. Paul two years later an Associated Press dispatch is headlined, "Minnesota All Set for Annual Carnival of Ice Kings and Queens and Revelry on Ice." Among the features described is this cryptic item: "Paul Bunyan, legendary giant of the north country, will bring his blue ox, Babe, and his 'lullaby band' of several hundred drummers for a parade Wednesday night.[2] Wisconsin matched this program by announcing "Paul Bunyan to Frolic at Sports Fete," in a special dispatch from Ephraim.

Ghosts of Wisconsin's greatest legendary figure, Paul Bunyan, will frolic at the Wonderland pageant to be staged here Saturday night as part of the Door County Winter Sports carnival Feb. 18 and 19. An elaborate raised stage, with a natural background of evergreens, is being constructed at Nicolet bay in Peninsula State park to provide a proper setting for Bunyan, the Ogre, and the rest of the legendary figures. There will be a cast of 48, mostly high school students.[3]

Summer and fall festivals with a lumberjack motif invariably adopted Old Paul as their figurehead. A feature article described in detail the log-birling contests that attracted chief attention at these "rolleos," in which husky lumberjacks tried to outlast their opponents on rapidly twirling logs. "Mythical Paul Bunyan Again Prepares for the Birling Matches that Enliven Life in the Great North Woods," the illustrated piece began.[4] San Francisco and Oakland newspapers previewed such an attraction, planned for the Labor Day weekend, with the heading, "Paul Bunyan Returns."

Fort Bragg, lumber center in Mendocino County, has a "natural" with its Paul Bunyan celebration this week-end. The patron saint of the lumbering industry, the Paul Bunyan to whom no feat of strength was impossible, is a loved figure out of the North woods. Countless are the tall tales spun of Paul, his blue ox, and the others who were in his company. This Bunyan person was one who could seize a redwood, chew its roots to a point, dip it into a volcano and sign his name in fire on the skies above. He was a man!

Tomorrow, Sunday and Monday, Fort Bragg puts on a show, "The Return of Paul Bunyan." The prodigious Paul will be there, and lumberjacks from all points on the Coast will compete in typical contests. As Calaveras is entitled to its jumping frogs, Fort Bragg has a right to take over the gay business of exploiting Paul Bunyan in pageantry and fun.[5]

Another article showed "Paul Bunyan (otherwise Charles Buck)" sawing a log, and stated, "The legendary hero of the Northwoods will be a feature of the Return of Paul Bunyan Celebration to be held at Fort Bragg Sept. 2, 3 and 4, with a program devoted to ax throwing, log rolling, log chopping, hi-pole climbing, greased pole climbing and log bucking, staged under the rules of the Pacific Logging Congress." Still another illustration showed an attractive young lady atop the Blue Ox.[6]

In the east meanwhile a similar fete was held at Turkey Pond, Concord, New Hampshire, on September 16, 1939, and designated "Paul Bunyan Day." On that day the Manchester (N.H.) *Union* commented:

What is believed to be the biggest roundup of lumberjacks ever held in New Hampshire is scheduled for today in Concord. . . . Men expert in log rolling, boom jumping, log bucking and sawing will compete for state championship titles and in addition to events of this nature the topnotch fire line construction and pump crews will battle it out for individual and district titles. . . . Paul Bunyan exploits will be heard over the public address system throughout the afternoon.

Another paper pointed out the eastern origin of the titular hero.

Paul Bunyan, after whom the affair is named is, for the benefit of the uninitiated, the mythical hero of all lumberjacks. Tales of this legendary giant, born in Maine and who performed many of his great feats in New Hampshire, aided and abetted by his pet ox, "Babe," have been told and retold through lumber camps throughout the country until they have attained epic qualities. [7]

The handout leaflet listing the events for Paul Bunyan Day carried the same vaunt, and promised that some of the men on hand had actually worked for Old Paul.

A climax to lumberjack contests came in the national rolleo held at Longview, Washington, in mid-August 1939. Paul Bunyan and his wife Pauline, chosen from among twelve contestants, ruled over the celebration. An extended announcement of the rolleo and its attractions included references to Bunyan as "the logger who, with his famous Blue Ox, performed such feats as scooping out the present Hood Canal to form the rugged Olympic Mountains or swinging his huge ax so mightily as to fell the trees on a dozen acres with a single blow." Commenting on a pancake-frying contest, another release noted, "The legendary Bunyan was a lover of pancakes and often would eat 300 at a single meal, covering them with 50 pounds of butter and 50 gallons of rich maple syrup and then washing them down with bucket after bucket of black coffee." [8]

Log-rolling contests reached down into Kansas City, where one paper announced "Bunyan's Sport—Log Rolling—Comes to K. C.," and went on to say:

Log rolling, the sport fictitious Paul Bunyan invented, will be a feature of the Sportsmen's Show in the main arena of Municipal Auditorium beginning May 2.

Paul Bunyan was champion of everything around the logging camps. He was in his prime as a log roller at his camp on the Big Onion at the fork of the Little Garlic in the year of the Blue Snow. He once got a log birling so fast he churned it right out from under him. In doing this, though, so many bubbles were churned up that Paul Bunyan walked ashore on 'em without getting wet above the shoe tops. At least that's the way the loggers tell it. [9]

Outdoor festivities of various sorts, framed by forests and lakes, borrowed the magic of Bunyan's name. The Edenville, Michigan, Lumberjack Picnic brought a crowd of sixty thousand for its rolleo events, old-time music and dance, and huge lumber-camp dinner. The subtitle to the newspaper story read, "Frank Wixom's Annual Party Again Proves Great Revival of Paul Bunyan Memories," and the story continued:

Fabulous Paul Bunyan must have stirred uneasily today in his gargantuan grave, wrestling to cast off immortality and become again the mortal hero of lumber camp and river drive as thousands of Michigan folk flocked to this hamlet to pay tribute to the memory of the hardy race of lumberjacks and rivermen who for two generations ruled the pine forests of Michigan. . . . Children listened open-mouthed as their elders spun yarns of Paul Bunyan's heroic deeds, standing in the shadow of the huge double-bitted ax sunk deep in the end of a huge pine stump.[10]

Youngsters enjoyed a Paul Bunyan day at the Wisconsin state YMCA Camp Manitowish. "Bunyan, the legendary hero of the lumberjacks, makes his appearance in a huge replica. Babe, Paul's big blue ox (boys dressed as the mighty beast) cavorts. And the campers put on their loudest shirts, their boots, and sprout false whiskers for the big day." A color photograph shows the replica of Old Paul. At Laona, Wisconsin, the third annual Paul Bunyan logging exposition was held from July 27 to July 30, 1939, against the background of a large hardwood sawmill.[11]

Finding Paul Bunyan so successful a magnet in winter time, Minnesota apparently decided to recruit his services in the summer as well. Bemidji, possessor of the giant concrete statue of Paul and center of the Paul Bunyan Playground Area, devised a Fourth of July weekend festival for tourists with water sports, boat races, entertainment, and a big-fish contest, announced in the papers as the Paul Bunyan Summer Carnival.

Old Paul Bunyan, Minnesota's legendary lumberjack whose feats of strength have spread the fame of the state's North Woods far and wide, will wave the Stars and Stripes over his old playground haunts on the Fourth of July. Tribute to this patron saint of the timber workers, whose blue ox, Babe, was so strong he pulled the kinks out of the logging roads, and whose seven axmen cut all the tall timber off North Dakota, will be paid in a three day celebration starting Friday at Bemidji.

Patrick (Paddy) Donovan, 90-year-old veteran of the timber country and president of the Bemidji Lumberjacks' Last Man's club, is set to don his gilded derby and, with a blow torch, set off the giant Paul Bunyan firecracker as a starting signal. [12]

Pictures accompanying the story showed Paddy with the Paul Bunyan firecracker towering over him, a girl speaking over a giant Paul Bunyan telephone, and a pair of teamster's wagon wheels, said to have come from Paul's baby carriage.

From the Bemidji carnival a Paul Bunyan Canoe Derby started out down the Mississippi River to finish ten days later at the Minneapolis Aquatennial celebration. This race attracted considerable newspaper interest, since the eventual winners were accused of paddling an illegal plywood craft instead of a conventional canoe. References to the derby by midwestern sports columnists splashed Paul Bunyan's name in many newspapers.

The city of Hoquiam, Washington, celebrated its fiftieth birthday with a Paul Bunyan festival in August 1939. Washington and Oregon newspapers provided full advance publicity.

Giant figures 15 feet tall of Paul Bunyan, his blue ox, of Pauline Bunyan, and other Bunyan characters, will be employed in staging Hoquiam's Paul Bunyan festival, August 6 to 12, and make it into one of the most unusual and colorful celebrations in Northwest history.

A public wedding between Paul Bunyan and Miss Pauline Bunyan August 7, will be one feature. All of the giant figures will appear in the celebration's street parade August 8. This parade will be different than anything heretofore held in the state, inasmuch as it will stop every few blocks with vaudeville shows being put on at each street intersection during these halts. This parade will be three hours long.

Crowning feature of the celebration will be a three-night "Paul Bunyan Spectacle," August 10, 11 and 12, with a cast of 750. [13]

The impending nuptials of Paul Bunyan called for a special news release from Hoquiam, headed "Paul Bunyan Denies Troth."

Paul Bunyan, famed mythical logger, in whose honor Hoquiam will stage a Paul Bunyan festival on August 6 to 12, scored the press this week for reports that Mrs. Pauline Bunyan was coming to Hoquiam for the celebration and to meet him, her husband.

"There ain't no Mrs. Bunyan," Paul declared. "I'm a single man. The lady who is coming to Hoquiam is Miss Pauline Bunyan, a seventh cousin of mine, and she is coming to Hoquiam to be my bride at a public wedding to be staged outdoors Tuesday night, August 8."

Bunyan said that, "according to her pictures, which I got from a matrimonial bureau, she is a 'purty' gal and about my own height, which is 15 feet 3 inches."

Paul declared he was a little "skeered" at venturing matrimony so late in life, but said he never was afraid of a gamble.

According to a later dispatch, approximately fifteen thousand persons witnessed the wedding fete.[14]

Another sidelight of Hoquiam's celebration to reach the press was the initiation of Paul into a fraternity of local fishermen. A picture showed his towering figure—a singularly saturnine and long-nosed dummy—receiving a Liar's License from the club. The accompanying story said:

Grays Harbor fishermen this week recognized Paul Bunyan as the world's greatest liar by initiating him into the Grays Harbor Sinkers' Club, an organization of sports fishermen. Two thousand persons saw the ceremony which was conducted in the open air with three orchestras furnishing music for the occasion. . . .

Coincident with Paul Bunyan's initiation into the Sinkers' Club, the Hoquiam Elks announced a nationwide Paul Bunyan liars contest. Lies of less than 200 words dealing with Bunyan exploits will be eligible to compete. Replies should be addressed to the Hoquiam Elks lodge, Hoquiam.

Elk officers said by limiting the lies to 200 words Paul Bunyan would be barred from competing, since he never told a lie that was shorter than 10,000 words.[15]

The idea of describing a Bunyan celebration in Bunyanesque terms occurred to the correspondent for the Ashland, Wisconsin, *Press*. His first notice reported on preparations, under the head, "Paul Bunyan Dinner Out Next Sunday."

Plans for the Paul Bunyan picnic here are going rapidly forward with Paul himself heading the committee. The "dinner out" will be on Sunday at the Tribovich logging camp near Sand Bay in the town of Russell about ten miles north of here [Bayfield].

One of the first big steps necessary for the picnic to go on has been taken. The dishes are washed. The scene of the great wash was on the waterfront where Paul with one blow of his heel knocked an acre hole in the ice sheet. Several hundred fishnets were borrowed from the commercial fishermen and stretched across the opening to hold the dishes. Paul then began to take the top plates off the 290 foot stacks and chief washer Einar Miller and his helpers Harvey Gildersleeve, Brit Burtness, Skedgie Feldmeier, "Butch" Lodie and Ole Holm went to work.

A ton of spoons fell through the meshes and were carried out to sea, but chief cook Gus Weber said it didn't matter because the tea he is brewing for the occasion will be too thick to stir.

Russell Rowley, Paul Tribovich and Bob Feldmeier are in charge of the new Bunyan camp site and the logging roads and operations. Babe, the big blue ox, has been called in to help with the snow plowing and to pack down the snow in camp.

Mystic Knights of the Blue Ox of Superior Camp No. 7 and Mining Camp No. 14 will be present as well as Knights from throughout the Chequamegon Bay region. Johnny Inkslinger will be at the gate with a hundred foot time sheet to register them as they come.[16]

Four days later the correspondent happily announced "Paul Bunyan Rests after a Great Big Day," and wrote:

The morning was spent logging the countryside which manages to grow up each year between the Bunyan logging operations. The morning's goal had been set at ten trainloads, but with Paul and the Blue Ox leading the way, twelve trainloads of logs were moving by noon.

When high noon was marked by Paul's huge sun dial 8 feet in diameter, a mighty blast was blown on the dinner horn by J. P. O'Malley. A few lumber-jacks, who happened to be standing too near, were blown a mile over the hill into a snowdrift, and were an hour late getting back for dinner. . . . Second, third and fourth helpings were in order and Paul himself had 22. The Blue Ox, thirsty from his morning's work, drank a tank full of tea. . . . Most of the time was spent swapping stories of the good old days when dinner out was an everyday occurrence and Paul had 2,000,000 camps scattered throughout the country. Paul recalled the winter of the blue snow and his meeting with Johnny Inkslinger. Johnny himself took a half day off for the party, but when he found that Gus Weber's thick tea was as good to write with as ink he went back to work.

A set of photographs portrayed pretty "lumberjills" preparing relics for the Paul Bunyan Dinner-Out celebration. These oversized objects included a giant axe, rolling pin, and store teeth fashioned out of a barrel, all purportedly belonging to Paul. The same paper, in reporting the speeches that followed the dinner, noted Bayfield's claim to Old Paul.

Paul Bunyan in the News

Historians came to bat with research into Paul's early life. Bayfield, which blissfully ignores the claims of other localities, maintains that Paul Bunyan was born here. In fact Paul's cradle still is here. It was measured according to the distance between the eyes of Babe, Paul's blue ox, and thus is 40 axhandles and a plug of tobacco from rocker to rocker.

Other historians related that when Paul kicked the slats out of his cradle (which is how the saying originated) there was such a splashing in Lake Michigan that the British sent their navy over to see what it was all about.

But (and somebody always has to get serious) this was brought out too: That Paul Bunyan has an authentic niche in Americana, his worship is untainted by commercialism, and it all "really is something connected with the timbering industry which old timers, their sons and elder brothers like to recall."[17]

This story beautifully illustrates the ambivalent attitude that surrounds Paul Bunyan. His exploiters wish to realize the full cash value of their hero, and at the same time to honor his unsullied folk character. The timber deity satisfies the twin American strains of materialism and idealism.[18]

Paul Bunyan in the Arts

The graphic arts, from sculpture to wood carving, music, drama, choral operetta, ballet, radio, and films, explored the Paul Bunyan theme during the period considered. A heroic sculpture of Paul and Babe displayed at the New York World's Fair of 1939 received substantial publicity, and a number of papers carried a picture of the idealized pair, under the heading, "Myth Enlivens New York Fair," and with the explanatory lines underneath, "Portraying vigor and efficiency, Paul Bunyan, genial and legendary titan of the northwoods, is the subject of this sculpture by Edmond Amateis. As one of an American folk-lore group, it will adorn the façade of the Health Building of the New York World's Fair 1939. With him is shown his ox, Blue Babe, and Shanty John, a woodsman friend perched on the giant's arm."[19] *The Daily Worker*, always partial to Paul as a workingman's hero, blew up the illustration to quarter-page size, and added the note, "Legend has it that Bunyan could hitch Babe to a crooked eight-mile road and stretch it out to twenty miles, skin a tree while Babe pulled the trunk out and cut down an extra tree on the back stroke of his 2-edged axe." Another New York paper reproduced the figure of Johnny Appleseed as well as Paul, and still another showed all three in the group, the third being Strap Buckner.[20] The sculptor, Amateis, intended Bunyan to represent Efficiency, Johnny

299

Appleseed Benevolence, and Strap Buckner depicted getting whipped by the Devil, Humility.[21]

Other sculptors besides Amateis expressed interest in American folklore subjects. A twenty-seven-year-old winner of the Prix de Rome award in sculpture, Robert Pippenger, said in an interview that "American mythology and folk lore offer an inexhaustible source of supply for ideas." He had already completed a work on Paul Bunyan with his blue ox Babe, and planned others on Johnny Appleseed and Rip Van Winkle.[22] The reviewer of the Los Angeles County Fair in 1941 singled out Carroll Barnes for mention, and lauded his dream to "carve Bunyan and Babe the Blue Ox on the grand scale."

Two years ago he carved a 40-inch figure of Paul Bunyan, legendary logging hero, in Carolina cherry. But he itched to carve Bunyan big. Months ago Barnes found a 15-foot chunk of sequoia. To get it out of the woods he needed the hundred bucks. He couldn't raise it.

But now with the third prize of two hundred and fifty dollars he could satisfy his ambition.

In Milwaukee a school board commissioned Ulrich Langanegger to carve three reliefs in stone over the entrances to the Frederick J. Gaenslen school. He selected themes from children's storybooks, and one about Paul shown in an illustration, is thus described: "Paul Bunyan striding along in his mile long gait, carrying his famous ox in a sling attached to an uprooted tree; under his other arm, a fat pig. Off in the corner looking like a pigmy, Paul's mother, with the cradle he now so completely dwarfs, beside her. And in the background, a battered forest that was foolish enough to get in the way of the mythical giant."[24]

The crayon-stone lithograph of "Paul Bunyan" by William Gropper received a good share of newspaper publicity when it was placed on exhibit in various galleries. A reproduction shows an elongated man with a foolish grin and his shirt out carrying a great log on his shoulder. A story on Gropper's exhibit at the American Congress of Artists Gallery devoted special attention to Bunyan.

Paul Bunyan is the theme of a series of drawings, which show the same vigorous, affirmative spirit. Bunyan strode through the woods with seven-league steps, chopped down a tree with one stroke of his fabulous axe, shouldered a mighty monarch of the forest and carried off his 10,000 feet of lumber. Of course, he also denuded the American mountain slopes, bringing about a laborious conservation program. But essentially Bunyan is a symbol

300

of the upsurge of American life, that crude physical energy which conquered the frontier. One may add that in this sense, Bunyan is a symbol of the workingman without whom the American wilderness never could have been brought under cultivation.

Gropper feels this romance and sets it down in simple, straightforward pictures.

A later release announces that the Bunyan lithograph was chosen for inclusion at the 114th annual exhibition of the National Academy by a jury of prominent artists.[25]

Smaller notices refer to a hand-carved statue of Paul Bunyan made by a boy patient in the Herman Kiefer Hospital and presented to the Paul Bunyan Club of Detroit; to wood carvings of Paul Bunyan in the Montana exhibit at the Golden Gate International Exposition; to drawings on Paul Bunyan subjects by Walter Quirt.[26] A Paul Bunyan exhibition in ceramics at the Oregon Ceramic Studio in Portland earned special comment.

Ceramics, textiles, display tables and room decor all have been keyed to the Paul Bunyan theme. All colors used are in the cool northwest palette of tree and earth colors. Glazes have been specially developed from typical northwest plant and tree forms, and shapes of pottery for table use based on conical forms. . . . In the exhibition Babe, the Blue Ox, predominates, in a wall decoration by Emma Lou Davis, in small glazed figures of Babe done by Lydia Herrick Hodge as an experiment in glaze colors, and in a group featuring Paul Bunyan and Babe, done by Arthur Pulos.[27]

In the field of musical composition, a "Paul Bunyan Suite" by William Bergsma won praise when it was performed at the eleventh annual Festival of American Music in Rochester, New York, by the Eastman School Senior Symphony Orchestra. Dr. Howard Hanson conducted. One critic wrote, "The 'Paul Bunyan Suite' by Bergsma, talented 20-year old Californian, was taken from his ballet 'Pioneer Saga,' presented in its entirety during the 1939 festival. The enormity of the mythical Bunyan's ox, Babe, dominates the first excerpt in true 'program music' style."[28] The same paper on the same day had another more technical review by Arthur Cohn, and the Rochester *Democrat* had a review, also for April 30, by Stewart S. Sabin. An announcement of the broadcast of the Paul Bunyan Suite appeared in the Houston, Texas, *Post*, March 23, 1939. A brief note tells that Woody Herman, the orchestra leader, has written a song about the exploits of

Bunyan, and a photograph shows him receiving a Paul Bunyan statuette as an award at the Minneapolis Aquatennial.[29]

Paul starred in a new play in the summer of 1939. A banner headline announced, "Professor Presents Paul Bunyan, Babe, His Blue Ox, on the Stage," with a smaller caption, "Author of Midwestern Plays Is Immortalizing Old Legends of Logger." The detailed summary follows.

Elsworth Conkle, the Iowa university professor who dramatized the plight of the Alaskan pioneers from the middle west and who wrote a successful play about Lincoln, "Prologue to Glory," has come up with another play from the midwest. It is "Paul Bunyan and the Blue Ox" and was given a premiere at the University of Iowa recently.

The play shows the winning of the loggers away from Paul by the inroads of farming, family life and machinery.

Any play which attempts to present the "colossal" quality of the Bunyan legend offers the producers a challenge. In this play by the use of an elevated backstage for Paul and clever scene painting tricks which reversed the perspective, the illusion of his immensity as compared with his loggers was achieved without masks or padding. An amplifier is used to give Bunyan the booming voice he uses occasionally. Babe, the blue ox, appears in the play as a part of the painted back drop and is accented by lighting as he is important to the scene.

The number of Bunyan legends which Mr. Conkle has woven into the lines of his play attest to his industry. Patrons are told of the pancakes so large that they were greased by Negro boys skating about on them with hams on their feet; of the prowess of Paul as a logger, and many more of the "tall stories," which lumberjacks have credited to their hero.

Many emotions are played upon in the drama. There is fun in the calculations of Johnny Inkslinger, Paul's secretary; pity for Paul as he is duped by the king of Europe; uncomfortable delight in the winning of the loggers to the ways of "civilization."

While the purely fairy tale quality of the Bunyan stories is never neglected, the characters have many of the characteristics of human nature which cause them to be identified with actual types. Paul's desire to have the best, that is, what is "best" in his opinion, for his men, reminds one of many community leaders. Johnny Inkslinger's enormous capacity for research and his "willingness" to expound on his findings picture certain ineffectual scholars.

One can scarcely see "Paul and the Blue Ox" without being reminded of the Greek plays. There is the protagonist, Paul, who has demigod qualities and plays in a story which is already known to the audience. There is the chorus composed of loggers who inform the audience of events and admonish and console the hero. The hero moves on to the end, which cannot be happy for him.

The play has entertainment value. In the commercial theater, the size of the cast and of the production staff would constitute a problem.[30]

The same paper later carried a picture of the leading actor, Robert L. Frederick of Sparta, Wisconsin, dressed for the role of Paul Bunyan. A notice elsewhere dates the "world premiere" on July 17.[31]

Drama and music fused unhappily in a Paul Bunyan creation launched under impressive auspices. Described as a "choral operetta" and "chamber opera," the composition bore the title "Paul Bunyan" and owed its book to the English poet W. H. Auden and its score to the English composer Benjamin Britten. The premiere was given on May 4, 1941, at Brander Matthews Hall, Columbia University, by the Columbia Theater Associates and the Department of Music of the University. Reviews were carried in the New York *Times, Herald-Tribune, World Telegram, Sun, Mirror, Daily Worker,* and the Brooklyn *Eagle.* The *New Yorker* for May 17 and the *Musical Courier* for June also offered notices. The consensus can be summed up in the heading to Virgil Thomson's review in the *Herald-Tribune* (May 6): "Musico-Theatrical Flop." The *Daily Worker* headlined, "Sugar Water Version of Great American Epic" (May 7). The work was described as dull, turgid, incongruous, jumbled, pretentious. Only the *Mirror* applauded "Opera 'Paul Bunyan' Catches Spirit of U.S." (May 7). Several reviewers pointed out the misinterpretation of Bunyan by the English pair. "What it lacks pre-eminently," wrote Irving Kolodin in the *Sun* (May 5), "is fantasy, the kind of improbable, exaggerated wonder-working that makes Bunyan merely one in a line of amiable American braggarts along with John Henry and Lightnin' Bill Jones." Ralph Warner in the *Daily Worker* said positively:

Mr. Auden misinterprets the meaning of Paul Bunyan. The folk-hero typifies those masses of pioneers who literally strode across the continent in seven-league boots, ripping away the forests, creating cities, dams, highways, factories, digging beneath the soil for precious metals. The Bunyan of this operetta is a leader to whom the masses look for guidance. Although the program calls him "a projection of the collective mind of a people . . ." he gives orders, punishes, and imposes his will upon the assembled lumbermen. And when his task is done, the forest cleared and the new industrial day about to begin, he speaks a farewell to pioneer freedom and asks for a new discipline which is never qualified by the word "democratic."

However, James Whittaker in the *Mirror* felt that the conception of Bunyan did "sense the larger meanings of our native legend of a friendly Gargantua whose place in our folk-lore is the same as that of Prometheus in the lore of Greece—that of an earthborn demigod who steals from Heaven to help unfortunate man."

A newspaper article on American contributions to the ballet mentions Jerome Moross as having "chosen to do a ballet about Paul Bunyan, hero of the logging camps . . . the prize character in American folklore."[32]

Poetry is represented with the verses of Louis C. Jones, "Paul Bunyan Is Back," published in the New York *Times Magazine* for August 24, 1941, with an accompanying sketch of the giant. The news value of the poem lay in associating the spirit of Paul Bunyan with American resolution in a time of world crisis.

Moving from the creative to the popular arts, we find Paul represented in films and radio. Ernie Pyle writes in his syndicated column about a friend in the movie department at the University of Minnesota, Robert Kissack, who was producing animated cartoon pictures in brilliant colors. "One is the legend of the mighty Paul Bunyan . . . I've seen the start of the Paul Bunyan picture, and it's marvelous." A locally famous character from Harrison, Michigan, anticipated Hollywood gold with a movie script on Paul Bunyan. The news account says:

Spikehorn Meyers, Harrison bear trainer and teller of tall tales, has written a scenario for the movies. The three principal characters in the movie are Paul Bunyan, his blue ox Babe, and Spikehorn. The time is laid in the year of the big snow, when snow fell for 109 days without even stopping for lunch. The climax of the film is reached when Bunyan (assisted by Spikehorn) teeters a hill to make a riverful of hot water run in a circle to cook fish for the breakfast of the other 208 characters in the cast. "All I need now is to borrow $25,000 to get the film produced," Spikehorn says.[33]

"Paul Bunyan to Have His Day on 30 Stations," a heading declared, to introduce this item:

Paul Bunyan, the mythical lumberjack of gigantic deeds, will be bigger than those who sang of his prowess in days gone by ever dreamed. He'll "stomp" into homes throughout the entire northwest all at the same time when he comes to life behind the microphone Monday, February 13, as part of a weekly series of two hour programs featuring a wide variety of entertainment.

With WTCN as the key station, the program will go to 30 stations in Minnesota, North and South Dakota, Wisconsin, Iowa, Montana and Nebraska over the North Central Broadcasting system. . . . Paul Bunyan will come in for his quarter hour in a section of the program to be called "Tall Tales of the Tall Timber." The scene will be a modern lumber camp and one of the oldtimers will tell of "as how he logged with the great Paul."

One of these radio broadcasts was also offered as a stage performance. "The Bunyan dramatization will be one of six acts to be presented on the stage of the Lyceum theater for a visual as well as a radio audience in a two-hour radio show."[34]

Paul Bunyan Speakers

The newspapers report a number of persons who publicly relate Paul Bunyan tales; these speakers may or may not be authors of books about him. The principal of South Intermediate school in Saginaw, Maurice M. Guy, though not an author, seems to have pleased a number of audiences with his recitals, for announcements record his speaking to the DeMolay Alumni Club, an Evangelical father-son banquet, the Port Huron branch of the American Association of University Women, and a husband's night for a YWCA group.[35]

The stories told by another speaker are suggested in a news item.

It took five storks to carry Paul Bunyan, mythical north woods lumberjack, at birth. They fluttered vigorously but the elephantine infant was too much for them, and they dropped him five miles from his birthplace. The baby covered that five miles at such a clip that the weary stork barely got to his birthday party in time.

N. W. Roeder of the public museum's extension department, in a lecture at the museum Wednesday night, told the stories to illustrate the lumberjack's sense of humor.

Sour Dough Sam, Paul Bunyan's equally famous cook, is the ideal of all lumber camp cooks, Roeder said.

"The cook in the lumber camp was a law unto himself," he explained. "He tolerated no talking at meals. Conversation interfered with his efficiency. Even the superintendent's conversation was restricted to 'Pass the beans'." . . .

Roeder told of the organization of lumber camps in the seventies and eighties, when lumbering was in its prime.[36]

At the thirty-ninth annual reunion dinner of former campers of Camp Tousey, a YMCA summer center, Professor John E. Hart of the Syracuse University mathematics department spoke on "Tales of Paul Bunyan."[37]

Among Paul Bunyan authors, Glen Rounds appears to have been especially active. He gave illustrated talks on "Paul Bunyan, the

American Legend," in the art gallery of the New Rochelle Public Library, and in Rochester at the Memorial Art Gallery for a children's and an adult group. James Stevens told stories of Paul Bunyon [*sic*] to the Seattle Association of Classroom Teachers at a session devoted to forest resources and the lumbering industry. A reading from her book, *Ballad of Paul Bunyan,* was given by Mrs. Mabel Natalie Erickson of Bemidji at a meeting of the League of Minnesota Poets.[38]

Carl Sandburg used Paul Bunyan material in his recitals of American folktales and folksongs. A new announcement of one such presentation states, "Sandburg will present folklore from the background of Abraham Lincoln, tall tales and imaginative follies joined to the exploits of such living American creations as Paul Bunyan, Pecos Pete [*sic*], Steamboat Bill, and Casey Jones.[39]

In a talk on the folklore of upstate New York to the New York Historical Association, in Cooperstown, Harold W. Thompson included tall stories of Cal Corey and Paul Bunyan.[40]

The death of a celebrated Paul Bunyan storyteller from Michigan was noticed in a United Press release carried in a number of papers.

One by one the old-time story tellers who conquered both man and beast with their mighty feats of strength are dropping away from the cracker barrel—never to return.

Latest of. the story-telling clan to die is Jack Fathey, long known as Midland's master of the Paul Bunyan logging yarns.

Year after year Fathey would draw a crowd to some Midland stove and there—with a face so straight it cracked—enliven the winter night with his stories of the days when men were mighty.

Fathey used to tell of the night when he was top-loading for Bunyan and piled his sleigh so full of logs the moon was caught against the pile. The world, Fathey said, was wondrously dark on one side but marvelously light on the other. Finally Fathey said he permitted the moon to continue its journey by taking off 20 logs.

One of Fathey's favorites was the saw-billed pike that cut logs for the Bunyan camp all one winter. He was partial also to the mosquitoes who combined in lots of 20 to carry boats on portages. And he never forgot the acrobatic 'coons that joined together to form a facsimile of a tree.

Midland's residents say they miss the yard-long Fathey stories. And they say that next winter the old stove and cracker barrel won't seem quite the same.[41]

Some unsuspected kinds of Paul Bunyan raconteurs are reported. An article on narrative techniques used by the storytelling staff of the New York Public Library states that fifty storytellers related stories to some 40,000 children in New York City in playgrounds and gardens of branch libraries. Two illustrations from James Stevens' *Paul Bunyan* accompanied the article. In one instance mothers were impressed into service as Bunyan narrators. A Buffalo paper reported, "The tall tales of Paul Bunyan are starting to circulate around the country in preparation for the suggested Cubbing theme for March. Some packs have planned to have the Den Mothers tell a Bunyan story at the first Den meeting. The second meeting will feature a tall tales contest among the boys, and another one among the mothers."[42]

Paul Bunyan Books

Two new books and one reprint swelled the Bunyan literature during this period, and spread the name and image of Paul across newspaper reviews and promotional releases. The hometown paper of one author showed him at work designing sketches for his book, and provided this story under the caption, "Children Will Meet Bunyan."

Thousands of children throughout the world will learn for the first time about the adventures of Paul Bunyan, through a book written by a Seattle man which is being published today.

It's the work of Dell J. McCormick, Seattle lighting fixture salesman, who has made a study of the legendary hero of the northwoods ever since the days he spent in lumber camps as a boy.

The book, *Tall Timber Tales*, published by the Caxton Printers, Ltd., of Caldwell, Idaho, is the second of its kind which McCormick has written. His first, *Paul Bunyan Swings His Axe*, is about to go into its fifth edition. It is also being translated into French—which is proving no mean task because of the lack of any French equivalent for most of the logging terms which are used.

The tales trace back to the same lore as that in the Paul Bunyan book which James Stevens, the celebrated Seattle author, wrote a number of years ago. But they were written for a different audience, as McCormick relates them with the same simplicity that characterized his original impression of the fables.[43]

The reviews of *Tall Timber Tales* took the form of blurbs for Bunyan as America's foremost folk-hero, and used their space to offer a few sample stories. Characteristic comments are: "The Bunyan stories are among the soundest of American legends"; "Dell J. McCormick's stories about Paul Bunyan, the mighty logger, and his faithful Babe, the blue ox, come straight from the heart of America.

They epitomize this country's lusty folklore (of which there is far too little, regrettably)"; "Paul Bunyan is the only authentic mythological creation of American culture."[44] The only discordant note comes from the Lowell, Massachusetts, *Courier-Citizen,* which on September 1 observed, "we must confess to finding a good deal of the Bunyan literature rather stupid."

The West Coast put forth another entry in 1941, this time from Oregon, a point emphasized in the Portland *Oregonian* on April 1.

Newest contribution to the ancient lore of the American lumberjack will make its bow here Tuesday when Binford & Mort, Portland publishing house, releases the first edition of *Paul Bunyan, the Work Giant.*

The new volume is the work of Ida Virginia Turney, ex-University of Oregon English instructor, who has spent a large part of her life studying the Paul Bunyan legend and writing about it.

The book is illustrated in three colors, with original drawings by Norma Lyon of Marshfield, a recent University of Oregon graduate, and master drawings by Harold L. Price, Portland, a 1937 Oregon graduate.

So enthusiastically has the volume been received that the first printing of 3300 copies already has been sold, L. B. Prillaman, Binford & Mort editor, said.

"We're very, very proud of this volume," Prillaman declared. "And the reason we're so proud is that it is really an all-Oregon product in every way. Author, artists, editor and publisher all are Oregonians."

Paul Bunyan, the Work Giant, is listed as a children's book, but has undoubted appeal for adults also. It develops Miss Turney's pet thesis that Paul Bunyan is the only legitimate American folk character, and her further thought that he is the symbol of the American workman.

Miss Turney's first volume, *Paul Bunyan Comes West,* was published while she was still teaching at the University of Oregon, and was later republished by Houghton Mifflin. She is now preparing a thesis on Paul Bunyan for a doctorate at the University of California.

Again the reviews are eulogistic, and convey the impression that anyone who writes about Paul Bunyan necessarily performs a patriotic service. This time the quarto-size colored pictures receive special praise.[45] The July 13 review in the San Francisco *Chronicle* illustrates the patriotic attitude toward the lumberjack hero:

Paul Bunyan is probably our best known and most authentic folk character free of European or Indian origins. For a long time his epic story was the almost exclusive property of James Stevens who wrote some masterly tales of the great workgiant of the logging camps. But today Paul Bunyan has been presented to the reading public in many ways by many different hands . . .

This is an ideal book for children, combining as it does amusement with folklore, but it is not without value for the busy adult reader who may wish to become familiar with the highlights of Paul's mythical career in quick condensed form; for the story touches all the spots from his origin in the Maine woods to his final glorification in the Pacific Northwest of the Douglas fir, containing such tales of his odyssey across the country and his sojourns in the Great Lakes region and in the great Michigan and Wisconsin white pine forests as are worthy to stand beside those of Baron Münchausen and Gargantua.

The reprint of Esther Shephard's *Paul Bunyan* in 1941, seventeen years after the original edition, was not reviewed, but some papers reproduced the new Rockwell Kent illustrations. One commented, "Paul Bunyan, the fabulous frontiersman, has met his match: an American artist who can do justice to his noble proportions." Notices of the book by Olive Beaupré Miller, *Heroes, Outlaws and Funny Fellows of American Popular Tales*, 1939, mentioned its inclusion of Paul Bunyan.[46]

Paul Bunyan Tales

Although most newspaper references to Paul Bunyan content themselves with such statements as "In American lumber camp legend Paul Bunyan was the hero of a series of tall tales, current through the timber country from Michigan westward,"[47] occasionally the texts of tales are given. A United Press release from Bemidji, Minnesota, in the winter of 1940, connected Paul Bunyan stories with the town's annual winter Paul Bunyan carnival.

An old timer, who likes to spin yarns of the great Paul Bunyan, sat in the back room of a Bemidji store.

A severe cold wave, driving down from the Arctic, had dropped the temperature to 30 degrees below zero.

"Bathin' weather," the old timer sneered.

He cocked his feet on the stove rail and inquired: "Ever hear about Paul Bunyan and the Year of the Two Winters?"

And then, over the crackle of the fire, he told of a winter so cold the snow turned blue.

The tale is only one of the many that compose the legend of the mythical Paul Bunyan.

Bunyan yarns now are being spun by the hundreds because this week Bemidji will celebrate its annual Paul Bunyan winter carnival. Every man in town must grow a beard for the carnival, at which the winter sports enthusiasts will seek to rival the feats of the mythical Bunyan.

According to old timers:

Bunyan built Lake Huron as a corral for milk whales when he learned whales were mammals.

He started the Mississippi river by emptying a pan of dishwater.

He built a fire under a lake in which he dumped a carload of peas and a herd of oxen, and made pea soup for his logging crew. (He brought a paddle wheel steamer from New Orleans to cruise around the lake and stir the soup.)

He brought the Swedes to Minnesota after selling the state to the king of Sweden.

And went through the longest, coldest winter ever heard of.

It was so cold the snow turned blue, and it grew progressively colder until next fall, when winter set in again.

Loggers in Paul Bunyan's day grew beards to protect their faces, and the beards grew to tremendous lengths.

"Some of the boys had the ends of 'em knitted into sox," the old timer said.

A low lying cloud bank was swiftly converted into a mountain of solid ice. That was the first of the glaciers.

The mercury in Bunyan's thermometer dropped so low it was three years climbing back to zero. Snow fell so heavily Paul had to dig down to find the forests, and loggers were lowered on ropes to fell the trees.

"It was so cold," the old timer said, "the wind froze up in sheets."

Bunyan then had it saved and stored in chunks for summer.

A fire had to be kept going full blast seven days and seven nights before it grew warm enough to burn paper. It took a month to fry a steak, and even then it was rare. Cooks had to plan a roast several months in advance, and a two-minute egg for Monday breakfast wasn't ready until Thursday.[48]

Fifteen months later when Bemidji held a Fourth of July Paul Bunyan festival the same set of stories went the rounds, with only minor variations. Lake Superior replaces Lake Huron as the corral for milk whales. One sentence is expanded: "And he went through the longest, coldest winter ever recorded, which was so cold 'that the coffee froze solid while it was scaldin' hot.' " A new sentence is inserted: "Work was slowed because the 'jacks were distracted by icicles oozing from their pores." For the summer readers this concluding paragraph is added: "Paul liked the annual log drive. His fast footwork made him a good man 'on the round stuff' despite his great weight. It was said in camp that Paul, who was 70 feet tall, could spin a log until the bark came off, then run ashore on the bubbles."[49]

From Bemidji also comes a story by Eldon Roark, a Scripps-Howard staff writer, that includes some Paul Bunyan fictions.

Paul Bunyan in the News

I want to give you a report on Paul Bunyan. I have done some under-cover work, and I have the lowdown.

This is the home town of the legendary Bunyan. He was born here, and he is buried here. That great hill west of town is his grave. The trees on the hill are so tough that no ax or saw has ever been found that can even scratch the bark. I tried it myself and the teeth of my 20-foot saw popped off as if they were the teeth of a comb.

As you enter the business section of Bemidji, coming from the south, you are greeted by colossal statues of Paul and his blue ox, Babe. They stand on the shore of the lake, with a wide parking space all around, and a steady stream of tourists flows by the spot, pausing to pay homage to the man and the ox who created this vacation land—and to photograph them.

Paul and Babe no doubt would rate a place in any list of "the most photographed things in America." Every group wants its picture made standing between Paul's mighty legs, or under Babe's broad belly. And it's a problem. Your folks run and start posing, and before you can snap your camera you discover they are all mixed up with some farmers from Iowa or a group of teachers from Indiana.

But I'm getting away from my promise—the lowdown on Paul Bunyan.

Well, I've had a few heart-to-heart, man-to-man talks with natives, and they have confessed that some of the amazing stuff about Paul Bunyan that they hand out to us tourists is exaggerated. We eat it up, so they keep feeding it to us.

Take the tale about Paul and Babe and the 10,000 Minnesota lakes. It says that while gallivanting around the state they left huge tracks which filled up with water and formed the lakes. As a matter of fact, only 6389 of the lakes were formed in that manner. The rest are in parts of the state where Paul and Babe never set foot, and they are not genuine Paul Bunyan lakes at all. They are fakes.

And take that story about Paul's being such a whopping big baby that it took five storks, working overtime, to deliver him. That shows how stories grow. It really took only three storks and one pelican.

They tell me that, as a general rule, if you will discount a Paul Bunyan story about 25 per cent you will be near the truth—all except the one about Paul's putting out a forest fire by spitting on it. That's the plain, unvarnished truth. [50]

The geographic feats of Paul Bunyan provided good publicity for the California Fair of 1939 held at San Francisco. James Stevens is credited with "new" and "amazing" tales, one of which, the whale corral, also appears in the Bemidji release.

Paul Bunyan could have saved Uncle San a lot of time and trouble if they had just called on him when they started to dig out Treasure Island.

311

He could have scooped the Island up off the bottom of the Bay in a couple of hours and had time left over to hand a couple of girders up to the fellows building the Bay Bridge.

Take it on the solemn word of James Stevens, whose book, "Paul Bunyan," a compilation of the manifold legends of that gigantic lumberman of the Pacific Northwest, and his huge blue ox, "Babe," has delighted thousands of readers since its publication in 1925.

Stevens, now associated with the West Coast Lumbermen's Association, whose exhibit at the Golden Gate International Exposition may be seen in the Homes and Gardens Building, visited the Fair yesterday and spun some new and amazing Bunyanesque tales.

Building Treasure Island would have been child's play to Paul, who was the fellow who dug out Puget Sound to make a corral for whales. He needed the whales to milk for Babe, who was sick just then and couldn't get enough milk to drink except from the cetaceans.

And the 50,000,000 feet of lumber used in building the exhibit palaces on the Island—why, Paul Bunyan could have taken his big ax and cut that lumber in no time at all, run the logs through his nine-story band saw and built the whole Fair practically overnight.

Babe, that big blue ox who measured 42 ax handles from stem to stern, would have made quite an exhibit at the Exposition, too.

The largest barbecue pit in the West, at Tex Cameron's Happy Valley Ranch on the Gayway, capable of holding 15 steers and 15,000 gallons of beans, wouldn't even be big enough to hold Babe's tail.

The meal just described might make a snack for Paul Bunyan, however, but couldn't satisfy for very long the man who used to hold his coffee pot over Mount Lassen to bring it to a boil, and strands of whose whiskers were used for cables in the Bay Bridge. [51]

Another paper gives further elaboration of the tales.

James Stevens, who gathered the immortal Bunyan tales in print, was at the Exposition to represent the great hero who is now supposed to be under Mount Lassen cooking a pot of beans.

To the many Bunyan tales, Stevens had this one to add:

Paul, according to one school of thought, never shed his whiskers in the spring. The engineers on the two San Francisco bay bridges, stumped for a strong and sturdy core for the suspension cables, looked up one of Bunyan's spring shedding grounds. And it is the Bunyan whiskers that now support the transbay traffic. . . .

"This Fair is truly a Paul Bunyan job," said Stevens. Although of course Paul Bunyan wouldn't have taken so much time to do the job.

"Paul Bunyan used to have a sawmill, you know, nine stories high, with a bandsaw running through the whole nine floors. That way they could saw logs on every floor with the same saw."[52]

A story by James Stevens designed for the Christmas trade, "The First Christmas Trees," 1500 words long, appeared in 1939. With puerility of invention, Stevens has Paul Bunyan invent Christmas trees by prettying up pines, firs, and spruces with ribbons and candles, to stop them crawling into the bunkhouses with the loggers.[53]

The *Daily Worker* twice ran an interpretive selection of Bunyan tales. Once they appeared under "Paul Bunyan, Child of Rebellion," story and silhouette by Eric Lucas, in the children's department "Junior America." In order to suggest proletarian philosophy, the writer refers to tales which "roundly ridicule the swivel-headed boss," and gives one example. In attempting to make Paul Bunyan a symbol for the workingman, the *Daily Worker* suffered from the disadvantage that Bunyan was a boss-hero, and far more useful to management than to workers. The tales are of the conventional exaggeration type, although the references to Paul's wife and son are unusual.

"Who was Paul Bunyan?" asks the tenderfoot.

An old lumberjack looks up through his shaggy eyebrows.

"Who? Paul Bunyan? Why, he wuz an all-powerful giant, the mightiest logger that ever lived, the inventor of the lumber industry. . . ." He squints one weatherbeaten eye. "Why, my grandpop logged with him at Bullfrog Lake near Onion River County."

"Onion River County?"

"Yep, that's jest this side o' Candy Mountain where it dips into Garlic Crik. My grandpop said that one time Paul Bunyan. . . ."

There is a ritual to telling Paul Bunyan tall stories. The speaker is in dead earnest. His listeners pretend to believe his every word. Invariably the yarn-spinner had an uncle or grandpop who worked right along with Paul Bunyan himself. The yarn is richly built up by the listeners. . . .

There are those who say Paul Bunyan hailed from Canada, that he started the French Canadian Papineau Rebellion of 1827 against the English Queen. They say he and his loggers, armed with mattocks, axes and wood forks steamed and warped into hooks, stormed to victory. But wherever Paul was born, he grew up in the forests of America.

Oh, we've had legends about Buffalo Bill, Jesse James, Kit Carson, Dan'l Boone and a host of others, but Paul Bunyan, he's different, he never really lived outside the virile imagination of the rank and file pioneer. . . .

The "camp" of Paul Bunyan held many wondrous figures. There was Big Joe, "6 foot 32 inches tall who, in the cold year of the Five Winters, set the boiling coffee pot on the stove that froze so quick that the ice was hot!"

And there was Paul's son Jean who used to lift logging trains past one another on a single-track railroad. Then there was Sourdough Sam, the cook, who built a griddle so big that to grease it took 80 men skating around with slabs of bacon hitched to their feet.

The "camp" also held Paul's Blue Ox, "Babe," who measured "42 ax-handles and a plug of tobacco between the eyes." Why, Babe could pull anything that had two ends to it. Babe pulled the kinks out of a crooked road, and a chain of three-inch links into a straight bar! One time Babe kicked Paul's boss in the head "so the brains all run out but the cook happened to be handy and he filled the hole up with hotcake batter and plastered it together again and he was just as good as ever!"

Paul Bunyan's cow gave milk so strong that the boys used it for cough syrup. And there are tales of Paul's wife, too. It took "thirteen" Hudson Bay blankets to make her a skirt and the sail of a full rigged ship to make a waist. She wasn't so different from other women, but the measurements were different—that was all—feet stead of inches . . . . She parted Paul's hair with a handaxe and combed it with a crosscut saw!

And as for Paul Bunyan, himself! Why, he cut his teeth on a peavy hook and drove logs down the Kennebec River in his first pair of pants. He marked his logs by pinching a piece out of each with his fingers. Paul could blow out the bunk house light and get into his bunk before it was dark; yes, and he could run around on floating logs and "could spin 'em so fast 'til the bark came off and then run ashore on the bubbles"; and he rode water so rough "that it would tear an ordinary man in two to drink out of the river!"

Other tales roundly ridicule the "swivel-headed boss," boast of the smart loggers "standin' up fer their rights," still others sing of the poetry of these builders of America. "I logged for Paul," goes one tale, "and it was fine loggin', too, in them ol' times. When the trees used to be standin' tall and thick so that the on'y way you could look was straight up, an' all you could see was a little patch of blue right above you, an' all you could smell was the smell of firs an' balsam pine an' all you could hear was the squirrels an' chickadees, an' the scrape of the lumberjacks' saws an' the bite of their axes. That was fine loggin'. . . ."

The legends of old Paul Bunyan have traveled to other out-of-doors American industries—to farming, hunting, trapping, even to mining in far-off Alaska. . . . But today the radio, the pulp magazines, the phonograph in the bunk house, the "jazz shack" in the village have stolen away many of those who once sang his praise. Today Paul Bunyan lives mostly in the hearts of the men of our outdoors. He is the symbol of the workers' power. His limitless strength is felt and heard in heated talks on politics, in stirring words like "org'nize" and "union" . . . . Yes, the powered footfalls of Paul Bunyan are still felt and heard, crashing through the wilderness, building, in their stride, a happier America.[54]

The *Daily Worker* had already used this piece, in slightly longer form for adults, in a feature article by Eric Lucas (April 9, 1939). Its title read, "Paul Bunyan: This legendary hero of the American worker lives forever in the stories of the tall-timber country of the West." Two additional introductory paragraphs describe Bunyan as the "sinew and brain, courage and soul of America's frontier folk." A few phrases and sentences appear which were cut for the children's version, such as the reference to "richly obscene" tales—a strangely authentic note—and this little incident. "It took a good man to pull the saw in heavy timber when Paul was on the other end. Paul used to say to his fellow-sawyer: 'I don't care if you ride the saw, but please don't drag your feet.' "

Only one clipping actually indicates an oral source for Bunyan stories, a human interest article on a school janitor, who had farmed and worked in the woods in his youth. Charles H. Almy of Saginaw remembered hearing Bunyan tales sixty years before in the lumber camps in the Saginaw Valley. "I had forgotten all about them until one day when I heard Principal Guy of South Intermediate school [see under "Paul Bunyan Spe .kers"] tell some Paul Bunyan stories. Then I remembered how we used to hear them around the fires in the lumber camps at night—stories of Paul and Babe, the big blue ox, and they used to say the moon was Paul Bunyan's sun because he worked so hard and so long. I can hear them now telling the stories while the teamsters were looking after their horses and maybe some of the boys were sharpening their axes."[55]

One item essays some interpretation of the tales. It comments on the celebrity attained by the "god of the woodsmen," and mentions some of his exploits. "According to the lumberjacks, who never tire of recounting the Bunyan feats, the Mississippi River is the old log trail down which Babe hauled logs when Paul cleared the western plains." Then the editorial compares Bunyan to the gods and heroes of the Greeks, and speculates that modern science and invention have rendered obsolescent the old gods; puny man has now become a giant, reality has surpassed myth, and Babe the blue ox is headed for the slaughter house while a tractor takes his place.[56]

Finally, some tall stories unconnected with Bunyan which enter the newspapers use his name. A whopper about large mosquitoes at Fort Benning, Georgia, is labeled "Bunyanese." The story runs, "the 'skeeters noted the guard's two sleeping companions and immediately went into a huddle. Said the first to the second, 'Should we take one with us and come back for the other?' 'No,' the second mosquito advised. 'If we did that somebody else would come along and get him. We'd better just eat both here.' " Two policemen turned amateur gardeners who boast about their produce are introduced with the line, "Shades of Paul Bunyan!!!" One explains that he doesn't dig his carrots, but plants Mexican jumping beans with them. "When they're ready I put baskets in the rows and the carrots jump into them."[57] The following item appeared under the heading, "Tall Story Dept."

Used to be that when folks in Flagstaff, Ariz., heard of the amazing adventures of Mr. Paul Bunyan, who was so powerful that he could use a giant redwood for a toothpick, they would say, "That's nothing, wait until you hear this one." And then they would tell how the mile-deep gorge of the Grand Canyon was created by a Scotchman digging for a nickel lost in a gopher hole.

Well, last week, Bob Evans, geology student in Arizona State Teachers College, discovered the coin at the very bottom of the canyon during an exploration trip. Said the date was worn off the nickel so that it was impossible to say just when the thrifty Scot dug the canyon, though. [58]

A humorous letter in dialect from "Cutover, Wisconsin," describes a lying bout in the deacon seat of Miller's store. Mention is made of the hoop snake which bit a peavy handle and caused it to swell, so that Charlie Agnew cut a million feet of second growth hickory from it; and of the agropelter that dropped limbs on passerby, and the tote-road shagamaw which had claws on its front feet and hoofs behind, and lived on red and green plaid mackinaws. When Old Man Simpson is accused of getting his stories from "them silly Paul Bunyan books wich city peepul thinks is true," he exclaims, "Hell, I wrote the books."[59]

Paul Bunyan Persons

Fabulous characters, exceedingly strong or tall men, and folk-heroes both foreign and American are linked with Paul Bunyan, as a quick means of pigeonholing them for newspaper readers. Since no figure, no matter how famous locally or abroad, enjoyed the status of Paul Bunyan, any new name could rise at least temporarily from obscurity by riding on the coattails of the household demigod.

The papers show pictures and print items about human giants who enact Paul Bunyan. In Brainerd, Minnesota, it is "the town's most famous fisherman, George Roth, a six-foot, seven-inch giant who weighs better than 225 pounds and plays Paul Bunyan in the annual Brainerd pageants." In Idaho it is Leo L. Hartley, from near Sandpoint, "known as the Paul Bunyan of the north Idaho woods," who speaks at a Scandinavian-night program of his life in the woods. The clipping states, "Paul Bunyan will appear in his woods costume of a red sweater and a coonskin cap and swinging a large ax. Bunyan is 6 feet 10 1/4 inches tall, weighs 287 and wears a No. 12 shoe." On another occasion Hartley assisted the aluminum committee of Coeur d'Alene, in his mythical role. The caption to a picture of Hartley dwarfing a tin figure reads, "Paul Bunyan Aids Aluminum Drive," and the note underneath explains:

Paul Bunyan came down from the hills of northern Idaho Monday, climbed into his store suit and headed for Coeur d'Alene to open the Lake City's aluminum drive. On arrival at the aluminum stockade in front of the Wilma theater, the giant woodsman (in private life his name is Leo L. Heartley [sic]) found the committee in charge of the drive had set up a heroic figure of a man in tin to symbolize Paul Bunyan. So Heartley [sic] himself took over the task. Armed with his huge ax, he warned passersby to bring in their aluminum. [60]

Still another flesh and blood Bunyan comes to light under the headline, " 'Paul Bunyan' Elected Mayor."

A "Paul Bunyan" was elected mayor of South International Falls [Minnesota] Monday night.

He's registered as Len Costley for legal purposes, but most people here know him as the second legendary northwoods figure. He stands six feet, ten inches tall and weighs 275 pounds. Attired in typical Bunyan regalia, he portrays the mythical lumberjack on festive occasions. [61]

In a separate category fall robust and colorful personalities whose lives have already acquired a mist of legend, worthy of Paul Bunyan himself. In an obituary piece with the heading, "Crozier Writes Eulogy on Fogg Coffey, a Fabulous Character of the Old West," the writer, Harry B. Crozier, draws several comparisons between his subject and Paul Bunyan.

I was born and reared here within sight of the early Indian paintings on a rocky cliff that gave the village and county seat its name [Paint Rock, Texas]. Over coffee and a morning newspaper I had learned of the death and forthcoming funeral of Fogg Coffey and 70 miles out of my way I came to be there. Fogg Coffey had been the most storied man of my infancy and youth. In manhood I had known him for the most superlative hyperboles I had ever heard from the lips of man and that did not exclude Will Rogers. . . . It occurred to me: I was going to the funeral of literally the last of the original white inhabitants of a bounteous country larger than most of the states of these United States. . . . There is a thought that Paul Bunyan is entirely a creature of fancy; some writer's imaginative capability. The truth is that Paul Bunyans exist and flourish in the soil that is theirs. Fogg Coffey was one and gifted with greater speech than any of Bunyan's chroniclers have ever conceived. Fogg and his brother Bill, dead these 25 years, already are legends. Together they weighed a good 500 pounds. They could take a horseshoe by its two ends and bend it straight or in any fashion to please an audience. Bill was the larger of stature and the more consummate in Paul Bunyan feats of strength; Fogg was the more nimble of words and author of more aphorisms than greedy wordsmiths among the authors have ever caught up with.

Fogg, in an ardent moment of maturity, say when he was a man of 30, would bet that he could stand flatfooted in a corral and rope any four-footed beast, horse, cow or anything else and break its neck. . . . And so in passing on swift tires I breathed a prayer of thankfulness for Fogg Coffey, the only Paul Bunyan that I had known in the flesh. The bounding waters of the Concho had gone with the processes of settling up. The buffalo had gone and the Indian had gone. Fogg Coffey was still there and by the eternals he had preserved the prairie dog. God plant the spirit of Fogg Coffey with folk over there; Paul Bunyan, Will Rogers and the others.[62]

The discovery of oil near New Orleans evoked an article on a fabled figure in the oil business who had recently died. "Oil's Paul Bunyan Won't Lead Jacketed Horde Into Orleans," the caption lamented.

Every business has its Paul Bunyan, but the Paul of the oil field will not be in New Orleans. He died last March, at least that is the report.

All the oil boomers knew him as Jim Biggers, although that was not his name. His real name was not used in so many years that it was forgotten but his feats will always be remembered.

Probably his greatest accomplishment was at old Sunshine Hill, near Electra, Tex., back at the time the United States was participating in the war.

Jim, by some means, acquired a few hundred acres of leases on Sunshine Hill, which was really in the producing territory. Instead of developing the field, however, he drew up maps outlining the field and setting off 20 foot square plots of ground. Jim went to Wisconsin where the German population was thickest, and plenty of good German cheese was being marketed under the name of "Liberty Cheese."

A few days in this dairy country and Jim had sold all his 20 foot square plots of ground.

When the purchasers went to Texas to investigate their acquisition, they found that Jim had been correct in telling them that an oil well was only 24 inches in diameter, but they also found that a derrick floor was 21 feet square, and more room was needed for the tool house, boilers, engine house, slush pits and other needs. Only those who had bought outside tracts were able to drill, and then only by cutting down on the size of their equipment.

It took almost 20 years of court fights to untangle that scrap.

Jim was also an accomplished "doodle bugger." He even invented a new locating method at one time. After trying out the water witch idea, dressing it up with a red rag soaked in kerosene or gasoline, and the bottle of oil on a string that would swing when over oil pools, Jim invented "smellology."

Using a pointed walking cane he would stroll over a plot of ground, stick the cane in the soil, then smell the end. For a fee, he would tell the landowner if oil was present or not. This may sound crazy, but Jim actually made more than $4000 in Jones county, Texas, before he pulled out for parts unknown.

When a Negro landowner had "Mr. Escrow" paged in a hotel lobby in Tyler one night, the oil men started laughing and saying that Jim Biggers had promised a new well to someone.

Jim died, but his accomplishments will live as long as the shine rod works in the pump jack of the old fields. His comment on art was confined exclusively to the saloon classic of "Custer's Last Stand." After a few drinks of Choctaw Beer, the power dive of dry Indian Territory, Jim would tell all who were within earshot that he was quarter breed Cherokee Indian, and had never been able to understand why it was that when the white troops won a battle it was always a "glorious victory," but when the Indians won it was invariably a "horrible massacre."

The oil fraternity will have another Jim Biggers some day, but at present they are mourning over the original who is now in the happy hunting grounds, where leases are passed out at breakfast, and people never speculate on the value of the ragged oil man's word.[63]

This character differs considerably from Gib Morgan, the spinner of oilfield whoppers, and falls into the tradition of the Yankee schemer, an aspect of Paul Bunyan seldom emphasized.

A tantalizingly meager reference to "Buck, known as the Paul Bunyan of the Bayous," occurs in a piece about the composer Robert MacGimsey, who drew inspiration from the Negro spirituals of his native Louisiana swamp country. Curiously, Senator Ellender of Louisiana is also referred to as "the Paul Bunyan of the bayous and the cane brakes," and "the rarin', ragin', snortin' Paul Bunyan of the Louisiana political wilds," but in highly sarcastic fashion. An uncomplimentary text accompanies two photographs that show Ellender punching a bag and rolling on a medicine ball, and contrasts the politician's self-portrait as a "regular Paul Bunyan" with his disappointing record in Washington.[64]

319

Folk-heroes from Europe unknown to Americans are regularly identified with Bunyan. A war correspondent on the Russo-Finnish front writes, "I have finally tracked down the Paul Bunyan of the Finnish army, the man whose feats with a rifle have made his name a byword in this army where expert shots are the rule instead of the exception." He then goes on to describe the record of Corporal Simo Hayha, reputed to have shot down five hundred or more Russians. An article on the "Slavonian" oystermen and fishermen of the Mississippi Gulf coast recounts the deeds of their folk hero, Kralyevich Marko, an "early Paul Bunyan of the Balkans." A Russian folk hero is likened to Bunyan, in a music review. "The Gliere symphony has as program the life and exploits of the legendary hero after whom it is named, 'Murometz', Russ counterpart of France's Gargantua, our own Paul Bunyan, the Big Guy, the man who eats an unskinned bear for breakfast and uproots a tree to brush his teeth." The Argentinian hero of an epic poem by José Hernandez, *The Gaucho—Martin Fierro*, "like Paul Bunyan, became a fabulous folk-figure."[65]

American folk demigods too are continually linked to Bunyan. John Henry began to attract newspaper notices in 1939, in connection with the Broadway production of a play, *John Henry*, by Roark Bradford and Jacques Wolf, and the releases identified him as the "Paul Bunyan of Negroes," "the Paul Bunyan of his race, a gigantic river roustabout whose Herculean feats of work and living are part of America's folk lore," "the Paul Bunyan of the black race," "the Paul Bunyan of Southern Negroes."[66] A column of Pecos Bill stories explains that "Pecos Bill was to the early cowboys—and still is—what Paul Bunyan was to the lumberjacks." In his department, "Mainly About Manhattan," John Chapman wrote, "Paul Whiteman is looking for data on Big Mose Humphreys, the Paul Bunyan of the Bowery," and proceeds to give some Mose tall tales. A news story on the folklore material collected by the Federal Writers Project used the headline, "Tall Tale Collection Reveals Many Rivals to Paul Bunyan," and offered some items about Febold Feboldson, Antoine Barada, Joe Magarac, and John Henry.[67]

Allusions, Similes, References

Many newspaper references to Paul Bunyan take the form not of complete news items or stories about the giant logger, but of casual and incidental allusion. His name comes to be used in an adjectival sense, to emphasize a mammoth object or undertaking, or to suggest lumbering operations or north-woods vacation lands.

Objects of extraordinary dimensions are regularly associated with Paul. The world's largest strawberry sundae, made in a dish eight feet long, four feet high, and four feet wide, as a feature of the Golden Jubilee Strawberry Festival of Burlington, Washington, is said to be "built in Paul Bunyan proportions." The largest cheese in the world, a 2,250-pound cyclinder of Wisconsin-made American cheese displayed in Washington, D.C., during Wisconsin week, is headlined as "Paul Bunyan Sized." The biggest cigar in the world, weighing 76 pounds, which took four men three weeks to make, on exhibit at the Weinberger Drug Company in Cleveland, is thus introduced: "If you see a man loafing about Playhouse Square and smoking a cigar six-and-a-half-feet long he will probably be Paul Bunyan, giant of the lumber camp legends." The world's largest sailing-ship masts, one hundred and fifty feet high, were made in an Oregon timber mill, where "Paul Bunyan would have enjoyed working." A giant chess set at the University of Wisconsin, with kings four feet high, and a board thirty feet square, so that spectators could look down upon it from a gallery and see the experts play, is one in which "Paul Bunyan, fabulous figure of Wisonsin's lumbering industry, would have delighted." A corn stalk ten feet three inches high is called "Knee High? Sure, to Paul Bunyan," in a news item pointing out that corn is supposed to be knee high by July 4. The snow cruiser built for Admiral Byrd "looks as if Jules Verne had turned out a custom job for Paul Bunyan"; the vehicle had ten-foot tires a yard thick, was fifteen feet longer than the longest bus, and two feet higher than the tallest railroad boxcars.[68]

Prodigious feats merit comparison with those performed by Paul. A widely printed release states, "The Paul Bunyan pancake crown went to Perry C. Hill, Jr., of Milwaukee, after he downed 31 standard-sized pancakes . . . Before attacking cakes, Hill first ate, as required by pancake derby rules, the standard Paul Bunyan breakfast—fruit, cereal and cream, toast, eggs and bacon" (papers in Florida, Kansas, Delaware, New York, Wisconsin, Minnesota, Ohio, July, 1941; the pancake derby was a summer tourist feature in Ephraim, Wisconsin). Thefts on a grand scale raised the question, in one paper, "Paul Bunyan Back?"

Paul Bunyan, as every good lumberman knows, ruled the North West from the time of the Blue Snow to the time of the Rain that Came Up from China.

And then he vanished from the earth.

Or did he?

The people in Kootenay district are wondering if he isn't lurking in the woods somewhere. For the thefts from Cranbrook and elsewhere the last few months have been nothing short of gargantuan. First, six miles of copper wire disappeared. Then it was a twelve pounder gun, weighing over a ton, the property of the 24th Field Brigade. And again, two and a half tons of power line.

Maybe Paul Bunyan is still alive. It would be good to think he was still wandering around with Babe the Blue Ox, who measured forty-two axe handles and a plug of chewing tobacco between the horns. He would probably like to go down and see the Grand Coulee dam, and compare it with the job of work he did when he dug out Puget Sound.

But, no, maybe he belongs better in history. For today, we speak of conserving the forests, and we can't catch a fish without a permit. And the authorities wouldn't tolerate Paul Bunyan going around pulling up a Douglas fir every time he wanted a toothpick.[69]

An act of vandalism in Hammond, Indiana, that laid seventy-eight decorative trees low, was put on the wires by the International News Service with the opening sentence, "The ghost of Paul Bunyan, legendary woodsman of the North country, plagued Hammond police today." Consequently, newspapers carrying the release used such headlines as "Police Hunt 'Paul Bunyan' "; "Paul Bunyan Outdone by Tree-Chopping Vandals"; "Paul Bunyan's Ghost Haunts Hammond, Ind."; "Paul Bunyan's Ghost Plagues Police Officials"; "Ghost of Bunyan Visiting Indiana?".[70]

A misprint that credited a farmer with amazing profits from one hundred instead of his actual seven hundred acres led to the correction "No Paul Bunyan," and the apology that, due to the error, "the story took on a Paul Bunyan tinge." An article on American cotton distribution, attempting to convey its size, says, "Something so big that it takes a Paul Bunyan brain to encompass it all."[71]

Large-scale enterprises of various sorts secure attention in the papers with lead-off sentences invoking Paul Bunyan. Examples are: "Paul Bunyan performed some incredible feats in his day, but so far as I know he never attempted to subdivide the north woods into 50-foot building lots"; "Uncle Sam might well draft the services of a Paul Bunyan in building the new lock in the government dam at Hastings"; "Paul Bunyan, Gargantua, Lemuel Gulliver, and the Giant in Jack and the Beanstalk are just members of a troupe of Singer's midgets compared with the man who runs the motor vehicle service of the Post

Office Department—the biggest enterprise of its kind anywhere on the face of the earth"; "Paul Bunyan, that mythical colossus of the lumber camps whose feats of strength and endurance are part of America's rich folklore, has found a collective rival in the men of the United States Forest service who are carrying out so successfully a scheme that was widely declared to be utterly fantastic and doomed to failure when it was started just five years ago" (the article refers to planting trees in the Dust Bowl).[72]

Before getting into the statistics of timber salvage following the 1938 hurricane, a county agricultural agent makes extensive use of Bunyan to capture reader interest.

The story of Paul Bunyan, the great woodsman of the North Country, is most fascinating reading for all lovers of the woods and woodsmen. The large scale woods operation as related by Paul Bunyan just brings to one's mind what a story he might have written about the hurricane of 1938 if he were only living. I presume Paul would have told in most realistic terms of the gigantic gusts of winds and crackling of the branches as our forests fell in groups or windrows, leaving the whole root system exposed for birds to find a roosting place. Then what a time Paul and his crew of woodsmen and the great Blue Ox would have had logging out the hurricane-felled trees and hauling them to the ponds or dry sites. When it came to cleaning up the slash or brush, Paul Bunyan would merely have laughed at such a little job. As to danger from forest fires which we all recognize in this dry time—why Paul and his great Blue Ox team would probably have hauled a whole pond of water to the scene of the fire and smiled as the fire and smoke were subdued.

But, to our great regret, Paul Bunyan and his great Ox Team were not living at the time of our 1938 hurricane, thus it was left to our generation of woodsmen, men of the forestry departments and other leaders to organize, develop and carry out the plan of timber salvage.[73]

To impress the reader with the most powerful short-wave radio station in the United States, a newswriter said, "Paul Bunyan, fabled northwest giant, could cup his hairy hands around his mouth and bellow something fierce. But Bunyan, wonder lad of his time, wouldn't rate much amazement in 1941, because 20 miles north of Cincinnati, at Mason, Ohio, is another maker of sound so gigantic that its voice is heard clearly in the mountains, plains, deserts and great modern cities of . . . Latin American countries."[74]

News items and features about the lumber industry frequently use Paul Bunyan as a synonym for the old-time lumberjack or for the industry itself. A sketch of a giant lumberjack vigorously striding forward with a sheaf of papers labeled "Capacity Orders" in one hand, and "Northwest Lumber Industry" blazoned across his shirt, bore the caption, "Paul Bunyan Walks Again." The note underneath reads: "There is general rejoicing over the strides being taken by the lumber industry of the Pacific Northwest as national business moves toward recovery and building moves forward. Paul Bunyan is on the march again through the woods. Let us hope that he has learned from experience in regions which he has left devastated in the past and that in his operations here he will harvest the current timber crop with a minimum of waste and set about to grow a new crop."[75]

The same note is repeated in other news releases, with Paul Bunyan sometimes epitomizing the forward march of the lumber industry, and sometimes representing the old-fashioned methods of logging now outmoded by modern methods. In the latter vein, Stewart Holbrook writes, to lead off an illustrated feature article, "The late Paul Bunyan was a great and mighty logger who mowed down whole forests with a swish of his ax and, on one occasion, when the Winters got too cold to suit him, moved the Temperate Zone a thousand miles north; but not even the gargantuan Paul in his palmiest days ever conceived anything like the vast ocean-going rafts [of lumber] that emerge every few months from the mouth of the Columbia River out in Oregon." The advance of science over Bunyan is also underlined in this item.

> Paul Bunyan was a fine frontiersman in his Minnesota timbering days. His giant ax hewed down forests he thought inexhaustible; he made Minneapolis at one time the lumber capital of the world. Great guy, Paul. But he was weak on planting. Where he stripped the land of tall pines, brush and poplar grew. Worthless stuff. At least, that's what folks said for a long time. But after Paul came other frontiersmen. Wonder what Paul would have thought if he could see them at work? Forest rangers, CCC, and, strangest of all, the chemists in the laboratory. . . . And before long, out of Paul Bunyan's "wastelands," may come explosives for America's fighters, plastics for her planes, film for her camera . . . the chemical industry, instead of a Paul Bunyan, appears as the state's new frontiersman.[76]

Still another rebuff comes in this story.

> Even Paul Bunyan, the mythical giant of the lumber world, would stop to stare at the impressive fleet of massive GMC Diesel lumber trucks which passed through Fort Wayne last week en route to Westwood, Calif., where they will be put to work by the Red River Lumber company.
> This fleet of 22 General Motors trucks, all powered by General Motors six-

cylinder, two-cycle Diesel engines, is a far cry from the crude hauling equipment in use during the legendary Paul Bunyan days, when "Babe," Paul's colorful blue ox, was called upon to do most of the transportation work.

These huge trucks will be called upon to do rugged work by the Red River Lumber Company, which, incidentally, uses the term, "Paul Bunyan's Pine," as a trade name.[77]

The fiction that Paul still rules the timber business is maintained, however, in some notes. "This guy Paul Bunyan, who's been running around the Pacific Northwest the past century with a big ax in his hand and chips on his shoulders, and in his beard, too, may not know it yet, but he's been loafing. Paul's got a big job ahead of him the balance of this year. That job is national defense. And it's going to keep him busy—too busy to go around scooping out holes in the ground to make places like Puget Sound." The piece goes on to say that the lumber industry is rapidly turning to meet the demands of national defense.[78] Apparently Paul stopped loafing, for six weeks later a paper reported:

Paul Bunyan, mythical giant doer of big jobs, and symbol of the West Coast lumber industry, is enjoying a great revival in 1941. Never since the year he worked so hard he sweat out the Great Salt Lake, according to the loggers, has he done more big things all at once. Typical of Paul's productions for national defense are Douglas fir keel timbers for the navy's new fleet of minesweepers, of which a few are pictured on a truck-haul. Each stick is 110 feet long, 16½ inches wide and 10½ inches thick. "Just two axhandles short of being as long as Paul Bunyan's backbone," says the oldtime timberman.[79]

The identification of Paul Bunyan with logging operations is made surprisingly, in Georgia, in an illustrated feature story on the termination of lumbering in that state. The headline declares, "Paul Bunyan Leaves Georgia," and one sketch shows Paul looking down at his logging camps through binoculars.

The brawniest figure in American folklore is Paul Bunyan, the mythical hero of the lumberjack. He originated years ago in the great logging camps of the wild northwoods. The rough-hewn lumberjacks amused themselves by spinning yarns, and somewhere in the telling of tall tales, the superhuman personage of Paul Bunyan emerged. The legend grew as the roughshod Homers of the logging camps vied with each other in attributing fantastic exploits to Paul Bunyan, the greatest logger of all time. He became the patron saint of the lumberjacks. Wherever the great trees are hurtling to the ground, logging locomotives shrilling, the shuddering forest in full retreat before huge logging enterprise—there the invisible presence of Paul Bunyan watches with all-consuming interest. He personifies the American lumberjacks; their tribe is diminishing but he lives on, a symbol of their prodigious deeds.

It may not be known to a whole lot of people in the state, but this same titan of the tall timber has frequented the mountains of Georgia for some 30 years. After the lumberjacks had whittled the northwoods down to bush size, they had to move to fresh fields. Then big lumbering concerns with the heavy armaments of the logging business came to reap north Georgia's virgin forests. Paul Bunyan, of course, was right in there with them. He never did fool around with any but the large-scale outfits big enough to use logging railroads and to maintain whole settlements of loggers way up in the woods. In these logging camps were found the "dyed-in-the-woods" lumberjacks, men who grew up on logging and neither knew nor cared about any other occupation. These were Paul's folk.

Without a doubt, he is the most amazing fellow ever to set a phantom foot in Georgia. Paul Bunyan—the giant who shaves with a huge hand ax, combs his hair with a crosscut saw, and uses Hudson Bay blankets for handkerchiefs—he is the man who invented logging, and all the tools that go with it. And can he use these tools. Know why there are no trees on the Great Plains? Paul logged off that entire country, did it all from one camp in North Dakota, too. He hauled water to this camp from Niagara Falls in enormous tanks. When one of them sprung a leak in Minnesota, he just let it set, and it created the Mississippi River.

Another time, he had a logging railroad that was so full of curves the engine master would get dizzy and fall out of the cab. Paul hitched his big blue ox to one end of the road, and straightened it out. He had enough railroad left over to supply the Union Pacific with a right-of-way across Nebraska. One Sunday when he wasn't busy he dug Puget Sound and piled up the dirt to make snow-topped Mount Rainier. In short, the bigger the proposition, the better he liked it. And to tell the truth, he is kind of in a hurry to finish up all his jobs in this territory so he can spend more time logging those overgrown trees on the west coast. When a tree is so big you can only get one log on a railroad car, that is really something. When Paul first saw it he got so excited he kicked up a hundred acres of stumps and tied a knot in a fair-sized river.

Ridge-hemmed Jack's river, in Fannin county, now presents the final scene in north Georgia of Paul Bunyan's "big time" lumbering with logging railroads. A dozen years back there was an even bigger job going on at Helen, Ga., with a logging ridge clear up to the North Carolina line. Paul's lumberjacks gave that ridge a face-lifting, too—made the south side look like a plucked chicken, in fact. But they ran out of timber and folded, leaving the company in Fannin county to carry on for Paul in Georgia.

One is always impressed by the seemingly impossible undertakings that characterize railroad logging in the mountains. Individually, the logger may not impress, but collectively he removed forests with a sweep that excites the imagination. There have been some full-blooded lumberjacks at the Jack's river logging camp all along. They drift in from logging camps in West Virginia and other places, and, as the job in Georgia nears the end, they will be drilling out to logging camps in other states.

Maybe it's a good thing Paul has got his mind all wrapped up in that western timber. Because something has been happening up there in the covers of Fannin county that would disconcert him if he knew about it. Paul is plenty proud of the fact that he is just about the he-est he-man there is. That goes for his lumberjacks, too. It would hurt Paul to hear that his lumberjacks were not way ahead of everybody in sight when it comes to being tough. However, up on Jack's river, a group of mountain farmers, working as loggers during off days on their farms, have risen head and shoulders above the lumberjacks as iron men. These mountaineers would walk five miles over steep mountain trails to reach the camp before daylight. They would work all day felling trees and "bruting" logs down the mountain sides—the most strenuous work. Then they would tramp the five miles home. I used to see them on the trail, carrying lanterns to find the path. The lumberjacks down in the camp wondered how anybody could stand a routine like that.

I've a hunch Paul would be disturbed if he knew his lumberjacks had been playing second fiddle on rugged performance. Maybe it's well he's leaving before he sees too much. And, along the same thought, maybe it's well for Paul those Georgia mountaineers haven't worked up their legendary hero yet. When they do, Paul may have to look to his laurels.[80]

The identification of Bunyan with the individual lumberjack, as well as with the whole lumber industry, recurs in newspaper comments. In reviewing the book *Logging Town: The Story of Grand Rapids, Minnesota,* James Gray writes, "The legendary Paul Bunyan was created by the lumberjacks to satisfy their yearning for a giant who could perform with ease and pleasure fabulous feats of strength like those which were exacted each day of their own merely human flesh. He was a humorous enlargement of their egos. Yet to the modern reader each lumberjack however humble or obscure he may have been seems to have led a strutting, strenuous existence on a scale almost as gigantic as that of the great god Paul." Even the staid New York *Times* continued to identify Paul Bunyan with the lumberjack, in spite of new mechanical methods. In an illustrated page on logging techniques, it used the heading, "Modern Paul Bunyans," and remarked:

The thud of the axe and the song of the two-man saw are echoing through the woods. Saws in mills long idle and rusty are screaming through logs, biting out the boards. Paul Bunyan has prodigious stories to tell in every bunkhouse. For the Army has ordered 1,500,000,000 board feet of lumber, the first part of more than 5,000,000,000 board feet that the lumber industry expects to sell to the government for national defense purposes during the next two years.

There is more machinery in the woods now than there was in the days of Paul Bunyan, but the machinery has not changed the men. Lumberjacks are still cut to Bunyan's measure—strong men who love their jobs because the work is dangerous. They are tireless at the saws, bucking tree trunks into log lengths.[81]

Many references to Paul Bunyan and Babe in the newspapers connect the mythical pair with the resort areas of northern Wisconsin and Minnesota, a result of the high-powered promotion to make the public think of the northern woods and lakes as a Paul Bunyan vacation land. A typical release says:

Paul Bunyan and his blue ox "Babe," mythical figures in the early history of northern Wisconsin and Minnesota, would be plenty surprised if they were to see today the scenes of their former activities.

The thousands of lakes still would be there, the vast wooded areas would be unchanged, except for the trees being smaller, the sun would be shining as brightly and the nights just right for relaxing and refreshing sleep.

The great change Bunyan and his "Babe" would note would be in the number of out-of-state visitors pouring into the section from all parts of the nation. Verily the rest of the country has discovered what a grand and glorious area this is in which to spend a summer vacation.[82]

Similar allusions link particular cities with Bunyan. "Brainerd, 'Capital of Paul Bunyan's Playground,' is headquarters of one of the most popular and alluring resort regions in Minnesota," one paper states, and repeats two years later, "About 25% of the state's resorts are within a 50-mile radius of this Paul Bunyan city." A travel article declares, "Bemidji is the mythological location of the Paul Bunyan country, Lake Itasca being formed when Babe, the blue ox, tipped over the water tower. The small, clean town derives its living from the tourist trade."[83]

A Boston columnist, stopping off at Madison, Wisconsin, sends back a column headed "Paul Bunyan Country," in which she begins with brief Paul Bunyan tales, and then comments, "this is Paul Bunyan's country I'm in now. People order milk by the gallon, not by the pint. They give away free buttermilk at the University of Wisconsin dairy, they have the biggest cheese factory, the greatest dairy country, and more timber than any place in the country."[84] Michigan also bids for the hero's name, with the heading "Paul Bunyan Land Lures Many Writers," and the release, "To the land of Paul Bunyan and giant blue ox Babe this summer will come writers, photographers and artists, intent on learning in a short school course how to get the ax-swinging, tobacco-chewing atmosphere of the lumberman into their arts. The wilderness village of Nahma, Mich. . . . which consists of the Bay de Noquet lumber center and resort enterprises, has planned a vacation school for authors and illustrators from Aug. 13 to Aug. 26." Photographs of Paul and Babe in their concrete likenesses at Bemidji always provided filler to illustrate the scenic attractions of northern Minnesota. A Paul Bunyan State Forest in Minnesota and a Paul Bunyan's Toad Stool in central Wisconsin relate place names to scenery and folklore.[85]

The Pacific Northwest strongly contested the claims to Paul Bunyan land held out by promoters in the Midwest. The president of the Seattle Grade School Teachers' Club, hoping to attract the National Education Association to Washington in 1943, offered them this bait:

When it was suggested in the Northwest that Seattle would like to be host to the N.E.A. convention in 1943, we began seeking for the best manner in which to present our invitation. The question went outside Seattle into the confines of the virgin forests and the fastnesses of the Olympic Peninsula, until it finally reached the ears of Paul Bunyan, the beloved patron of all big things in our region. Now, if his best-loved Northwest wanted a big thing very badly, Paul was ready to help, though it takes a really big thing to lure him and his Blue Ox out of their retirement on the Olympic Peninsula.

We recognize the fact out West that Paul did some very fine cadet work in his trek westward through the north woodlands, but it is in the Northwest where he did his life work and where he now lives in retirement. His accomplishments are too enormous to contemplate in these few minutes, but as an example we will just mention how he dug out Puget Sound to make a waterway for his boom of logs. Such an immense quantity of earth had to be removed, that he and the Blue Ox piled it into a heap which we call Mount Rainier.

What we are trying to tell you is that the Northwest does things in a big way. We want you to come out and see our mountains with their up-pointing crowns of eternal snow, our glaciers, our lakes, our forests, our flowers. Above all, we want you to experience the delights of our incomparable summer weather—a dream climate to those who do not know of its perfection.

Paul and the Blue Ox have come across the continent to invite you West.

Their spirits symbolize the very bigness of our desire to have you. They have promised to drag Alaska, Hawaii, Oregon and California within sight of Seattle that summer for your pleasure and convenience.[86]

Still other examples can be given of various ways in which the name of Paul Bunyan is brought into the news. Columnists sometimes refer to Bunyan. Describing a conceited lady-killer, a female columnist says, "Cocky Carl swings along like Paul Bunyan in his prime." "Daniel Webster had a good start to be the Paul Bunyan of American statesmanship," a literary column begins, and points out that Webster never achieved his destiny. A man-about-town columnist refers to "Herbert Stoltz, a one-time Paul Bunyan among Rhodes scholars who shinnied up a drainpipe to a height of three stories at Oxford and miraculously regained his sleeping quarters." A sports columnist attacking the control exerted by Mike Jacobs over the boxing world, asserts, "Paul Bunyan himself, or the prodigious John Henry, couldn't become heavyweight champion of the world without Mike's cooperation."[87]

Paul's name often creeps into the notes beneath tricky news photographs. "Shades of Frankenstein! Or is it Paul Bunyan? No; it's the eighty-foot shadow of a normal man, cast upon the upstream face of Grand Coulee Dam when a photographic flash globe was exploded at a considerable distance," explains the text under a weird shadowy figure of enormous proportions. "Paul Bunyon [*sic*] Trick" reads the caption to a picture of a champion wood chopper shaving a champion log roller with an ax. A picture of a trout derby queen holding the mounted head of a toothed fish proves to be the "first tobacco chewing fish caught since the days of Paul Bunyan." Adjacent photographs of a giant railroad girder and an office building are tied with the statement, "If Paul Bunyan, the legendary lumberjack, were around to stand the giant steel ruler on end, it would just about reach the parapet of the Hills building, as indicated by the arrow."[88]

Paul Bunyan Editorials

An article appeared in the March 1940 issue of *Minnesota History* by Carleton C. Ames entitled "Paul Bunyan, Myth or Hoax?" which pointed out the obvious lack of any evidence that old-time lumberjacks told Bunyan tales before 1890. The following Minnesota papers commented vigorously on the article in their editorial columns:

St. Paul *Pioneer Press,* April 10, 1940, "Debunking Paul Bunyan."

Minneapolis *Star-Journal,* April 11, "In Defense of Paul Bunyan."

Bemidji *Daily Pioneer,* April 13, "Yes, Carleton, There is a Paul Bunyan."

Duluth *Herald,* April 17, "Paul Bunyan's Age."

Lake Wilson *Pilot,* April 18, "In Defense of Paul Bunyan."

Minneapolis *Times-Tribune,* April 19, "Paul Bunyan Lives."

Bemidji *Daily Pioneer,* May 1, "Comment That's Meant." (Prints a detailed letter from W. B. Laughead.)

Itasca *Iron News,* Coleraine, Jan. 16, 1941, "Origin of Paul Bunyan Stories Still in Doubt."

Itasca *Iron News,* Coleraine, Feb. 13, 1941, "Tracing Paul Bunyan to His Lair."

These editorial observations particularly interest the student of Bunyan, since they deal directly with the question of the origin and authenticity of the Bunyan legend, a matter either taken for granted or ignored by the press. Minnesota had raised perhaps the loudest voice of any state in claiming and promoting the giant lumberjack, and her newspapers revealed the strong sentimental and financial bonds she felt for the impugned demigod. "The debunking of Paul Bunyan is simply too painful to be true," the St. Paul *Pioneer Press* mourned. "Surely the proofs exist somewhere." Next day her sister paper, the Minneapolis *Star-Journal,* thought of a way out. "Minnesota won't give up Paul Bunyan," an editor wrote defiantly. "Somebody has to invent fables or we wouldn't have any. And if the old loggers didn't have the imagination to do so, more credit goes to those who thought up Paul Bunyan later on. The test of a legend is its folk flavor, its capacity for stirring the imagination. Paul Bunyan and his story have long since passed that test."

This appealing if specious argument won immediate favor. The Lake Wilson *Pilot* reprinted the editorial, and in spoofing vein quoted sixteenth-century tall tales about Gargantua to demonstrate the lineage of Paul. Horrified at the thought of the town losing its patron saint and meal ticket, Bemidji's newspaper likened Bunyan to Santa Claus, and asserted it was sacrilege to ask for documentary proof of either.

We admit that no person may have seen Paul roll his cigars from patent tar roofing, but who has ever seen the robust Santa Claus descend through a twelve-inch chimney?

Yes, Carleton, there is a Paul Bunyan and no amount of scoffing will ever convince the residents of logging countries that there is not. The books dealing with his prowess have been among the best sellers. His statue here in Bemidji is the most photographed scene in northern Minnesota. His name will always be used as indicative of outstanding achievement in the great outdoors. . . .

It is too bad that there is always someone who tries to debunk history, always someone who wants to take the romance out of the tales we love to tell about our great figures of history.

We are very much afraid we will have to relegate Mr. Ames . . . to the muckrakers who can find nothing but dirt in the lives of our past presidents.

Paul Bunyan is going to live in the memories of those who have delighted in his adventures and we hope that Bemidji will always keep him prominently in the minds of those who visit our city.[89]

In kindlier tone the Duluth *Herald* noted that Ames was only inquiring into the age of the Bunyan stories. "But even if he proves his point—that Paul Bunyan was not invented until a comparatively recent date—it will only make the Bunyan stories more remarkable. Old folklore is common enough; brand new folklore is a mighty rare article. Mr. Ames may prove to be the best friend Old Paul ever had. In the meanwhile he is waiting for evidence."

The evidence was slow to come in. It took no more substantial form than the following contribution. "One bit of evidence in favor of the early origin of the Paul Bunyan stories comes from Fred Staples, who started working in the woods bordering on the St. Croix when he was sixteen years old, and reports that he heard about Paul Bunyan the first year he worked."[90] Nothing more! The Itasca *Iron News* became engaged in an intramural debate between its columnist, Dad Lammon, who insisted that the Paul Bunyan stories originated with the old Itasca Logging Company, an isolated and savage little logging kingdom, and its editor, Paddy Pederson, who asserted a French-Canadian origin. In the February 13, 1941, issue Pederson wrote:

However, we doubt that Paul Bunyan originated here or in Wisconsin or in Michigan. As far back as we can remember, which is more than 30 years, we have heard stories of Paul and these were brought from the east, the down east provinces of Canada and the state of Maine. Just to verify this we checked with Jim Robb who comes from Ottawa and John Pinette from the state of Maine. Jim says that his first log drive, in the year 1892 in Canada, was enlivened by the tales of the Round River Drive and many other Paul Bunyan stories which we have today. The legend even then was well established. John Pinette says the foreman on the first log drive on which he worked in Maine was a big man called Paul Bunyan although his name was Lawler. He remembers his uncles and others telling tales of the prowess of Paul, which would place Paul in the state of Maine and eastern Canada as early as 1860 or '70 before the pine forests of Michigan or Wisconsin were even touched.

Our guess is that Paul originated in the minds of the French-Canadians of eastern Canada. The French are an imaginative people. They were the peasant French, fresh from the old country, steeped in superstition and folk-lore. They were used to things on small scale. Their cultivated fields were small tracts, every inch of which was cultivated by their own hand; their trees were numbered and counted. When they came here where land was measured in areas as large as their provinces at home and the trees were reckoned in the thousands of acres instead of by the piece, with everything else on an accordingly magnificent scale, what is more natural than that their fertile imagination would create a superman in scale with the new country? That creation, in our estimation, was Paul Bunyan.

The name itself smacks of French origin. Paul is a very common French Christian name. The French name "Gagnon" is pronounced "Gonya." By sounding of the final letter "n" in Bunyan which would be natural with the English, the Irish and the Scotch, as they intermingled with the French, we have the "yan" of Bunyan. Not too great a corruption to expect in a name in two or three generations.

While Paul did not originate here, we firmly believe that after his travels all over the country, he quit logging and homesteaded in Itasca county and that was his and Babe's last earthly residence. After all, that's what usually establishes claim to a celebrity.

The person most qualified to speak about the early development of the Bunyan legend, W. B. Laughhead of the Red River Lumber Company, Westwood, California, wrote a detailed letter to the Bemidji *Daily Pioneer* which was printed in their editorial column, May 1, 1940. An introductory note states that Mr. Laughead "is also an artist and painted the large canvas now on display in the Elks Club of this city, picturing Paul Bunyan and his Blue Ox in their native habitat."

I thank you for your letter enclosing the fine editorial in the Pioneer of April 13th replying to the review "Paul Bunyan, Myth or Hoax" from the March issue of "Minnesota History."

If the review quoted in your editorial gives Mr. Ames' position correctly he has apparently arrived at a conclusion on incomplete evidence. He quotes Stewart Holbrook's phrase "the madeup tales of Paul Bunyan." They must have been "made up" unless we accept as geological and historical fact that Paul dug the Great Lakes, started the Mississippi and logged off North Dakota. The question is, when were they made up and by whom.

Mr. Ames objects to the variations in detail and locale of the different versions and the introduction into some of them of modern machinery. These very differences would tend to establish them as myth, the work of many narrators not limited to time or place. A true myth is a living thing, taking on local color as it grows. If the stories were struck off at one time by some individual there would be few discrepancies.

Without getting into a discussion of the technical distinctions of fable, legend, myth and folklore we might quote an authority, John Fiske, "While a legend is usually confined to one or two localities and is told of not more than one or two persons, it is characteristic of a myth that it is spread over a large part of the earth, the leading incidents remaining constant while the names and often the motives vary with each locality."

The fact that Mr. Ames' father and grandfather did not hear of Paul Bunyan in the camps of the Upper Mississippi is also inconclusive. If they had never happened to see a blacksmith with red hair would that prove that there never was a red headed blacksmith? The oral transmission of a tale, unaided by printer's ink, is slow and its distribution is spotted.

When the Red River Lumber Company started using Paul Bunyan stories in their advertising in 1914 it was soon learned that Paul was unknown to the general public and to the distributors and sawmill people of the lumber industry. The stories were known only to loggers and many loggers had not heard of them. My own experience in the camps around Bemidji and on the upper Mississippi dated from 1900 and that is where I first heard of Paul Bunyan. In 1901 I heard the tales again from Michigan loggers in California. These men had gone to California from Michigan some 15 years before that time.

In 1920 Mr. Henry L. Neall, then well along in years, wrote to The Red River Lumber Company that he had heard Paul Bunyan stories when a boy in his grandfather's camps in Pennsylvania and that his grandfather referred to them as old traditions.

Paul's exploits are seldom told in narrative form. Someone in a group refers to something Paul did in a casual, offhand way as if to some well known event like Washington crossing the Delaware or Columbus discovering the New World. Another takes it up, perhaps arguing about some detail. Extemporaneous embellishments come into the conversation which becomes a lying contest. In this way local color and modernization creep in.

There is an extensive version in the oil fields full of the trade slang of the drillers, "The Buttermilk Gusher," "The 48-inch Casing from India," etc. Some of the old pine loggers ranged wide as itinerant laborers, sticking to frontiers, and evidently some strays reached the oil fields. It is said that there are locally colored stories of Paul Bunyan in the West Indies.

Research by individuals and institutions have [sic] failed to reveal the origin of the Paul Bunyan stories. They appear in the Eastern States prior to the Lake States era of the pine industry. Mention of Paul Bunyan occurs in letters to newspapers and lumber trade journals but so far as shown by investigation up to this time the publications of the Red River Lumber Company dating from

1914 were the first compilations in book form. Their book "Paul Bunyan and His Big Blue Ox" (1922) has gone through ten printings of 5,000 to 10,000 each up to and including 1939.

I regret that I can add no conclusive evidence but none has come my way in 25 years of contact and correspondence with students of the Paul Bunyan myth.

Yours sincerely,
W. B. Laughead

Mr. Laughead, whom I interviewed in California in 1939, had a vested interest in Paul Bunyan, because as advertising agent for the Red River Lumber Company he had conceived the idea of using stories and pictures of the giant lumberjack to promote his product. Professors corresponded with him and, like Joel Chandler Harris, he found himself regarded as an authority on folklore.

Conclusions

The evidence presented here completely alters the accepted view of Paul Bunyan. He is the pseudo folk-hero of twentieth-century mass culture, a conveniently vague symbol pressed into service to exemplify "the American spirit." He means different things to different vested interests: the soul of the workingman to the *Daily Worker* and author Turney; the efficiency of American capitalism to sculptor Amateis and the lumber companies; a gargantuan comic dummy for resort promoters; the invincible brute strength of America to some artists; a braggart and a blowhard, a fantasy, a performer of enormous tasks, a deified woodsman, to other segments of the American people. But no one knows very much about the legends of Paul and Babe. A few simple exaggerations circulate in the press, but the tales are the least part of the myth. When the natives of the northern woods country make inquiries for oral origins, they find the thinnest of spoors. Mr. Laughead, who writes freely to the Bunyan scholars,[91] recalls only minor motifs from oral tradition, and his letter to the Bemidji *Daily Pioneer* shows a surprising sophistication in matters of folklore study.

The mass media care nothing about academic questions of origin. As one of their functions, they provide mass heroes for the public, Paul Bunyan and Davy Crockett, Johnny Appleseed and Jesse James. In Paul Bunyan the nation's newspapers found good copy, appealing to hazy aesthetes and hard-headed businessmen, patriots and liberals, and mass-readers avid for sensations and stunts. The advertising pamphlets of Laughead and the juvenile Bunyan books reached thousands of readers, but the newspapers reached the millions. In the early 1920s Paul Bunyan columns in the Seattle *Star* and the Portland *Oregonian* helped publicize the legend.

Besides making the name of Paul Bunyan a household word, the newspapers inform us of serious creative efforts by artists to perceive deeper meanings in this loudly trumpeted native myth. Their attempts fail, because they are pursuing a chimera; there is no myth, just a vacuous giant and his vacuous ox. But this all-pervasive interest in the timber god, from intellectuals as well as from hucksters, testifies to his vital role in twentieth-century America. The maturing of American society and the crystallization of American nationalism have generated the desire for a New World Thor or Hercules or Gargantua, with no taint of foreign genesis. And Paul Bunyan, breaking into public view in the 1920s, filled the bill. A tremendous promotion campaign spread his name across the land, broadly but thinly, with a few associated cliches about his uniqueness in American mythology. The hullabaloo penetrated all corners of American life, and even impressed the lumberjacks. Professors and critics and composers swallowed the myth as eagerly as the man in the street. The explanation for this phenomenon lies largely in the staple reading fare of the country and the century, the newspaper, whose reporters had found a lusty, 100 percent American symbol in Paul Bunyan. Journalism, not folklore, has nourished Old Paul in the hearts of his countrymen.

Notes

Selected Bibliography

Index

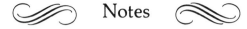 Notes

Folklore, Academe, and the Marketplace

1. *Commentary* 50 (October 1974): 20, 22; the book reviewed was *The British Folklorists.*

2. William R. Ferris, in the American and Afro-American Studies Programs at Yale, and Peter Seitel, in the anthropology department at Princeton, both Ph.D.'s from the University of Pennsylvania, and Barbara Kirshenblatt-Gimblett, in the linguistics department at Columbia, with her Ph.D. from Indiana University.

3. Wallace Stegner, *The Uneasy Chair: A Biography of Bernard DeVoto* (Garden City, N. Y.: Doubleday, 1974), p. 237.

4. Critical reviews I have written of such works have appeared as follows: Carl Carmer, *America Sings: Songs and Stories of Our Country's Growing,* in *California Folklore Quarterly* 2 (1943): 230-231; Stan Newton, *Paul Bunyan of the Great Lakes,* in *Western Folklore* 6 (1947): 397-399; B.A. Botkin, *A Treasury of New England Folklore,* in *American Literature* 20 (1948): 76-78; B.A. Botkin, *A Treasury of Southern Folklore,* in *Journal of American Folklore* 63 (1950): 480-482; Harold Felton, *Legends of Paul Bunyan,* in *Journal of American Folklore* 64 (1951): 233-235; B.A. Botkin, *A Treasury of Mississippi River Folklore,* in *Minnesota History* 35 (1956): 39-40; Maria Leach, *The Rainbow Book of American Folk Tales and Legends,* in *Kentucky Folklore Record* 4 (1958): 180-182; Frank R. Kramer, *Voices in the Valley: Mythmaking and Folk Belief in the Shaping of the Middle West,* in *Wisconsin Magazine of History* 57 (1964): 344-346; Duncan Emrich, *Folklore on the American Land,* in *Western Folklore* 32 (1973): 141-143.

5. Richard M. Dorson, *America in Legend* (New York: Pantheon, 1973), pp. 169-170.

6. Richard M. Dorson, "Folklore and Fake Lore," *American Mercury* 70 (1950): 335-343; James Stevens, "Folklore and the Artist," *ibid.,* pp. 343-349.

7. Professional folklorists now sometimes employ the neologism "fakelore" without emotive bias, and consider that fakelore itself is worth studying.

See, e.g., Tristram P. Coffin, *Uncertain Glory* (Hatboro, Pa.: Folklore Associates, 1971), "Fakelore Goes to War."

8. A variant of "Tag, you're it" is in the Indiana University Folklore Archives, told on a traveling salesman tagged by a gorilla (Folder 69-12 under "Negative Legends," collected in 1969 by Charlotte Sluss of Unionville, Indiana, on the Bloomington campus from Glen Salmon). A text localized in Morganfield, Kentucky, is printed in *Hoosier Folklore Bulletin* 3 (1944): 68-69, no. 18, "Surprise."

9. Archer Taylor, "A Long-Sought Parallel Comes to Light," *Western Folklore* 16 (1957): 48-51; Richard M. Dorson, "The Legend of Yoho Cove," *ibid.* 18 (1959): 329-331.

10. The Baughman motif number is X1215.7 (a) "Dog runs beside train, cools off the hot boxes."

11. Publications of mine resulting from the field trip are: "Collecting Folklore in Jonesport, Maine," *Proceedings of the American Philosophical Society* 101 (June 1957): 270-289; "Maine Down-Easters," in *Buying the Wind* (Chicago: University of Chicago Press, 1964), pp. 21-105; "Mishaps of a Maine Lobsterman," *Northeast Folklore* 1 (1957): 1-7; and "The Folktale Repertoire of Two Maine Lobstermen," in *Internationaler Kongress der Volkserzählungsforscher in Keil und Kopenhagen* (Berlin: de Gruyter, 1961), pp. 74-83.

12. John Gould, *The Jonesport Raffle* (Boston: Little Brown, 1969), p. 11.

13. Jules Zanger, "Bogies of American Folklore: A Report on the Eleventh Newberry Library Conference on American Studies," *Newberry Library Bulletin* 5 (April 1961): 227-239.

14. *Congressional Record,* Proceedings and Debates of the 87th Congress, First Session, vol. 107, no. 82, pp. 7695, 7714, 7719, reporting the proceedings for May 17, 1961.

15. Richard M. Dorson, "Folklore and the NDEA," *Journal of American Folklore* 75 (1962): 160-164.

16. During the season of campus unrest, a graduate student in anthropology published in a 1969 issue of the *Spectator,* the Indiana University radical student newspaper, a violent attack upon Professor Dorson whom he called a "prostitute" for seeking funds from the federal government fighting a barbarous war in Vietnam. The anonymous author quoted various passages from my published letter to Senator Morse and highlighted my quotation from the New York *Times Magazine* on communist techniques of infiltrating into South Vietnam through manipulation of folklore.

17. John Williams, "Radicalism and Professionalism in Folklore Studies: A Comparative Perspective" and "Comment" by Richard M. Dorson, *Journal of the Folklore Institute* 11 (1974): 211-234, 235-239.

18. *North Carolina Folklore Journal* 21 (1973): 157-159; 22 (1974): 35-41.

19. Wigginton in *ibid.,* p. 38.

20. *Journal of American History* 61 (March 1975): 1072-1073. In *America in Legend*, p. 87, I quoted a contemporary indictment of Mike Fink as a savage ruffian for playing a brutal prank on his wife. Drinnon cites the prank and ignores the quotation. Richard Drinnon, *White Savage: The Case of John Dunn Hunter* (New York: Schocken, 1972) is an absorbing study of the authenticity of Hunter's captivity narrative. Drinnon's bias shows in his emotional review of Michael Paul Rogin, *Fathers and Children: Andrew Jackson and the Subjugation of the American Indian*, in *New York Times Book Review*, June 15, 1975, pp. 21-22. On faddism of historians see the excellent statement by Michael Lodwick and Thomas Fiehrer, "Undoing History; or, Clio Clobbered," *AHA Newsletter* 13 (May/June 1975): 4-5.

21. Review by Laura D. S. Harrell of Moritz Jagendorf, *Folk Stories of the South*, in *New York Times Book Review*, January 27, 1974.

Folklore in the Modern World

1. A. Gillies, *Herder* (Oxford: Basil Blackwell, 1945), p. 45n, quoted in R. M. Dorson, *Folktales of Germany* (Chicago: University of Chicago Press, 1968), p. vi.

2. Quoted in *ibid.*, pp. vi, viii.

3. Quoted in R. M. Dorson, ed., *Peasant Customs and Savage Myths*, 2 vols. (Chicago: University of Chicago Press, 1968), I, 7, 53.

4. *Ibid.*, pp. 55-56.

5. Quoted in R. M. Dorson, *The British Folklorists; A History* (Chicago: University of Chicago Press, 1968), pp. 5-6.

6. Quoted in Dorson, *Peasant Customs*, I, 219, 231, 261.

7. Jouko Hautala, *Finnish Folklore Research 1828-1918* (Helsinki: Finnish Academy of Sciences, 1969), p. 25. Martti Haavio, "Elias Lönnrot," *Biographica: Nordic Folklorists of the Past* (Copenhagen: Nordisk Institut for Folkedigtning, 1971), p. 3. Juha Pentikainen, "Julius and Kaarle Krohn," *ibid.*, p. 15.

8. R. T. Christiansen, ed., *Folktales of Norway* (Chicago: University of Chicago Press, 1964), p. xli.

9. Nils-Arvid Bringéus, "Gunnar Olof Hyltén-Cavallius," *Biographica*, p. 90.

10. Lørn Piø, "Svend Grundtvig," *Biographica*, pp. 193, 207, 214. The English title is a translation of the long subtitle of Grundtvig's *Danske Folkeminder.*

11. Quoted by Bengt Holbek and Thorkild Knudsen, *ibid.*, p. 249.

12. Quoted in Y. M. Sokolov, *Russian Folklore*, tr. Catherine R. Smith (New York: Macmillan, 1950), p. 72.

13. Quoted in *ibid.*, pp. 112-113.

14. B. M. and Ju. M. Sokolov, "In Search of Folktales and Songs (From Travel Impressions)," in Felix J. Oinas and Stephen Soudakoff, ed. and tr.,

The Study of Russian Folklore, (The Hague: Mouton, 1975), p. 14.

15. Given in R. M. Dorson, ed., *Studies in Japanese Folklore* (Bloomington: Indiana University Press, 1963), p. 52.

16. *Ibid.,* p. 51.

17. Cecil J. Sharp, *English Folk Songs from the Southern Appalachians* (London, New York, Toronto: Oxford, 1960), "Introduction to the First Edition, 1917," pp. xxii-xxiii.

18. Emelyn E. Gardner, *Folklore from the Schoharie Hills, New York* (Ann Arbor: University of Michigan Press, 1937), p. 2.

19. *Folk-Lore Journal* 3 (1885): 117.

20. Arthur M. Schlesinger, *Paths to the Present* (New York: Macmillan, 1949), p. 228.

21. Donald McKelvie, "Aspects of Oral Tradition and Belief in an Industrial Region," *Folk Life* 1 (1963): 77-94, quotation pp. 79-80. See also McKelvie, "Proverbial Elements in the Oral Tradition of an English Urban Industrial Region," *Journal of the Folklore Institute* 2 (1965): 244-261.

22. McKelvie, "Aspects of Oral Tradition," p. 79.

23. Henry Mayhew, *London Labour and the London Poor,* 4 vols. (New York: Dover, 1968), I, 102; II, 117.

24. R. P. Dore, *City Life in Japan* (Berkeley and Los Angeles: University of California Press, 1958), p. 336.

25. Linda Dégh, "Two Old World Narrators in Urban Setting," *Kontakte und Grenzen, Festschrift für Gerhard Heilfurth zum 60 Geburtstag* (Göttingen: Otto Schwartz, 1969), pp. 71-86.

26. R. M. Dorson, "Is There a Folk in the City?" in Américo Paredes, and Ellen Stekert, eds., *The Urban Experience and Folk Tradition* (Austin and London: University of Texas Press, 1971), pp. 21-52.

27. *The Urban Experience and Folk Tradition,* p. 63.

28. Harriet M. Pawlowska, *Merrily We Sing! 105 Polish Folksongs* (Detroit: Wayne State University Press, 1961); Susie Hoogasian-Villa, *One Hundred Armenian Folktales* (Detroit: Wayne State University Press, 1966). Kenneth A. Thigpen, "Folklore and the Ethnicity Factor in the Lives of Romanian-Americans," unpublished diss., Indiana, 1973, I, 66.

29. Hermann Bausinger, "Folklore Research at the University of Tübingen," *Journal of the Folklore Institute* 5 (1968): 127, 130.

30. Gerhard Heilfurth, "The Institut für mitteleuropäische Volksforschung at the University of Marburg," *Journal of the Folklore Institute* 5 (1968): 138.

31. R. M. Dorson, "Foreword" to Linda Dégh, ed., *Folktales of Hungary* (Chicago: University of Chicago Press, 1965), pp. xv-xvi, citing Tekla Dömotor, "Principal Problems of the Investigation on the Ethnography of the Industrial Working Class in Hungary," *Acta Ethnographica* 5 (1956): 331-349.

32. Y. M. Sokolov, *Russian Folklore,* tr. Catherine R. Smith (New York:

Macmillan, for the Russian Translation Project of the American Council of Learned Societies, 1950), pp. 577-578.

33. *Ibid.,* pp. 649, 653.

34. Shire Publications (Tring, Herts., 1969).

35. George Korson, *Minstrels of the Mine Patch* (Philadelphia: University of Pennsylvania Press, 1938); *Coal Dust on the Fiddle* (Philadelphia: University of Pennsylvania Press, 1943); and *Black Rock* (Baltimore: Johns Hopkins University Press, 1960).

36. Mody C. Boatright, *Gib Morgan, Minstrel of the Oil Fields,* Texas Folk-Lore Society Publication XX (1945), and *Folklore of the Oil Industry* (Dallas: Southern Methodist University Press, 1963). Mody C. Boatright and William A. Owens, *Tales from the Derrick Floor* (New York: Doubleday, 1970).

37. T. P. Coffin and H. Cohen, eds., *Folklore from the Working Folk of America* (New York: Doubleday, 1973).

38. Betty Messenger, "Picking Up the Linen Threads: Some Folklore of the Northern Irish Linen Industry," *Journal of the Folklore Institute* 9 (1972): 18-27.

39. See Stewart Sanderson, "The Folklore of the Motor-car," *Folklore* 80 (1969): 241-252; and the following texts and discussions of automobile legends in *Indiana Folklore:* Linda Dégh, "The Hook" and "The Boy Friend's Death," and Carlos Drake, "The Killer in the Back Seat," 1 (1968): 92-109; Xenia Cord, "Further Notes on 'The Assailant in the Back Seat,' " 2 (1969): 47-54.

40. Raphael Patai, *Myth and Modern Man* (Englewood Cliffs, N.J.: Prentice-Hall, 1972), pp. 229-230, 257.

41. Priscilla Denby, "Folklore in the Mass Media," *Folklore Forum* 4 (1971): 113-114.

42. Tom Burns, "Folklore in the Mass Media: Television," *Folklore Forum* 2 (1969): 103.

43. Fall 1972, accession number STU-187.

44. Hermann Bausinger, "Folklore Research at the University of Tübingen," *Journal of the Folklore Institute* 5 (1968): 131.

45. Walter Havernick, "The Hamburg School of Folklore Research," *Journal of the Folklore Institute* 5 (1968): 121 n11.

46. Quoted in R. M. Dorson, "Foreword" to Kurt Ranke, ed., *Folktales of Germany* (Chicago: University of Chicago Press, 1966), pp. ix, xix, quoting Louis L. Snyder, "Nationalistic Aspects of the Grimm Brothers' Fairy Tales," *Journal of Social Psychology* 23 (1959): 219-221.

47. Quotations are cited in Christa Kamenetsky, "Folklore as a Political Tool in Nazi Germany," *Journal of American Folklore* 85 (1972): 221-235.

48. William A. Wilson, "Folklore and National Consciousness in Pre-Nineteenth Century Finland."

49. Quoted in R. M. Dorson, "Introduction" to *Folktales of Norway,* pp.

vi-vii, xiv, x, from Dasent's "Introductory Essay on the Origin and Diffusion of Popular Tales," *Popular Tales from the Norse*, 2nd ed. (London: Routledge, n.d.).

50. R. M. Dorson, "The Question of Folklore in a New Nation," *Journal of the Folklore Institute* 3 (1966): 293, and "Foreword" to Sean O'Sullivan, ed., *Folktales of Ireland* (Chicago: University of Chicago Press, 1966), pp. xv-xxii.

51. Al. N. Oikonomides, "Foreword" to John C. Lawson, *Modern Greek Folklore and Ancient Greek Religion* (New York: University Books, 1964), p. vii.

52. Felix J. Oinas, "Folklore and Politics," *Slavic Review* 32 (1973): 45-58; "The Problem of the Aristocratic Origin of Russian Byliny," *ibid.* 30 (1971): 513-522; "Introduction" to Y. M. Sokolov, *Russian Folklore*, tr. C. R. Smith (Hatboro, Pa.: Folklore Associates, 1966), pp. v-xvi; and "Folklore Activities in Russia," in R. M. Dorson, ed., *Folklore Research Around the World* (Bloomington: Indiana University Press, 1961), pp. 76-84.

53. Sokolov, *Russian Folklore*, pp. 39, 141.

54. James W. Fernandez, "Folklore as an Agent of Nationalism," *African Studies Bulletin* 5 (1962): 3-8.

55. Gyula Ortutay, *Hungarian Folklore Essays* (Budapest: Akadémiai Kiadó, 1972), p. 9.

Mythology and Folklore: A Review Essay

1. Burton Feldman and Robert D. Richardson, *The Rise of Modern Mythology, 1680-1860* (Bloomington and London: Indiana University Press, 1972).

2. Raphael Patai, *Myth and Modern Man* (Englewood Cliffs, N.J.: Prentice-Hall, 1972). Claude Lévi-Strauss, *The Raw and the Cooked*, tr. John and Doreen Weightman (New York: Harper and Row, 1969; originally published in 1964 in France as *Le cru et le cuit*).

3. Joseph Campbell, *The Flight of the Wild Gander: Explorations in the Mythological Dimension* (New York: Viking, 1969); *Myths To Live By* (New York: Viking, 1972).

4. Campbell, *Flight of the Wild Gander*, p. 251.

5. Campbell, *Myths To Live By*, p. 253.

6. Lévi-Strauss, *The Raw and the Cooked*, pp. 340-341.

7. *Ibid.*, pp. 1, 64.

8. Geoffrey S. Kirk, *Myth: Its Meaning and Functions in Ancient and Other Cultures* (Berkeley: University of California Press, 1970).

9. Jouko Hautala, *Finnish Folklore Research, 1828-1918* (Helsinki: Finnish Academy of Science, 1968).

10. Richard M. Dorson, *The British Folklorists: A History* (Chicago: University of Chicago Press, 1968).

11. Richard M. Dorson, ed., *Peasant Customs and Savage Myths*, 2 vols. (Chicago: University of Chicago Press, 1968).

12. Dag Strömbäck et al., eds., *Biographica: Nordic Folklorists of the Past* (Copenhagen: Nordisk Institut für Folkedigtning, 1971), p. 67.

13. Ruth Michaelis-Jena, *The Brothers Grimm* (London: Routledge and Kegan Paul, 1970).

14. Murray B. Peppard, *Paths Through the Forest: A Biography of the Brothers Grimm* (New York: Holt, Rinehart and Winston, 1971), p. 64.

15. Duncan Wilson, *The Life and Times of Vuk Stefanović Karadzić, 1787-1864* (Oxford: Clarendon, 1970), p. 7.

16. Américo Paredes and Richard Bauman, eds., *Toward New Perspectives in Folklore* (Austin and London: University of Texas Press, 1972).

17. Pierre Maranda and Elli Köngäs Maranda, eds., *Structural Analysis of Oral Tradition* (Philadelphia: University of Pennsylvania Press, 1971), pp. 295, 316, xxix.

18. Elli Köngäs Maranda and Pierre Maranda, *Structural Models in Folklore and Transformational Essays* (The Hague: Mouton, 1971).

19. Richard M. Dorson, *American Folklore and the Historian* (Chicago: University of Chicago Press, 1971); *Folklore: Selected Essays* (Bloomington: Indiana University Press, 1972).

20. Richard M. Dorson, ed., *Folklore and Folklife: An Introduction* (Chicago: University of Chicago Press, 1972).

21. Munro S. Edmonson, *Lore: An Introduction to the Science of Folklore and Literature* (New York: Holt, Rinehart and Winston, 1971), p. 234.

22. Keith Thomas, *Religion and the Decline of Magic* (New York: Scribner's, 1971), p. x.

23. Alan Macfarlane, *Witchcraft in Tudor and Stuart England* (New York: Harper and Row, 1970), pp. 107, 206, 250-251.

24. Katharine Briggs, *A Dictionary of British Folktales*, 4 vols. (Bloomington: Indiana University Press, 1970-1971).

25. G. Ewart Evans, *Where Beards Wag All: The Relevance of the Oral Tradition* (London: Faber and Faber, 1970); G. Ewart Evans and David Thomson, *The Leaping Hare* (London: Faber and Faber, 1972).

26. Wayland D. Hand, ed., *American Folk Legend: A Symposium* (Berkeley, Los Angeles, and London: University of California Press, 1971).

27. Tristram P. Coffin, *Uncertain Glory: Folklore and the American Revolution* (Hatboro, Pa.: Folklore Associates, 1971).

28. Gene Bluestein, *The Voice of the Folk: Folklore and American Literary Theory* (Amherst: University of Massachusetts Press, 1972).

29. George Carey, *A Faraway Time and Place: Lore of the Eastern Shore* (Washington and New York: Luce, 1971).

30. Eliot Wigginton, ed., *The Foxfire Book* (Garden City, N.Y.: Doubleday Anchor, 1972), p. 144.

31. Bill C. Malone, *Country Music, U.S.A.* (Austin and London: University of Texas Press, 1968).

32. Archie Green, *Only a Miner* (Urbana: University of Illinois Press, 1972).

33. R. Serge Denisoff, *Great Day Coming: Folk Music and the American Left* (Urbana, Chicago and London: University of Illinois Press, 1971).

34. Harry M. Hyatt, *Hoodoo-Conjuration-Witchcraft-Rootwork*, 3 vols. (Hannibal, Mo.: Western Publishing, 1970-1973). Harry Oster, *Living Country Blues* (Detroit: Folklore Associates, 1969). Bruce Jackson, *Wake Up Dead Man: Afro-American Worksongs from Texas Prisons* (Cambridge, Ma.: Harvard University Press, 1972). John Lovell, *Black Song: The Forge and the Flame* (New York: Macmillan, 1972). Alan Dundes, ed., *Mother Wit from the Laughing Barrel* (Englewood Cliffs, N.J.: Prentice Hall, 1973).

35. Duncan Emrich, *Folklore on the American Land* (Boston and Toronto: Little, Brown, 1972).

36. Vance Randolph, *Ozark Folklore: A Bibliography* (Bloomington: Indiana University Folklore Institute Monograph Series, vol. 24, 1972).

37. Ruth Finnegan, *Oral Literature in Africa* (Oxford: Clarendon, 1970).

38. Richard M. Dorson, ed., *African Folklore* (Garden City, N.Y.: Doubleday Anchor, 1972).

39. Bacil F. Kirtley, *A Motif-Index of Polynesian Narratives* (Honolulu: University of Hawaii Press, 1971); Hiroko Ikeda, *A Type and Motif Index of Japanese Folk-Literature* (Helsinki: Suomalainen Tiedeakatemia Academia Scientiarum Fennica, 1971).

Is Folklore a Discipline?

1. Robert Klymasz, "Folklore Studies at the National Museum of Man, Canada," *Folklore Forum* 5 (January 1972): 11-13.

2. *Folklore* 2 (1891): 111.

3. *Journal of the Folklore Institute*, special issue on American Folklore Historiography, 10:1-2 (1973).

4. Published in P. D. Olch and F. C. Pogue, eds., *Selections from the Fifth and Sixth National Colloquia on Oral History* (New York: Oral History Association, 1972), pp. 40-49.

5. Charles Sanders Peirce, *Chance, Love, and Logic: Philosophical Essays* (New York: Harcourt, Brace, 1923).

Oral Literature, Oral History, and the Folklorist

1. See Milman Parry, *The Making of Homeric Verse: The Collected Papers of Milman Parry*, ed. Adam Parry (Oxford: Oxford University Press, 1971).

2. Bela Bartók and Albert B. Lord, *Serbo-Croatian Folk Songs* (New York: Columbia University Press, 1951); and *Serbo-Croatian Heroic Songs*, 2 vols. (Cambridge, Mass.: Harvard University Press, 1953-54).

3. Francis P. Magoun, "The Oral-Formulaic Character of Anglo-Saxon Narrative Poetry," *Speculum* 28 (1953): 446-467. See the critique of Larry D.

Benson, "The Literary Character of Anglo-Saxon Formulaic Poetry," *Publications of the Modern Language Association* 81 (1966): 334-341.

4. *Forum for Modern Language Studies* 10 (July 1974): 187-209.

5. See "The Oldest Form of Creative Achievement," *Harvard Magazine* 76 (March 1974): 11-12.

6. David E. Bynum, "Child's Legacy Enlarged: Oral Literary Studies at Harvard since 1856," *Harvard Library Bulletin* 22 (July 1974): 237-248.

7. Allan Nevins, *The Gateway to History* (New York: Appleton-Century, 1938), p. iv; quoted in Elizabeth B. Mason and Louis M. Starr, eds., *The Oral History Collection of Columbia University* (New York: Oral History Research Office, 1964), p. 9.

8. *Oral History: The First Twenty Years* (New York: Columbia University, ca. 1970), p. 1.

9. Allan Nevins, "The Uses of Oral History," in *Oral History at Arrowhead: Proceedings of the First National Colloquium on Oral History* (Los Angeles: Oral History Association, 1967), p. 35.

10. Studs Terkel, *Division Street America* (1966), *Hard Times: An Oral History of the Great Depression* (1970), and *Working* (1974), all published by Pantheon Books, New York.

11. Charles W. Crawford, "Oral History—the State of the Profession," *Oral History Review 1974* (New York: Oral History Association, 1974), pp. 1-2.

12. The information on Mamman Shata derives from Abdulkadir Dandatti, "The Role of the Oral Singer in Hausa-Fulani Society," unpublished diss., Indiana University, 1975.

13. Henry Glassie, Edward D. Ives, and John F. Szwed, *Folksongs and Their Makers* (Bowling Green, Ohio: Bowling Green University Popular Press, [1971]).

14. Edward D. Ives, *Larry Gorman: The Man Who Made the Songs* (Bloomington: Indiana University Press, 1964); and *Lawrence Doyle: The Farmer-Poet of Prince Edward Island* (Orono: University of Maine Press, 1971).

15. Linda Dégh and Andrew Vaszonyi, "The Memorate and the Proto-Memorate," *Journal of American Folklore* 87 (1974): 225-239.

16. The stories told by Curt Morse about himself I printed in "Mishaps of a Maine Lobsterman," *Northeast Folklore* 1 (1958): 1-7.

17. Stuart A. Gallacher, "Franklin's *Way to Wealth*: A Florilegium of Proverbs and Wise Sayings," *Journal of English and Germanic Philology* 47 (1949): 229-251.

18. Arthur Palmer Hudson, "The Singing South: Folksong in Recent Fiction," *Sewanee Review* 44 (1936): 268-295.

19. Jeff Opland, "*Imbongi Nezibongo*: The Xhosa Tribal Poet and the Contemporary Poetic Tradition," *Publications of the Modern Language Association* 90 (1975): 185-208.

20. Kenneth Goldstein described and played tapes of monologues in his paper "Oral Recitations" presented at the annual meeting of the American Folklore Society, Portland, Ore., November 1, 1974. It should be noted that a written (typed, mimeographed, Xeroxed) traditional literature *does* exist; see Alan Dundes and Carl R. Pagter, *Urban Folklore from the Paperwork Empire* (Austin, Tex.: American Folklore Society, 1975).

21. Albert Lord, "Perspectives on Recent Work on Oral Literature," *Forum for Modern Language Studies* 10 (July 1974): 202-203.

22. See, e.g., James H. Jones, "Commonplace and Memorization in the Oral Tradition of the English and Scottish Popular Ballads," *Journal of American Folklore* 74 (1961): 97-112; Bruce A. Beatie, "Oral-Formulaic Composition in the Spanish Romancero of the Sixteenth Century," *Journal of the Folklore Institute* 1 (1965): 92-113; Bruce A. Rosenberg, *The Art of the American Folk Preacher* (New York: Oxford University Press, 1970); David Evans, "Techniques of Blues Composition among Black Folksingers," *Journal of American Folklore* 87 (1974): 240-249.

23. Bruce Jackson, *"Get Your Ass in the Water and Swim Like Me": Narrative Poetry from Black Oral Tradition* (Cambridge, Mass.: Harvard University Press, 1974).

24. The geologist Dorothy Vitaliano has combined geology and folklore, and coined the term geomythology, in *Legends of the Earth* (Bloomington: Indiana University Press, 1974).

25. G. S. Kirk, "The Search for the Real Homer," *Greece and Rome*, n.s. 20 (October 1973): 126.

26. Joseph A. Russo, "Homer Against his Tradition," *Arion* 7 (1968): 279-295.

27. William A. Hansen, *The Conference Sequence: Patterned Narration and Narrative Inconsistency in the Odyssey* (Berkeley, Los Angeles, London: University of California Press, 1972). Works on Homer that are insufficiently grounded in folktale scholarship include Rhys Carpenter, *Folk Tale, Fiction and Saga in the Homeric Epics* (Berkeley and Los Angeles: University of California Press, 1958), and Denys Page, *Folktales in Homer's Odyssey* (Cambridge, Mass.: Harvard University Press, 1973).

28. *The Odyssey*, Book II, verses 101-134 (Oxford Classical Text Edition).

29. R. M. Dorson, *Buying the Wind* (Chicago: University of Chicago Press, 1964), p. 39.

30. Robert A. Georges, "Addenda to Dorson's 'The Sailor Who Went Inland,' " *Journal of American Folklore* 79 (1966): 373-374.

31. Wayland D. Hand, "Definitions of Oral History," in *Oral History at Arrowhead*, pp. 11-19, 26-27, 33; *The Third National Colloquium on Oral History* (New York: Oral History Association, 1969), the contribution of Roger Welsch to "Interdisciplinary Views on Oral History," pp. 18-22, 35-36, 37-38; *Selections from the Fifth and Sixth National Colloquia on Oral History*

(New York: Oral History Association, 1972), the symposium on "The Oral Historian and the Folklorist," chaired by Richard M. Dorson, with William L. Montell, Henry Glassie, and William Ivey, pp. 40-62. The English journal *Oral History*, published at the University of Essex since 1972, has similarly included contributions on folk tradition by G. Ewart Evans.

32. Paul Bullock, "Oral History in the Ghetto," *Selections from the Fifth and Sixth National Colloquia*, pp. 85-89.

33. Courtney Brown, "Oral History and the Oral Tradition of Black America: The Kinte Foundation," *Oral History Review 1973*, pp. 26-28.

34. Alex Haley, "Black History, Oral History and Genealogy," *Oral History Review 1973*, pp. 1-25.

35. David W. Cohen, "A Field Study of Traditional African History," in Gould P. Colman, ed., *The Fourth National Colloquium on Oral History* (New York: The Oral History Association, 1970), pp. 88-97.

36. *Negro Folktales in Michigan* (Cambridge, Mass.: Harvard University Press, 1956), pp. 85-86; *Bloodstoppers and Bearwalkers* (Cambridge, Mass.: Harvard University Press, 1952), pp. 38-39; "Tales of a Greek-American Family on Tape," *Fabula* 1 (1957): 119-120.

37. See, e.g., Ebiegberi Joe Alagoa, "Oral Tradition Among the Ijo of the Niger Delta," *Journal of African History* 7 (1966): 405-419; Kwame Y. Daaku, "History in the Oral Traditions of the Akan," in R. M. Dorson, ed., *Folklore and Traditional History* (The Hague: Mouton, 1973), pp. 42-54.

38. Barrett has written *Tales from the Fens* (1963), *More Tales from the Fens* (1964), and his autobiography, *A Fenman's Story* (1965), all edited by Enid Porter and published in London by Routledge and Kegan Paul.

39. Barbara Tuchman, "Ventures in Oral History," in Colman, *Fourth National Colloquium on Oral History*, p. 129.

40. Robert W. Lowie, "Oral Tradition and History," *American Anthropologist*, n.s. 17 (1917): 596-599; reprinted in Lowie, *Selected Papers on Anthropology* (Berkeley: University of California Press, 1960), pp. 115-118.

41. Dorson, *Negro Folktales in Michigan*, pp. 90-94.

42. Leonard Roberts, *Up Cutshin and Down Greasy* (Lexington: University of Kentucky Press, 1959).

43. Barrett, *Tales from the Fens*, pp. 148-149.

44. *The Dewar Manuscripts*, vol. 1, *Scottish West Highland Folk Tales*, ed. John MacKechnie (Glasgow: William MacLellan, 1964).

45. Gladys-Marie Fry, *Night Riders in Black Folk History* (Knoxville: University of Tennessee Press, 1975).

46. Barbro Klein, "The Testimony of the Button," in Dorson, *Folklore and Traditional History*, pp. 55-74.

47. Walter Goldschmidt, George Foster, and Frank Essene, "War Stories from Two Enemy Tribes," *Journal of American Folklore* 3 (1939): 141-154.

48. Richard A. Gould, "Indian and White Versions of 'The Burnt Ranch Massacre,' " *Journal of the Folklore Institute* 3 (1966): 30-42.

49. Lord Raglan, *The Hero: A Study in Tradition, Myth and Drama* (New York: Oxford University Press, 1937).

50. Louis Dupree, "The Retreat of the British Army from Kabul to Jalalabad in 1842: History and Folklore," *Journal of the Folklore Institute* 4 (1967): 50-74.

Sources for the Traditional History of the
Scottish Highlands and Western Islands

1. Numbers in parentheses refer to the catalogue entries for cited tape recordings in the School of Scottish Studies, Edinburgh. I am grateful to the staff of the School for their generous assistance on this project, which depended in large part on their resources.

2. For variants told me by a Maine lobsterman and a French-Canadian widow in upper Michigan see Richard M. Dorson, *Buying the Wind* (Chicago: University of Chicago Press, 1964), pp. 87-88, and "Aunt-Jane Goudreau, Roup-Garou Storyteller," *Western Folklore* 6 (1947): 27. Aili Johnson has given me an unpublished text of types 1281A + 1739 collected from a Finnish informant in Ohio.

3. John Prebble, *Glencoe: The Story of the Massacre* (London: Secker and Warburg, 1966), pp. 231-232, 245.

4. *Ibid.*, pp. 222, 238, 240, 246.

5. *The Dewar Manuscripts*, vol. 1, *Scottish West Highland Folk Tales*, collected originally in Gaelic by John Dewar, translated into English by Hector MacLean, edited with introduction and notes by the Reverend John MacKechnie (Glasgow: William MacLellan, 1964). Regrettably the editor has deferred providing information about the tradition tellers and given no explanations for the order and arrangement of the volume. Campbell of Islay furnished a table giving useful data on the narrators of his *Popular Tales of the West Highlands*.

6. MacKechnie cites Alwyn and Brinley Rees, *Celtic Heritage* (London: Thames and Hudson, 1961), pp. 225 ff., and B. Z. Goldberg, *The Sacred Fire* (London: Jarrolds, 1931), p. 51.

7. Richard M. Dorson, "Negro Folksongs in Michigan from the Repertoire of J. D. Suggs," *Folklore and Folk Music Archivist* 9 (1966): 11-13.

8. Alasdair Alpin MacGregor, *The Peat-Fire Flame* (Edinburgh and London: Ettrick, 1947), p. 312.

9. John Lorne Campbell, ed., *Tales of Barra Told by the Coddy* (Edinburgh: printed by W. and A. K. Johnston and G. W. Bacon, 1960), pp. 26-27.

10. *Ibid.*, pp. 81-88.

11. John Francis Campbell, *More West Highland Tales*, transcribed and translated by John G. McKay, ed. W. J. Watson and H. J. Rose (Edinburgh and London: Oliver and Boyd, 1940), p. 394.

12. *Tales of Barra*, p. 91.

13. *Ibid.*, pp. 95-97.

14. Angus MacLellan, *Stories from South Uist*, tr. John Lorne Campbell (London: Routledge and Kegan Paul, 1961), p. 84.

15. *Tales of Barra*, pp. 63, 66.

16. MacLellan, *Stories from South Uist*, no. 35.

17. *Tales of Barra*, pp. 141-143. Cf. Richard M. Dorson, *American Negro Folktales* (New York: Fawcett, 1967), p. 376, no. 243, "The Irishman and the Frogs."

18. Some of these motifs are identified in the discussion of Hugh Miller in Richard M. Dorson, *The British Folklorists: A History* (Chicago: University of Chicago Press, 1968), pp. 146-149.

19. In a contract research report prepared in 1961 for the Indian Land Claims section of the Department of Justice, United States Government, on "The Historical Validity of Oral Tradition."

In the Field

1. C. Vann Woodward, review of Shelby Foote, *The Civil War: A Narrative*, vol. 3, in *New York Review of Books* 22 (6 March 1975): 12.

2. For folkloric collections and analyses of Jewish dialect stories see Richard M. Dorson, "Jewish-American Dialect Stories on Tape," in Raphael Patai, Francis Lee Utley, and Dov Nov, eds., *Studies in Biblical and Jewish Folklore*, Indiana University Folklore Series, No. 13 (Bloomington, 1960), pp. 111-174; Richard M. Dorson, "More Jewish Dialect Stories," *Midwest Folklore* 10 (1960): 133-146; Ed Cray, "The Rabbi Trickster," *Journal of American Folklore* 77 (1964): 331-345; Naomi Katz and Eli Katz, "Tradition and Adaptation in American Jewish Humor," *Journal of American Folklore* 84 (1971): 215-220; Dan Ben-Amos, "The 'Myth' of Jewish Folklore," *Western Folklore* 32 (1973): 112-131.

3. "Danish Dialect Stories of the Mormon Church" as told by Hector Lee, in R. M. Dorson, *Buying the Wind* (Chicago: University of Chicago Press, 1965), pp. 515-520.

4. Here is a text told me by Austin Fife. Juan is sitting in the plaza under the hot noonday sun, his back propped against a tree, his head resting on his arms, his arms resting on his knees, his sombrero tipped back on his head. Pedro wanders into the plaza, resplendent in military uniform, beribboned and bemedaled. "Hello, Pedro, where you've been?" asks Juan [high singsong voice]. "I've been in de war, I've got maddles, Juan." "For what you've got maddles, Pedro?" "I got maddles for gonnery [gunnery]." "Dat's fonny, I've got gonnery and I ain't got no maddles."

Collecting in County Kerry

1. See Caoimhín Ó Danachair, "Irish Folk Narrative on South Re-

cords," *Laos* 1 (1951): 180-186; J. H. Delargy, "The Gaelic Story-Teller," *Proceedings of the British Academy* 31 (1945): 177-221; Seamus Ó Duilearge (idem), "Irish Stories and Storytellers," *Studies* 31 (1942): 31-46; David O'Neill, "Voices of Remote Time," *Columbia* (September 1951): 5, 23-24, and condensed as "The Ancient Voice of Ireland," *Catholic Digest* 16 (November 1951): 50-54; Francis Shaw, "The Irish Folklore Commission," *Studies* 33 (1944): 30-44; Stith Thompson, "Folktale Collecting in Ireland," *Southern Folklore Quarterly* 2 (1938): 53-58. The present article was written in 1953.

2. George W. Potter, *An Irish Pilgrimage* (Providence: Providence Journal Co., 1950). For a purely folklore work by Alfred Williams see *Studies in Folksong and Popular Poetry*, with a prefatory note by Edward Clodd (London, 1895).

3. Translated from Tadhg Ó Murchadha, "Béaloideas ó Uibh Ráthach," *Béaloideas* 8 (1938): 178-179 ("Folklore from Iubh Rathack"—a barony in southwest Kerry). The belief in "overlooking" in Ireland and Gaelic Scotland has deep roots and a wide acceptance. It can be found in the pre-Christian legend of Balor that still survives orally; A. H. Krappe, *Balor with the Evil Eye* (New York: Columbia University Press, 1927), p. 9. For collections of Irish and Scottish evil-eye stories see Lady Gregory, *Visions and Beliefs in the West of Ireland*, 2d ser. (New York and London: Putnam's, 1920), I, 127-166, "The Evil Eye—the Touch—the Penalty"; Lady Wilde, *Ancient Legends, Mystic Charms, and Superstitions of Ireland*, 2 vols. (Boston, 1887), I, 36-48, "The Evil Eye"; R. C. Maclaglan, *Evil Eye in the Western Highlands* (London: David Nutt, 1902). These collectors agree that the action of the evil eye is often independent of the will of the possessor (Gregory, I, 131-132; Wilde, I, 43; Maclaglan, p. 35). A superb series of verbal charms to banish the evil eye can be found in Alexander Carmichael, *Carmina Gadelica: Hymns and Incantations with illustrative notes on words, rites, and customs, dying and obsolete: orally collected in the Highlands and Islands of Scotland and translated into English* (Edinburgh: Norman Macleod, 1900), II, 43 ff. Maclaglan, in *Evil Eye*, found that more "overlooking" stories dealt with cattle than with any other beasts (pp. 53-61); for the idea of banishing the evil to another spot see p. 214, "Putting Elsewhere."

4. Maclaglan, *Evil Eye*, p. 88, "Conversion to Belief in Evil Eye"; Lady Gregory, *Visions and Beliefs* I, 134, gives practically the same episode.

5. Dennis Casey, like Stephen O'Shea, is a charm-setter, with power to counteract the overlooker; cf. Maclaglan, *Evil Eye*, p. 98, "Hurter and Healer."

6. This anecdote specifies the words of the evil-dispelling prayer. Cf. Maclaglan, *Evil Eye*, p. 104, "Forms of Incantation"; he refers to W. Mackenzie, *Gaelic Incantations, with Translations* (Inverness, 1895). James Napier, *Folk Lore: Or, Superstitious Beliefs in the West of Scotland within this Century* (Paisley, 1879), pp. 36-37, gives a detailed ritual to remove "a blink of an ill e'e," known as *scoring aboon the breath*.

7. Lady Wilde, *Ancient Legends*, I, 37-38, tells of a nameless man with so powerful an evil eye his neighbors compelled him to wear a black patch over it; to help a weeping boy whose pet pigeon had flown to the top of a castle, he removed the patch, gazed at the pigeon, and caused it to fall unharmed to the ground. Black, *Folk Medicine*, pp. 21-22, cities a Lancashire man whose glances withered a pear tree.

8. These samples of demonic legends bear out the assertion of Douglas Hyde that the Devil and witches, so prevalent in England and on the Continent, rarely appear in Ireland, which has its own special creatures; *Legends of Saints and Sinners*, coll. and trans. from the Irish by Douglas Hyde (Dublin, Cork and Belfast, n.d.), p. ix. Yeats also remarks on the absence of Devil-compact stories; Lady Gregory, *Visions and Beliefs*, I, 276, n. 11.

9. Translated from *Béaloideas* 8 (1938): 176, see n. 7. The informant was an 83-year-old native of Call-a-ghoirtan. Cf. Séan O Súilleabháin (O'Sullivan), *A Handbook of Irish Folklore* (Dublin: Folklore of Ireland Society, 1942), p. 482, "Spirits in Female Form." In "Saved by a Pipe," in *Peasant Lore from Gaelic Ireland*, collected by Daniel Deeny (London, 1890), pp. 19-22, Charley Ann tells how his father met a stranger on horseback late at night, to whom he gave a pipe of tobacco, mentioning God's name, whereon he disappeared in a lump of fire, shortly reappearing, however, to save him from a hideous thing that jumped on his mare.

10. T. Crofton Croker first introduced the "Phooka" (sic) to English readers ("The Spirit Horse,") in *Fairy Legends and Traditions of the South of Ireland*, ed. Thomas Wright, 5th ed. (London, 1898), pp. 130-135. Yeats thus describes him: "The Pooka, *rectè Púca*, seems essentially an animal spirit. . . . He has many shapes—is now a horse, now an ass, now a bull, now a goat, now an eagle. Like all spirits, he is only half in the world of form"; *Irish Fairy and Folk Tales*, ed. W. B. Yeats (New York: Modern Library, n.d.), p. 100. Yeats prints two pooka stories: "The Piper and the Púca," pp. 101-103, an original Gaelic tale translated by Douglas Hyde, in which the Púca teaches a semi-idiot to play the pipes; and "The Kildare Pooka," pp. 112-115, reprinted from Patrick Kennedy, *Legendary Fictions of the Irish Celts* (London, 1866), in which the pooka resembles the Scandinavian house goblin. Similarly, Lady Wilde's "The Phouka" (*Ancient Legends* I, 87-90) follows the formula of the fairy helper who ceases domestic work when rewarded with fine clothes. Kennedy in his original note (p. 126) recognized the un-Irish character of the Kildare pooka, but his story of "The Pooka of Murroe" (pp. 124-126), in which an aerial he-goat drops on a benighted traveler, runs to form. See also Ó Súilleabháin's *Handbook*, pp. 485-486. In *Irish Popular Superstitions* (Dublin, 1852), p. 14, W. R. Wilde refers to the belief that the "pooca" defiles the blackberries as he rides over them at Michaelmas and Holly-eve. Popularized collections containing pooka stories are D. R. McAnally, *Irish Wonders* (Boston and New York, 1888), pp. 17-35, "Taming the Pooka"; Barry O'Connor, *Turf-Fire Stories and Fairy Tales of Ireland* (New York, 1890), pp. 305-311,

"The Phooka"; John O'Hanlon, *Irish Folk Lore* (Glasgow and London, 1870), pp. 20-29, "Lackeen Castle, O'Kennedy, and the Phooka."

11. The fairy shoemaker appears under various similar names. Croker called him the Cluricaune (*Fairy Legends,* pp. 127-219); Lady Wilde, the Leprehaun (*Ancient Legends* I, 103-105); Kennedy, the Lurikeen (*Legendary Fictions,* pp. 130-131); Tobias Kavanagh, the Luaracans in his series of Kilkenny folktales, *Béaloideas* 2 (1929): 16-17. Kavanagh gives nine references, in English and Gaelic. Other names are given in Ó Súilleabháin's *Handbook,* p. 492.

12. The informant, an 86-year-old native of Ardgroon, County Cork, told Tadhg this story on September 17, 1951. As Lady Wilde explains this type of tradition, "The souls of the dead who may happen to die abroad greatly desire to rest in Ireland. And the relations deem it their duty to bring back the body to be laid in Irish earth. But even the dead will not rest peaceably unless laid with their forefathers and their own people, and not amongst strangers" (*Ancient Legends* I, 153). Cf. Ó Súilleabháin's *Handbook,* pp. 491-492, "Supernatural Funerals"; Caoimhín Ó Danachair, "The Funeral Path," *Béaloideas* 17 (1947): 224; Deeney, *Peasant Lore,* pp. 8-11, "A Midnight Funeral."

13. This fragmentary tale belongs to the cycle of fairy traditions involving the Magic Ointment, discussed by E. S. Hartland in *The Science of Fairy Tales* (London: Methuen, 1925), pp. 59 ff.

14. As the *Handbook* points out, "In Irish tradition the dead and the fairies appear to be inextricably mingled. People who tell stories about them are not always quite clear as to whether the fairies or the dead are being spoken of" (Ó Súilleabháin, pp. 245-246). See *ibid.,* "The Return of the Dead," pp. 244-250, esp. p. 247, "Dead Seek Help"; Yeats, *Irish Fairy and Folk Tales,* pp. 139-155, "Ghosts"; Jeremiah Curtin, *Tales of the Fairies and of the Ghost-World* (London, 1895); Kennedy, *Legendary Fictions,* pp. 180-192.

15. The cycle of London Bridge legends was treated at length by George Laurence Gomme in *Folklore as an Historical Science* (London: Methuen, 1908), pp. 13-33, in an attempt to prove the ancient importance of London as reflected in folk tradition. He gives no Irish examples, although the legend gets attached to many bridges. See Antti Aarne and Stith Thompson, *The Types of the Folk-Tale* (Helsinki: Suomalainen Tiedeakatemia, 1928), no. 1645, "The Treasure at Home." Close parallels that contain the final episode of the poor scholar are Caoimhín Ó Danachair, "The Hidden Treasure," *Béaloideas* 17 (1947): 222-223, which also refers to Balls (sic) Bridge, Limerick; and Lady Gregory, *Visions and Beliefs* II, 35. Cf. also Croker, *Fairy Legends,* pp. 293-304, "Dreaming Tim Jarvis"; Padraig Ó Tuathail, "The Crock of Gold," *Béaloideas* 7 (1937): 75-76.

16. See Ó Súilleabháin's *Handbook,* p. 521, under "Historical Tradition—Individual Personages—Oliver Cromwell."

17. This type of Indo-European humorous story was treated at length by W. A. Clouston in *The Book of Noodles* (London, 1888).

18. This tale has been reprinted in Sean O'Sullivan, *Folktales of Ireland* (Chicago: University of Chicago Press, 1966), no. 38, for which I supplied the following note, pp. 278-279: "A rich legend complex lies behind Séan Palmer's narrative. The theme of a visit to a foreign country with the fairies is represented in a separate file of the archives of the Irish Folklore Commission, clasified as the 'Hie over to England (London, Dublin, Paris, Spain, Scotland, etc.)' type. An early chapbook version, 'Manus O'Mallaghan and the Fairies,' is reprinted in 'The Royal Hibernian Tales,' *Béaloideas* 10 (1941): 172-175. Manus visited both Spain and Rome and was granted a request by the Pope. Other printed texts are in B. Hunt, 'The Voice at the Door,' *Folk Tales of Breffny* (London: Macmillan, 1912), pp. 137-142, in which an Irish youth, abducted by the fairies because of his fine singing voice, says he has seen America, France, and Spain; Seumas Mac Manus 'The Adventurer,' *Bold Blades of Donegal* (London, n.d.), ch. 13, pp. 138-150, in which the fairies take an Irish lad to Philadelphia (where he buys tobacco), then to China and Spain; Philip Dixon Hardy, 'Hie over to England,' *Legends, Tales, and Stories of Ireland* (Dublin, 1837), pp. 134-148, where an Irish mason flies with the fairies to Lancashire and as in the preceding tale, saves himself from hanging by putting on his red cap, which transports him home; Patrick Kennedy, *Legendary Fictions of the Irish Celts* (London, 1891), pp. 148-150, condensed version of the above; Patrick Kennedy, 'Tom Kiernan's Visit to France,' *The Fireside Stories of Ireland* (Dublin, 1870), pp. 144-145, where an Irish servant boy brings back a goblet from a French wine cellar."

Tales of Two Lobstermen

1. Leonard Roberts, *South from Hell-fer-Sartin* (Lexington: University of Kentucky Press, 1955); Marie Campbell, *Tales from the Cloud Walking Country* (Bloomington: Indiana University Press, 1958); Richard Chase, *The Jack Tales* (Boston: Houghton Mifflin, 1943), and *Grandfather Tales* (Boston: Houghton Mifflin, 1948).

2. These four texts are printed in Richard M. Dorson, "Collecting Folklore in Jonesport, Maine," *Proceedings of the American Philosophical Society* 101 (1957): 288 f., with a fifth anecdote about Captain Horace by another informant, Stuart Alley.

3. Examples of this tale are in the Indiana University Folklore Archives.

4. Two texts are printed in Dorson, "Collecting Folklore in Jonesport, Maine," p. 279.

5. Richard M. Dorson, *Bloodstoppers and Bearwalkers* (Cambridge, Mass.: Harvard University Press, 1952), p. 145.

6. Ernest W. Baughman and Clayton A. Holaday, "Tall Tales and

'Seils' from Indiana University Students," *Hoosier Folklore Bulletin* 3 (1944): 68-69, no. 18.

7. The texts mentioned above are printed in Richard M. Dorson, "Mishaps of a Maine Lobsterman," *Northeast Folklore* 1 (Spring 1958): 1-7.

8. References are given in my *Negro Folktales in Michigan* (Cambridge, Mass.: Harvard University Press, 1956), pp. 229-230, no. 147.

9. Dorson, "Collecting Folklore in Jonesport, Maine," pp. 276, 283.

Comic Indian Anecdotes

1. Albert Keiser, *The Indian in American Literature* (New York: Oxford University Press, 1933). Stith Thompson, *Tales of the North American Indians* (Cambridge, Mass.: Harvard University Press, 1928). Constance Rourke, *The Roots of American Culture* (New York: Harcourt, Brace, 1942), pp. 60-75. See also Roy Harvey Pearce, *Savagism and Civilization: A Study of the Indian and the American Mind* (Baltimore: Johns Hopkins Press, 1965).

2. George Catlin, *Illustrations of the Manners, Customs, and Condition of the North American Indians*, 10th ed. (London, 1866), I, 84-85. Peter Martyr quoted in John T. Lanning, *The Spanish Missions of Georgia* (Chapel Hill: University of North Carolina Press, 1935), pp. 29-30. Charles Waterton, *Wanderings in South America* (London, 1836), p. 38. John Lawson, *A New Voyage to Carolina* (London, 1709), quoted in William M. Smallwood, *Natural History and the American Mind* (New York: Columbia University Press, 1941), p. 22. "Sam Hide," in the *Rutland Herald* 12 January 1835, credited to the *Norfolk Advertiser*.

3. The Maushop legend is in Alice A. Ryder, *Lands of Sippican on Buzzards Bay* (New Bedford, Mass.: Reynolds Printing, 1934), pp. 5-6; *Gazette of Maine*, 13 January 1971, "Origin of the Island of Nantucket: An Indian Tradition"; and *Journal of American Folklore* 11 (1898): 162, and 54 (1941): 83. The Big Bear story is from "Indian Fun," in Francis Chase, ed., *Gathered Sketches from the Early History of New Hampshire and Vermont* (Claremont, N.H., 1856), pp. 97-98. The Deacon Nauhaught story is in Charles F. Swift, *History of Old Yarmouth* (Yarmouth Port, 1884), pp. 171-173.

4. General Wayne tale in George Turner, *Traits of Indian Character; as generally applicable to the aborigines of North America. Drawn from various sources;—partly from personal observation of the writer*, 2 vols. (Philadelphia, 1836), I, 28. Whitejohn tale in Samuel G. Drake, *The Book of the Indians*, 9th ed. (Boston, 1845), p. 18, credited to the *Universal Museum* for 1763. Rum and cider tale in Nathan Daboll, *The New-England Almanack, 1804* (New London, n.d.); Robert B. Thomas, *The Farmer's Almanac, 1815* (Boston, n.d.). Metallak tale in Ernest E. Bisbee, *The White Mountain Scrap Book* (Lancaster, N.H.: Bisbee, 1939). John Tutson tale in Turner, *Traits of Indian Character*, I, 62-63; and Drake, *The Book of the Indians*, p. 27.

5. Joseph O. Goodwin, *East Hartford: Its History and Traditions* (Hartford, 1879), p. 36.

6. Mug of flip tale from "An Indian's Joke," in *Indian Anecdotes*, a sixteen-page booklet, with no given author or place or date of publication; a copy is in the Houghton Library of Harvard University. Grand Rapids tale in Charles S. Larzelere, *The Story of Michigan* (Lansing: Michigan Education Company, 1928), p. 214, quoting from the *Michigan Pioneer and Historical Society Collections* 30 (1906): 187, Dwight Goss, "The Indians of the Grand River Valley." Potawatomi warrior tale in Turner, *Traits of Indian Character*, I, 33-34. Portland, Michigan, tale in Franklin Everett, *Memorials of the Grand River Valley* (Chicago, 1878), p. 297.

7. Samuel Peters, *General History of Connecticut* (New York, 1877), pp. 115-118. William Cothren, *History of Ancient Woodbury, Connecticut* (Woodbury, 1872), II, 883-884.

8. Pima tale in Jay J. Woodman, *Indian Legends: being a choice collection of the best legends, stories and traditions as told by the warrior and the squaw to the papoose and showing how the young Indian of the olden time was educated* (Boston: Stratford, 1906), p. 686. Scalping tale in Turner, *Traits of Indian Character*, I, 163-164. Buffalo Bill tale in Norman B. Wood, *Lives of Famous Indian Chiefs* (Aurora, Ill.: American Indian Historical Publishing Co., 1906), p. 686.

9. Kiskauko tale in Turner, *Traits of Indian Character*, I, 40-41. "Me all face" tale in William C. Hatch, *A History of the Town of Industry, Franklin County, Maine* (Farmington, Maine, 1893), p. 272; Vinal A. Houghton, *The Story of an Old New England Town* (Wilton, Maine: Nelson, 1926), p. 24; and Turner, *Traits of Indian Character*, II, 35, credited to Timothy Flint, "Sketches of Indian Character," in the *Western Monthly Review*; and see Cecily Hancock, "The 'Me All Face' Story: European Literary Background of an American Comic Indian Anecdote," *Journal of American Folklore* 76 (1963): 340-342. "Me no work now" story told by Walter Gries in a talk before the Rotary Club of Lansing, Michigan, Nov. 30, 1945, on "Legends and Lore of the Upper Peninsula."

10. Turner, *Traits of Indian Character*, I, 33. *John Long's Voyages and Travels in the Years 1787-1788*, ed. Milo M. Quaife (Chicago: R. R. Donnelley and Sons, 1922), pp. 205-206.

11. *Boston Evening Post*, 2 August 1736.

12. Skeleton tale in Turner, *Traits of Indian Character*, II, 15. Susquehanna Indian story in *ibid.*, II, 20-21. Father Abraham story in *John Long's Voyages and Travels*, pp. 38-39, from Peter Kalm's Travels; *The American Magazine of Wit* (New York, 1808), pp. 19-20. For the Adario motif see Percy G. Adams, *Travelers and Travel Liars 1660-1800* (Berkeley: University of California Press, 1962), pp. 199-201.

13. Deceptive land purchase story in Mabel Burkholder, *Before the*

White Man Came: Indian Legends and Stories (Toronto: McClelland and Stewart, 1923), pp. 20, 23; and Woodman, *Indian Legends*, p. 9.

14. Dream contest in *The Merry Fellow's Companion; or American Jest Book* (Harrisburgh, 1797), p. 26; *John Long's Voyages and Travels*, pp. 112-113; and *The Percy Anecdotes*, II, 24-25, "Dreaming Match."

15. Log splitter story in *The Percy Anecdotes*, rev. ed. *To which is added a valuable collection of American Anecdotes, original and select*, 2 vols. (New York, 1845), II, 135-136; and Earl Newton, "Lovewell's 'Capture,' " *Granite Monthly* 57 (April 1925): 169-170. Yankee trick story in Woodman, *Indian Legends*, p. 145.

16. Headwork story in *The American Jest Book* (Harrisburgh, 1796), p. 12; and *The Child's Picture Book of Indians* (Boston, 1833), pp. 87-89. Gunpowder Harvest story in Drake, *The Book of the Indians*, p. 21; and *The Percy Anecdotes*, II, 84. Ouiattanon story in Turner, *Traits of Indian Character*, I, 139.

17. Sam Hide story in Drake, *The Book of the Indians*, pp. 21-22; *The American Jest Book*, pp. 5-6; *Gazette of Maine*, 13 January 1791; *The Child's Picture Book of Indians*, pp. 115-116; *Rutland Herald*, 12 January 1835; and Wood, *Lives of Famous Indian Chiefs*, pp. 700, 703.

18. Sane-day story in *Indian Legends*, by Pupils of Haskell Institute, United States Indian Training School (Lawrence, Kans., 1914), pp. 37-38, "Indian and White Man," by John Bosin, a Kiowa.

19. Receipt story from "The Indian Receipt," in Robert B. Thomas, *The Farmer's Almanac, 1809* (Boston, n.d.). Genesis story in *The Child's Picture Book of Indians*, pp. 44-46.

20. Wood, *Lives of Famous Indian Chiefs*, pp. 698-699; as told by Black Horse, second chief of the Comanches, to an Indian Agent.

21. Edmund Fuller, ed., *Thesaurus of Anecdotes* (New York: Crown, 1942), pp. 460-461.

22. Federal Writers' Project, *New Hampshire: A Guide to the Granite State* (Boston: Houghton Mifflin, 1938), p. 119.

23. Fuller, *Thesaurus of Anecdotes*, p. 162; Powers Moulton, *2500 Jokes for All Occasions* (New York: New Home Library, 1942), p. 49.

24. Wood, *Lives of Famous Indian Chiefs*, p. 716.

25. *The American Magazine of Wit*, pp. 49-50.

26. Wood, *Lives of Famous Indian Chiefs*, p. 683.

27. Captain Johnny story in Edward Eggleston and Lillie E. Seelye, *Tecumseh and the Shawnee Prophet* (New York, 1878), p. 265. Chickasaw story in Turner, *Traits of Indian Character*, I, 40.

28. Ysabel F. Rennie, *The Argentine Republic* (New York: Macmillan, 1945), p. 12.

29. Chokun story in John C. Wright, *The Crooked Tree: Indian Legends and a Short History of the Little Traverse Bay Region*, 3rd ed. (Harbor Springs, Mich.: J. C. Wright, 1917), pp. 90-93, "Outwitting a White Man."

Courtship story in Woodman, *Indian Legends,* p. 54. Second courtship story in *Rutland Herald,* 9 May 1837, "Indian Marriage Promise."'

30. Thomas B. Williams, *The Soul of the Red Man* (n.p., 1937), p. 392.

The Career of John Henry

1. Bascom, "Ballads and Songs of Western North Carolina," *Journal of American Folklore* 22 (1909): 249. Perrow, "Songs and Rhymes from the South," *ibid.* 26 (1913): 163-165. John Lomax, "Some Types of American Folk-Song," *ibid.* 28 (1915): 14.

2. John Harrington Cox, "John Hardy," *Journal of American Folklore* 32 (1919): 505-520; and *Folk-Songs of the South* (Cambridge, Mass.: Harvard University Press, 1925), pp. 175-188. The same identification of John Henry with John Hardy was made by Dorothy Scarborough, *On the Trail of Negro Folk-Songs* (Cambridge, Mass.: Harvard University Press, 1925), pp. 218-222.

3. Newman I. White, *American Negro Folk-Songs* (Cambridge, Mass.: Harvard University Press, 1928), pp. 189-191, "John Henry."

4. Howard Odum and Guy B. Johnson, *Negro Workaday Songs* (Chapel Hill: University of North Carolina Press, 1926).

5. Louis W. Chappell, *John Henry: A Folklore Study* (Jena: Frommann-sche Verlag, Walter Biedermann). Between the two monographic studies of Johnson and Chappell, various related items were published. Chappell demanded an explanation from Johnson in *American Speech* 6 (December 1930): 144 ff. Lowry C. Wimberly wrote a note in admiration of Johnson's *John Henry* and praised the ballad as great literature, for its theme "of the individual pitting his lone strength and courage against an environment" and "its ringing hammer music" and portrayal of "the struggle of sentient humanity against the unfeeling machine" (B. A. Botkin, ed., *Folk-Say, a Regional Miscellany* [Norman: Oklahoma Folk-Lore Society, 1930], "Steel-Drivin' Man," pp. 413-415). Gordon H. Gerould in *The Ballad of Tradition* (Oxford: Clarendon, 1932), pp. 264-268, discussed the confusion of "John Henry" with "John Hardy," speculated that "John Henry" was of Negro origin, and reprinted a 22-stanza text from Johnson, pp. 289-292. Louise Pound lauded Johnson's *John Henry* in her review in the *Journal of American Folklore* 43 (1930): 126-127.

6. Johnson, *John Henry,* p. 150.

7. Roark Bradford and Jacques Wolfe, *John Henry: A Play* (New York and London: Harper, 1939). Josh White played the part of Blind Lemon, a folksinger, and in his twenty-fifth anniversary album (ca. 1955) recorded "The Story of John Henry," based on songs in the stage production (Elektra Records 123-A).

8. *Time* and *Newsweek* carried notices on January 22, 1940, and *Thea-*

tre Arts in its March 1940 issue (vol. 24, pp. 166-167). Roark Bradford wrote a piece for *Collier's* on "Paul Robeson in John Henry" (January 13, 1940): 105 f.

9. Odum and Johnson, *Negro Workaday Songs*, p. 221; Carl Sandburg, *The American Songbag* (New York: Harcourt, Brace, 1927), p. 24 ("In southern work camp gangs, John Henry is the strong man, or the ridiculous man, or anyhow the man worth talking about, having a myth character somewhat like that of Paul Bunyan in work gangs of the Big Woods of the North"); R. M. Dorson, "Paul Bunyan in the News, 1939-1941," *Western Folklore* 15 (1956): 193, citing newspaper notices of the Bradford-Wolfe music-drama in which John Henry was likened to Paul Bunyan.

10. The chapter, "John Henry, the Steel Driving Man," in Frank Shay, *Here's Audacity!* (New York: Macaulay, 1930), pp. 245-253, was based on Guy B. Johnson's chapter "John Henry: A Negro Legend," in Charles S. Johnson, ed., *Ebony and Topaz: A Collectanea* (New York: Opportunity, National Urban League, 1927), pp. 47-51. The titles in juvenile works are Carl Carmer, *The Hurricane's Children* (New York and Toronto: Farrar and Rinehart, 1937), "How John Henry Beat the Steam Drill Down," pp. 122-128; Olive Beaupré Miller, *Heroes, Outlaws and Funny Fellows* (New York: Doubleday, Doran, 1939), "John Henry's Contest with the Big Steam Drill," pp. 147-157; Anne Malcolmson, *Yankee Doodle's Cousins* (Boston: Houghton Mifflin, 1941), "John Henry," pp. 101-107; Carl Carmer, *America Sings* (New York: Knopf, 1942), "John Henry," pp. 174-179; Walter Blair, *Tall Tale America* (New York: Coward-McCann, 1944), "John Henry and the Machine in West Virginia," pp. 203-219; Maria Leach, *The Rainbow Book of American Folk Tales and Legends* (Cleveland and New York: World, 1958), "John Henry," pp. 33-35.

11. One such volume, *Their Weight in Wildcats* (Boston: 1946), carried only the name of the illustrator, James Daugherty, on the title page. This selection of reprinted hero tales was made by an editor, Paul Brooks, at Houghton Mifflin, the publisher. For John Henry he reprinted the statements of one of Guy B. Johnson's informants, Leon R. Harris of Moline, Illinois. Brooks saw in John Henry only "brute strength and dumb courage" (p. 170).

12. B. A. Botkin, *A Treasury of American Folklore* (New York: Crown, 1944), pp. 230-240; *A Treasury of Southern Folklore* (New York: Crown, 1949), pp. 748-749; *A Treasury of Railroad Folklore* (New York: Crown, 1953), pp: 402-405. The Editors of Life, *Life Treasury of American Folklore* (New York: 1961), pp. 168-169. Other popular publications to retell the story of John Henry and reprint a ballad text are Freeman H. Hubbard, *Railroad Avenue* (New York: McGraw Hill, 1945), pp. 58-64, "The Mighty Jawn Henry"; Langston Hughes and Arna Bontemps, eds., *The Book of Negro Folklore* (New York: Dodd, Mead, 1958), "John Henry," pp. 345-347; *American Heritage* 14 (October 1963): 34-37, 95, Bernard Asbell, "A Man Ain't Nothin' but a Man."

13. Alan Lomax, *The Folk Songs of North America* (New York: Double-day, 1960), pp. 551-553. For the work song, cf. Chappell, p. 99. Support for Lomax's position is given by Roger D. Abrahams in his note and ballad text on John Henry as a sexual hero of South Philadelphia Negroes; *Deep Down in the Jungle* (Hatboro, Pa.: Folklore Associates, 1964), p. 80. John Greenway, *American Folksongs of Protest* (Philadelphia: University of Pennsylvania Press), p. 107; reprinted as paperback by A. S. Barnes and Co. (Perpetua edition, 1960).

14. Odum and Johnson, *Negro Workaday Songs*, pp. 238-240. There is no connection between the trickster John cycle and John Henry, as Alan Lomax suggests (*Folk Songs of North America*, p. 553). For folktales of John the slave and his Old Marster, see R. M. Dorson, *Negro Folktales in Michigan* (Cambridge, Mass.: Harvard University Press, 1956), ch. 4, and *Negro Tales from Pine Bluff, Arkansas, and Calvin, Michigan* (Bloomington: Indiana University Press, 1958), pp. 43-62.

15. W. C. Hendricks, ed., *Bundle of Troubles and Other Tarheel Tales* (Durham, N.C.: Duke University Press, 1943), pp. 37-51, "John Henry of the Cape Fear" (told by Glasgow McLeod to T. Pat Matthews). Hurston, *Mules and Men* (Philadelphia and London: Lippincott, 1935), p. 306; she prints nine "verses of John Henry, the king of railroad track-laying songs," pp. 80-81, 309-312.

16. Information on copyrighted John Henry songs was kindly supplied to me by Joseph C. Hickerson, Reference Librarian in the Archive of Folk Song, Library of Congress. Field-collected texts are reported by G. Malcolm Laws, *Native American Balladry* (Philadelphia: American Folklore Society, 1950), p. 231. "John Henry" is 11 in his index. He refers to thirty-nine recordings from eleven states and the District of Columbia in the Library of Congress folksong archives, including five releases. He cites, in addition to works already mentioned, Mellinger E. Henry, *Folk-Songs from the Southern Highlands* (New York: J. J. Augustin, 1938), pp. 441-442, 446-448, for a text and many references. In *Folk-Songs of Virginia, A Descriptive Index and Classification* (Durham, N.C.: Duke University Press, 1949), p. 294, Arthur K. Davis lists six John Henry texts collected between 1932 and 1934. Only one full text of eight stanzas is presented in *The Frank C. Brown Collection of North Carolina Folklore*, vol. 2, *Folk Ballads* (Durham, N.C.: Duke University Press, 1952), pp. 623-627. The editors, H. M. Belden and A. P. Hudson, say, "Few if any folk songs of American origin have been so extensively and intensively studied as John Henry." Some representative examples of commercially released "John Henry" recordings currently available, which appear indebted at least indirectly to traditional southern Appalachian sources, are Laurel River Valley Boys, *Music for Moonshiners* (Judson L3031); Mainer's Mountaineers, *Good Ole Mountain Music* (King 666); Bill Monroe and His Blue Grass Boys, *New John Henry Blues* (Decca 45-31540); George Pegram and Walter Parham, *Banjo Songs from the Southern Mountains* (Riverside

RLP 12-610); Harry Smith, *Anthology of American Folk Song* (Folkways; rerecordings of early hillbilly and race records), No. 18, Williamson Brothers and Curry, "Gonna Die with my Hammer in my Hand," and No. 80, Mississippi John Hurt, "Spike Driver Blues"; Merle Travis, *Back Home* (Capital T891). Neil Rosenberg and Mayne Smith kindly furnished me information for this list from their personal record collections.

17. Philips Barry, review of L. W. Chappell, *John Henry*, in *Bulletin of the Folk-Song Society of the Northeast* 8 (1934): 24-26. As further evidence of "non-tunnel" influences, Barry cites a "John Hardy" tune transferred to "John Henry" but known only to white mountaineers.

18. That new surprises are still possible in the career of John Henry was shown in the remarkable paper by MacEdward Leach presented at the regional meeting of the American Folklore Society at Duke University on April 23, 1964, "John Henry in Jamaica," suggesting the possibility that the tradition originated among Jamaican Negroes.

Paul Bunyan in the News

1. St. Paul *Sunday Pioneer Press*, 10 January 1937.

2. Bozeman, Mont., *Chronicle*, 22 January 1939.

3. Milwaukee *Sentinel*, 13 February 1939.

4. *Denver Post*, 6 August 1939; and Seattle *Times*, same day, by C. S. Van Dresser.

5. Oakland, Calif., *Tribune*, 1 September 1939.

6. San Francisco *News*, 29 August 1939. San Francisco *Call-Bulletin*, 2 September 1939.

7. Concord *Daily Monitor and N.H. Patriot*, 15 September 1939.

8. Seattle *Post Intelligencer*, 6 August 1939. Cleveland *Plain-Dealer*, 7 May 1939.

9. Kansas City, Mo., *Journal-Post*, 12 April 1941.

10. Saginaw, Mich., *News*, 23 August 1939, by Robert T. McMillen.

11. Milwaukee *Journal Roto Section*, Sunday, 31 August 1941. Chicago *Tribune*, 23 July 1939; Milwaukee *News*, 14 July 1939.

12. St. Paul *Pioneer Press*, 29 June 1941, by Jack Newman.

13. Tacoma, Wash., *News-Tribune*, 26 July 1939. Other stories appeared in the Seattle *Star* on August 7 and 10, in the Seattle *Times* on August 6, and in the Portland *Oregonian* on July 16, which carried a picture of Paul and Babe.

14. Portland *Oregonian*, 23 July 1939. Tacoma *News-Tribune*, 9 August 1939.

15. Seattle *Times*, 25 June 1939.

16. Ashland, Wisc., *Press*, 23 March 1939.

17. St. Paul *Press*, 26 March 1939, 28 March 1939.

18. Still other references to Paul Bunyan affairs appear in the news-

papers. News headings state: "Paul Bunyan and Blue Ox Coming to Circus" (Spokane, Wash., *Spokesman-Review*, 29 January 1939); "Paul Bunyan Presides" (over the Forestry Club's annual banquet at Oregon State College: Saginaw, Mich., *News*, 23 March 1939; also Passaic, N.J., *News*, 31 March; Louisville, Ky., *Journal*, 31 March; Columbus, Ohio, *Dispatch*, 14 April); "Paul Bunyan Club Plans Banquet" (a sportsmen's father-and-son banquet: Detroit *Free Press*, 23 February 1941); "Flyers Will Join Paul Bunyan Clan" (pilots from the middle west will be initiated at the legendary camp of Paul Bunyan: Chicago *Tribune*, 22 June 1941); "Bunyan Club Cooks Up Tall Tales in Park" (first annual outdoor flapjack feast of a sportsmen's Paul Bunyan Club: Detroit *Free Press*, 29 September 1941). A pageant conducted by the City Recreation Department of Toledo as a climax to its summer playground programs featured representations of both Paul Bunyan and John Henry, played by masked boys on stilts (Toledo, Ohio, *Blade*, 8 August 1941, with photographs). Under the captions "Job For Paul," "Paul Bunyan Motif at 'Y' Drive Dinner," and " 'Y' Bunyanites Ready," Minneapolis papers reported a YMCA membership drive highlighted by a dinner in lumberjack costume and setting, with Paul Bunyan as chairman, and Johnny Inkslinger as bookkeeper (Minneapolis *Journal*, 10 and 19 October 1939; Minneapolis *Tribune*, 9 October).

19. Union, N.J., *Register*, 26 January 1939; Kingston, N.Y. *Leader*, 15 February; Port Jefferson, N.Y., *Record*, 23 March; Hackensack, N.J., *Republican*, 20 April; Brooklyn *Citizen*, 28 April.

20. New York, *The Daily Worker*, 30 April 1939. *Post*, 29 April 1939. *Mirror*, 30 April 1939.

21. New York *World Telegram*, 25 February 1939.

22. Indianapolis *Star*, 6 May 1939; also Muncie, Ind., *Star*, 28 May.

23. Los Angeles *Times*, 14 September 1941, by Arthur Miller; Elaine St. Maur also praises his wood sculpture of Paul Bunyan and Johnny Appleseed in the Los Angeles *Examiner*, 16 February 1941.

24. Milwaukee *Journal*, 18 June 1939.

25. New York *World Telegram*, 22 July 1939. Springfield, Mass., *Union*, 26 February 1939. Ossining, N.Y., *Citizen-Register*, 16 March 1940.

26. Detroit *Free Press*, 28 March 1941. Bozeman, Mont., *Chronicle*, 4 March 1939. Milwaukee *Journal*, 29 October 1939.

27. Portland *Oregonian*, 6 April 1941, by Catherine Jones. The same paper carried other notices on March 30, April 13, April 20, and April 27.

28. Rochester *Times-Union*, 30 April 1941, by R.J.L.H.

29. Minneapolis *Star-Journal*, 6 May 1941.

30. Milwaukee *Journal*, 5 August 1939.

31. *Ibid.*, 1 September 1939. Sioux City, Iowa, *Journal*, 2 July 1939.

32. Cincinnati *Enquirer*, 12 March 1939, by Frederick Yeiser.

33. Cleveland *Press*, 18 August 1941. Detroit *Free Press*, 22 November 1939, from the column "It Happened in Michigan," by Donald F. Schram. I

met Spikehorn in 1946 and wrote down a Paul Bunyan story he told me.

34. Minneapolis *Journal*, 29 January 1939. Minneapolis *Tribune*, 12 February 1939.

35. Saginaw *News*, 31 January and 25 February 1939; Port Huron, Mich., *Herald*, 22 March 1939; Saginaw *News*, 3 March 1940.

36. Milwaukee *Journal*, 23 March 1939.

37. Syracuse, N.Y., *Herald*, 1 April 1939.

38. New Rochelle, N.Y., *Star*, 25 October 1939; Rochester *Democrat*, 4 March 1940; Rochester *Times-Union*, 15 March 1940. Seattle *Post-Intelligencer*, 19 February 1939. St. Paul *Press*, 26 February 1939.

39. Cleveland *Plain-Dealer*, 12 November 1939.

40. Franklin, N.Y., *Dairyman*, 24 November 1939.

41. Indianapolis *Star*, 17 August 1941, "Teller of Bunyan Tales Is Dead"; also Wilmington, Del., *Star*, 17 August; Milwaukee *Journal*, 26 August; Bronx, N.Y., *Home News*, 2 September.

42. New York *Times*, 13 August 1939; Buffalo *Courier-Express*, 16 February 1941.

43. Seattle *Post-Intelligencer*, 21 August 1939.

44. Charlotte, N.C., *News*, 20 August 1939; Denver, Colo., *News*, 28 August; Lowell, Mass., *Courier-Citizen*, 1 September; Hartford, Conn., *Times*, 2 September; South Bend, Ind., *Tribune*, 3 September; Fort Worth, Tex., *Star-Telegram*, 3 September; Cincinnati *Enquirer*, 9 September; Waterbury, Conn., *American*, 6 October; New Haven, Conn., *Journal*, 22 November; Denver *News*, 20 August 1939; Carl E. Zimmerer in South Bend *Tribune*, 3 September 1939; Hartford *Times*, 2 September 1939.

45. New York *Times*, 13 April 1941; Minneapolis *Tribune*, 20 April; New York *Herald-Tribune*, 25 May; San Francisco *Chronicle*, 13 July; Seattle *Post-Intelligencer*, 8 August; illustration in *PM*, New York, 6 April.

46. Columbus, Ohio, *Dispatch*, 28 September 1941; similar praise accompanies the reproduction in the Springfield, Mass., *Republican*, 28 September 1941; New York *Post*, 11 November 1939; New York *Herald-Tribune*, 3 December 1939.

47. Gloversville, N.Y., *Leader*, 26 March 1939; New Milford, Conn., *Times*, 19 October 1939.

48. Canton, Ohio, *Repository*, 15 February 1940, under the caption, "Weather Can't Freeze Out Those Paul Bunyan Legends"; also Middletown, Conn., *Press*, 24 February 1940.

49. Province, R.I., *Journal*, 8 June 1941; also, Canton, Ohio, *Repository*, 1 June 1941; Addison, N.Y., *Advertiser*, 10 July 1941.

50. Washington, D.C., *News*, 23 September 1941; also Cincinnati *Post*, 24 September 1941.

51. Oakland, Calif., *Tribune*, 21 March 1939, by Robert Blum.

52. San Francisco *Chronicle*, 21 March 1939.

53. Warrensburg, N.Y., *News*, 21 December 1939.

54. New York, *Daily Worker*, 20 April 1941. This article is reprinted entire, the ellipses being in the text.

55. Saginaw, Mich., *News*, 14 March 1941.

56. Columbus, Ohio, *Journal*, 13 October 1941, "Myth and Reality."

57. White Plains, N.Y., *Dispatch*, 16 July 1944; Syracuse, N.Y., *Post Standard*, 1 June 1941.

58. Brooklyn *Eagle*, 20 July 1941.

59. Milwaukee *Journal*, 22 June 1941.

60. Minneapolis *Journal*, 19 November 1939, " 'Paul Bunyan' Shows City Policemen Some Fishing!"; Spokane, Wash., *Spokesman-Review*, 15 April 1941, 22 July 1941.

61. St. Paul, Minn., *Dispatch*, 9 August 1939.

62. Dallas, Tex., *Dispatch*, 31 July 1939.

63. New Orleans *Item*, 7 May 1939.

64. Rochester, N.Y., *Times-Union*, 30 April 1941; New Orleans *States*, 19 and 23 February 1940.

65. New York *News*, 7 March 1940, by Donald Day; New Orleans *Times-Picayune*, 13 April 1941, "Gulf Anglers Recall Deeds of Serb Hero," by Arthur Halliburton; New York *Mirror*, 20 March 1940; New York *Times*, 25 June 1939.

66. Union City, Ind., *Gazette*, 24 July 1939; Kingston, N.Y., *Leader*, 24 July 1939, by the United Press; Raleigh, N.C., *News and Observer*, 29 January 1939; New Orleans *States*, 31 January 1939.

67. Rome, N.Y., *Sentinel*, 28 February 1940; New York *News*, 10 February 1939; Providence, R.I., *Bulletin*, 4 February 1939.

68. Seattle *Times*, 17 June 1939; Milwaukee *Journal*, 19 April 1939; Cleveland *News*, 12 March 1940; Portland *Oregonian*, 10 October 1941; Milwaukee *News-Sentinel*, 11 August 1941; Minneapolis *Times*, 17 July 1941; Chicago *News*, 16 October 1939.

69. Calgary, Canada, *Herald*, 26 July 1939. The Seattle *Times* reported "Bunyan Thief Takes Half-Ton" on 17 July 1939.

70. McKeesport, Pa., *News*; St. Louis *Star*; Lowell, Mass., *Sun*; Worcester, Mass., *Gazette*; Saginaw, Mich., *News* (all 26 October 1939).

71. Memphis, Tenn., *Appeal*, 13 July 1941; Montgomery, Ala., *Advertiser*, 11 August 1941.

72. Lowell, Mass., *Leader*, 24 March 1941; St. Paul *Dispatch*, 31 July 1941; Cincinnati *Enquirer*, 25 February 1940; Springfield, Mass., *Sunday Union and Republican*, 25 February 1940.

73. Exeter, N.H., *News-Letter*, 20 July 1939, "If Paul Bunyan Were Only Living," by James A. Purington.

74. Niagara Falls, N.Y., *Gazette*, 1 March 1941.

75. Seattle *Post-Intelligencer*, 5 October 1939.

76. Oakland, Calif., *Tribune*, 18 June 1939; Minneapolis *Times*, 28 May 1941.

77. Ft Wayne, Ind., *Journal-Gazette*, 20 April 1941.

78. Seattle *Times*, 27 July 1941, by Robert Barr.

79. Tacoma, Wash., *News-Tribune*, 9 September 1941.

80. Atlanta, Ga., *Constitution* Sunday Magazine and Feature Section, 7 May 1939.

81. St. Paul, Minn., *Pioneer Press*, 1 August 1941; also St. Paul *Dispatch*, 31 July; New York *Times* Magazine, 23 March 1941.

82. Cleveland *News*, 16 July 1941; also Pittsburgh *Press*, 13 July; Boston *Globe*, 13 July; Boston *Post*, 13 July; Cincinnati *Times-Star*, 23 July; Cincinnati *Enquirer*, 27 July; Indianapolis *Star*, 27 July.

83. Minneapolis *Tribune*, 21 May 1939 and 8 June 1941; Madison, Wis., *Capital Times*, 22 June 1941.

84. Boston *Daily Globe* and Boston *Evening Globe*, 22 July 1941, by Nell Giles.

85. Pittsburgh *Press*, 14 July 1939; Red Wing, Minn., *Republican*, 7 July 1939; Chicago *News*, 26 April 1941; New York *Post*, 25 July 1939; Cincinnati *Enquirer*, 25 May 1941.

86. Seattle *Times*, 6 July 1941, quoting Mrs. Lilla C. Norman.

87. Pittsburgh *Press*, 23 June 1941, by Maxine Garrison; Springfield, Mass., *Union*, 7 November 1939, by A. L. S. Wood; Los Angeles *Times*, 26 February 1941, by Bill Henry; Seattle *Times*, 28 February 1940, by Dale Harrison.

88. *Ibid.*, 24 August 1941; St. Paul *Press*, 22 February 1939; Milwaukee *Journal*, 10 August 1941; Syracuse, N.Y., *Post Standard*, 31 March 1941.

89. Bemidji *Daily Pioneer*, 13 April 1940.

90. Itasca *Iron News*, 16 January 1941.

91. See his letters to Louise Pound, *Southern Folklore Quarterly* 7 (1943): 139, n. 12; to Max Gartenberg, "W. B. Laughead's Great Advertisement," *Journal of American Folklore* 63 (1950): 447; and to Daniel G. Hoffman, *Paul Bunyan: Last of the Frontier Demigods* (Philadelphia: University of Pennsylvania Press, 1952), pp. 80-81.

Selected
Bibliography
of Works Cited

Aarne, Antti, and Stith Thompson. *The Types of the Folk-Tale*. Helsinki: Suomalainen Tiedeakatemia, 1928.

Abrahams, Roger. *Deep Down in the Jungle: Negro Narrative Folklore from the Streets of Philadelphia*. Hatboro, Pa.: Folklore Associates, 1964; new ed., Chicago: Aldine, 1970.

Apuleius, Lucius. *The Golden Ass*. Tr. Robert Graves. Harmondsworth, Eng.: Penguin, 1950.

Baker, Ronald L. *Folklore in the Writings of Rowland E. Robinson*. Bowling Green, Ohio: Bowling Green University Popular Press, 1973.

Barrett, W. H. *A Fenman's Story*. London: Routledge and Kegan Paul, 1965.
——— *More Tales from the Fens*. London: Routledge and Kegan Paul, 1964.
——— *Tales from the Fens*. London: Routledge and Kegan Paul, 1963.

Bartók, Bela, and Albert B. Lord. *Serbo-Croatian Folk Songs*. New York: Columbia University Press, 1951.
——— *Serbo-Croatian Heroic Songs*. 2 vols. Cambridge, Mass.: Harvard University Press, 1953-54.

Bassett, Fletcher. *Legends and Superstitions of the Sea and of Sailors in all Lands and at all Times*. Chicago, 1885.

Baughman, Ernest W. *Type and Motif-Index of the Folktales of England and North America*. The Hague: Mouton, 1966.

Bausinger, Hermann. *Volkskultur in der technischen Welt*. Stuttgart: Kohlhammer, 1961.

Bernstein, Barton J., ed. *Dissenting Essays in American History*. New York: Pantheon, 1968.

Bianco, Carla. *The Two Rosetos*. Bloomington: Indiana University Press, 1974.

Blair, Walter. *Tall Tale America*. New York: Coward-McCann, 1944.

Bluestein, Gene. *The Voice of the Folk: Folklore and American Literary Theory*. Amherst: University of Massachusetts Press, 1972.

Selected Bibliography

Boatright, Mody C. *Folklore of the Oil Industry.* Dallas: Southern Methodist University Press, 1963.

────── *Gib Morgan, Minstrel of the Oil Fields.* N.p., Texas Folklore Society, 1945.

────── and William A. Owens. *Tales from the Derrick Floor.* New York: Doubleday, 1970.

Bolte, Johannes, and Georg Polívka. *Anmerkungen zu den Kinder- und Hausmärchen der Brüder Grimm.* 5 vols. Leipzig: Dieterich, 1913-32.

Botkin, B. A., ed. *The Pocket Treasury of American Folklore.* New York: Pocket Books, 1950.

────── *A Treasury of American Folklore.* New York: Crown, 1944.

────── *A Treasury of New England Folklore.* New York: Crown, 1947.

────── *A Treasury of Southern Folklore.* New York: Crown, 1949.

────── and Alvin C. Harlow, eds. *A Treasury of Railroad Folklore.* New York: Crown, 1953.

Bradford, Roark. *John Henry.* New York and London: Harper and Brothers, 1931.

────── *Ol' Man Adam an' His Chillun.* New York and London: Harper and Brothers, 1928.

Brand, John. *Observations on Popular Antiquities.* London, 1777.

Briggs, Katharine. *A Dictionary of British Folk-Tales.* 4 vols. Bloomington: Indiana University Press, 1970-1971.

Brown, Charles E. *"Cousin Jack" Stories: Short Stories of the Cornish Lead Miners of Southwestern Wisconsin.* Madison: Wisconsin Folklore Society, 1940.

The Frank C. Brown Collection of North Carolina Folklore. 7 vols. Durham, N.C.: Duke University Press, 1952-64.

Burkholder, Mabel. *Before the White Man Came: Indian Legends and Stories.* Toronto: McClelland and Stewart, 1923.

Cambiaire, Celestin Pierre. *East Tennessee and Western Virginia Mountain Ballads.* London: Mitre, 1934.

Campbell, John Francis. *More West Highland Tales,* ed. W. J. Watson and H. J. Rose. Edinburgh and London: Oliver and Boyd, 1940.

────── *Popular Tales of the West Highlands.* 4 vols. Edinburgh, 1860-62.

Campbell, John Lorne, ed. *Tales of Barra Told by the Coddy (John MacPherson, Northbay, Barra, 1876-1955).* Edinburgh: printed for the editor by W. and A. K. Johnston and G. W. Bacon, 1960.

Campbell, Joseph. *The Flight of the Wild Gander: Explorations in the Mythological Dimension.* New York: Viking, 1969.

────── *The Masks of God: Creative Mythology.* New York: Viking, 1968.

────── *Myths to Live By.* New York: Viking, 1972.

Campbell, Marie. *Tales from the Cloud Walking Country.* Bloomington: Indiana University Press, 1958.

Carey, George. *A Faraway Time and Place: Lore of the Eastern Shore.* Washington and New York: Luce, 1971.

Selected Bibliography

Carmichael, Alexander. *Carmina Gadelica, Hymns and Incantations.* 2 vols. Edinburgh: Norman Macleod, 1900; 2nd ed., 5 vols., Edinburgh and London: Oliver and Boyd, 1928-54.

Chambers, Robert. *Traditions of Edinburgh.* London: Chambers, 1869.

Chappell, Louis W. *John Henry, A Folklore Study.* Jena: Biedermann, 1938.

Chase, Richard. *Grandfather Tales.* Boston: Houghton Mifflin, 1948.

————— *The Jack Tales.* Boston: Houghton Mifflin, 1943.

Child, Francis James, ed. *The English and Scottish Popular Ballads.* 5 vols. in 10. Boston, 1882-98.

Christiansen, Reidar, ed. *Folktales of Norway.* Chicago: University of Chicago Press, 1964.

Clodd, Edward. *Memories.* London: Watts, 1926.

————— *Tom Tit Tot: An Essay on Savage Philosophy in Folk-Tale.* London, 1898.

Clouston, W. A. *The Book of Noodles.* London, 1888.

Coffin, Tristram P. *Uncertain Glory: Folklore and the American Revolution.* Hatboro, Pa.: Folklore Associates, 1971.

————— and Hennig Cohen, *Folklore from the Working Folk of America.* New York: Doubleday, 1973.

Colman, Gould P., ed. *The Fourth National Colloquium on Oral History.* New York: Oral History Association, 1970.

Cox, George W. *Introduction to the Science of Comparative Mythology and Folk-Lore.* London, 1881.

Cox, John H. *Folk-Songs of the South.* Cambridge, Mass.: Harvard University Press, 1925.

Cox, Marian. *An Introduction to Folklore.* London: Nutt, 1904.

Curtin, Jeremiah. *Tales of the Fairies and the Ghost World.* London, 1895.

Dégh, Linda, ed. *Folktales of Hungary.* Chicago: University of Chicago Press, 1965.

Denisoff, Serge R. *Great Day Coming: Folk Music and the American Left.* Urbana: University of Illinois Press, 1971.

DeVoto, Bernard. *The Year of Decision 1846.* Boston: Houghton Mifflin, 1961.

The Dewar Manuscripts, vol. 1, *Scottish West Highland Folk Tales,* ed. John MacKechnie. Glasgow: MacLellan, 1964.

Dore, R. P. *City Life in Japan.* Berkeley and Los Angeles: University of California Press, 1958.

Dorson, Richard M., ed. *African Folklore.* Garden City, N.Y.: Doubleday Anchor, 1972.

————— *America In Legend.* New York: Pantheon, 1973.

————— *American Folklore and the Historian.* Chicago: University of Chicago Press, 1971.

————— *American Negro Folktales.* Greenwich, Conn.: Fawcett, 1967.

————— *Bloodstoppers and Bearwalkers.* Cambridge, Mass.: Harvard University Press, 1952.

—— ed. *The British Folklorists, a History.* Chicago: University of Chicago Press, 1968.

—— *Buying the Wind.* Chicago: University of Chicago Press, 1964.

—— ed. *Folklore and Folklife: An Introduction.* Chicago: University of Chicago Press, 1972.

—— ed. *Folklore and Traditional History.* The Hague: Mouton, 1973.

—— ed. *Folklore Research Around the World.* Bloomington: Indiana University Press, 1961.

—— *Folklore: Selected Essays.* Bloomington: Indiana University Press, 1972.

—— *Negro Folktales in Michigan.* Cambridge, Mass.: Harvard University Press, 1956.

—— ed. *Peasant Customs and Savage Myths.* 2 vols. Chicago: University of Chicago Press, 1968.

—— ed. *Studies in Japanese Folklore.* Bloomington: Indiana University Press, 1963.

Drake, Samuel G. *The Book of the Indians.* 9th ed., Boston, 1845.

Dundes, Alan. *The Morphology of North American Indian Tales.* Helsinki: Suomalainen Tiedeakatemia Academia Scientiarum Fennica, 1964.

—— ed. *Mother Wit from the Laughing Barrel.* Englewood Cliffs, N.J.: Prentice Hall, 1973.

—— and Carl Pagter. *Urban Folklore from the Paperwork Empire.* Austin: American Folklore Society, 1975.

Edmonson, Munro S. *Lore: An Introduction to the Science of Folklore and Literature.* New York: Holt, Rinehart and Winston, 1971.

Emrich, Duncan. *Folklore on the American Land.* Boston and Toronto: Little, Brown, 1972.

Evans, Ewart. *Where Beards Wag All: The Relevance of the Oral Tradition.* London: Faber and Faber, 1970.

Falnes, Oscar J. *National Romanticism in Norway.* London: P. S. King and Son, 1933.

Feldman, Burton, and Robert D. Richardson, eds. *The Rise of Modern Mythology, 1680-1860.* Bloomington and London: Indiana University Press, 1972.

Finnegan, Ruth. *Oral Literature in Africa.* Oxford: Clarendon, 1970.

Flanagan, John, and A. P. Hudson, eds. *Folklore in American Literature.* Evanston, Ill.: Row, Peterson, 1958.

Folklore Institute of Japan. *Japanese Folklore Dictionary.* Compiled under the supervision of Kunio Yanagita. Tokyo: Tokyoso Publishing, 1951. Tr. Masanori Takatsuka; ed. George K. Brady. University of Kentucky Press Microcards, Series A: Modern Language Series, no. 18, 1958.

Fry, Gladys-Marie. *Night Riders in Black Folk History.* Knoxville: University of Tennessee Press, 1975.

Fuller, Edmund, ed. *Thesaurus of Anecdotes.* New York: Crown, 1942.

Selected Bibliography

Gardner, Emelyn E. *Folklore from the Schoharie Hills, New York.* Ann Arbor: University of Michigan Press, 1937.

Gillies, Alexander. *Herder.* Oxford: Blackwell, 1945.

Glassie, Henry, Edward D. Ives, and John F. Szwed. *Folksongs and Their Makers.* Bowling Green, Ohio: Bowling Green University Popular Press, 1971.

Gomme, George Laurence. *Folklore as an Historical Science.* London: Methuen, 1908.

———— *Folk-Lore Relics of Early Village Life.* London, 1883.

———— *Handbook of Folklore.* London, 1890.

Gould, John. *Farmer Takes a Wife.* New York: Morrow, 1946.

———— *The House That Jacob Built.* New York: Morrow, 1947.

———— *The Jonesport Raffle.* Boston: Little, Brown, 1969.

Green, Archie. *Only a Miner: Studies in Recorded Coal-Mining Songs.* Urbana: University of Illinois Press, 1972.

Greenway, John. *American Folksongs of Protest.* Philadelphia: University of Pennsylvania Press, 1953.

Gregory, Lady. *Visions and Beliefs in the West of Ireland.* 2nd ser. New York and London: Putnam's Sons, 1920.

Grimm, Jacob. *Deutsche Mythologie.* Göttingen, 1835. (Translated from the 4th ed. [1875-78] by James S. Stallybrass as *Teutonic Mythology,* 4 vols., London, 1882-88.)

Grimm, Jacob and Wilhelm. *Kinder- und Hausmärchen.* 3 vols. Berlin, 1812-22.

Hand, Wayland D., ed. *American Folk Legend: A Symposium.* Berkeley, Los Angeles, and London: University of California Press, 1971.

Hansen, William A. *The Conference Sequence: Patterned Narration and Narrative Inconsistency in the Odyssey.* Berkeley, Los Angeles, and London: University of California Press, 1972.

Hardy, Philip Dixon. *Legends, Tales, and Stories of Ireland.* Dublin, 1837.

Hartland, Edwin Sidney. *The Legend of Perseus.* 3 vols. London, 1894-96.

———— *The Science of Fairy Tales.* London: Methuen, 1925.

Hautala, Jouko. *Finnish Folklore Research 1828-1918.* Helsinki: Finnish Academy of Sciences, 1969.

Hazard, Thomas R. *The Jonny-Cake Letters.* Providence, R.I., 1882.

Henry, Mellinger Edward, ed. *Folk-Songs from the Southern Highlands.* New York: Augustin, 1938.

Hoffman, Daniel G. *Paul Bunyan, Last of the Frontier Demigods.* Philadelphia: University of Pennsylvania Press for Temple University Publications, 1952.

Hoffman, Frank, *Analytical Survey of Anglo-American Traditional Erotica.* Bowling Green, Ohio: Bowling Green University Popular Press, 1973.

Hoogasian-Villa, Susie. *One Hundred Armenian Folktales.* Detroit: Wayne State University Press, 1966.

Selected Bibliography

Hunt, B. *Folk Tales of Breffny*. London: Macmillan, 1912.

Hurston, Zora Neale. *Mules and Men*. Philadelphia and London: Lippincott, 1935.

Hyatt, Harry M. *Hoodoo-Conjuration-Witchcraft-Rootwork*. 3 vols. Hannibal, Mo., Western Publishing, 1970-73.

Hyde, Douglas, ed. *Beside the Fire: A Collection of Gaelic Folk Stories*. London, 1890.

—— *Legends of Saints and Sinners*. Dublin, Cork, and Belfast, n.d.

Ikeda, Hiroko. *A Type and Motif Index of Japanese Folk-Literature*. Helsinki: Suomalainen Tiedeakatemia Academia Scientiarum Fennica, 1971.

Indian Legends, by Pupils of Haskell Institute, United States Indian Training School, Lawrence, Kansas, 1914.

International Volkskundliche Bibliographie. See Wildhaber.

Ives, Edward D. *Larry Gorman, The Man Who Made the Songs*. Bloomington: Indiana University Press, 1964.

—— *Lawrence Doyle, The Farmer-Poet of Prince Edward Island*. Orono: University of Maine Press, 1971.

Jacobs, Melville. *The Content and Style of an Oral Literature*. New York: Wenner-Gren Foundation for Anthropological Research, 1959.

Jackson, Bruce. *"Get Your Ass in the Water and Swim Like Me": Narrative Poetry from Black Oral Tradition*. Cambridge, Mass.: Harvard University Press, 1974.

—— *Wake Up Dead Man: Afro-American Worksongs from Texas Prisons*. Cambridge, Mass.: Harvard University Press, 1972.

Johnson, Guy B. *John Henry: Tracking Down a Negro Legend*. Chapel Hill: University of North Carolina Press, 1929.

—— and Howard W. Odum. *Negro Workaday Songs*. Chapel Hill: University of North Carolina Press, 1926.

Keightley, Thomas. *The Fairy Mythology*. London, 1828.

Keil, Charles. *Urban Blues*. Chicago: University of Chicago Press, 1966.

Keiser, Albert. *The Indian in American Tradition*. New York: Oxford University Press, 1933.

Kennedy, Patrick. *The Fireside Stories of Ireland*. Dublin, 1870.

—— *Legendary Fictions of the Irish Celts*. Dublin, 1870.

Kirk, Geoffrey S. *Myth: Its Meaning and Functions in Ancient and Other Cultures*. Berkeley: University of California Press, 1970.

Kirtley, Bacil F. *A Motif-Index of Polynesian Narratives*. Honolulu: University of Hawaii Press, 1971.

Kittredge, George Lyman. *The Old Farmer and His Almanack*. Cambridge, Mass.: Harvard University Press, 1924.

Korson, George. *Black Rock: Mining Folklore of the Pennsylvania Dutch*. Baltimore: Johns Hopkins University Press, 1960.

—— *Coal Dust on the Fiddle: Songs and Stories of the Bituminous Industry*. Philadelphia: University of Pennsylvania Press, 1943.

Selected Bibliography

———— *Minstrels of the Mine Patch: Songs and Stories of the Anthracite Industry.* Philadelphia: University of Pennsylvania Press, 1938.

Krappe, Alexander H. *Balor with the Evil Eye.* New York: Columbia University Press, 1927.

———— *The Science of Folklore.* London: Methuen, 1930.

Laws, G. Malcolm. *Native American Balladry.* Philadelphia: American Folklore Society, 1950; new ed., 1964.

Lawson, John C. *Modern Greek Folklore and Ancient Greek Religion: A Study in Survivals.* New York: University Books, 1964. (Originally published 1910)

Lean, Vincent Stuckey. *Lean's Collectanea.* 4 vols. Bristol: Arrowsmith, 1902-04.

Lévi-Strauss, Claude. *The Raw and the Cooked.* Tr. John and Doreen Weightman. New York: Harper and Row, 1969.

Life Treasury of American Folklore. New York: Time Incorporated, 1961.

Lomax, John A. and Alan. *American Ballads and Folk Songs.* New York: Macmillan, 1934.

———— *Folk Song U.S.A.* New York: Duell, Sloan and Pearce, 1947.

———— *The Folk Songs of North America.* New York: Doubleday, 1960.

———— *Our Singing Country.* New York: Macmillan, 1941.

Lord, Albert B. *The Singer of Tales.* Cambridge, Mass.: Harvard University Press, 1960.

Lovell, John. *Black Song: The Forge and the Flame.* New York: Macmillan, 1972.

McCormick, Dell J. *Paul Bunyan Swings His Axe.* Caldwell, Idaho: Caxton Printers, 1936.

———— *Tall Timber Tales: More Paul Bunyan Stories.* Caldwell, Idaho: Caxton Printers, 1939.

Macfarlane, Alan. *Witchcraft in Tudor and Stuart England.* London: Routledge and Kegan Paul, 1970.

MacGregor, Alasdair Alpin. *The Peat-Fire Flame; Folk-Tales and Traditions of the Highlands and Islands.* Edinburgh and London: Ettrick, 1947.

MacKenzie, W. *Gaelic Incantations, with Translations.* Inverness, 1895.

Maclaglan, R. C. *Evil Eye in the Western Highlands.* London: Nutt, 1902.

MacLellan, Angus. *Stories from South Uist.* Tr. John Lorne Campbell. London: Routledge and Kegan Paul, 1961.

Malone, Bill. *Country Music U.S.A.* Austin and London: University of Texas Press for the American Folklore Society, 1968.

Maranda, Elli Köngäs, and Pierre Maranda, eds. *Structural Models in Folklore and Transformational Essays.* The Hague: Mouton, 1971.

Maranda, Pierre, and Elli Köngäs Maranda, eds. *Structural Analysis of Oral Tradition.* Philadelphia: University of Pennsylvania Press, 1971.

Mason, Elizabeth B., and Louis M. Starr. *The Oral History Collection of Columbia University.* New York: Oral History Research Office, 1964.

Selected Bibliography

Mayhew, Henry. *London Labour and the London Poor.* 4 vols. New York: Dover, 1968.
The Merry Fellow's Companion; or American Jest Book. Harrisburgh, 1797.
Michaelis-Jena, Ruth. *The Brothers Grimm.* London: Routledge and Kegan Paul, 1970.
Miller, Hugh. *My Schools and Schoolmasters.* Edinburgh, 1859.
—————— *Scenes and Legends of the North of Scotland: or the Traditional History of Cromarty.* Edinburgh, 1881.
Miller, Merle. *Plain Speaking.* New York: Berkley Publishing, distributed by Putnam, 1974.
Miller, Olive Beaupré. *Heroes, Outlaws and Funny Fellows of American Popular Tales.* New York: Doubleday, Doran, 1939.
Montell, William Lynwood. *The Saga of Coe Ridge.* Knoxville: University of Tennessee Press, 1970.
Napier, James. *Folk Lore: or, Superstitious Beliefs in the West of Scotland within this Century.* Paisley, 1879.
Nevins, Allan. *The Gateway to History.* New York: Appleton-Century, 1938.
Nutt, Alfred. *The Fairy Mythology of Shakespeare.* London: Nutt, 1900.
O'Sullivan, Seán, ed. *Folktales of Ireland.* Chicago: University of Chicago Press, 1966.
—————— *Handbook of Irish Folklore.* Dublin: Folklore of Ireland Society, 1942.
Oinas, Felix J., and Stephen Soudakoff, eds. *The Study of Russian Folklore.* The Hague: Mouton, 1975.
Olch, P. D., and F. C. Pogue, eds. *Selections from the Fifth and Sixth National Colloquia on Oral History.* New York: Oral History Association, 1972.
Ong, Walter J. *The Presence of the Word.* New York: Simon and Schuster, 1970.
Oral History at Arrowhead: Proceedings of the First National Colloquium on Oral History. Los Angeles: Oral History Association, 1967.
Oral History: The First Twenty Years. New York: Columbia University, ca. 1970.
Ortutay, Gyula. *Hungarian Folklore Essays.* Budapest: Akademiai Kiado, 1972.
Oster, Harry. *Living Country Blues.* Detroit: Folklore Associates, 1969.
Paredes, Américo, and Richard Bauman, eds. *Toward New Perspectives in Folklore.* Austin and London: University of Texas Press for the American Folklore Society, 1972.
—————— and Ellen Stekert, eds. *The Urban Experience and Folk Tradition.* Austin and London: University of Texas Press for the American Folklore Society, 1971.
Parry, Milman. *The Making of Homeric Verse: The Collected Papers of Milman Parry,* ed. Adam Parry. Oxford: Oxford University Press, 1971.
Patai, Raphael. *Myth and Modern Man.* Englewood Cliffs, N.J.: Prentice-Hall, 1972.

——— and Robert Graves. *Hebrew Myths*. New York: McGraw-Hill, 1966.

——— Francis Lee Utley, and Dov Nov, eds. *Studies in Biblical and Jewish Folklore*. Indiana University Folklore Series, no. 13. Bloomington, 1960.

Pawlowska, Harriet M. *Merrily We Sing! 105 Polish Folksongs*. Detroit: Wayne State University Press, 1961.

Pearce, Roy Harvey. *Savagism and Civilization: A Study of the Indian and the American Mind*. Baltimore: Johns Hopkins University Press, 1965.

Peppard, Murray. *Paths Through the Forest: A Biography of the Brothers Grimm*. New York: Holt, Rinehart and Winston, 1971.

The Percy Anecdotes, rev. ed., *To which is added a valuable collection of American Anecdotes, original and select*. 2 vols. New York, 1845.

Perrault, Charles. *Contes de ma Mere l'Oye*. Paris, 1697.

Potter, George W. *An Irish Pilgrimage*. Providence: Providence Journal, 1950.

Prebble, John. *Culloden*. New York: Atheneum, 1962.

——— *Glencoe: The Story of the Massacre*. London: Secker and Warburg, 1966.

——— *The Highland Clearances*. Harmondsworth, Eng.; Penguin, 1970.

——— *The Lion in the North: A Personal View of Scotland's History*. New York: Coward, McCann and Geoghegan, 1971.

Propp, Vladimir. *Morphology of the Folktale*. Bloomington, Ind.: Research Center of the Language Sciences, 1958.

Raglan, Lord. *The Hero: A Study in Tradition, Myth and Drama*. New York: Oxford University Press, 1937.

Randolph, Vance. *Ozark Folklore: A Bibliography*. Indiana University Folklore Institute Monograph Series, vol. 24. Bloomington, 1972.

——— *The Ozarks: An American Survival of Primitive Society*. New York: Vanguard, 1931.

Ranke, Kurt, ed. *Folktales of Germany*. Chicago: University of Chicago Press, 1966.

———, ed. *Internationaler Kongress der Volkserzählungsforscher in Kiel und Kopenhagen*. Berlin: de Gruyter, 1961.

Rees, Alwyn and Brinley. *Celtic Heritage*. London: Thames and Hudson, 1961.

Roberts, Leonard. *South from Hell-for-Sartin: Kentucky Mountain Folk Tales*. Lexington: University of Kentucky Press, 1955.

——— *Up Cutshin and Down Greasy: Folkways of a Kentucky Family*. Lexington: University of Kentucky Press, 1959.

Rosenberg, Bruce A. *The Art of the American Folk Preacher*. New York: Oxford University Press, 1970.

Rourke, Constance. *American Humor: A Study of the National Character*. New York: Harcourt, Brace, 1931.

——— *The Roots of American Culture*. New York: Harcourt, Brace, 1942.

Sandburg, Carl. *The American Songbag*. New York: Harcourt, Brace and World, 1927.

Scarborough, Dorothy. *A Song Catcher in Southern Mountains: American Folk Songs of British Ancestry.* New York: Columbia University Press, 1937.

Schlesinger, Arthur M. *Paths to the Present.* New York: Macmillan, 1949.

Schmidt, Otto. *Volkstumsarbeit als politische Aufgabe.* Hamburg: Hanseatische verlagsanstalt, 1943.

Scholes, Robert, and Robert Kellogg. *The Nature of Narrative.* New York: Oxford University Press, 1966.

Sharp, Cecil J. *English Folk Songs from the Southern Appalachians.* London, New York, and Toronto: Oxford University Press, 1960.

Shay, Frank. *Here's Audacity! American Legendary Heroes.* New York: Macaulay, 1930.

Shephard, Esther. *Paul Bunyan.* New York: Harcourt, Brace, 1924.

Sokolov, Y. M. *Russian Folklore.* Tr. Catherine Ruth Smith. New York: Macmillan, 1950.

Springer, George T. *Yumpin' Yimminy: Scandinavian Dialect Selections.* Long Prairie, Minn.: Hart, 1932.

Stevens, James. *Paul Bunyan.* New York: Knopf, 1925.

——— *The Saginaw Paul Bunyan.* New York: Knopf, 1932.

Strömbäck, Dag, et al., eds. *Biographica: Nordic Folklorists of the Past.* Copenhagen: Nordic Institute Folkedigtning, 1971.

Terkel, Studs. *Division Street America.* New York: Pantheon, 1966.

——— *Hard Times: An Oral History of the Great Depression.* New York: Pantheon, 1970.

——— *Working.* New York: Pantheon, 1974.

Thiselton-Dyer, Thomas F. *Folk Lore of Shakespeare.* London: Griffith and Farran; New York: Dutton, 1884.

Thomas, Keith. *Religion and the Decline of Magic.* New York: Scribner's, 1971.

Thompson, Stith. *Motif-Index of Folk Literature.* 6 vols. Bloomington: Indiana University Press, 1955-58.

——— *Tales of the North American Indians.* Cambridge, Mass.: Harvard University Press, 1928.

Turner, George. *Traits of Indian Character; as generally applicable to the aborigines of North America.* 2 vols. Philadelphia, 1836.

Turney, Ida Virginia. *Paul Bunyan Comes West.* Boston: Houghton Mifflin, 1928.

——— *Paul Bunyan, the Work Giant.* Portland, Ore.: Binsford and Mort, 1941.

Tyler, Moses Coit. *The Literary History of the American Revolution, 1763-1783.* 2 vols. New York and London, 1897.

Vansina, Jan. *Oral Tradition: A Study in Historical Methodology.* Tr. H. M. Wright. Chicago: Aldine, 1965.

Vitaliano, Dorothy. *Legends of the Earth.* Bloomington: Indiana University Press, 1974.

Wheeler, Mary. *Kentucky Mountain Folk-Songs.* Boston: Boston Music, 1937.

White, Newman I. *American Negro Folk-Songs.* Cambridge, Mass.: Harvard University Press, 1928.

Wigginton, Eliot, ed. *The Foxfire Book.* Garden City, N.Y.: Doubleday Anchor, 1972.

—— *Foxfire 2.* Garden City, N.Y.: Doubleday Anchor, 1973.

Wilde, Lady. *Ancient Cures, Charms, and Usages of Ireland.* London, 1890.

—— *Ancient Legends, Mystic Charms, and Superstitions of Ireland.* 2 vols. Boston, 1887.

Wilde, W. R. *Irish Popular Superstitions.* Dublin, 1852.

Wildhaber, Robert, ed. *Internationale Volkskundliche Bibliographie.* Bonn: Rudolf Habelt, 1965-1972. The five volumes of this series issued to date cover the years 1961-62, 1963-64, 1965-66, 1967-68, and 1969-70. All volumes carry three concurrent titles: *Internationale Volkskundliche Bibliographie, International Folklore Bibliography,* and *Bibliographie Internationale des Arts et Traditions Populaires;* in the most recent the English title has been changed to *International Folklore and Folklife Bibliography.*

Williams, Alfred. *Studies in Folksong and Popular Poetry.* London, 1895.

Williams, Phyllis H. *South Italian Folkways in Europe and America.* New Haven: Yale University Press, 1938.

Wilson, Duncan. *Vuk Stefanović Karadzić, 1787-1864.* Oxford: Clarendon, 1970.

Wood, Norman B. *Lives of Famous Indian Chiefs.* Aurora, Ill.: American Indian Historical Publishing, 1906.

Woodman, Jay J. *Indian Legends.* Boston: Stratford, 1906.

Yanagita, Kunio. *Studies in Fishing Village Life.* Tr. Masanori Takatsuka; ed. George K. Brady. University of Kentucky Press Microcards, Series A: Modern Language Series, no. 1, 1954.

—— *Studies in Mountain Village Life.* Tr. Masanori Takatsuka; ed. George K. Brady. University of Kentucky Press Microcards, Series A: Modern Language Series, no. 2, 1954.

Yeats, W. B., ed. *Irish Fairy and Folk Tales.* New York: Modern Library, n.d.

Index

Index

comic Indian, 269-282; from Maine
lobstermen, 213-215; of racial
discrimination, 262; of sailor tired of
seafaring, 138
*Ammerkungen zu den Kinder- und
Hausmärchen der Brüder Grimm*
(Bolte and Polívka), 118
Appalachia, 43, 44, 54, 96, 97
Apuleius, Lucius, 191
Arnason, Jón, 82
Asbjörnsen, Peter Christen, 2, 38, 70
Aubrey, John, 35

Baker, Ronald L., 28-29
Ballads: *byliny*, 40, 41, 71, 72; of
Lieutenant Calley, 64; of John
Henry, 283-284, 287, 288, 290;
studies of, 42-43, 44, 125, 127, 128
Barbeau, Marius, 110
Baring-Gould, Sabine, 119
Barrett, W. H., 140-141
Barry, Phillips, 290
Bartók, Bela, and Albert B. Lord, 127
Bascom, Louise Rand, 283
Basset, Fletcher S., 106, 107
Baughman, Ernest W., 11, 12
Bauman, Richard, 85, 86
Bausinger, Hermann, 56, 57, 67
Beach, Joe, 265
Beaton, Tom, 230, 231, 232, 233, 241
Bedny, Demian, 71
Ben-Amos, Dan, 85, 86
Benedict, Ruth, 2
Beowulf, 128
Beside the Fire (Hyde), 188, 190
Bianco, Carla, 29
Biographica (Strömbäck), 82
Black folklore. *See* Afro-American
folklore
Black, William G., 191
Blair, Walter, 15, 17
Blankenship, W. T., 284
Bloodstoppers and Bearwalkers
(Dorson), 53
Bluestein, Gene, 94, 95, 96
Boas, Franz, 2, 45, 74
Boatright, Mody C., 16, 60

Boberg, Ingrid, 185
Bogatyri (Bedny), 71
Bolte, Johannes, and Georg Polívka,
118
Bonny Prince Charlie, 146-151, 173,
178, 179, 180
Bontemps, Arna, and Jack Conroy, 12
Boorstin, Daniel J., 15
Botkin, Benjamin A., 5, 120; *Pocket
Treasury of American Folklore*, 94-
95; *Treasury of American Folklore*,
5, 7, 12, 287; *Treasury of Railroad
Folklore*, 61, 287; *Treasury of
Southern Folklore*, 287
Bowman, James Cloyd, 286
Bradford, Roark, 285, 286, 320
Brand, John, 35, 51, 183, 190
Briggs, Katharine, 92, 103, 121
British folklorists, biographies of, 120
The British Folklorists (Dorson), 81,
109
The Brothers Grimm (Michaelis-Jena),
83
Brown, Courtney, 139
Brown, Frank C., 102
Brunvand, Jan, 104, 110, 119
Buckley, Bruce, 111
Bullock, Paul, 139
Bunyan. *See* Paul Bunyan
Burns, Tom, 65, 67
Buying the Wind (Dorson), 15, 161
Byliny, 40, 41, 71, 72
Bynum, David, 128, 135

Cambiaire, Célestin Pierre, 44
Cambridge University, 110
Camden, William, 81
Campbell, John Francis (Campbell of
Islay), 37, 145, 168, 175
Campbell, John Lorne, 171, 172, 173,
175, 176
Campbell, Joseph, 75, 76, 77, 84
Campbell, Marie, 213
Canada, 110
Carey, George, 96
Carl XII's: död, 142
Carmichael, Alexander, 145

Index

Index

Folklife, 118, 135, 136
Folk Life Studies, 49
Folklore: as academic discipline, 26,
31, 74, 101-123; in the city, 48-55;
contemporaneity of, 46-48, 71, 117;
distortion of, 5, 119; and ideology,
17, 19-20, 24, 67, 71-72; in industry,
56-61; in mass media, 61-67; in
modern world, 31, 46, 48-73; as out-
moded survivals, 33, 35. *See also*
Fakelore; Methodology; Studies,
folklore; Theory, folklore
Folklore and Folklife (Dorson), 88, 118
Folklore and Legends (Hartland), 119
Folklore as an Historical Science
(Gomme), 37
*Folklore from the Schoharie Hills, New
York* (Gardner), 44
*Folklore from the Working Folk of
America* (Coffin and Cohen), 60
Folklore in American Literature
(Flanagan and Hudson), 17
*Folklore in the Writings of Rowland E.
Robinson* (Baker), 28-29
The Folk-Lore Manual, 106
Folklore of Shakespeare (Thiselton-
Dyer), 119
Folklore of the Oil Industry (Boat-
right), 60
Folklore on the American Land
(Emrich), 99
Folk-Lore Relics of Early Village Life
(Gomme), 37
Folklore Research Around the World
(Dorson), 21
Folklore: Selected Essays (Dorson), 87
Folklorismus, 58, 123. *See also* Fake-
lore
The Folk-Lorist, 106
Folklorist, academic, 3-4, 8, 15;
attacked by Williams, 22-24;
dialogue with colleagues, 15-17; field
techniques of, 13, 14; goals of, 10-
11, 13; and nonacademic folklorist,
4, 5, 23; province of, 117-118; type
and motif indexes, 11, 12
Folk-Medicine (Black), 191
Folksongs and Their Makers (Glassie,

Ives, Szwed), 132
*Folk-Songs from the Southern High-
lands* (Henry), 44
The Folk Songs of North America
(Lomax), 287
Folk-Songs of the South (Cox), 283,
284
*Folktales and Songs of the Belozernsk
Region* (Sokolov), 41
Folktales of Ireland (O'Sullivan), 104
The Foxfire Book (Wigginton), 24, 25,
96
The Foxfire Magazine (Wigginton), 25
Foxfire 2 (Wigginton), 24
France, 2, 105, 106
*The Frank C. Brown Collection of
North Carolina Folklore*, 102, 103
Franklin, Benjamin, 93, 94, 133
Frazer, James G., 76
Freitas, Florinda Pereira, 55
French-Canadian dialect, 226-227
French dialect, 226-227; jokes, 265;
stories, 228-241
Fry, Gladys, 29, 142

Gaidoz, Henri, 105, 106
Gallacher, Stuart, 133, 240
Gardner, Emelyn E., 44, 45
Garrison, Lucy M., 45
The Gateway to History (Nevins), 128
Germany, 2, 34, 56-57, 68, 123
Glassie, Henry, 132
Glencoe: The Story of the Massacre
(Prebble), 146, 158, 159
Glencoe, traditions of, 146, 152-159,
179, 180
The Golden Ass (Apuleius), 191
Goldstein, Kenneth, 85, 134
Gomme, George Laurence, 37, 42, 81,
106, 109, 190
Gossen, Gary, 86
Gould, John, 8-15
Great Day Coming (Denisoff), 72, 98
Great Team, 46, 81, 109, 118, 123;
criticism of popularizers of folklore,
119; definition of folklore by, 36-37;
and doctrine of survivals, 117; need
for study of, 120

383

Index

Greece, 70
Greek Americans, 140
Green, Archie, 62, 97
The Green Mountain Songster
(Flanders), 93
The Green Pastures (Connolly), 285
Greenway, John, 288
Gregory, Lady, 70
Gries, Walter F., 162, 228, 229, 246,
250, 251, 252, 254, 255, 256, 257,
258, 260, 264, 266
Grimm, Jacob, 34, 68, 75, 83, 84, 85
Grimm, Jacob and Wilhelm, 26, 46, 79,
86, 87; biographies of, 83-84, 85;
and English antiquaries, 35; *Kinder-
und Hausmärchen*, 34, 84, 102, 103,
161; *Naturpoesie* concept, 34;
Norwegian collectors, 38; and
polished texts of, 84, 125; recon-
struction of Germanic past, 34, 67-
68, 117; Volkskunde establishment,
2
Grimm, Wilhelm, 34, 83
Grundtvig, Svend, 39, 82
Gusev, V. E., 20
Guthrie, Woody, 22, 72, 98

Haley, Alex, 139
Halpert, Herbert, 111
Handbook of Folklore (Gomme), 190
Handbook of Irish Folklore (O'Sulli-
van), 184, 187, 190
Hand, Wayland D., 92
Hansen, William, 137
Harrington, Dan, 238, 246, 249, 257,
261, 265
Harris, Joel Chandler, 16, 45, 107
Hartland, Edwin Sidney, 36, 46, 47, 81,
109, 119; *Legend of Perseus*, 37;
Science of Fairy Tales, 190
Harvard University, 3, 42, 127, 128,
130, 135
Hautala, Jouko, 38, 80, 82, 103
*The Haymes Bibliography of the Oral
Theory*, 128
Hazard, Thomas R., 215
Head comics, 65-66
Heilfurth, Gerhard, 57

Henderson, Hamish, 105
Henry, Mellinger Edward, 44
Herder, Johann Gottfried, 34, 94
Here's Audacity! (Shay), 286
*Heroes, Outlaws and Funny Fellows of
American Popular Tales* (Beaupré),
309
Heroic saga, 163; of Big Archibald
MacPhail, 166, 168; of Big Auchry,
162, 163; of Big John, 164; of Big
Malcolm MacIlvain, 163, 164; of
Fierce John, 164; of Grettir the
Strong, 163
The Highland Clearances (Prebble),
146
Hilferding, A. F., 41
Hirayama, Toshijiro, 42
Historians, radical, 22
Historical-geographical method, 38, 80
Hoffman, Bambi, 243, 245, 261
Hoffman, Daniel, 7
Hoffmann, Frank A., 29
Holbek, Bengt, 83
Homer, 136, 138; and formulaic
epithets, 127, 134; and tradition, 137
Hori, Ichiro, 108
The House that Jacob Built (Gould), 8
Howard, Romey, 139
Hudson, Arthur Palmer, 133
Hungary, 57-58
Hurston, Zora Neale, 288
Hyatt, Harry M., 13, 98, 102
Hyde, Douglas, 70, 188, 190
Hyltén-Cavallius, Gunnar Olof, 39
Hymes, Dell, 85, 86, 125

Ideology, and folklore, 19, 20, 21, 71-
72
Ikeda, Hiroko, 100
Iliad, 127, 136
Indexes of folklore, 100
Indiana University: Archives of the
Folklore Institute, 63, 65, 114;
Archives of Traditional Music, 114,
130; development of folklore pro-
gram at, 113-115, 116; Folklore
Institute, 52, 69, 88, 114, 115; Folk-
lore Students Association, 116; folk-

Index

lore studies at, 2, 8, 26, 52, 60, 69, 74, 104, 108, 113, 114, 115, 143. See also *Journal of the Folklore Institute*

Industrialism, and folklore, 56-61

Internationale Volkskundliche Bibliographie (Wildhaber), 118

An Introduction to Folklore (Cox), 118

Introduction to the Science of Comparative Mythology and Folk-Lore (Cox), 118

The Invisible Man (Ellison), 95

Ireland: fieldwork in, 182, 183-190; folk beliefs in, 191; folklore societies of, 185, 190; folklore studies in, 104; folklore texts collected in, 191-211; Gaelic League, 70; Irish Folklore Commission, 14, 104, 182, 184, 185, 190; nationalism and folklore research, 70

Irish dialect jokes, 219, 264-265

Irish stories: about America, 203-211; about demonic beings, 194-199; about evil eye, 191-194; about local traditions, 199-203

Italian dialect stories, 260-261

Ives, Edward, 28, 132, 133

Ivey, William, 112

Jackson, Bruce, 98, 134

Jackson, Glenn W., 259

Jackson, Kenneth, 105, 109, 135, 188

Jacobs, Melville, 8, 16, 109

Jagendorf, Maurice, 27

Japan, 41-42, 51-52, 106, 107, 108

Japanese Folklore Institute (Minzokugaku Kenkyūshō), 42, 107

Jason, Heda, 86

Jewish dialect story, 181, 182

John Henry, 268, 283-290; in ballad tradition, 283-284, 287, 288, 290; in children's books, 286-287; as folk hero, 286; in folk-tale tradition, 288; historicity of, 284; associated with Paul Bunyan, 285, 320; psychoanalytic interpretation of, 287-288, and southern mountain song tradition, 290; steam-drilling contest, 283-288, in work song tradition, 290

John Henry (Blankenship), 284

John Henry (Bradford), 285, 286

John Henry (Chappell), 284

John Henry and His Hammer (Felton), 286

John Henry and the Double-Jointed Steam Drill (Shapiro), 286, 287

John Henry, the Rambling Black Ulysses (Bowman), 286

Johnson, Guy, 284, 298

The Jonesport Raffle (Gould), 14

The Jonny-Cake Letters (Hazard), 215

Jordan, Philip, 15

Journal of American Folklore, 8, 13, 19, 21, 120, 143, 283; issue on New Perspectives in Folklore, 85; issue on urban folklore, 53-54

Journal of the Chicago Folk-Lore Society, 106

Journal of the Folklore Institute, 49, 74, 104, 120

Jul (Feilberg), 83

Jung, Carl, 76, 79

Juslenius, Daniel, 69

Kalevala (Lönnrot), 38, 69, 80, 81

Karadzić, Vuk, 2, 79, 84, 85

Keightley, Thomas, 35, 190

Keil, Charles, 62

Keiser, Albert, 269

Kellogg, Robert, 125

Kentucky Mountain Folk-Songs (Wheeler), 44

Killens, John Oliver, 287

Kimball, J. Golden, 183

Kinder- und Hausmärchen (Grimm), 34, 84

Kirk, Geoffrey S., 78, 79

Kirk, Grayson, 136

Kirshenblatt-Gimblett, Barbara, 55

Kirtley, Bacil F., 100

Kittredge, George Lyman, 95, 128, 262

Klein, Barbo, 142

Klymasz, Robert, 110, 111

Korpela, Heino, 266

Korson, George, 60

Koskerjaako, A. A., 82

Kotila, Bob, 241, 242

Index

Politics, and folklore, 67, 72-73
Poor Richard's Almanac (Franklin), 133
Pop, Mihai, 104
Popular culture, 122. *See also* Mass media
Popular Culture Association, 122
Popular Tales of the West Highlands (Campbell), 37
Prebble, John, 146, 158, 159
Princeton University, 3
Printed sources: comic-heroic folk types in, 268; for comic Indian anecdotes, 269-282; for stories of Paul Bunyan, 291-336, for stories of John Henry, 282-290; for Scottish Highland traditions, 145-180
Propp, Vladimir, *Morphology of the Folktale*, 137

Qvigstad, Just Knud, 82

Raglan, Lord, 143
Randolph, Vance, 13, 44, 99
The Raw and the Cooked (Lévi-Strauss), 76, 77
Reichborn-Kjennerud, Ingjald, 82
Relic areas, 14
Religion and the Decline of Magic (Thomas), 47, 88
Reuss, Richard, 72
Richardson, Robert D., 75
Riehl, Wilhelm, 68
The Rise of Modern Mythology, 1680-1860 (Feldman and Richardson), 75
Roberts, Leonard, 44, 141, 213
Robinson, Rowland E., 28-29
Roche, A.C., 263
Rourke, Constance, 94, 95, 269
Russia, folklore studies in, 40-41. *See also* Soviet Union
Russo, Joseph, 136
Rybnikov, P. N., 41

The Saga of Coe Ridge (Montell), 24, 28
The Saginaw Paul Bunyan (Stevens), 6
Salmelainen, E., 80, 103

Salminen, V., 80
Sandburg, Carl, 286
Sandklef, Albert, 142
Sawyer, E. G., 266
Scandinavia, 2, 38-40
Scarborough, Dorothy, 44
Scenes and Legends of the North of Scotland (Miller), 177, 178
Schlesinger, Arthur, Sr., 4, 48
Schmidt, Otto, 68
Scholarship, mythology, 74-79
Scholes, Robert, 125
The Science of Fairy Tales (Hartland), 190
The Science of Folklore (Krappe), 119
Scotland, 104, 145-180, 187
Sébillot, Paul, 59, 105, 106
Seeger, Pete, 22, 72, 98
Seki, Keigo, 108
Serbo-Croatian Folk Songs (Bartók and Lord), 127
Serbo-Croatian Heroic Songs (Bartók and Lord), 127
Setälä, E. N., 80
Shapiro, Irwin, 286, 287
Sharp, Cecil, 42, 43, 44, 102
Shay, Frank, 286
Shephard, Esther, 7, 309
Smith, Alan, 59, 60
Smith, Henry Nash, 95
Smith, Robert J., 86
Sokolov, Boris, 41
Sokolov, Jurij, 41
A Song Catcher in Southern Mountains (Scarborough), 44
South Italian Folkways in Europe and America (Williams), 48
Soviet Union, 18; All-Union Congress of Soviet Writers, 71; folklore and ideology, 71-72; folklore as propaganda weapon in, 19, 20, 21; folklore studies in, 2, 58-59. *See also* Russia
Spencer, Dave, 253
Springer, George T., 258, 259, 260
State University of New York, 111
Stekert, Ellen, 54
Stevens, James, 5, 6, 7, 286, 307, 313

389

Index

97-98, 132; regional fieldwork in, 96-97, 99, 212-266, theoretical works of folklore, 92-96
University College, Dublin, 104, 184
University of Bucharest, 104
University of California at Los Angeles, 3, 116; Center for Folklore and Comparative Mythology, 116
University of Edinburgh, 104, 105; School of Scottish Studies, 104, 145, 151, 188
University of Hamburg, 67
University of Helsinki, 38, 80, 103
University of Marburg, Institute for Central European Folk Research, 57
University of Maryland, 107
University of Massachusetts, 112
University of Pennsylvania, 2, 8, 23, 26, 49, 72, 74, 105, 116
University of Texas, 105, 116; Afro-American Studies Center, 122
University of Tokyo, 108
Upper Peninsula, 223-266
Urban Blues (Keil), 62
The Urban Experience and Folk Tradition, 122
Urban folklore: in East Chicago, Indiana, 52, 53; fieldwork, 54-55; *Journal of American Folklore* special issue on, 53-54; studies, 48-54, 103, 122
Utley, Francis Lee, 16

Vansina, Jan, 140
Victorian folklorists, 4, 89, 119. *See also* Great Team
Vigeant, Pete, 231
Vivian, Jim, 264

The Voice of the Folk (Bluestein), 94
Volkskultur in der technischen Welt (Bausinger), 56
Volkstumsarbeit als politische Aufgabe (Schmidt), 68
Vuk Stefanović Karadzić 1787-1864 (Wilson), 84

Ware, Charles P., 45
Wayne State University, 53, 54
Wells, Herman B, 19
Western Kentucky State University, 72
Wheeler, Mary, 44
Where Beards Wag All (Evans), 92
Whisky Galore (Compton), 177
White, Newman I., 284
Wigginton, Eliot, 24, 25, 26, 96
Wilde, Lady, 191
Wildhaber, Robert, 113
Wilgus, D. K., 54
Williams, John, 21, 22, 23, 24
Williams, Phyllis H., 48, 49
Wilson, Duncan, 84
Wilson, Edward M., 103, 109
Wilson, William A., 69
Witchcraft in Tudor and Stuart England (Macfarlane), 89, 90, 91
Witchcraft: 89, 90, 91, 92, 215
Woodward, C. Vann, 181

Yale University, 3, 121
Yanagita, Kunio, 41, 42, 100, 107, 108
Yankee humor, 168-169, 227, 270, 274, 319
The Year of Decision: 1846 (DeVoto), 4
Yugoslavia, 127, 128, 134
Yumpin' Yimminy (Springer), 258